THE CROWN
AND
THE PEOPLE

1. *King George VI and Queen Elizabeth in Westminster Hall on the opening of the rebuilt House of Commons in 1950*

THE
CROWN
AND THE
PEOPLE

Allan A. Michie

London
SECKER AND WARBURG
1952

Made and printed in Great Britain by
William Clowes and Sons Limited
London and Beccles
and
first published
1952
by
Martin Secker and Warburg Limited
7 John Street, London, W.C.1

To
MY WIFE, BARBARA
and Children
BARBARA, JANET and ALLAN
who waited patiently

CONTENTS

THE APPARATUS OF MAJESTY

POSTSCRIPT

LIST OF ILLUSTRATIONS

THE SYMBOL

9

AUTHOR'S NOTE

THE first purpose of this book is to explain the modern British concept of monarchy, unique in man's political story down through the ages, an institution that is both paradoxical and mystifying and yet practically suited to Britain's needs. In some lands monarchy is regarded as a feudal anachronism. Britain's monarchy *is* a survival of medievalism in the twentieth century; but it not only survives—it functions.

As a constitutional monarch Queen Elizabeth II not only has a job to do but, like her father before her, she does it superbly well. The second purpose of this book is to explain what that job is and how she does it.

An English constitutional legist, initiating me in the symbolism of the crown, once put it this way: "The institution of monarchy is the important thing, but a good man helps." He might have added, "and a good family helps even more." For if George VI was easily the most popular monarch Britain has ever had, it is equally true that his family has captured the affection of the nation to a unique degree. This book, therefore, must be the story of a family.

As correspondent and editor in Britain since 1939 for a succession of American magazines—*Fortune, Time, Life, The Reader's Digest* and *Collier's*—it has been part of my assignment to observe the monarchy in action and occasionally to write about it, and in the course of that work I have been privileged to make a wide circle of royal and political contacts. In writing this book I have drawn on these sources, and although they must remain nameless—for reasons which they will understand—I wish to express my thanks to them.

During the early war years I wrote a close-up of Queen Elizabeth, now the Queen Mother, for *Life* (March 17, 1941), and in 1949 I wrote a profile of George VI for *The Reader's Digest*

11

("The People's King," November, 1949). I have taken the liberty of incorporating some of that earlier material in this book.

ALLAN A. MICHIE

London
September, 1952

THE INSTITUTION

I

THE KING IS DEAD: LONG LIVE THE QUEEN!

IT began as a rumour about 9.30 on the cold, grey morning of February 6, 1952, and nobody would believe it. "You and your 'King dead'. Get away with you," scoffed an indignant London housewife at a milkman who had heard it from a taxi driver who had picked up a fare outside Buckingham Palace.

The editors of London's afternoon newspapers, whose sensitive reportorial feelers had picked up the first rustles of the rumour, busily sought confirmation while they made ready the special obituary pages held in hand since George VI's critical lung operation the previous September ; but even at Sandringham, the royal country home in Norfolk where the King had been in residence, there were no outward signs of anything unusual. "Here now, don't you go around spreading silly rumours like that," cautioned a burly policeman at the main gate as an early-bird reporter nosed for news.

At 10.30 came the confirmation. The Buckingham Palace press office telephoned the announcement to London's two chief press agencies and requested a 15-minute embargo to allow official notices to reach their destinations. At 10.45 bells rang on the news tickers as they clacked out the sad flash: "The King, who retired to rest last night in his usual health, passed peacefully away in his sleep early this morning." Five minutes after the deadline the news was circling the world.

At 11.15, when London's afternoon papers had their special editions on the streets, the British Broadcasting Corporation made its announcement in its own good time. Swiftly the news spread over the land. Buckingham Palace sped the message to Prime Minister Winston Churchill. The Lord Mayor of London,

15

by ancient prerogative one of the first to be informed, ordered the flag on his Mansion House lowered to half-mast and sent a dispatch rider to St. Paul's asking the bell-ringers to toll "Great Tom," the hour bell of the Cathedral, every minute for two hours. Gradually, from the spires of the smaller churches which Sir Christopher Wren scattered around his masterpiece, from the steeples of the multitude of other churches in London and from the grand and humble towers in the cities and countryside of Britain other bells joined in the dismal chorus. In the big underwriting room at Lloyd's the famed Lutine Bell—historic herald of bad news—clanged once and the underwriters stopped business for the day. At the Stock Exchange jobbers symbolically turned their price boards to the wall, and a great hush, a Sabbath stillness, descended over the busy City of London.

As Union Jacks fluttered to half-mast the news spread in ever-widening circles. Over and over the four-word message was repeated—"The King is dead." Chalked on empty coal tubs, it reached the coal-face workers deep down in the earth; spoken over factory loudspeakers, it rose over the clatter of machinery; phoned from house to house, it overwhelmed the telephone system; hurled into the ether, it reached out to ships at sea and aircraft in flight.

At Sandringham the news slowed down to country pace. The butcher, the baker and the milkman on their rounds carried it from cottage to cottage, from hamlet to village tucked away amid the pine trees and rolling heathland of the royal estate. Farm hands tramping in from the King's fields for their midday dinner saw the village church flag at half-mast and wondered, but still did not guess what it meant.

Coming so soon after reports of George VI's improving health, the news was at first received by Britons in bewilderment and disbelief, but as the tragic truth settled each gave thought to his own personal sorrow. For no monarch had been nearer to his people than George VI.

Where words were spoken, they were simple, homely tributes. "He was a good man, and a good King." Not much more could be added to that. Up in the grey-green Chiltern Hills of Buckinghamshire an aged road ditcher heard the news in stunned silence. Taking his pipe from his mouth, he said, "There weren't ever no better King, I suppose," and then bent back to his work.

2. The King's last farewell to
Princess Elizabeth

3. Elizabeth returns to London
Airport as Queen

4. Accession of Queen Elizabeth II is proclaimed at the Tower of London

5. *The pomp of national requiem: the last vigil over the body of King George VI
during the lying-in-state at Westminster*

6. *The naval escort waits to receive the coffin*

7. *Four royal dukes walk in funeral procession*

8. *The cortege winds its way through the sorrowing heart of London*

9. *Last homage as the funeral train departs for Windsor*

Kings have had prouder epitaphs, but none that came more from the heart.

At the great house at Sandringham the tragic discovery had been made soon after 7.30 that morning. Not having received the usual summons to the King's bedroom, assistant valet James Macdonald waited a decent interval and then went to wake his master with an early-morning cup of tea. He found George VI lying tranquilly in his bed. The King had been dead for some hours.

Macdonald hurriedly summoned an officer of the royal household, who sent the lady-in-waiting to awaken Queen Elizabeth and Princess Margaret. Queen Elizabeth went at once to the bedside of her husband. Though her face was twisted with misery, she did not weep. Trained by her years as a royal person to control her emotions, she leaned down and kissed the forehead of the dead King. Then, straightening up, she said: "We must tell Elizabeth." She hesitated, then corrected herself: "We must tell . . . the Queen."

"The King is dead: long live the Queen" (adapted in this case to allow for the female succession) is no mere monarchic paradox. It encompasses the constitutional principle that the throne is never vacant: at the very instant of the death of the monarch the reign of the new sovereign begins. The formal proclamation of accession, the renewed oaths of allegiance and the coronation itself are but subsequent affirmations that the new monarch possesses all the powers of sovereignty.

Princess Elizabeth, George VI's elder daughter, thus became Queen without even knowing it as she sat through the dark night of an African forest. On the first leg of her projected five-month tour of Kenya, Ceylon, Australia and New Zealand, she had gone with her husband and two members of her staff to spend the night of February 5–6 in a tree-hut in Kenya's Royal Aberdare Game Reserve, watching big game gather at the jungle water-hole below. In the morning, after an exciting night spying on nocturnal visitors to the water-hole, she thanked her hosts for her experience, one of the rare moments of relaxation on her tour to date, and, still unaware of her high position, vowed to return soon and bring her father.

It was not until almost 3 o'clock Kenya time that afternoon that the new Queen heard the momentous news that changed her life. It was telephoned by a local newspaperman to an equerry at Sagana Royal Lodge, the cedar-log house (given to Elizabeth and her husband as a wedding present by the people of Kenya) where the royal couple were resting after their night's outing. The Duke of Edinburgh sent the equerry to phone London for confirmation, then led his wife down to the edge of the little Sagana River that runs through the estate and gently told her the news. Like any young girl who has lost her father in death, Elizabeth broke down and cried. She returned to the lodge in full command of herself, however. "She took it like a Queen," said one of her staff.

By early evening the new Queen, accompanied by her husband, was airborne, en route to the capital of her British realm.

Meanwhile, back in Britain—where all power derives from the sovereign—a variety of adjustments were being made to fit the crown to its new head. The continuity of the crown first declared itself in the courts of law. At Durham's Assize Court, where the trial for an alleged murder was in progress, the court adjourned for ten minutes on news of George VI's death and when it resumed the barristers who had begun the case as King's Counsel continued the trial as Queen's Counsel. As the Assizes ended the day the judges marshal closed the court with the words, "God save the Queen and my lords the Queen's justices." A justice of the peace being sworn in at Belfast took his oath of allegiance to the Queen. His Majesty's Government became, automatically, Her Majesty's Government and the diplomatic couriers of the Foreign Office changed over from King's Messengers to Queen's Messengers. That night at the Tower of London the traditional nightly ritual of the Keys was altered for the first time since the death of Queen Victoria. "Who goes there?" called out the sentries. "The Queen's Keys," came the new answer.

Constitutionally, the demise of the crown sets in motion a series of legal steps providing for the immediate continuity of kingship and as soon as George VI's death was made known the procedure was meticulously observed.[1]

The House of Commons, in the midst of a bitter partisan

1 The notes *throughout* are grouped under the relevant chapters at the end of the book.

debate on foreign policy, met briefly while the Prime Minister communicated the sad news (which the members already knew) and then recessed until the evening. In the Lords the Lord Privy Seal announced the death of the King. That afternoon the Accession Council, a convocation with a history almost as old as the monarchy itself, met at St. James's Palace, solemnly affirmed that Elizabeth was the rightful successor to the throne and ordered her proclamation as Queen. Their task was complicated by the fact that Elizabeth was still some 4,500 air miles distant from London and thus unable to sign the oath of accession in accordance with constitutional usage, and so public proclamation of her accession was held over for two days.[2] That evening when the Commons again assembled the Speaker, wearing his white cuffs of mourning, swore the traditional oath of allegiance to the new sovereign. He was followed by the Prime Minister and then the other members. In the House of Lords the Lord Chancellor heard the oath of allegiance taken by the peers. Before the peers met one of the two thrones which George VI and his Queen Consort had used was removed from the throne dais, a reminder that the new Queen's husband has no status in the constitutional monarchy.

On the afternoon of February 7, just seven days and four hours after she had flown away from London airport as Princess, Elizabeth returned to London as Queen, dressed in her makeshift mourning (a black velvet hat and black coat hiding her greyish-blue dress). Even at a time of great personal and family grief, however, duty came first as she stepped into her life of service. On her return to Clarence House from the airfield she was handed a batch of state papers before she could even compose herself. The business of the crown never pauses. Later she received the two royal officials who have charge of state ceremonial, the Duke of Norfolk, in his capacity of Earl Marshal, and the Earl of Clarendon, her Lord Chamberlain, and approved their tentative plans for her father's funeral.

Next morning the new Queen, dressed in deep mourning and followed at a discreet distance by her consort and officials of her household, walked along the snow-flecked garden path from Clarence House to St. James's Palace to receive the homage of her Accession Council, meeting for the second time, and make her accession declaration. In her clear, girlish voice she read

19

out the personal declaration which custom decrees for each sovereign:

"By the sudden death of my dear father I am called to assume the duties and responsibilities of sovereignty. At this time of deep sorrow it is a profound consolation to me to be assured of the sympathy which you and all my peoples feel towards me, to my mother, and my sister, and to the other members of my family.

"My father was our revered and beloved head as he was of the wider family of his subjects: the grief which his loss brings is shared among us all. My heart is too full for me to say more to you today than that I shall always work, as my father did throughout his reign, to uphold constitutional government and to advance the happiness and prosperity of my peoples, spread as they are all the world over.

"I know that in my resolve to follow his shining example of service and devotion I shall be inspired by the loyalty and affection of those whose Queen I have been called upon to be, and by the counsel of their elected parliaments. I pray that God will help me to discharge worthily this heavy task that has been laid upon me so early in my life."

Elizabeth then signed the oath of accession, took and subscribed the oath relating to the security of the Church of Scotland, and withdrew. The veteran statesmen and politicians who made up the Council, the youngest of them (except for her husband, the Duke of Edinburgh) more than twice her age, marvelled at her composure. During the poignant ceremony, which brought memories of her father flooding back, only once did a lone tear appear and trickle down her cheek.

As the musical notes of St. James's Palace clock struck 11, reinforced by the distant bass of Big Ben from across the park, the 300-year-old royal residence burst forth in a blaze of pageantry that rolled back the centuries and lifted, for a brief interlude, the sodden grief which lay heavy on the land. Out on to the Tudor balcony above Friary Court (the same balcony from which Elizabeth's great-great-grandmother, Victoria, had been proclaimed Queen) stepped a medieval tableau—the Earl Marshal, resplendent in the scarlet gold-braided coat and black beaver cocked hat of his office; Lord Halifax, the High Steward of Westminster, in his ancient uniform; then the three Kings of Arms, six Heralds and three heraldic Pursuivants, decked out in their quartered gold, blue and scarlet stiff satin tabards emblazoned with the royal arms and looking as if they had just stepped from the illuminated pages of Froissart's " Chronicles"; and, finally, four state trumpeters of the Household Cavalry in gold-laced tabards and the sergeants-at-arms carrying their maces.

The guard of honour of Coldstream Guards in the courtyard below snapped to attention. Raising their long silver horns, the trumpeters blew a spine-tingling fanfare and as the notes leaped and fell over the heads of the huge crowd and then died away in the cold, crisp morning air Garter Principal King of Arms unrolled his large parchment scroll and began to read the sonorous, nobly phrased proclamation:

"Whereas it hath pleased Almighty God to call to His Mercy our late Sovereign Lord King George the Sixth of Blessed and Glorious Memory by whose Decease the Crown is solely and rightfully come to the High and Mighty Princess Elizabeth Alexandra Mary: We, therefore, the Lords Spiritual and Temporal of this Realm, being here assisted with these of His late Majesty's Privy Council, with representatives of other members of the Commonwealth, with other Principal Gentlemen of Quality, with the Lord Mayor, Aldermen and Citizens of London, do now hereby with one voice and Consent of Tongue and Heart publish and proclaim that the High and Mighty Princess Elizabeth Alexandra Mary is now, by the Death of our late Sovereign of Happy Memory, become Queen Elizabeth the Second, by the Grace of God, Queen of this Realm and of all Her other Realms and Territories, Head of the Commonwealth, Defender of the Faith, to whom Her lieges do acknowledge all Faith and constant Obediance, with hearty and humble Affection ; beseeching God, by whom Kings and Queens do reign, to bless the Royal Princess Elizabeth the Second with long and happy Years to reign over us. God Save the Queen."

The band struck up the national anthem and the thousands of spectators joined in the refrain that had not been heard for 51 years—"God Save Our Gracious Queen." As the anthem died away the royal standard flying above the chimney pots of St. James's was hauled down from half-mast and then run up to the mast-top, taut in the icy wind. All over London the half-staffed flags climbed upward to full-mast, there to remain for the rest of the day in honour of the new Queen. In the background came the boom of cannon as the gunners at the Tower of London, in Hyde Park and at Woolwich saluted the new sovereign.

The scarlet and gold tableau then dissolved and reassembled again in a fairy-tale cavalcade of five state landaus. Escorted by the glittering troops of the Household Cavalry it moved off down the Mall, crowd-packed and lined with Guards, to complete the ritual of proclaiming Queen Elizabeth II at other key points in London.[3] At the same time the proclamation was read with ceremonial flourishes to the people of Scotland, Wales and Ulster at Edinburgh, Cardiff and Belfast, in provincial towns and cities of the United Kingdom and in the principal cities throughout the far-flung Commonwealth of Nations which had pledged allegiance to the new Queen.

Thus proclaimed, Elizabeth II was at last free to comfort her mother and sister and pay her last respects to her father. That afternoon, accompanied by Philip, she entered her stately, crested Rolls-Royce and headed for Sandringham.

At Sandringham the solemn but splendid ceremonial that attends the death of a monarch had begun on a simple theme. To the workers on the royal estate and the nearby villagers in this pine-scented corner of Norfolk George VI was first of all the squire and then the King, and it was as a well-beloved country gentleman and master that he was honoured and mourned.

Carpenters on the royal estate had laboured throughout the night of February 6 on their dolorous task of fashioning a simple coffin of seasoned oak cut from the Sandringham forests. When it was finished they carried it to the great hushed house and up to the first-floor bedroom. There the body of George VI was laid out. It was there that the new Queen went, after greeting her mother and sister and kissing her children, and knelt alone by the coffin when she arrived at Sandringham on the afternoon of February 8. Later her husband joined her, and when they had left the old family servants filed quietly into the room.

As darkness fell six black-suited carpenters, their hands roughened in the service of the King, carried their master's body out through the north door of the house and gently placed the coffin on a wheeled bier. Led by the King's pipe major skirling the heart-tearing Scottish lament "Flowers o' the Forest," and followed by the Queen, her mother, the Duke of Edinburgh, Princess Margaret, and a handful of household officials and senior servants, the cortege—lighted by estate workers carrying torches —wound its eerie way a few hundred yards down the tree-lined path, George VI's favourite evening walk, to the little estate church of St. Mary Magdalene, where the King and his father and grandfather before him had worshipped. There the casket was placed on simple trestles in the chancel before the magnificent silver altar. Over the coffin was draped the royal standard, which was to accompany him to the grave. Wreaths and flowers from the estate filled the richly-decorated chapel, but on the bier were only three wreaths, addressed not to a King but to a father and a husband. On the floor of the chancel, at the foot of the coffin, lay a white offering from Princess Margaret, inscribed: "Darling Papa, from his ever-loving Margaret." At the head of the bier was an all-white wreath from the new Queen and her husband, addressed: "Darling Papa, from his loving and devoted daughter and son-in-law, Lilibet and Philip." On the coffin rested a wreath of white orchids, white lilies and white carnations from the Queen Mother, marked: "Darling Bertie, from his always loving Elizabeth."

For the next two days George VI lay in the vigil of his tenantry. Gamekeepers and foresters from the estate, dressed in their Sandringham uniforms of green country tweeds, gaiters and boots, and builders, carpenters, cowherds and dairymen from the King's fields and farms, stiffly dressed in their Sunday black, took their turns standing guard in two-hour shifts, four at a time, one at each corner of the coffin, throughout the night and every hour of the day. Singly, in twos and threes, in little family groups the estate workers and the village folk who were his neighbours filed silently past the simple bier to pay their last respects to their squire and King.

The funeral of a British sovereign is a deliberate, complex ritual, governed by long-honoured protocol, which only gradually approaches its processional climax. On Monday, February 11, when the body of George VI was taken from his Sandringham birthplace on its last sad journey to his London Palace of Westminster, the pomp of national requiem began. At first it overlapped and then it displaced the homely, intimate, country leave-taking of his family, his tenants and his friends.

The Queen and her family attended a short service that morning in the church of St. Mary Magdalene and as the estate choir sang the slow, solemn music of the *Nunc dimittis* the coffin was borne from the chapel. This time it was carried high on the shoulders of eight tall Guardsmen of the King's Company of the Grenadiers, and laid upon a gun carriage drawn by six bays of the King's Troop of the Royal Horse Artillery. As the casket was placed upon the caisson the King's piper again struck up the sorrowful lament "Flowers o' the Forest." As the first notes filtered through the trees a brace of startled pheasants flashed up into the blue and white metallic sky.

At walking pace the solemn procession made its way along the meandering two-and-a-half-mile road to the little pseudo-Tudor railroad station at Wolferton, where the first of the dead King's funeral trains waited. Behind the caisson walked the Dukes of Edinburgh and Gloucester, bareheaded, carrying their black silk hats. Behind them, in a closed limousine, rode the Queen, the Queen Mother and Princess Margaret, and behind them, in stolid ranks, marched the estate workers who had served the King. Along the tree-lined road, in hushed thousands, stood the friends and neighbours and country folk who had come to bid farewell.

At King's Cross Station in London, the sooty grime mercifully hidden behind black and purple hangings, the imperial crown of state was carried into the hearse-coach when the train arrived and firmly fixed atop the coffin. George VI was no longer a father mourned by the family he had left, a deceased country squire: he was a dead sovereign, a symbol, in the keeping of his soldiers, and from now until his committal at Windsor five days hence his burial rites would move to their climax amid military panoply, with the thunder of guns, the thud of drums, the heart-throbbing beat of funeral marches and the vivid colours of state pageantry, in sharp yet stirring contrast to the grieving mood of his people.

A guard of honour mounted by the three fighting services presented arms as the Guardsmen bearers lifted the coffin on to another gun carriage drawn by the King's Troop for the three-mile journey through the rain-soaked, sleety streets of London to the Palace of Westminster, where the body of George VI would lie in state. Behind the cortege again walked the Duke of Edinburgh and the Duke of Gloucester, and behind them, completing the short and simple procession, walked eight male members of the royal household. Along the streets hundreds of thousands of Londoners stood in hushed, mute homage. No bands played: not a hand waved.

At Westminster the coffin was slowly carried on the linked arms of the bearers into the great stone Hall, the shrine of almost 900 years of Britain's history.[4] There it was placed on a six-tiered, purple-covered catafalque in the centre of the Hall, under the great oaken arches of the hammer-beamed roof. Atop the casket, still draped in the rich scarlet, blue and gold of the royal standard, rested the imperial state crown, the bejewelled royal sceptre and gold orb, and, at the head of the coffin, the floral offering of the King's wife. Around the bier were placed five massive candlesticks from the Unknown Warrior's tomb in Westminster Abbey and, at the head of the casket, the glittering Wanamaker cross from the Abbey. Reverently, but with the quiet possessiveness of their ancient privilege, the members of the King's bodyguards moved like life-sized chessmen into the positions of their last vigil —at the corners of the catafalque four scarlet-and-black-clad Yeomen of the Guard, their antique partisans reversed ; above them, on the third tier, four officers of the Household Cavalry, brilliantly attired in the scarlet-and-white and blue-and-white of the Life Guards and the Royal Horse Guards ; and, at the head of the coffin, two of the Gentlemen-at-Arms, standing statuesque in their dark blue and scarlet uniforms, their white plumes cascading down from their golden helmets.

After a short service Britain's three Queens—Queen Mary, the Queen Mother and Queen Elizabeth II—who had patiently endured one more ritualistic, planned stage of the state ending of one who was to them a son, a husband and a father, withdrew from the Hall with the lesser members of the royal family and the homage began. First the Archbishop of York, deputizing for the ailing Archbishop of Canterbury, made a deep obeisance to his dead sovereign. Then the Heralds stood around the coffin and bent their heads in unison. Then two processions moved slowly along each side of the Hall, the Lords Spiritual, in black and white lawn, and some 500 of the Lords Temporal on one side, the members of the Commons, unidentifiable in unrelieved black, on the other. In symbolic demonstration of the unifying presence of the crown the parliamentarians walked side by side,

Tory with Socialist, as they circled the purple island of the cata-falque and bowed low to the bier. Daylight had gone from the high windows at the ends of the Hall and the tall candles around the catafalque sent shadows leaping up to the eaves when the privileged official mourners were admitted to pay homage—members of the diplomatic corps, the late King's doctors and nurses who had attended him in his many illnesses, then upwards of 1,000 royal household servants, butlers, pages, housemaids, stable hands from the royal homes and palaces.

For the next three days George VI belonged to his people. Moved by some dramatic mass impulse, they came in their thousands to pay their respects to the great and good King who was gone. Neither rain nor snow nor the penetrating damp of that leaden week could deter them from joining the endless line of patient, waiting mourners, a great queue that at its peak periods stretched for almost four miles and doubled and redoubled its way across the bridges of the Thames.

Once inside the great gaunt Hall, cold with the chill of cen-turies, they paused at the top of the stone stairs to take in the theatrical, surprisingly colourful yet majestically dignified tableau of the catafalque, and then, shuffling forward slowly, as if to prolong their leave-taking as long as possible, they moved forward in a double line past the bier. Around the coffin the ten guards stood rigid, like figures in a waxworks. Every 20 minutes they came to life as the watch was changed in a ceremony of slow precision.[5]

Every now and then the slow, steady file of the mourners past the coffin was interrupted by some dramatic little touch, some small scene of devotion—a legless man carried past by attendants, a party of blind ex-servicemen, their guides describing the scene to them in hushed whispers. Once a woman sank to her knees abreast of the coffin and whispered a prayer. A clergyman behind her in the queue helped her to her feet and led her, in tears, from the Hall. Occasionally a woman curtsied and a man bowed deeply to the bier. Men, women and children furtively carried posies hidden under their coats and surreptitiously dropped them as they passed the catafalque. People were not explicitly forbidden to bring flowers, though it was understood there were to be no wreaths in the Hall except those from the royal family, but the policemen on duty around the bier did not interfere and by the early morning hours, when the doors were briefly closed before the next day's queue began, the grey carpet around the catafalque was strewn with bootlegged little flowers, faded and withered from long hours of clutching in the queue.

Throughout the lying-in-state the great and near-great of Britain and foreign lands came to a side door of the Hall to pay their tribute—among them the three Queens of Britain, the Duke of Edinburgh, Princess Margaret, Holland's Queen Juliana and Prince Bernhard, King Haakon of Norway, the Duchess of Kent and her children, General Eisenhower, President Auriol of France and Dean Acheson of the United States—but they stood dwarfed and unnoticed in the shadows. For this was a people's ceremony. Queen Mary, with her unerring judgment, quickly sensed this when she came with her son, the Duke of Windsor, and daughter, the Princess Royal, to view the coffin. As the police considerately halted the files of mourners to give her a better look at the catafalque, the aged Queen spoke to a police official at her side. "Have the people been stopped because of us?" she asked. "There is no reason for that. Let them go on, please."

By 6 a.m. on Friday, February 15, when the doors of the Hall were finally shut in order to prepare the start of the funeral procession a few hours later, 305,806 people had filed past the remains of George VI.[6]

For Elizabeth II it was a week of activity in the midst of mourning, for the business of the state moves inexorably ahead. On February 10, from Sandringham, she announced that her court would go into mourning until June 1. On February 12 she received in audience Prime Minister Churchill, and the next day at Buckingham Palace received a deputation from the Commons presenting an address of loyalty and condolence. From Elizabeth went a series of formal messages of thanks to the Lords and Commons, to the armed services, the Dominion Governments, the Colonial Service and the Civil Service. On Churchill's advice she dispensed with the unseemly tradition of a state banquet on the eve of the funeral for visiting foreign dignitaries, but she went through the wearisome formality of receiving for a brief audience her Commonwealth High Commissioners and foreign heads of state and their representatives. Each day she devoted three to four hours to state affairs as the routine business of the crown went on. On the day before the funeral she approved the appointment of a new Puisne Judge in Hongkong and approved the appointment of one new member and the reappointment of three members to the court of the Bank of England.

Now the octave of grief neared its end. On the morning of February 15, the ninth day after his death, the body of George VI was carried through the streets of his capital for the last time and conveyed by train to his Castle at Windsor, there to be lowered into his place in history alongside the remains of nine of his royal forbears who lie at St. George's Chapel.

At a slight sign from the new Queen as the hands of Big Ben approached 9.30 the sombre pageantry began and the silence that hung over the heart of London was shattered by the bark of military commands: "Guard of Honour. Royal Salute. Present Arms!" Bayonet points flashed in the weak morning sun that peeped through the banks of clouds and mist. Riding high on the shoulders of the eight bareheaded Guardsmen pallbearers, the coffin appeared, still wrapped in the gold, azure and gules of the royal standard, surmounted with the crown of state on its cushion of royal purple, the orb and the sceptre, the King's insignia of the Order of the Garter, and the Queen Mother's white wreath. As one man the escort of white-gaitered Royal Navy bluejackets waiting fore and aft of the dull green gun carriage doffed their caps in unison and sank their heads to their breasts in obeisance to the coffin. The high, shrill wail of naval bosuns as they piped their Admiral "aboard" split the hushed air with poignant sound as the bearers slid their burden on to the caisson with tender, reverent care. As the throaty boom of Big Ben's minute bell rang out in the first of 56 strokes that told the King's age the naval gun crew strained at the pipe-clayed drag-ropes and the body of George VI moved off across the cobbled courtyard, leaving for ever the Parliament of his people.[7]

Elizabeth II, followed by her mother, Princess Margaret and the Princess Royal, entered the waiting scarlet, gold and glossy black Glass Coach, and as their carriage pulled away so the pieces in the processional tableau took up their appointed places. Behind the Queen's coach walked the four royal Dukes—the Duke of Edinburgh, in naval uniform, the Duke of Gloucester, in army uniform, the Duke of Windsor, in the uniform of Admiral of the

Fleet which he last wore as the uncrowned King, and the teen-aged Duke of Kent, in formal mourning. Behind them walked the male members of the British and foreign royal families, heads of state, the High Commissioners of the Dominions and the heads of foreign delegations, and behind them came six carriages carrying the aged King of Norway, the Queens of the Nether-lands, Sweden and Denmark, the Grand Duchess of Luxembourg, Princess Astrid of Norway, women members of the British royal family and ceremonial female attendants of the royal households.

As the gilded coaches drew slowly away drums thudded in the distance and up near the head of the procession, which reached to the Mall, the band of the Welsh Guards struck up the first notes of Handel's Dead March from "Saul" as the military con-tingents, arms reversed, moved off in processional step, the magnificent stiff-legged march at half-time, at which Britain's military forces are unequalled.

Up through the heart of royal London—from Whitehall, across the parade ground of the Horse Guards, along the wide Mall and up St. James's Street to Piccadilly—the sad cavalcade wound its way. In the centre of the mile-long procession (which took 35 minutes to pass), separated from the marching contin-gents by a mounted escort of Household Cavalry, came the gun carriage, closely flanked now by the late King's equerries, his Yeomen of the Guard and his Gentlemen-at-Arms. At Marl-borough House, overlooking the Mall, all the blinds were drawn save one. In that window sat silver-haired Queen Mary, binoculars to her eyes. When the cortege came abreast she drew herself erect and raised her right hand in a quick gesture of fare-well to her dead son. The black-clad ladies in the Queen's coach bowed toward her and the four royal Dukes saluted. The old Queen bowed stiffly in reply.

Through Hyde Park, where gunners of the King's Troop fired minute guns to mark off the years of George VI's life, past the Marble Arch and up the Edgware Road to Paddington the slow-moving river of scarlet and gold, khaki and black flowed through Britain's shabby, cheerful masses, standing in countless silent thousands along the route. The only sounds that broke the in-credible stillness of the morning were the measured crunch of marching feet beating out the hypnotic rhythm of the slow march on the sanded roadway, the jingle of harness and breastplates as the

Household Cavalry passed, the mournful notes of the alternating funeral marches and the keening music of the massed pipe bands.

At Paddington Station, transformed from a busy railway terminus into a mausoleum of purple hangings and potted greenery, the high notes of the bosuns' pipes signalled the Admiral "over the side" as the bearers gently lifted the coffin and carried it into the waiting funeral train. As the hearse-coach was sealed the pipe bands played their Highland lament, "Flowers o' the Forest," and then the haunting "Skye Boat Song." Five minutes before the funeral train departed a blind in the royal rail carriage was suddenly lifted and the new Queen peered out. Unveiled, she watched the scene until the train drew slowly out of the station to the farewell strains of Chopin's Funeral March.

At Windsor, where another naval escort of 150 sailors waited, caps off and heads bowed, to carry their King, medieval pageantry replaced the military precision of London. The shortened procession was stripped of much of its military escort, and in its place walked the Kings of Arms, the Heralds and Pursuivants in the emblazoned tabards of their historic offices. As the funeral train glided to a stop the Union Jack flying at half-staff above the grey walls of the Castle was hauled down and the royal standard fluttered up to the top of the mast, signifying that the new Queen had brought her father's body to the royal borough which gave his dynasty its name.

Although the Castle walls are but a stone's throw from the station the procession wound its way through the narrow streets of Windsor half a mile past the fortress to the Cambridge Gate, into the imposing Long Walk and so back to the Sovereign's entrance to the Castle. As it entered the grounds saluting guns barked across the Thames-side meadows, counting off the years of the King's life, and from the Round Tower of the Castle the great Sebastopol bell, the Crimean relic which is tolled only for the funeral of a sovereign, beat like a mighty hammer on the air every 30 seconds. Once inside the ancient walls the procession crossed the quadrangle, passed through the Norman Gate by the Round Tower and then down the gentle slope to the lower ward and St. George's Chapel. Over the soft tread of the procession came the swelling lament of the massed pipe bands, bouncing back from the grey stone battlements, as the pipers played their King to rest with "My Home" and then slipped easily into "The

Mist Covered Mountains of Home" and finally, as the gun carriage came to a halt before the Chapel, "Flowers o' the Forest."

St. George's Chapel, a sacred architectural gem of the Renaissance, wrought by master craftsmen in ageless Cotswold stone, soared skyward on a carpet of colour. Piled against its grey walls and covering the green slopes around them in a magnificent array were the wreaths, bouquets and bunches of flowers, more than 3,000 in all, which had been sent in tribute from all over the world. Like the lying-in-state, it was a classless display. Intermingled with the elaborate floral tributes from overseas and from the towns and boroughs and institutions of the King's realms—a floral model of the George Cross, inscribed "For Gallantry," from the British Government ; a model of its badge in flowers from H.M.S. *Vanguard* ; a Welsh harp in golden daffodils from Cardiff ; a yard-square Union Jack worked in flowers from the city of Nice ; crossed floral swords from Jordan's Arab Legion ; a model of the *Golden Hind* with broken mainmast from Plymouth—were the modest offerings of the King's people, each with its personal inscription—a bunch of daffodils "to His Majesty with deep respect from a working girl" ; a floral cross "from a few ordinary insurance clerks" to "a really magnificent King" ; a handful of snowdrops "from a little boy of six from his garden." Side by side lay the tribute from the King of Kings of Abyssinia and the flowers from the stationmaster and staff at Windsor. Alongside the wreath from the recently-enthroned King Idris of Libya stood a floral crown sent by the street traders of Fulham.

For the last time the keen of bosuns' pipes shrilled through the still air as the naval party from H.M.S. *Vanguard*, on which George VI had sailed happily to South Africa, piped their Admiral "over the side." The Guardsmen inched the casket to their shoulders and slowly bore it up the broad stone steps to the great west door, where the officiating clergy waited to receive the body. "I am the Resurrection, and the Life," sang the choir and, as the poignant music floated upward past the carved stalls and the blazing heraldic banners of the Knights of the Garter to lose itself among the traceried stonework of the lofty roof, the coffin was borne along the blue-carpeted pathway of the nave, between the ranks of the privileged congregation, through the oaken screen and into the candle-lit chancel, where it was placed upon the funeral bier, a tall pedestal draped in purple, at the foot of the altar steps. The Queen and her mother remained standing at the head of the coffin, facing the altar. Behind them stood the other royal ladies and the Dukes and the ranks of kings, princes and heads of foreign states. At the foot of the coffin stood the Archbishop of Canterbury, Primate of All England, in his cope of deep purple spangled with silver, the Lord Chamberlain and the Garter King of Arms, and on the sides the King's personal servants and household officials who had escorted their master to the end. Guardsmen removed the jewelled emblems from the coffin and placed them on a purple-draped stand at the side, for these were now the symbols of the new reign.

Except for royal interpolations at the end, the King's burial service, the simple ceremony of the order for the burial of the dead from the Church of England's Book of Common Prayer, was the same as that which commits any commoner to the grave, thus proclaiming to the end the kinship between sovereign and people. When the coffin was made ready for the grave the Lord Chamberlain symbolically broke his staff of office by unscrewing it in the middle and reverently placed one piece on the coffin to show that he no longer held his authority from his dead monarch. An officer handed the Queen a square of crimson silk, the King's Colour of the King's Company of the Grenadier Guards, the regiment of which George VI had been colonel-in-chief, and Her Majesty laid it over the head of the coffin.

And then, as the Archbishop spoke the ancient, consoling words of the committal, "Forasmuch as it has pleased Almighty God of His great mercy to take unto Himself the soul of our dear brother here departed, we therefore commit his body to the ground ; earth to earth, ashes to ashes, dust to dust," the coffin sank slowly from sight through the floor to the royal tomb house below.[8] The young Queen took from the Master of the Household a small silver bowl and, stepping to the lip of the chasm, sprinkled a few small handfuls of Windsor earth on the disappearing coffin.

One royal formality remained. The Garter King of Arms, as is his right, stepped forward and recited over the grave the titles of the dead King and immediately repeated the stately styles of his successor:

10. *St. Edward's Crown*

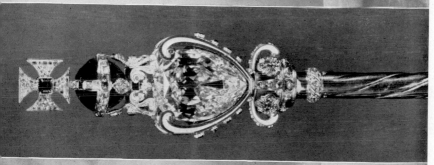

11. *Sceptre with Cross*

12. *The Crown of State*

13. *George VI is crowned in Westminster Abbey on May 12, 1937: in the homage rite the nobles swear fealty to the new King*

14. *The bejewelled Gold Orb*

15. *The Ampulla and Anointing Spoon*

"Thus it hath pleased Almighty God to take out of this transitory life unto His Divine Mercy the late Most High, Most Mighty, and Most Excellent Monarch, George the Sixth, by the Grace of God, of Great Britain, Ireland, and the British Dominions beyond the Seas, King, Defender of the Faith, and Sovereign of the Most Noble Order of the Garter.

"Let us humbly beseech Almighty God to bless with long life, health, and honour, and all wordly happiness, the Most High, Most Mighty, and Most Excellent Monarch, our Sovereign Lady, Elizabeth the Second, now, by the Grace of God, of Great Britain, Ireland, and the British Dominions beyond the Seas, Queen, Defender of the Faith, and Sovereign of the Most Noble Order of the Garter. God Save the Queen!"

The choir sang the dimissory anthem, "God be in my heart and in my understanding," and the Archbishop pronounced the benediction. Elizabeth II and the Queen Mother walked to the space in the chapel floor, looked down for a last painful moment at the coffin, and then dropped deep, reverent curtsies. And then, one by one, the princesses and the royal dukes and the royal mourners from overseas and all those within the chancel came in turn to bow and curtsy in tribute at the square where the coffin had disappeared.

Hardly had the last mourner left the chapel when court officials arrived to inspect and pack away the crown jewels.

The new Elizabethan age had begun.

As the cortege of George VI rolled across London the presence of the bent, greying figure of the Duke of Windsor marching behind the bier of his brother seemed to turn the hand of time back to the abdication of 1936.

"And now we all have a new King," said Edward VIII in the peroration of his last broadcast before stepping down from the throne he had occupied for only 325 days. And, he might have added, a new kind of king. Few then thought that George VI, the shy, unimposing, unmajestic younger brother, could restore the broken confidence in the throne. Untrained for the highest responsibilities, a comparative unknown who had much leeway to make up in impressing his people with his personality, he obviously abhorred personal prominence, seemed easily flustered when things went wrong, and stammered agonizingly when

3

making public speeches. His maiden radio address to his people was interrupted with pauses in which he struggled audibly for the power to continue and during those moments of "dead air" sympathetic listeners felt that the fate of the monarchy hung in the balance.

It is necessary to go far back in history to discover a monarch who took the throne of Britain under comparable testing circumstances. The sixtieth in the long list of British sovereigns since the days of Egbert, who was probably the first (in 809) to receive the homage of all the other English kings, no reign witnessed wider external conflict than that of George VI. None since the days of Elizabeth I passed through greater peril.

When he stepped up to the throne, an unprepared understudy, the crown itself had been shaken by the bitter, angry disappointment over Edward VIII's defection, which split the country into two camps. The international situation was already ominous and it was soon to bring the most parlous years in Britain's history: a desperate global war which raged for more than a third of his reign, far more devastating in its consequences than the First World War; a drastic shift in Britain's economic structure, bringing with it a loss of wealth, power and prestige—almost everything that Britons in the between-wars years regarded as their heritage; a bloodless revolution in Britain's social structure; and the sinister threat, while the nations were still convalescent from the last conflict, of a new menace to the free world.

And yet, as George VI went to his grave, a decade and a half after his accession, the monarchy had not only been restored to its ancient dignity but had been elevated to new levels of respect and affection; a political institution which many thought was in the stages of decline had acquired a significance far richer than anyone had deemed possible; the throne which Elizabeth II inherited was more securely established than at any time in the past 1,000 years of Britain's history; and the partnership of Commonwealth and Empire of which she became the head was more firmly knit than ever before.

Why this should be so is a prodigious fact, worthy of sober assessment. For in an age when few traditions are immune from challenge, when forms of government all over the globe have been going through violent or gradual change, any institution which commands such universal approval is not to be discounted.

34

II

THE CROWN AND THE PEOPLE

OVERWORK is not the occupational hazard usually associated in the public mind with the lives of royalty. King George VI's gradual but visible breakdown as a direct result of the heavy duties of kingship he had carried since ascending the throne—first with a serious arterial ailment in his legs in 1948 and then when he underwent a major operation for the removal of his cancerous left lung in September, 1951—therefore came as a profound shock even to his own subjects, most of whom had no idea that behind the elaborate façade of royal pomp their King's work was arduous.

Many Britons, and most citizens of other lands, had come to believe that in an age of democracy the sovereign in Britain had been reduced to a figurehead, a cipher in the affairs of the state. The premature death of George VI, when his tired and overtaxed heart finally gave way under the daily weight of his office, served as a belated and tragic reminder that the crown is not purely ornamental. Indeed, it is one of the ironies of the British system of government that, as despotic power has dwindled in the hands of its kings and queens, the growth of a parliamentary democracy has converted the ruling monarch into the busiest official in the kingdom.

When George VI was first stricken with the arterial ailment that was to lead to his death three years and three months later his doctors, while they declined to define his affliction (a variant of Buerger's disease), privately described his complaint as a "tired businessman's disease," peculiar to over-zealous executives who work and worry too hard and too long at their jobs. This description was not clinically precise but in the King's case it was singularly true.

A great legal authority once characterized George V as being

"as good as a trusty family solicitor for the British Empire."
George VI preferred to think of his job in the more modern sense
as that of board chairman of the British Commonwealth, a wide-
flung enterprise embracing some 610,000,000 people, more than
one quarter of the world's population, scattered at strategic intervals around the globe. But, unlike the president of a world-
wide corporation, whose job his own resembled, the King was in
the unenviable position of having no deputy to stand in for him
while he had a yearly rest. Nor, like the President of the United
States, could he look forward to retirement. The King was king
24 hours of every day, seven days of every week, 52 weeks of
every year, as long as he lived. Never, after becoming a king by
force of circumstance when he took up his brother's burden late
in 1936, did George VI enjoy a real holiday free from state
responsibilities, or even a week-end that he could call his
own.

George VI could never close the office door. As the fount of all
authority, his regal sign-manual—altered in the eleventh year of
his reign from George R.I. to George R. when India and Pakistan
became independent—was the starter impulse without which
Britain, the Dominions and the Empire could not tick over. No
matter where he went—shooting in the Scottish hills around
Balmoral, celebrating the traditional family Christmas at his
country house at Sandringham, or week-ending quietly at Royal
Lodge, his family home in the parkland of Windsor Castle—
always present were the "boxes," the steel-lined, leather-covered
dispatch cases, containing state papers, reports from Cabinet
Ministers and other documents needing his study and signature,
which followed him everywhere he went. Even on the royal tour
of South Africa in 1947 a cipher clerk travelled constantly with
him to deal with messages continuously demanding the monarch's
attention. As an English commentator once remarked, "There is
no trade union for kings."

This is the life of service, a never-ending job relentless in its
demands on time and person, upon which Queen Elizabeth II has
now embarked.

The monarchy, which runs back in time a thousand years to
the half-legendary kings of Wessex who presided over the misty
beginnings of English history, is Britain's oldest institution,

older by far than Parliament, more ancient even than its laws, yet it has evolved and altered so much in character down the centuries that it is today one of the country's most modern institutions, fulfilling a role far broader and far more meaningful than ever before.

Constitutionally, Britain is a parliamentary democracy with a limited constitutional monarchy. Any contradictions that arise between the two systems are generally resolved in favour of democracy. This triumphant reconciliation of two apparent irreconcilables, in itself a remarkable example of the British genius for compromise, has been in the making for several hundred years, most of them marred by the long struggle for power between the ruling monarch and the representatives of his people. But, as the London *News Chronicle* editorially commented in 1948: "It has been the great achievement of the British nation that out of tyranny it has won constitutional monarchy without tearing apart the fabric of society. . . . It [the monarchy] has become the emblem of our capacity for ordered change, the stability of our society and our enduring love of freedom."

Stretching back over the centuries from the present time to the days of the Saxon Witenagemot, a council of wise men who were summoned to give counsel to the king, is a long record of successive attempts to secure a form of government that would be "broad-based upon the people's will" and to curb the power of those elements in the state which attempted to interfere with this.

The Plantagenet kings engaged in a struggle with the landholding aristocracy they had created, and at the same time the Great Councils, which were purely feudal bodies, became gradually transformed into something that was more representative of the nation as a whole. In 1215 the barons gathered at Runnymede, the meadow below Windsor on the Thames, to force from King John the cornerstone of English liberties, the Magna Carta, in which he reluctantly agreed to respect the law of the land by refraining from imposing feudal dues (with certain exceptions) "save by the common council of the realm. . . ." In the year 1254 each county sheriff was bidden to send two knights, chosen by the county "to consider what aid they would give to the King in his great necessity." In this way there began to develop the power to grant or withhold supplies, an important safeguard against royal tyranny, which was continually used by the people's representatives in their struggle against the sovereign and his executives.

It was Simon de Montfort's Parliament of 1265 which contained for the first time not only knights of the shire, but also citizens and burgesses representing the cities and boroughs, and Edward I's Model Parliament thirty years later laid the foundations on which the structure of the modern British Parliament was built. Parliaments upon this first model were frequently summoned thereafter, and with their consent the king enacted statutes. Three centuries after the Magna Carta the lusty, powerful Tudor monarchs broke the power of their great lords, and when Elizabeth I died in 1603 and was succeeded by the Stuarts the struggle became one between the kings and Parliament. By the end of the century Parliament had won this fight and the powers of the kings became limited, particularly with the passing in 1689 of the Bill of Rights, which forbade unlawful acts and the suspension of laws by the king, and the imposition of taxation without Parliament's consent. The coming of the Hanoverian dynasty brought about the rise of Cabinet government, which developed mainly because the earlier Georges, who had not mastered English, were content to leave much of the work of government to their Ministers. Choleric George III made strong efforts to reassert royal powers and Queen Victoria acted with a good deal of independence, but throughout the nineteenth century, along with a succession of Reform Acts which broadened the franchise, the personal intervention of the monarch in the mechanics of government slowly diminished. However, it was not until the reign of George V that the modern position of the monarchy became stabilized.

In this concept, although all powers and responsibilities of government are vested in Parliament, the crown is recognized as the ultimate seat of authority and from it radiate outward all the offices and functions which feature in the British form of constitutional government.

But the crown is worn by the sovereign: without the person the crown is only a legal fiction, a useful but inanimate emblem. It is the living, breathing personality of the sovereign, who by virtue of his or her lineage and office is the living representative of the nation's history from its earliest days, that lifts the crown

38

above an abstraction and makes visible and audible to the subjects the continuity and the unity for which the crown stands.

In a sense which few foreigners fully comprehend, but which no Briton needs to understand, the sovereign *is* Britain. Standing above faction, party, class, nationality and race, he or she is everybody's king or queen, the chief of the nation.

Most foreign observers confess themselves puzzled to understand why the British accept as chief of their nation a personage to whom they concede little executive authority. Behind this apparent paradox, however, there is deep significance.

In the evolution of their constitutional monarchy the British have come to look upon their sovereign as their supremely representative person, the most British Briton of them all. Whatever the monarch says or does, he or she speaks and acts for the people; and when the British are given laws or receive orders in the sovereign's name, it is the people incarnate in the monarch that they obey. Thus it is today that members of the Cabinet are the Queen's Ministers, holding their offices as her servants and advisers and receiving their seals of office from her own hands [1]; the leader of the majority party in the House of Commons on becoming Prime Minister receives his trust from the sovereign and the Parliamentary Opposition is known as Her Majesty's Opposition; judges sitting with the royal arms over their heads administer the Queen's justice; the armed services are Her Majesty's Forces; civil servants are servants, not of their departmental Ministers, but of the crown; officers of the law keep the Queen's peace; and diplomatic couriers are called "Queen's Messengers." Government mail is franked "On Her Majesty's Service," the humble postmen carry Her Majesty's mails, and even Britain's scarlet mail-box pillars are monogrammed "ER" (Elizabeth Regina).

There is another aspect of this seeming paradox which is noteworthy. As the repository of the ultimate power of the people, the monarch is expected to be shown the utmost deference by those elected or nominated leaders to whom power has been temporarily delegated. Thus, Prime Ministers on addressing the sovereign "present their humble duty" and the military leaders stand respectfully to attention and salute in the monarch's presence.

Some 85 years ago the famed British constitutional scholar

Walter Bagehot, writing in the reign of Queen Victoria, observed that in theory the sovereign "could disband the army; she could dismiss all the officers . . . she could sell off all our ships-of-war and all our naval stores; she could make a peace by the sacrifice of Cornwall and begin a war for the conquest of Brittany. She could make every citizen in the United Kingdom, male or female, a peer; she could make every parish in the United Kingdom a 'University'; she could dismiss most of the civil servants, and she could pardon all offenders."

By the strict letter of the law, Queen Elizabeth II inherited all these rights—but in practice she can no more do these things than the humblest of her subjects. Although she personifies authority, she cannot wield it. She cannot override the will of Parliament or refuse to sign its bills—the veto power was last used in 1707 by Queen Anne, who was also the last sovereign to preside in person over meetings of the Cabinet—nor can she dismiss any of her Ministers, although Parliament can dismiss the sovereign, as Edward VIII discovered. And because she must not express a political preference in public, she cannot vote, a privilege denied her along with members of her family, prisoners, certified lunatics and peers of the realm. (The last monarch to intervene openly in the nation's politics was George III, who in 1780 personally electioneered in Windsor against the Whig candidate.) She cannot rent property from her subjects, nor can she appear as a witness in her courts. Although she is guardian of Britain's infants, idiots and lunatics the actual responsibility is carried out by the Lord Chancellor in her name. Pardons granted in the name of the sovereign to condemned persons or serving prisoners are actually granted by the Home Secretary. (George VI conscientiously read up many capital cases during his reign, but usually discussed them with his Home Secretary *after* pardons had been granted.)

Few royal prerogatives remain to Elizabeth II, but among them are the right to drive as fast as she likes upon the Queen's highways in a car which needs no licence and the right to ride in a horse-drawn carriage upon Hyde Park's Rotten Row, where others can only ride horseback. And in her courts, whose judges and magistrates are appointed in her name, she cannot be sued or arraigned for any crime, including murder.

The two Houses of Parliament meet in what is known as the King's Palace of Westminster,[2] a building which is royal property, yet the monarch by constitutional usage is not permitted to set foot in the House of Commons. He or she must confine royal appearances to the House of Lords. Even the sovereign's messenger, a frock-coated and gaitered functionary with the sinister-sounding title of Gentleman Usher of the Black Rod, must observe a time-honoured ritual whenever he delivers some official piece of news from the upper house to the Commons. When Black Rod arrives at the door of the Commons it is ceremoniously slammed in his face and the cry "Black Rod! Black Rod!" goes echoing down the corridors. The messenger thereupon knocks with his staff three times on the oak door—his marks are clearly visible—and is then admitted, bowing to the Speaker and the members as he approaches the Commons. None of the monarch's military forces are permitted within a certain distance of the Parliament buildings, and to cross the boundary for a procession or parade they must first get the permission of the Speaker of the Commons. These safeguards, perpetuated as proof of the treasured independence of the people's chamber from the crown, date back to 1642, when Charles I, engaged in a furious quarrel with the Commons, made his dramatic swoop into the House to seize five leading members he had impeached for high treason.

George VI could count himself luckier than any of his royal predecessors over the past 300 years, for in October, 1950, the day before the formal opening of the rebuilt House of Commons, which had been bomb- and fire-gutted by German bombers on May 10, 1941, an exception was made to the long-standing rule and with his wife and Queen Mary he was permitted to inspect the precincts of the new Commons.

III

THE MONARCHY IN ACTION

AS the embodiment of a medieval custom in modern government which not only survives but functions, the occupant of
the British throne has, in fact, three jobs in one.

Under the concept of a monarch who reigns but does not rule,
the king or queen is a servant of the people, paid to perform
certain well-defined constitutional duties within the United Kingdom without getting in the way of the fiercely democratic pro-
cesses of government. These duties, which far exceed the
sovereign's powers, are limited in scope but remorseless in their
demands on the monarch's time. Taken together, they comprise the
first of the jobs performed by the occupant of the British throne.

In her formal role in the government of the United Kingdom,
which is carried on in her name, Elizabeth II is an integral part
of Parliament, which correctly means the sovereign, the House of
Lords and the dominant partner, the House of Commons, acting
together to form the legislature. Parliament is summoned to take
up its duties by the Queen. Each session is opened by a personal
visit from the Queen, when her speech, written by her Ministers
in explanation of her Government's policies, is read from the
throne in the House of Lords by the monarch herself.[1] The
sovereign does not nowadays attend personally the end of each
session, but the monarch's prorogation speech is read by the
Lord Chancellor in the House of Lords and by the Speaker in the
Commons.

Before a Bill becomes an Act it must receive the monarch's
assent, which is still given in the traditional Norman French,
La Reine (or *Le Roy*) *le veult*. If the Bill is one sponsored by a
private member instead of by Her Majesty's Government the response is *Soit fait comme il est desiré*. As a historical note, the form
of rejection—*La Reine* (or *Le Roy*) *s'avisera*—has not been used

since the beginning of the eighteenth century when the sudden report of Jacobite unrest in Scotland caused Queen Anne, on the advice of her Ministers, to refuse a Bill introducing the militia to Scotland. It may now be regarded as defunct.

In legal theory, at least, the Queen is the only lawful origin of constitutional authority and in the interim between a change of government all power resides in her hands. Constitutionally, the sovereign retains two important functions. The first is to appoint the Prime Minister, although in practice the person designated is invariably the leader of the party that can command a majority in the Commons. About the only time when the sovereign now has a choice of action is when the majority party has no clearly-designated leader. For instance, when the ailing Bonar Law, the Conservative Prime Minister, resigned in 1923 he declined to tender advice as to his successor. His expected heir was his Foreign Secretary, Lord Curzon, who was the most senior member of the Conservative Party, but George V—after expert political advice—sent instead for Stanley Baldwin, the lesser-known Chancellor of the Exchequer in Bonar Law's Cabinet, to form a new Government. This choice was partly dictated by the realization that a Government could no longer be directed by a Prime Minister from the Lords, but the choice of Baldwin instead of the imperious Curzon contributed greatly to the settlement of the vexatious Irish problem of that time.

The second main function of the sovereign is to dissolve Parliament. In this the monarch is expected to be guided by the advice of the Prime Minister, although in exceptional circumstances, with an alternative Prime Minister available who could command a majority of the votes in the Commons, constitutional jurists agree that he or she could with propriety act contrary to official advice. Thus, for instance, when the world-wide financial crisis hit Britain suddenly in 1931 it was George V who talked Prime Minister Ramsay MacDonald out of his intention of resigning. The King felt an election at that time would be bad for the country and instead prevailed upon MacDonald to form a Coalition Government and then persuaded the Conservative and Liberal party leaders to cooperate with him.

Many of the monarch's remaining functions result from quirks or oversights in the development of the British Constitution. Unlike the Constitution of the United States, which can be

43

compressed into a few pages of print, the British Constitution is unwritten. It is an elastic, flexible, constantly changing collection of the innumerable Acts of Parliament, together with a large body of customs or conventions which are generally accepted although they may not appear in the statute books. For instance, though the office of Prime Minister had been in existence since 1721, it was not recognized by legislation until 1917—and then only because Parliament passed a Bill endowing the office of Prime Minister with its country house estate at Chequers. Today there is still no Act of Parliament laying down how the Prime Minister should be appointed or how many members there should be in the Cabinet; likewise nowhere is it laid down in law that the Prime Minister should be a member of the House of Commons rather than the Lords.

When anomalies appear, unless they are of such major importance as to necessitate a new Act of Parliament, they are generally referred to the sovereign. Thus George VI was asked in 1948 to give the supreme ruling in the case of a German prisoner-of-war in Britain who had been sentenced to death by an English military court for the murder of a fellow-prisoner: there was no higher court to which the convicted P.O.W. could appeal and, with the war over, there was no protective power acting for Germany to whom the findings of the military tribunal could be submitted. Parenthetically, it was a similar quirk in the British Constitution which spared Dr. Klaus Fuchs, the German-born British scientist who was convicted and sentenced to 14 years' imprisonment in 1950 for passing to Russia atomic information of value to a possible enemy. Britain has no death penalty for espionage in peacetime, because technically there can be no treason while the sovereign has no official enemies.

The ruler still retains the royal prerogative of mercy in dealing with British courts martial, under which a sentence may be mitigated or remitted or a free pardon granted whether or not an appeal against conviction has been made.

Apart from her participation in Parliament, Elizabeth II plays an intimate role in her country's constitutional government through Her Majesty's Privy Council, a unique, age-old body which, like the monarchy it serves, also demonstrates the peculiar British knack of putting new content into old forms.

Heir to a great tradition as old as the monarchy itself, the 300 or so royally-appointed Privy Councillors of today are the lineal successors of the courts of the Norman kings. In those times it was composed of the king's tenants-in-chief, his household officials and others whom he wished to summon. It did all the day-to-day routine work of central government and expanded whenever the king called in a greater number of his barons for more important business. By the reign of Henry VII this council had become the instrument of the crown. It was then composed of an inner ring of counsellors proper and an outer ring of technical experts and dignitaries frequently summoned for advice. From 1540, after Henry VIII reorganized it, the Privy Council had its regular staff of clerks and other officials and it was from this skeleton beginning that most of Britain's existing administrative system grew. Through the sixteenth and seventeenth centuries it had two main functions: first, it sat as a council of state, advising the crown on all matters of policy and taking administrative action through its permanent officials; second, reinforced by judicial assessors, it sat on certain days as a court of law.

As the task of government became more complex the Privy Council tended to increase in size and influential inner rings of Councillors took over the reins of government. Charles II, who followed Cromwell's brief dictatorship, trusted few of his 50-odd Councillors and relied mainly on an inner committee of five members, known as the Cabal from the initial letters of their names. From this originated the Cabinet as a small inner committee of the Privy Council, and as this system gained acceptance during the rule of the first two Georges gradually the Privy Council was reduced to formal business.

In their roles as temporal fathers to more than a quarter of the world's inhabitants, successive British monarchs have enlarged their Privy Councils until today the 300 or so life members, all of whom bear the title Right Honourable Privy Councillor, cover the Empire and the Commonwealth, with Ministers and ex-Ministers of the Dominions included in its ranks along with their counterparts in Britain. Membership is sometimes also conferred as a special honour on those who have done the state service. All Cabinet Ministers and ex-Cabinet Ministers are Privy Councillors (but, of course, all Privy Councillors are not Cabinet Ministers).

Until 1707 Privy Councillors were regarded as servants of the reigning monarch and their appointments came to an end with his death. In that year, in order to smooth the transition from one reign to the next, Parliament decreed that Privy Councillors should act for a further six months in the new reign. In 1910 another Act of Parliament decreed that Privy Councillors should hold office for life, so that a new monarch inherits his predecessor's Privy Council. Councillors have a ceremonial dress—a coat of blue with gold braid, knee breeches and a cocked hat—but it is now worn by a few members only on the highest state occasions.

While many functions of the Privy Council have fallen into disuse, three of its historical features remain. On a sovereign's succession to the throne, the full Privy Council (or as many members as can assemble in time) forms the main part of the Accession Council, which meets as the first act of a new reign in order to arrange the public proclamation of the new monarch and, as the first of the subjects, to take the oath of allegiance. The Accession Council, an even older body than the Privy Council, with origins traced back by some authorities to the ancient Witenagemot, is an *ad hoc* body which meets but once during a reign. It consists of members of the Privy Council, the Lords Spiritual and Temporal, the Lord Mayor, Aldermen and Citizens of London, individuals quaintly described as "numbers of other gentlemen of quality," and representatives from Commonwealth countries.

Because of her absence abroad when her father died, Elizabeth II's Accession Council broke with precedent and conducted its formalities in two stages. On the day of George VI's death the full Council met, proclaimed the new Queen and issued an Order in Council for the public proclamation to be made. On Elizabeth's return to London a second Council was held, from which, in accordance with custom, all but the Privy Councillors withdrew. Before them the new Queen read her Declaration of Accession, subscribed to the oath for the security of the Church of Scotland, in accordance with the Act of Union with Scotland, and signed her first Orders in Council.

The proclamation of the accession is the only occasion on which the full Privy Council is now summoned. The routine executive work of authorizing the official Orders in Council is now more or less a formality, which is periodically carried out by the sovereign

46

in person with the clerk and at least three other members of the Council present.

The Privy Council's most vital function is as a source of committees. The chief of these, of course, is the Cabinet itself. Others of its committees designated in the past have expanded and developed into full Government departments like the Board of Trade, though they are still technically committees of the Privy Council. Still others, like the Committee of Imperial Defence, which was formed in 1905, came into being as adjuncts of the Privy Council because there existed at that time no other policy-making body to coordinate the interests of the United Kingdom, the Dominions and the Empire. More recently the Privy Council has revived its earlier employment of technical experts by setting up among its varied members small specialized committees like the Medical Research Council. Reporting directly to the Queen, beholden to no department of the Government, these specialized bodies function unhindered by the compartmentalism which is inherent in a great bureaucracy.

Aside from the Cabinet, the Privy Council's most important remaining component is its Judicial Committee, which performs much the same function in the British Commonwealth as does the Supreme Court in the United States. It is the final court of appeal from the decisions and rulings of all British courts outside the confines of the United Kingdom, except in so far as some self-governing Dominions (Canada, Pakistan and South Africa) have taken steps since 1949 to abolish the right of appeal for their own nationals. (The House of Lords is the Supreme Court of Appeal in the United Kingdom and the Lords, in turn, delegate this function to a small committee of the Lords of Appeal in Ordinary and such peers as have held high judicial office.) [2]

The routine administrative duties, many of them reduced to empty form, none the less took a heavy toll of George VI's time and energy. For instance, under the omnibus Emergency Powers Defence Act by which Churchill's Coalition Government ruled during the Second World War, all rules and regulations had to be read aloud in the King's presence with at least three members of his Privy Council present. By the war's end the King, who was a stickler for every letter of royal protocol, had listened to and said "approved" to some 13,000 emergency decrees, ranging from blackout restrictions to the prohibition of kite-flying.

In his book "The English Constitution," Walter Bagehot observed that the British sovereign retained only "three rights— the right to be consulted, the right to encourage, the right to warn." A sensible monarch, Bagehot added, would want no others.

Despite the progressive loss of older powers, it is impossible to over-estimate the importance of the sovereign's role in Britain today. In a negative sense he (or she) stands as the final guardian of the liberties of his subjects. As king (or queen) in Council he is the watchman against any temptation of a bad Government to rule the country (or any of the Dominions) by means of undebatable Orders in Council, such as the emergency edicts of wartime, instead of by direct legislation approved by Parliament.

Although he reigned without governing, George VI nevertheless managed to exert a real and powerful influence behind the scenes in political life, but because of his restricted constitutional role his intervention was necessarily roundabout and unobtrusive.

Much of his influence stemmed from the potentialities rather than the realities of his position—that is, George VI *might* have taken a firm stand, risking further curtailment of the monarchy's power in a head-on clash between state and throne, but often the mere threat of it sufficed. Before any actual clash of personality took place between the King and one of his Ministers the private secretaries on each side would spar and fence and His Majesty's principal private secretary, Sir Alan Lascelles, a most powerful though little-known figure in Britain, would strongly press his master's views. As the next step, the King himself would call in the Minister for a face-to-face argument. In the final result, George VI would almost certainly give way on anything save a question of such major importance to the kingdom that it was worth risking the future of the crown itself. But long before that point had been reached the unpleasant consequences of making an enemy of the King and his influential friends, and the loss of rewards in the form of honours, would usually weigh heavily with any Minister.

In strict constitutional form, George VI's Ministers advised him, but in fact there are few of them who cannot recall occasions when they profited by his advice.

"It is one of the privileges of a Prime Minister to be able to discuss affairs of State with a man who is above the political

16. *The King's procession passes out of the Abbey after his coronation*

17. *The newly-crowned King and his family on the balcony of Buckingham Palace*

18. *King and Queen return to the Palace in the State Coach*

battle, and who has had a long and continuous experience both of things and persons," commented Clement Attlee after the King's death. "I knew, too, that I would always get from him a well-balanced judgment."

The court is no longer the headquarters for party politics, as it was in Hanoverian days, and by maintaining equally good relations with all major parties the King, like his father before him, did much to smooth down political bickering. By virtue of his central position and continuation in office while Governments came and went George VI was perpetually accumulating background and experience more varied than any party leader can hope to possess. He was privy to all the secrets of his Cabinets—indeed, they were technically his secrets—and whatever crises arose were first brought before him.

"I made certain he was kept informed of every secret matter," said Prime Minister Churchill after the King's death, "and the care and thoroughness with which he mastered the immense daily flow of state papers made a deep mark on my mind."

Like his mother Queen Mary, George VI had an astonishing capacity for gathering facts and remembering them and from this storehouse of information was frequently able to make valuable contributions to the policies of his Governments. Because of his brother's constitutional set-to with the Cabinet, George VI in the early years of his reign was careful not to venture into the twilight zone between the crown and the Government, but towards the end of the war and in the post-war years he exerted a growing influence in the area of political and international policy.

Like his grandfather Edward VII, whose royal diplomacy laid the sentimental basis for the *Entente Cordiale*, George VI consciously and deliberately used himself and his royal family to tighten the bonds that unite the free world, particularly the ties that bind Britain and the English-speaking nations of the Commonwealth and Britain and the United States.

He frequently used his personal influence to persuade British public figures to take on what appeared to be thankless assignments. For instance, it was on George VI's urging that his blue-blooded second cousin, Lord Louis Mountbatten, whose versatility and ability the King admired, agreed to take on the onerous job as the twenty-ninth and last Viceroy of India, charged with devising and implementing a solution that would meet Indian demands for independence. Mountbatten at first rejected the post when the Labour Government nominated him—"No one in his right frame of mind would dream of going out to try to settle an insoluble problem," he told Prime Minister Attlee—and only accepted the assignment when George VI personally asked him to take up the challenge.

More recently, just prior to his death, the King pressed for the appointment of Viscount Montgomery as supreme commander for Communist-infested Malaya. The appointment, proposed by Churchill's Cabinet and agreed to by Montgomery, later fell through because of the short-sighted opposition of Malayan planters, who feared that an all-out campaign against the Communists combined with a military regime which Montgomery's appointment implied would put a temporary end to their already restricted business activities in the Red-ridden areas.

Occasionally George VI exerted his influence in most unexpected directions. Just prior to D-Day for the invasion of France in 1944 Prime Minister Churchill plagued General Eisenhower with repeated requests to be allowed to travel along as a witness to the massive operation. Eisenhower strongly demurred in view of the extra precautions that would have been needed because of the Prime Minister's presence and the consequences in the unhappy event that he became a casualty. Churchill was persistent, however. At this point one of Eisenhower's aides tipped off Buckingham Palace, and George VI promptly sent word that if the Prime Minister felt it necessary to go on the expedition the King felt it his equal duty and privilege to participate at the head of his troops.

Later the King tactfully wrote Churchill saying he had decided "that it would not be right for either you or me to be where we planned to be on D-Day." Pointing out that their presence would be an embarrassment to those responsible for the fighting ship or ships on which they travelled, George VI said: "I have very reluctantly come to the conclusion that the right thing to do is what normally falls to those at the top on such occasions, namely, to remain at home and wait."

While he admitted Eisenhower's overall command of the operation Mr. Churchill doggedly contended that the Supreme Commander could not stop him, as Minister of Defence in Great Britain, from sailing on the invasion as a crew member of one of

His Majesty's ships and the old war-horse was all set to sail when another letter from the King overtook him.

"I am a younger man than you, I am a sailor, and as King I am head of all these Services," wrote George VI. "There is nothing I would like to do better than to go to sea, but I have agreed to stay at home; is it fair that you should then do exactly what I should have liked to do myself?"

That settled the matter. Both the King and his first Minister stayed in London and visited the Normandy beaches only after the landings had been accomplished.

British schoolchildren are still brought up to think of a large part of the world as coloured red on the map, but the children of today learn that this signifies a far different form of association than it did for their grandparents, for whom the red splashes all over the globe meant the British Empire during its heyday of greatest expansion in the latter half of the nineteenth century.

Over the last 50 years a succession of quiet constitutional changes has transformed the political character of the Empire, resulting in a Commonwealth of Nations [3] that is unique not only in the world of today but also in the history of the past—a functioning league of nations that binds together some 610,000,000 peoples of diverse races, creeds and colours, who profess a hundred and more religions, speak four or five hundred languages and are scattered to the far corners of the earth.

In the United States, for some reason, this still-continuing transmutation from imperialism to free association has been largely overlooked ("One often wonders how the British manage with little more than a few sticks and stones and a bit of glue and some swagger to keep an Empire together," confessed an American professor, Max Lerner, at the time of George VI's death), and it is startling but not unusual to encounter Americans whose notions of British imperialism are coloured by schoolbook stories of George III, still believing that one-time British possessions like Canada or Australia even now pay financial tribute to and are run by London.[4] In fact the actual relationship between the so-called British Dominions [5] and the Government of the United Kingdom is broadly on the same basis as the relationship between Washington and London. Under the Statute of Westminster of 1931, which formally ended what already in practice had become obsolete—i.e., the right of the United Kingdom Parliament to pass Acts binding the Dominions, save only by their own request and consent—the five Dominions of that time (Canada, Newfoundland, Australia, New Zealand and South Africa) were recognized as self-governing nations, independent, and equal in status with each other and with the mother country. Each of the major Commonwealth countries now has its own Parliament, and complete freedom to legislate and to make war and peace.

There is no federal constitution, no formal ties to hold these nations together, and each is free at any time to withdraw from the Commonwealth, as Eire and Burma have done. The linchpin which holds these scattered states in common bond is the crown, which the Statute of Westminster specifically recognized as "the symbol of the free association of the members of the British Commonwealth of Nations." If the crown were to be cast aside, the Commonwealth would cease to exist as a functional, organic unit.

Thus Elizabeth II embodies in her own person many monarchies: she is Queen of Great Britain, but she is equally Queen of Canada, Australia, New Zealand, Pakistan, South Africa and Ceylon. (India, on becoming a republic, decided to remain a full member of the Commonwealth. As a republic, she could not "owe allegiance to the crown," as do her associates, but she accepted the sovereign as the symbol of free association of the independent Commonwealth nations and Elizabeth II, as was George VI, is acknowledged in India as Head of the Commonwealth.)

This multiple kingship, the second of Elizabeth II's jobs, is in many ways more demanding than her role in the administration of Great Britain. As each new member state sets up on its own it increasingly exercises its right of direct access to the sovereign, either through the governor-general, the sovereign's representative in each of the major Commonwealth nations (except India), or direct to Buckingham Palace. Governors-general, formerly appointed on the recommendation of the United Kingdom Government, are now appointed by the sovereign on the recommendation of the Dominion Government concerned, but the monarch can (and George VI did) refuse to make appointments because of objections to the nominees on personal grounds. In the past the appointees were invariably public men or minor royalty from Britain, but increasingly the Dominions, sensitive to any suggestion that they are inferior in stature to the mother country, are suggesting public figures of their own for these high posts.

In 1947, when the Duke of Gloucester gave up his post as Governor-General of Australia, the then Prime Minister of Australia, Labourite Joseph B. Chifley, suggested a home-grown Governor-General as the Duke's successor. His choice was another Labourite, William John McKell, a butcher's son who had worked his way up from a boxer and a boilermaker to become a barrister and a Labour member of the New South Wales Parliament for more than 30 years. He was premier of New South Wales throughout the Second World War. George VI, who had nothing against Billie McKell personally, gently suggested that his representative be someone less identified with party politics, but Chifley insisted on the last word and overruled the King. Buckingham Palace officials were quietly horrified, but McKell filled his non-partisan job as the King's representative with such rectitude that the Liberal Prime Minister of Australia, Robert Menzies, extended his term of office for a sixth year. When McKell visited Britain in the summer of 1951 he was invited to join the house party at Balmoral in order to brief the King and Queen and Princess Margaret on their projected (and later cancelled) tour of Australia, and the royal family got along so well with the ex-boilermaker that the King later knighted McKell and invested him with the insignia of the Order of St. Michael and St. George.

As father of his world-wide family of co-equal nations that has grown up around the British throne, George VI conceived it his duty to be well posted on all Commonwealth problems, from racial difficulties in South Africa to the fate of the princely states of India. This added greatly to his paper work—for example, in a single year, 1944, the Dominions Office in London handled nearly 25,000 telegrams to and from the Dominions, many of which were read by the King—and the time he had to devote to fact-finding interviews, but it gave him the authority of an expert when he intervened, as he often did in a quiet way, in matters of Commonwealth policy.

"There is no doubt that of all the institutions which have

grown up among us over the centuries or sprung into being in our lifetime, the constitutional monarchy is the most deeply founded and dearly cherished by the whole association of our peoples," said Winston Churchill in his moving broadcast tribute on the death of George VI. Why this should be so has for long puzzled foreign observers—and been taken much for granted by the British, who seldom question the nature of their monarchy except in times of constitutional crisis. The death of the King provided a fresh opportunity to examine the meaning of the monarchy, and in their efforts to explain the almost universal response which George VI's passing stirred, not only in Britain and in the Commonwealth but in most countries of the free world, British newspapers and public figures proffered numberless reasons why this medieval survival should remain a living force in twentieth-century Britain. Of these, the most searching was undoubtedly that put forward by the London *Observer*.

"It is worth noting that the particular British form of Monarchy which has shown such exceptional powers, first of survival and then of renaissance, is one which was, in the last century, regarded as particularly weak and 'unreal' by the Continental Kings and Emperors of the day: a strictly constitutional form of Monarchy, wholly divorced from the political business of government," said the *Observer* editorial. "It is now plain that this divorce, far from weakening the Monarchy, has given it an unsuspected, immeasurable strength. The separation of the Monarchy from the field of 'affairs,' of political business, intellectual argument, and rival ambitions has cleared its channels to the subconscious and emotive strata of the collective soul where, we may suspect, lie the deep secret springs of national purpose, character, and living unity.

". . . It may well be that the millennium of European Monarchy, when its chief function was the business of ruling, was really a long interlude, and that we have here in Britain, by accident rather than design, stumbled back to the original, true, and abiding function of the Monarchy, which lay in the magical power of Kings—in modern language, in their power to represent, express, and affect the aspirations of the collective subconscious."

The editorial continued: "It may well be that without an organ to fulfil this function, a community and its State is like a body starved of some vitamin, and that this helps to explain the instability of so many recent Republics and their unpredictable propensity to sudden mass-mania, hero-worship and relapse into crude dictatorship. The existence of a constitutional Monarchy, by satisfying profound emotional needs, leaves the business of government to proceed in a quieter, more sober and more rational atmosphere.

"Democracy requires a Government which is not invested with an aura of sanctity; Ministers who can be criticized, and dismissed by popular vote. But that is not enough," concluded the *Observer*. "In the collective soul of the people there is also a deep craving for a figure who represents an ideal; an archetypal figure who, in a phrase originally legal but with a much wider significance, must not be criticized because he 'can do no wrong.'"

As a tentative venture into the still-unexplored field of political psychology the *Observer's* deduction probably comes close to the real meaning of the monarchy, although the ordinary folk who made up the majority of George VI's subjects would express their "craving for an archetypal figure" in more workaday language.

When he laid aside the crown, whose unshared burden he had found too heavy to bear, the Duke of Windsor in his farewell broadcast at the end of the abdication crisis commended his brother, the new King, and remarked that "he has one matchless blessing, enjoyed by so many of you, and not bestowed on me, a happy home with his wife and children." With this one phrase —which the Duke later revealed had been added to his manuscript by Winston Churchill—the abdicated Edward VIII underscored the reason why the majority of his subjects lamented but none the less approved his laying down the crown.

In its time the monarchy has been variously a byword for raffishness and scandal, but during the last five reigns at least, covering the past 100 years, it has increasingly come to stand for not only the unity and continuity of the British nation and Commonwealth but also the high moral and personal and, above all, family virtues which are recognized as the necessary foundations of modern political life. Ever since the idyllic example of Queen Victoria and her consort, Prince Albert, and their family, the idea of a family has become an integral part of the idea of monarchy, and the notion of a bachelor king—or a king with a thrice-married wife—seems to the British to smack of the musical comedy or Hollywood conception of monarchy.

The British are essentially a homey people, and nothing rejoices them more than to see their own ideal of family life realized in the monarchy. The royal family is thus a cross-section of the nation, in which flattered millions see reflected facets of their own lives. That is why in countless homes, in Britain and in the Commonwealth, both rich and poor, the milestones of family life —the great events of births and marriages and deaths—are marked off in relation to the public and private doings of the royal family.

Parenthetically, it is equally noteworthy that the royal family today is thought of throughout Britain *as a family* and not as a dynasty. This explains why the great personal occasions in the royal family's life, such as the silver wedding anniversary of George VI and Queen Elizabeth in 1948 and the birth of a son and heir to Princess Elizabeth the same year, are regarded as truly *national* events, and not, as in the old days of royalty, as of first and foremost importance to the dynasty.

In their own reign King George VI and his Queen, who shared her husband's qualities of dignified simplicity and quiet devotion to duty, provided in their own happy married life and wise upbringing of their two daughters a visible example of domesticity which served, to a surprising extent, as a model for their subjects. Churchill, with his talent for epitomizing, once said of them, "They have the rare talent of being able to make a mass of people realize, in a flash, that they are good."

This symbolic function, the third of the sovereign's jobs, involving as it does a monotonous round of public appearances and an almost complete lack of privacy in the lives of royal personages, is in many ways the most onerous of the monarch's roles. George VI found it the most trying of his triple functions, but he worked hard at it and gradually subordinated his own personality in the symbol of the sovereign. He even changed his Christian name on taking the throne. Named Albert to please his great-grandmother, who requested that all her male descendants bear the name of her beloved consort, he declined to become King Albert on ascending the throne because he felt it was too closely associated in the public mind with Victoria's husband and instead chose to be known by the last of his four Christian names, as a mark of respect for his father. He also changed his official birthday —December 14—so that it could be formally celebrated by the glorious Trooping the Colour ceremony in June, a better month for drawing trade and tourists to London than gloomy December.

To his relief, much court ceremony, particularly those social functions which draw reflected glory from royal sponsorship, was dispensed with during the Second World War and did not come back during the remainder of his reign.

By nature a shy, modest, retiring man, he grew up with no desire to flaunt his royal prerogatives. When a gardener at Windsor Castle insisted on addressing him as "Your Royal Highness," young Albert turned on him one day and pouted, "You can call me that once a day and no more. I am sick of it.' As Duke of York he preferred to leave the limelight to his father and the Prince of Wales. Detesting poses and humbug in any form, he ruefully confessed to a friend, "I'm just not palace-minded." On becoming King, however, his life unrolled upon an endless red carpet, but he successfully mastered the royal art of suffering boredom at public performances without showing it. After 1937 he and his family lived in a pitiless glare of publicity. He fiercely resented intrusion in his family life—remembering the hounding he suffered from the press at the time of his own marriage he kept photographers from bothering Princess Elizabeth and Philip on their honeymoon—but he personally learned to submit to public gawking without becoming "sucker sour."

Although the sovereign naturally bears the heaviest burden, the symbolic role of the monarchy is diffused in secondary measure over all members of the royal family. Like his father before him, George VI insisted that each member of his family except the youngest grandchildren shoulder his or her share of the appearances which royalty is expected to make, and he kept a wall map in Buckingham Palace which showed by tiny coloured flags where and when each visit had been made. In one three-year wartime period the wall chart showed a total of more than 3,000 public appearances, which caused the King to complain, "We are not a family; we are a firm!" Each member of the family also kept his or her own record of royal chores performed, and twice each year, at Christmas and in midsummer, the King examined the records and then equitably shared out the major events on the programme for the forthcoming six months.

Royal services are constantly in demand: royal visits stimulate trade, royal interest lends prestige to professional organizations, and royal patronage gives the national stamp of approval to a host of charitable institutions and worthy causes. Invitations and applications pour into "Buck House," as the monarch's London headquarters is sometimes known, in a never-ending stream—to unveil statues and lay foundation stones, to visit exhibitions, to inspect youth groups and welfare centres, to call on institutions for waifs and strays and the deaf and dumb, to address conferences and banquet with professional organizations, to tour museums and to open new roads and bridges and buildings and towns. George VI was compelled to reject the majority of these requests, but he accepted enough of them to keep himself and the main members of his family engaged in an endless round of public engagements.

In the summer of 1951, when the King's doctors finally persuaded him to forgo all public appearances and take a long convalescence to recover from a mild bout of influenza which had aggravated a patch of catarrhal infection in one of his lungs, it came to light that in a seven-week period during June and July the King and Queen and the two Princesses had been booked up for no fewer than 48 public engagements, taking them all over Britain. The King, under previous medical advice to spare himself the physical ordeal of these public occasions, was down for five of them, the Queen for eight and Princess Margaret for five, but Princess Elizabeth, deputizing for her father and in her own right, was obliged to carry out no fewer than 30 public engagements during this period. This revelation spurred at least one influential British newspaper (the London *Sunday Express*) to protest: "Not only the King but the whole royal family is being grossly overworked. . . . We are turning the royal family into royal drudges."

Few of their subjects are aware of the mental fatigue and physical exhaustion which the members of the royal family endure in these formal engagements, most of which involve prolonged standing or much walking and endless hand-shaking. For instance, when the Queen and Princess Margaret visited Northern Ireland at the time the King was in bed at home with influenza, they shook hands with and exchanged a few polite words of conversation with some 90 officials in the course of a five-hour tour that was non-stop except for a hurried ten-minute break for tea. When Princess Elizabeth visited Birmingham about the same time she was hustled through a seven-hour programme which included starting a rally of old-time cars, unveiling a statue, visiting a handiwork exhibition and seeing a sports demonstration, and in the course of it she had to meet 106 local civic dignitaries and citizens and some of their wives.

When Elizabeth brilliantly stood-in for her father at the 1951 Trooping ceremony the millions of admirers who saw her pictures in the newspapers and newsreels saw only a fairy-book princess sitting side-saddle on a horse, looking as if she had stepped from a Friml operetta. Few thought of the strain of keeping even a parade-trained horse almost motionless for nearly two hours, or the long hours of practice that went to make the ceremony precision-perfect.

Even the business of dressing to suit these royal appearances is a weariful chore. In the course of an ordinary day George VI perhaps changed from a lounge suit into one of his service uniforms, back into a business suit and finally into evening dress. Queen Elizabeth, Princess Margaret and the Queen Mother, whose outfits are eagerly conned by female readers in the next day's papers, can seldom get through a day without three or four changes of clothes.

It was popularly supposed that George VI's advisers and court officials were responsible for overloading the royal family with public engagements. This was not so. There is a spartan tradition of overwork in the royal family. King George had an almost passionate sense of public duty and in accepting the many engagements he did he was a slave to what he regarded as the inescapable lot of the sovereign and his family in the monarchic concept of today.

IV

THE MONARCHY ON PARADE

YOU get more free shows in London than anywhere else on
earth.

In its outward manifestations, the monarchy today is essentially a form of ceremonial. As they progressively stripped their
monarchs of political power the British—with their happy knack
of drawing on the best of the past to give authority and point to
the needs of the present—carefully retained much of the colour,
customs and traditions that are inalienably linked to their throne,
and it is the periodic display of this rich tapestry of the past—
history come alive in the form of medieval pageantry and public
ceremonial—that has made the symbolic role of the monarchy
popular and acceptable today.

Though the apparatus of the monarchy has changed and evolved
reign by reign, adapting itself to the times, until today it is an
essential part of the British political system, it is the preservation
of the spectacular, even anachronous ritual going back over the
centuries through Victorian and Georgian and Stuart and Tudor
reigns to Plantagenet and even Norman times that provides the
sense of continuity which the British recognize as the main contribution of the monarchy in a constitutional democracy. It is the
constant function of the British throne and its occupant to remind
the people of these arteries from the past.

In its modern symbolic role, moulded over the past 100 years,
the monarchy is expected to serve the people by its example since
it can no longer serve by direct political authority: the royal
family, revolving around the person of the sovereign, is therefore
expected to be the embodiment of virtue, a model of individual
and family behaviour for all the realms of the crown. But the
British are not content merely to respect their monarchy—they
like to enjoy it as well. Their reputation for suffering their

60

pleasures sadly does not apply to royal pomp and pageantry. A sense of history runs strongly in their blood, and few of them can resist the romance of military full-dress, historic paraphernalia, ermine and scarlet robes and gilded royal coaches that are reminders of a colourful and glorious past. For hours on end, usually at great personal discomfort, they will stand patiently in line, and feel rewarded with a flash of scarlet, a gleam of sabres and burnished breastplates or a fleeting glance at passing royalty.

Austerity may be their post-war way of life, yet the colour and gaiety provided by a royal spectacle meets with almost universal approval. The national dress is uniformly drab—to dress conspicuously is regarded as a breach of taste—and yet this inhibition is quickly forgotten when a full-dress ceremony provides the opportunity to enjoy and indulge in exhibition. The British are in no sense militarists, yet they glory in the outmoded vestiges of militarism which surround a royal procession. Much of the pomp and pageantry that remains has purely a fictitious function in the twentieth century, yet the fact that it has survived these apparent contradictions indicates that the magic and mystery and the medieval show provided by the monarchy on parade fills a deep need in the collective life of the nation by satisfying the emotional part of man in politics.

In any reign, the supreme pageantry is seen only in the ritualistic coronation rites, which embody many aspects of the meaning and function of kingship today.

At the time of writing the coronation of Elizabeth II, set for June 2, 1953, is still a distant prospect. The coronation of George VI and Elizabeth, crowned King and Queen on May 12, 1937, has passed into history, but a brief reconstruction of that ceremony can set the scene for the coronation of their daughter. The highly-stylized coronation service, each part of which arises from the history of the crown, remains unchanged from reign to reign, and, except for the fact that she will be a lone figure in the stately drama, the ceremony by which Elizabeth II will be crowned Queen will re-enact step by step the coronation of her father.

The coronation service is divided into three stages, each of which represents a different aspect of the relationship between the monarch and the people: first, the acceptance of their sovereign by the people and the taking of the oath by the monarch;

second, the purely religious ceremony, which includes the anointing and the crowning; and third, the rendering of homage in person by the Lords Spiritual and Temporal. The form of the service is as old as the monarchy itself. The earliest ritual that has been preserved dates from the eighth century and in the development of the ceremony down through the ages the main features of its Saxon prototypes have been faithfully retained. From the beginning this formalistic service has marked the consecration of the English King by the English Church, and although his domain has widened into the United Kingdom, the Empire and the Commonwealth, he is still consecrated and crowned for high office in accordance with the ancient English rites. Thus the main actor in the coronation drama is not the King or Queen but His Grace the Lord Archbishop of Canterbury, exercising his privilege as Primate of All England to crown his country's sovereigns. (The high place accorded the Church of England is further reflected in the fact that the Archbishop, whose appointment must be approved by the sovereign, sits in the House of Lords and takes precedence after the princes of the blood royal but before every peer of Parliament, including the Lord Chancellor.)

Traditionally since the reign of King Harold the Kings of England have been crowned in Westminster Abbey, itself a storehouse of history. In ancient days the King merely crossed from his Palace of Westminster on foot, accompanied by a magnificent secular procession of state officers, but George and Elizabeth, in the custom set by their predecessors of the last few reigns, rode in regal splendour in the great State Coach from Buckingham Palace to the Abbey through the streets of London that were jam-packed with an estimated 5,000,000 people.

On arrival, heralded by a trumpet fanfare, they were led in solemn procession, with the regalia borne before them, up the body of the church, through the choir to the theatre, where the ancient rites were unfolded stage by stage.

First came the ceremony known as the recognition, in which the great officers of state present the King to the assembled people who are asked to acclaim him their rightful sovereign. The Archbishop, the Garter King of Arms, the Lord Chancellor, the Lord Great Chamberlain, the Lord High Constable and the Earl Marshal moved first to the east side of the theatre, where the Archbishop called out, "Sirs, I here present unto you King

George, your undoubted King: Wherefore all you who are come this day to do your homage and service, are you willing to do the same?" According to form the people should then signify their acceptance of him by loud and repeated cries of "God Save King George," but by long custom this privilege is left to the King's Scholars of Westminster School, who act as representatives of the people on this day. The same proclamation and answer were then repeated at the south, west and north sides of the theatre while the King stood by his chair in the middle of the sacrarium and faced each side in turn. As the succession to the crown has for long been governed by the principle of hereditary descent, the recognition ceremony is pure formality, but it perpetuates a custom stretching back eleven centuries to the time when the king was presented to his Witenagemot of nobles and bishops and acknowledged king by their acclamations.

Then came another brilliant phrase from the trumpets. When the regalia had been placed upon the altar, the Archbishop stood before the King and administered the solemn coronation oath. The form of the oath has varied according to the political and religious customs of the realm, but its substance has remained the same since the earliest days of the monarchy. Kneeling before the altar, with his right hand on an open Bible held before him, the King promised and swore to govern his peoples in all their lands according to their respective laws and customs, to cause law and justice in mercy to be executed in all his judgments, to maintain the laws of God and the true profession of the Gospel, to maintain in the United Kingdom the Protestant Reformed Religion established by law, to maintain and preserve inviolably the settlement of the Church of England and the doctrine, worship, discipline and government thereof, and to preserve unto the bishops and clergy of England and to the churches committed to their charge all such rights and privileges as do by law appertain to them.

Following the communion service came the most ancient of all rites connected with kingship, the anointing, which is regarded as the central feature of the coronation with the actual crowning as its culmination. By his anointing the King is consecrated, and his donning of symbolic garments emphasizes the spiritual as well as the civil nature of the office to which he is admitted.

Having taken off, with the help of the Lord Great Chamberlain, his crimson robe and cap of state, these being indicative of the parliamentary rank in which he entered the Abbey, the King again advanced before the altar and took his seat on the ornate wooden throne known as King Edward's coronation chair, a venerable oaken relic that has been used for the crowning of almost every successive monarch since the reign of Edward I, who brought to the Abbey the ancient and famed object known as the stone of Scone,[1] which rests under the chair's seat. Four Knights of the Garter, wearing their mantles, came forward bearing a rich gold cloth canopy, which they held above the King's head. From the altar the Dean of Westminster took the ampulla, a small golden vessel shaped in the form of an eagle, filled with consecrated oil, and poured a small quantity into the gold, romanesque coronation spoon, which he handed to the Archbishop, who then anointed the King in the form of a cross—on the palms of his hands, on his breast and on the head.

The anointed King was thus ready to be invested with the sacerdotal vestments of his spiritual office and the robes and regalia of royalty. The Knights of the Garter withdrew their pall and the King rose while the Dean of Westminster draped about him first the *colobium sindonis*, a fine white cambric surplice without sleeves, which was the ancient dress of bishops and priests, and then the *supertunica*, a close-fitting surcoat with plain gold cloth, and finally a girdle of the same material, fitted with gold buckle and hangers to suspend the sword with which the monarch is girded. Then the King was presented with the attributes of royalty. First the Lord Great Chamberlain received from the altar St. George's spurs, richly-chased, solid gold ornaments that are symbolic of knightly chivalry, and, kneeling down, touched them to His Majesty's heels and then returned them to the altar.[2] Next the Archbishop, accompanied by the Archbishop of York and the bishops of the realm, took from the altar the jewel-encrusted state sword,[3] made for the coronation of George IV, and, placing it in the King's right hand as a symbol of knighthood, delivered his traditional prayer: "With this sword do justice, stop the growth of iniquity, protect the holy Church of God, help and defend widows and orphans, restore the things that are gone to decay, maintain the things that are restored, punish and reform what is amiss, and confirm what is in good order: that doing these things you may be glorious in all virtue:

and so faithfully serve our Lord Jesus Christ in this life, that you may reign for ever with him in the life which is to come."

When the prayer ended there occurred another of those flash-backs to the days of liegemen and knightly chivalry. The King arose, ungirded the sword and went and placed it on the altar, still in its scabbard. By tradition, the peer who had previously carried the sword then redeemed it for the price of 100 shillings, and on receiving it back from the Dean of Westminster, drew it from its scabbard and carried it naked before the King for the rest of the ceremony.

Then, in quick succession, the Officer of the Great Wardrobe brought forward the *pallium*, the royal cope of purple and gold brocaded tissue, and the *armill*, a stole of gold cloth lined with crimson, which the Dean draped around the King. The bejewelled king's orb, a ball of solid gold surmounted by a diamond-decorated cross, was brought from the altar and placed in the King's right hand by the Archbishop of Canterbury, signifying that independent sovereignty is subject to the power of the cross of Christianity. Next the Keeper of the Jewel House delivered to the Archbishop the King's ring—specially made to fit each sovereign —and the Archbishop carefully placed it on the fourth finger of the King's right hand, reminding his sovereign that this was the ensign of kingly faith and of defence of the Catholic faith, a seal to signify the marriage between king and people.

At this point the Lord of the Manor of Worksop came into his own. By tradition he is allowed to present the glove which the King puts on before receiving into his hand the royal sceptre. Having drawn on the glove, the King then received from the Archbishop in his right hand the priceless royal sceptre with the cross, signifying kingly power and justice, and in his left hand the gold sceptre, known as the rod with the dove, signifying equity and mercy.[4]

With the King thus anointed and invested with his regalia the stage was set for the most dramatic moment of the ceremony— his reception from the hands of the Archbishop of the ultimate symbol of sovereignty, the crown. Standing before the altar the aged Archbishop took St. Edward's crown into his hands for a solemn moment and then replaced it on the altar and asked its blessing. Then the Dean of Westminster carried the crown to King Edward's chair, where the King was sitting, head slightly bowed, and the Archbishop took the crown from him and carefully, reverently placed it on the new monarch's head. At that instant, playing their part in the tradition, the audience in the Abbey acclaimed King George VI with loud and repeated shouts of "God save the King"; and the princes and peers and the Kings of Arms simultaneously placed their coronets on their heads; the state trumpeters burst into a fanfare within the Abbey; bells pealed overhead; and, in the distance, the saluting guns rumbled from Hyde Park and the Tower of London.

Having been presented with the Holy Bible, which he held in his hands for a moment before giving it back to the Archbishop, the King then stood in front of King Edward's chair, waiting for the last two stages of the coronation, the inthronization and the homage, both of which trace back to the feudal ages when the bishops and the princes and nobles of the land rendered to their king their promises of service in return for lands or privileges granted to them by him. The Archbishops and the bishops and representative peers of the kingdom grouped around him and symbolically assisted him into the chair, and then all the great officers of the kingdom and those who had carried the regalia gathered about the steps of the throne while the Archbishop of Canterbury exhorted the monarch to "stand firm, and hold fast from henceforth the seat and state of royal and imperial dignity . . ." Then the Archbishop knelt before the King's knees and the rest of the ecclesiastics knelt in their places and spoke their vow of homage. The Archbishop, rising, kissed his King's left cheek and drew aside. Then the Duke of Gloucester, the first prince of the realm, and the Duke of Kent took off their coronets, knelt before the King and pronounced their words of homage. Then the two brothers arose and individually touched the King's crown and kissed him on the left cheek. After this the peers of the kingdom followed suit in rapid order, kneeling down in their places and removing their coronets: first the dukes, then the marquesses, the earls, the viscounts and then the barons, while the first member of each order knelt before the King on his throne. Having done their homage, the representative of each order ascended the throne dais, reached out to touch the King's crown and kissed their sovereign on the left cheek.

With a roll of the drums and another trumpet fanfare the long homage rite came to an end and the Abbey once more echoed to shouts of "God Save King George. Long Live King George. May the King live for ever." The Archbishop then returned to the altar, leaving the King alone on his throne.

The Queen's coronation which followed is a shorter form of the coronation of the King, and its origins are likewise traced to Saxon times. Advancing before the altar the Queen knelt on a faldstool set between the steps and King Edward's chair while four peeresses stood beside her and held above her head the canopy which had been held over the King. Taking the coronation spoon from the altar, the Archbishop poured the holy oil on her head. From the Keeper of the Jewel House he took the Queen's ring, which he placed on the fourth finger of her right hand. Then he took from the altar the magnificent Queen's crown and solemnly placed it on Elizabeth's head. At this signal the princesses and peeresses of the realm put on their coronets, as the princes and peers had done when the King was crowned. Into the Queen's right hand the Archbishop put the Queen's sceptre with the cross and in her left hand the Queen's ivory rod with the dove. Her Majesty then arose and, conducted by two bishops, went up the theatre to her throne placed at the left hand of the King. As she passed in front of the King she paused and bowed reverently to him.

Following the long communion service, the rites concluded with the "Te Deum." As the choir sang, the King, with the four swords carried before him, descended from the throne, carrying his sceptre and rod, and passed through a door on the south side of the altar into St. Edward's chapel, while the Queen, bearing her rod and sceptre, descended and passed into the chapel by the north side of the altar. There, standing before the chapel altar, the King and Queen and their officers handed over the regalia, which was replaced on the altar. The King then took off the *pallium* and put on his robe of purple velvet and at the same time exchanged the heavy St. Edward's crown for the lighter, but more magnificent imperial crown of state.[5] During this interval the royal procession reformed. Then the King and Queen, wearing their crowns—the King holding in his right hand the sceptre with the cross and in his left the orb, and the Queen carrying her sceptre and ivory rod—were conducted slowly through the choir, down the long aisle to the west door of the Abbey and so out to their waiting State Coach.

Each Parliament and each session of Parliament is opened by a personal visit from the sovereign, who gives a speech written for him by his Ministers outlining briefly the Government's policies. A normal session of Parliament lasts a year, and unless a general election—obligatory every fifth year except in wartime, although it may be called by the Government in power at any time during the five-year life of a Parliament—intervenes to upset the schedule, Londoners can look forward to an annual state opening ceremony, generally in late October or early November.

Although it celebrates an authority that no longer exists, the scene at the royal opening of a Parliament is an ancient and impressive ceremony that is second in pomp and pageantry only to the coronation itself.

At the time of writing Queen Elizabeth II has not personally opened her first Parliament, although she accompanied her father and mother as part of her apprenticeship for the throne, but the annual pageant in which she will participate has become almost as formalized as the coronation and it changes little from reign to reign.

On the morning of the appointed day the Queen will drive in state from Buckingham Palace to Westminster, escorted by the jingling cavalcade of the Household Cavalry, through streets lined by the Brigade of Guards in full dress. For great ceremonial occasions the monarch is expected to travel through the capital in the huge Gold State Coach, an ornately carved, gilded and panel-painted vehicle that weighs four tons and is pulled by eight grey horses. It was originally made for the coronation of George III, but George VI preferred to drive to the opening of his Parliaments in the Irish State Coach—so called because it was bought by Victoria at a Dublin exhibition—which is beautifully sprung and can be drawn at a trot.

There are actually two processions when Parliament is opened. First passes a single closed carriage, escorted by a non-commissioned officers' escort of Household Cavalry. Inside the carriage rests the imperial state crown, which is brought from the Tower of London to Westminster for the sovereign to wear while making the speech from the throne, and the troops lining the route present arms as this symbol of authority passes by. Then, about ten minutes later, the expectant hush that settles over the crowd is broken by staccato commands as the Guards come to attention and then present arms as the sovereign's coach (or, when the weather is bad, a stately motor-car flying the royal standard) comes abreast, and as the glittering cavalcade passes the cheers of the crowd swell to a welcoming roar that rolls along in time with the procession for the length of the route.

Inside the House of Lords, where the ceremony takes place, the atmosphere is decidedly social, reminiscent of the days when the king, as host, summoned the most important of his subjects for a parley in his Palace of Westminster, and the proceedings are impressively theatrical.

Before each opening ceremony a detachment of scarlet-and-gold-clad Yeomen of the Guard, carrying lanterns and pikes, solemnly search the cellars, galleries and corridors of Parliament, a ritual that goes back to the famous gunpowder plot of 1605 when Guy Fawkes and a few fellow hot-heads tunnelled under Parliament Square and planted 20 barrels of powder in one of the Lords' cellars, only to have their plot exposed when a conspirator sent a friendly warning to a peer.

Long before the royal arrival the red morocco benches and the galleries of the Lords' chamber are filled with a dazzling array of colour. Along the centre of the floor crowd the peers of the realm, the Temporal Lords in their heavy robes of scarlet and ermine, the Lords Spiritual in their state robes of crimson and long ermine hoods. Then there are the Law Lords, grey-wigged and resplendently-robed, the Lord Justices in black and gold, the Judges of Assize in red. On the tiers of benches along either side of the chamber sit the peeresses—not allowed to sit in the House of Lords in their own right—decked out in evening dress and tiaras, and in the galleries are the elaborately-uniformed ambassadors and ministers of foreign states and their ladies in evening gowns.

Having inherited the medieval genius for pageantry, the British know how to extract the last splash of colour from such an occasion. A salute of 41 guns will announce Queen Elizabeth's arrival at Westminster, where she will be met at the royal entrance and led in procession up the staircase to the chamber. First, dressed in the quartered satin tabards of their degree, will come the Heralds and Pursuivants, with their evocative, romantic titles—Portcullis Pursuivant, Bluemantle Pursuivant, Rouge Croix Pursuivant, Rouge Dragon Pursuivant, Windsor Herald and Richmond Herald, York, Chester, Somerset and Lancaster Heralds; then the members of the Queen's staff, her equerries-in-waiting and household officers; then the Kings of Arms decked in their fifteenth-century tabards; then the great state officers, the Lord Privy Seal, the Lord President of the Council, the Lord High Chancellor, the Earl Marshal, the Lord Great Chamberlain, the Garter Principal King of Arms and Black Rod; and finally the sword of state, carried high by a peer. Behind the Queen will come Buckingham Palace and household officials, who take it in turn to attend at ceremonies—generally the Mistress of the Robes, a lady-of-the-bedchamber, a woman-of-the-bedchamber and assorted ladies-in-waiting.

Just before the Queen enters the chamber the lights will be dimmed. Then, as a trumpet fanfare heralds the arrival of the stately procession, the lights will blaze full on as Her Majesty advances down the length of the House to take her seat on the great square-backed throne which stands under the high Gothic oak canopy behind the woolsack in the Lords. When her train has been arranged in a cascade down the steps of the red-covered throne dais the peers will bow to her and the peeresses curtsy, and the Queen will say, according to tradition, "My Lords, pray be seated."

With another of those historic falderals which the British perpetuate, the members of the House of Commons are then summoned to hear the monarch's speech. The Queen's messenger, Black Rod, proceeds to the Commons, where the door is ceremoniously shut in his face and not reopened until he gives the required three knocks. Then, led by the Speaker of the Commons, who represents them when the Lords and Commons meet together in the presence of the sovereign, as many members of the lower house as can be accommodated crowd along to stand at the bar at the far end of the Lords' chamber, this being the farthest that tradition allows them to go. They remain standing, in mock defiance, during the sovereign's speech.

When the Commons are assembled the Lord Chancellor then advances and on bended knee proffers the monarch the speech to be delivered. Although the sovereign may not add or subtract a word of this "Most Gracious Speech from the Throne," which is written by the Prime Minister or his staff, long usage requires it to be couched in personal terms. Thus it always contains such phrases as "It is the intention of my Government . . . Legislation will be submitted to you . . . My Ministers will ask you to approve . . ." and it traditionally concludes with the words, "I pray that the blessing of Almighty God may rest upon your counsels." Then the Lord Chancellor again approaches, bows, and takes the speech from the monarch's hand. Her speech read, Queen Elizabeth will then step down from the dais, bow first to the right and then to the left, and then walk out of the chamber.

No long ordeal like the coronation, the state opening of Parliament is a cut-and-dried affair which seldom lasts more than a quarter of an hour. George VI regarded it as the least onerous of his public ceremonies, although his father once crustily complained that he knew of few worse ordeals than having to deliver somebody else's speech while wearing a 39-ounce crown on his head.

The verses of A. A. Milne have helped to make the changing of the guard at Buckingham Palace the most familiar bit of ceremonial in the English-speaking world. There is a little of Christopher Robin in every visitor to London and few of them can resist the daily pageantry of toy soldiers coming to life to march and wheel and salute with mathematical precision. Rain or shine, there are always crowds of onlookers at Buckingham Palace, St. James's Palace, and the Horse Guards' building in Whitehall, the three places where the guard-changing display takes place, although few can distinguish any meaning in these time-honoured formalities.

Whether the Queen is in residence or not, every day of the year a guard is mounted at Buckingham Palace, her official home. Similar guards are maintained at two royal residences nearby— Marlborough House, Queen Mary's home, and Clarence House, destined to be the future home of the Queen Mother and Princess Margaret. Periodically during the day and every two hours throughout the night the Captain of the Queen's Guard, accompanied by a patrol, checks the sentries at their boxes before the royal dwellings to see that all is well. Although responsibility for guarding the Palace and the sovereign now rests with the Home Office, which delegates the task to Scotland Yard, the custom of maintaining vigil over the monarch's house goes back to the days when kings and queens employed their own household troops, the first beginnings of a standing army.

By long tradition the duty of mounting guard at the royal residences is the cherished privilege of the five foot regiments of the Brigade of Guards, while the two mounted regiments of the Brigade, the Royal Horse Guards and the Life Guards, which together make up the Household Cavalry, act as the sovereign's escort when he or she rides forth in state. Both George V and Edward VIII, as a gesture of respect for the rest of their military establishments, occasionally invited other troops to take a spell at guard duty, and during the Second World War George VI broadened this practice so that numerous troops had the brief honour of guard-mounting at the Palace, including such new-comers to military ranks as the Home Guard and the R.A.F. Regiment. Some of the glamour departed during the war years when the soldiers on duty wore their workaday khaki or blue battledress, but with the return of peace the traditional duties were resumed by the five foot regiments of the Household Brigade, which now take it in turn to mount guard in full military panoply.

Londoners take for granted the Guards' historic uniforms, though admittedly few of them can tell one regiment from another. The foot Guards wear scarlet tunics and towering bearskin head-dresses, popularly known as busbies, which are cut from the pelts of Canadian black bear. The Life Guards, when mounted, wear scarlet tunics, white breeches and silver breastplates and their shining helmets are adorned with streaming white plumes, while the Royal Horse Guards, known as "the Blues" because they wear blue tunics instead of the usual scarlet of the Guards, have red plumes to their helmets. Each regiment has its own dis-tinguishing emblems and its own proud military history and traditions. How hard traditions die is shown by the following true story: during the final campaigns of the Second World War the Colonel of the Regiment of Coldstreamers, an aged, veteran general whose distinguished Boer War service qualified him for this purely honorary post, solemnly issued this order to his unit: "Officers of the Coldstream Guards will shout 'Hurrah' and not 'Hooray' when storming a redoubt."

The Grenadier Guards, who received their title in 1815 as a reward for their service at Waterloo, wear a white plume on the left-hand side of their busbies; the Coldstream Guards, formerly

General Monck's Regiment of Foot and named after the village from which Monck led them from Scotland to England to restore the Stuart monarchy in 1660, have a red plume on the right of their bearskins; the Scots Guards, given their title in 1877, wear no plumes; the Irish Guards, created at the wish of Queen Victoria in 1902 in recognition of the services of her Irish regiments in the Boer War, have pale blue plumes on the right; and the Welsh Guards, formed in 1915 to satisfy the claims of Wales to be represented in the King's bodyguard, have white and green plumes on the left of their head-dresses. In addition, the foot regiments are recognizable by the buttons on their tunics, which are arranged in groups according to the number of the regiment in the Brigade: thus the Grenadiers, as the premier regiment, have their buttons evenly spaced, the Coldstreamers wear groups of two buttons, the Scots Guards three, the Irish four and the Welsh five.

The parade-ground ceremonial that accompanies the changing of the guard takes place every alternate morning at Buckingham Palace whenever the Queen is in residence. Preceded by its band, the new guard—which, in its full turnout, consists of the Captain of the Queen's Guard, three officers and an ensign to carry the Queen's colour, and 55 warrant officers, n.c.o.'s and Guardsmen—marches across from its barracks in Birdcage Walk and in the gravelled forecourt of the Palace the retiring guard and the new guard meet to exchange the Queen's colour, which is carried out with a drill display that makes the Guards' name synonymous with precision teamwork. When the Queen is not in London a similar guard-changing takes place daily at nearby St. James's Palace, commemorating the fact that it was a royal residence from 1698 to 1837—the Court of St. James's—although it is now largely used for royal offices and state functions.

The two regiments of the Household Cavalry have been the picked bodyguard of the sovereign since their formation after the restoration of the monarchy in 1660, thus giving them pride of place as the senior units of the British Army. The Life Guards are a survival of the Cavalier units that followed Charles II to his continental exile in 1651, and the Royal Horse Guards were created out of remnants of Oliver Cromwell's New Model Army.[6] They are the only two regiments possessing the proud privilege of being allowed, when on duty, inside the royal palaces.

Although their principal remaining function is to provide the monarch with a horsed escort on ceremonial occasions, one of the two regiments every 24 hours mounts what is known as the Queen's Life Guard Duty in the courtyard of the Horse Guards' building, a tradition that goes back to the reign of Charles II, when the Palace of Whitehall then existed as the personal residence of the King and the Horse Guards' building was its guardhouse. The Palace of Whitehall has long since disappeared, but the maintenance of the 300-year-old tradition, with the mounted, cuirass-carrying troopers wearing their uniforms of contemporary design, provides London with a spine-tingling touch of pageantry on the dullest of days.

Every day when the Queen is in residence at Buckingham Palace the "Long Guard" is mounted at the Horse Guards in Whitehall. An officer and 22 troopers ride on their beautiful chargers from their Hyde Park barracks down Constitution Hill, alongside Buckingham Palace, and as they draw abreast of the royal residence the mounted trumpeter in the lead sounds the royal salute. In the Horse Guards' courtyard the retiring guard is drawn up, mounted, and after a series of intricate manœuvres on horseback, the duties are exchanged and the old guard rides off. The troopers deftly station their horses inside the arched horse sentry boxes flanking the Horse Guards' entrance, where they and their reliefs remain on mounted guard all day. The old guard riding back from duty also sounds the royal salute as it passes the Palace. Each afternoon the guard is inspected on foot, a lesser ceremony but equally fascinating for the display of sword handling. When the Queen is not in London a "Short Guard" is mounted, consisting of ten mounted troopers and two n.c.o.'s, and no royal salutes are given on approaching the Palace.

This long tradition, which had come down without a break since 1661, was interrupted for a period during the Second World War, when every available trooper was needed for active service. The two regiments are no longer purely cavalry troops. Aside from their ceremonial duties, which occupy only a small part of each trooper's tour of duty, the two units are among the finest of the mechanized regiments of the British Army and in this role they saw much hard campaigning in the Second World War.

The magnificent climax to each year of guard-mounting is the annual ceremony of Trooping the Colour, London's favourite spectacle and accounted by military men the finest drill display in the world. The Trooping ceremony has now become a military review in honour of the sovereign's birthday and takes place on or near his or her officially-designated birth-date, generally in early June—when similar ceremonies go on all over the world where British troops are garrisoned—but the meaning and origins of the Trooping ritual are obscure in military history. Some military authorities believe that it derives from the custom of lodging the colours in a place of safety in event of a sudden attack. Household Brigade experts claim that it began during the great Duke of Marlborough's campaign in the Netherlands early in the eighteenth century, when the general discovered that the early-morning ceremony of parading the regimental colours through the lines had a sobering effect on still-tipsy soldiers. However, back in the seventeenth century trooping was apparently a daily ceremony, when the battalion providing the king's guard for the day trooped the colour, and the Brigade of Guards still perpetuates this old custom during the month of June, when the regiment assigned to guard duty troops the colour on the Horse Guards' parade ground before marching off to the Palace, a display which many onlookers mistakenly take to be a dress rehearsal for the birthday parade.

Whatever its origins, the ceremony has survived as a stirring reminder of the days when battles were fought with parade-ground precision. The traditional parade order, a solemn and complicated military ritual in which rows of Guardsmen march and wheel like rows of glittering chessmen, is divided into three parts. While the Queen and her Household Cavalry escort rides down the Mall the foot regiments of the Brigade are drawn up in arrow-straight ranks on the hard surface of the Horse Guards' Parade, an open space framed by St. James's Park, the back of Downing Street and the official buildings of Whitehall. Not a man moves, not a sound breaks the hushed quiet until the Queen and her clattering mounted escort ride on to the parade ground. Then, with a signalling thud from a drummer on watch, the massed bands blare out, staccato orders are barked over the ranks of the troops and the pageantry of scarlet and bearskin begins to move.

First the Queen rides along the lines, inspecting her Guards (normally George VI was also mounted for the Trooping ceremony, but in 1949 and 1950, because of his leg ailment, he rode in an open landau drawn by two greys, and in 1951 the then Princess Elizabeth, in her capacity of honorary colonel of the Grenadier Guards, deputized for him). Then, with the Queen on the saluting dais, the colour of the foot regiment mounting the guard of the day is carried high through the rigid ranks of Guardsmen and given full honours. With their massed bands marching and counter-marching across the square the full Brigade then parades the colour past the sovereign, first with the immaculate, rhythmic, ballet-like slow march step and then, after manœuvring and wheeling in line, in a quick march. Finally, with the Brigade again drawn up in lines as straight as if they had been made by a ruler, the officer in command rides up to the dais, salutes with his sword and announces, "Guards ready to march off." With a nod, the Queen gives her assent and the command rings out, "Guards, to your duties. . . . Quick march."

Then the Queen places herself at the head of her Guards and leads them back to Buckingham Palace. Here Her Majesty dismounts and, as a finale to the ceremony, stands at salute on a dais placed at the main Palace gate while the Household Cavalry, the bands and the foot regiments of Guards again march past her. On this day, too, the old and the new Palace guard are drawn up facing each other in the forecourt when the Queen returns from the Trooping parade. While the band plays "God Save the Queen" and the guard presents arms the Queen walks slowly between them and passes out of sight in the archway entrance to her official home.

The firing of royal salutes which marks most state occasions in London is a long-established ritual which is carried out with almost as much punctilio as the changing of the guard. The practice of firing salutes dates back to the early days of artillery, when it was apparently customary to empty the guns as an obvious gesture of friendliness whenever royalty visited the army. Nowadays, royal salutes are fired from Hyde Park and from the saluting base alongside the Thames at the Tower of London on the occasion of royal births, on the anniversary of the accession of the reigning monarch, the anniversary of his coronation, and on his official birthday, as well as on the actual birthdays of the Queen, the Queen Mother and Queen Mary. A salute is also fired in St. James's Park as well as at the Tower to mark the state opening of

Parliament, and is repeated if the sovereign prorogues or dissolves Parliament in person. On the death of a monarch a special salute—one round for each year of his life—is fired.

A royal salute fired from the saluting stations in Britain and overseas normally consists of 21 rounds, but in Hyde Park 41 rounds are fired and at the Tower the salute is sometimes 62 rounds,[7] the extra 21 commemorating the days when private citizens of London owned ordnance and joined in the salutes. The privilege of firing the salutes at the Tower belongs to the Honourable Artillery Company, a Territorial unit of part-time soldiers with a history dating back to 1537, which took over the duty when the regular Tower gunners were disbanded after the First World War, while the royal salutes fired in Hyde Park and St. James's Park are the proud task of the King's Troop of the Royal Horse Artillery, the only surviving mounted artillery in the British Army.

The superbly-mounted horsemen of the King's Troop, almost as dashing as the Guards in their gold-braided, Hussar-style deep blue jackets and plumed busbies, also enjoy the distinction of being allowed to wheel their gun carriages *through* London's Marble Arch, closed to all but royal traffic, when they ride from their St. John's Wood barracks to Hyde Park. George VI took a keen personal interest in this military survival from the days of horse-drawn artillery. Although it was absorbed into the mechanized artillery during the war years King George insisted on its recomposition when peace came. Until 1947 the unit was known as the Riding Troop, because it was directly descended from the body which had always trained mounted artillerymen, but when the King reviewed it at its headquarters he crossed out the old designation on the unit's visitor's book and personally wrote in the "King's Troop." Later, when it was proposed to make minor changes in the Troop's uniform, the commanding officer was requested to bring three troopers wearing the suggested variants to the Palace, where George VI paraded them around his study like male mannequins while he compared details of their dress. Queen Elizabeth, in recognition of her father's special interest, has decided that the unit shall continue to be called the King's Troop.

In addition to the Household Cavalry the monarch has two

ceremonial bodyguards, both of them heirs to a tradition that is older than the 300-year-old function of the Life Guards and Royal Horse Guards, as well as a special bodyguard which attends the sovereign in Scotland.

The Queen's Bodyguard of the Yeomen of the Guard, familiarly known as the "Beefeaters," is the oldest and most picturesque military body in Britain. Its formation goes back to 1485, when Henry Tudor defeated Richard III on Bosworth Field. Many of Henry's soldiers that day had served overseas with him when he was Earl of Richmond, and at the close of the battle he proclaimed them his bodyguard not only for his protection but "for the protection of the dignity and grandeur of the English crown for ever." In the reign of Henry VIII they numbered 600, for they were active soldiers then and fought in campaigns abroad. The last battle they took part in was that of Dettingen in 1743.

Today the Yeomen are limited to 100, though for economy reasons they now number only 74, all of them bemedalled, long-service veterans up to the rank of sergeant in the Army, Royal Marines or R.A.F. who have applied for and been accepted to serve—for £60 per year—as foot bodyguards to the sovereign on state occasions. No royal ceremonial would be quite complete without the splash of scarlet and gold provided by the Tudor uniforms of the "Beefeaters"—a nickname acquired back in 1669 when Count Cosimo, the Grand Duke of Tuscany, admired the fine stature of the Yeomen on a visit to London and attributed it to their diet. Their picturesque uniform has been modified only slightly since the time of Henry VII—an ornate, monogrammed and braided doublet of scarlet, breeches, monk-type shoes, with gaudy rosettes on garters and shoes, beribboned flat hats and the frilly white ruff added to the costume by Queen Elizabeth I (the ruffed collar was removed by Queen Anne, who didn't like it, and then replaced by the Georges, who did). An antique pikestaff, known as a partisan, is carried by each Yeoman on parade.

Until the brief reign of Edward VIII the Yeomen were required to grow Tudor-style beards. However, few recruits were applying for admission to the corps and when Edward heard that this was the result of an objection to beards from the wives of potential Yeomen he promptly abandoned the custom.

Her Majesty's Bodyguard of the Honourable Corps of Gentlemen-at-Arms shares with the Yeomen of the Guard the ceremonial duty of protecting the person of the sovereign on most important occasions of state in England. This corps was founded in 1509 by Henry VIII and is now composed of a handful of senior and distinguished officers from the fighting services, although the Captain of the Corps is traditionally a political appointee nominated by the Government as it comes to power. Their uniform, a composite of military styles from the past, is less picturesque but more dazzling than that of the Yeomen of the Guard. It consists of a gleaming gilt helmet from the high peak of which droop long swans' feathers, a scarlet coatee topped with gold epaulettes and encircled with a gold sash, and broad-striped, tight-fitting "overall" trousers of dark blue, designed to fit over Wellington boots, which are worn with straight gilt spurs. Each Gentleman-at-Arms on duty carries an ornately-tasselled halberd called an "axe," an implement similar to the old boarding weapons used when ships came alongside each other to fight their battles.

Duties similar to those performed by the Gentlemen-at-Arms in England are the proud responsibilities of the Royal Company of Archers whenever the sovereign is in Scotland. The Company was formed primarily in the interests of archery in 1676—and its members, drawn from Scotland's highest and oldest nobility, must still claim proficiency in the use of the long bow—but George IV gave it the added title of the King's Royal Bodyguard for Scotland when he visited there in 1822. When on duty, carrying their bows and quivers, the members wear a handsome green, braided doublet and a Kilmarnock bonnet topped with an eagle feather.

Much of the pageantry of each royal year revolves around the sovereign's relations with the City of London, which has a proud, independent history almost as old as the monarchy itself. This packed square mile in the heart of London, the centre of much of the world's finance, insurance and corporate business, has for centuries enjoyed many of the privileges of a state within a state. Even William the Conqueror signed a special treaty with the City, after the rest of England was in his hands, confirming rights which its citizens had enjoyed in Anglo-Saxon times, and in the Middle Ages the City won new rights for itself and its representatives by granting or withholding the financial aid which made and unmade monarchs. Thus the Lord Mayor of the City, elected for a one-year term as its chief administrator and chief magistrate, takes precedence over all except the sovereign within the City's boundaries, including even the heir to the throne and princes of the blood royal. He is automatically made a Privy Councillor, is the first to be consulted about the choice of a sovereign, and is also the first person, apart from members of the family, to be informed of a royal birth. The Queen is bound to send him the quarterly passwords to the royal palaces and to the Tower of London. Outside the City, the Lord Mayor has the ranking precedence of an earl.

No troops may cross the City boundaries without the Lord Mayor's permission and only six privileged regiments of the British Army may march through the City with "colours flying, drums beating and bayonets fixed." Like the monarch, the Lord Mayor has his own guard of honour for ceremonial occasions or when he receives the reigning monarch in the City. These are the Pikemen of the Honourable Artillery Company, veterans of the regiment who dress in the helmets and breastplates as worn by the pikemen and musketeers of Cromwellian times. On occasion, the whole City Corporation, the Court of Aldermen and the Court of Common Council, 232 strong, exercises its ancient right to present an address to the Queen at her palace and is received by Her Majesty in person.

Whenever a royal procession arrives at Temple Bar, one of the boundaries to the City, it comes to a halt for the ceremony of the sword, a tradition mellowed by the centuries, in which the Lord Mayor presents the sovereign with the City's Pearl Sword, which is the symbol of the monarch's justice in the City. First enacted in Plantagenet days, this ritual has been repeated at Temple Bar every time that a monarch has sought to enter the precincts of the City. On this site posts and chains, erected by the consent of Henry III, stood across the riverside road which is now Fleet Street. These later gave way to a bar of timber and then a gate and it was here that Wren's Temple Bar of stone was erected after the Great Fire of London in 1666 destroyed the old landmark. For ease of traffic, Temple Bar was removed in 1878, and nowadays the boundary is marked for royal processions by a crimson silken cord stretched across the road by two constables until the procession arrives. The Lord Mayor, resplendent in his

19. *A royal procession approaches Buckingham Palace along the broad avenue of the Mall.*

20. *The Irish State Coach takes the Queen to the opening of Parliament*

21. *George VI participating in the ceremony of the sword at Temple Bar*

gold-encrusted robe, takes up his position at the roadside, 1 by his Serjeant-at-Arms bearing the impressive mace a sword-bearer carrying the four-foot-six-inch sheathed swo surrounded by deputations from the Court of Aldermen and Court of Common Council. As the Queen's carriage halts at the pavement's edge the Lord Mayor advances, sword in hand, and presents its hilt to Her Majesty. The Queen touches it in acknowledgment that it is indeed hers, and then gives it back to the Lord Mayor.

It is sometimes thought that this bit of symbolism signifies a right of the City to exclude the monarch from its privileged ground if displeased with him and that the sovereign must ask permission to enter its precincts. In fact, no sword may be borne in the realm except in the sovereign's service, and the ceremony of the sword is a historic reminder of the days when the monarchs lived within the City's walls and often required protection from their enemies. The Pearl Sword, symbolic of the King's justice, is entrusted to the Lord Mayor as the sovereign's representative for the punishment of wrongdoers and the defence of the City's privileges. According to the tradition, whenever the Lord Mayor is informed that a cavalcade is approaching the City's boundary he seizes the sword and hurries to meet the approaching column in case it should be the sovereign's enemies. When he finds that it is the monarch himself who seeks admission he surrenders the sword in case the King should wish to wield it, and the King, after touching it in token that it is his weapon, gives it back to the Lord Mayor, thus indicating that the monarch is well pleased with the officer to whom it has been entrusted. Thereafter the Lord Mayor holds it aloft before the monarch, indicating that within the City he is responsible for guarding his sovereign's life.

By a strange quirk of history, the one place where the sovereign's own troops stand guard inside the City is in the City's holiest of holies, the Bank of England. By British standards, this tradition is relatively new, going back only 171 years. It originated by necessity in 1780 when, after Parliament passed a bill enabling Roman Catholics to purchase and inherit land in England if they willingly abjured the sovereignty of the Pope, fierce anti-Catholic riots—known as the Gordon riots because they were led by Lord George Gordon—broke out. Rioters invaded Parliament, attacked foreign embassies and assaulted the Bank of England.

George III, who had seen one rebellion lose him his American colonies, called out his troops to quell the riots and sent soldiers to ward off the attacks on the Bank. And so from that day to this, in the way the British have of letting necessity become a habit until it becomes a tradition, the Brigade of Guards has provided a daily Bank Picket or patrol. In time the tradition gave birth to its own traditions. During the early years the Bank's directors customarily provided the guard with greatcoats, blankets and provisions and the officer in charge was allowed to invite two guests to dine and spend the evening with him in the Bank. Nowadays, no coats or blankets are furnished, but the Bank still pays each sergeant two shillings per picket, corporals one shilling and sixpence, and Guardsmen and drummers one shilling for their courtesy, and the officer on duty may have one guest in to dinner.

The changing of the guard provides London with its daily outward show, but it is to the historic old Tower of London that one must go to see the traditional ritual of the oldest royal pageantry in the nation.

Built by order of William the Conqueror for the purpose of controlling and protecting the City, the original Tower was erected within the Roman city walls, but later enlargements carried its boundaries eastward so that today it is partly within the City, partly outside. In its grim, bloody past it has served as fortress, palace, execution ground, torture chamber and prison (even in the Second World War it was used for a time to detain Rudolf Hess) and the names of its victims who were justly or unjustly incarcerated, beheaded or murdered within its castellated walls—the kings' enemies, the kings' friends, kings and queens themselves: young Edward V, Henry VI, Anne Boleyn, Katherine Howard, Lady Jane Grey, Elizabeth I, Sir Thomas More, Sir Walter Raleigh, Archbishop Laud, Judge Jeffries and Guy Fawkes among them—spell out the turbulent history of the monarchy in its evolution to its constitutional role of today. The Tower was occupied as a palace by the kings and queens down to the reign of James I, and even afterwards it was the custom for each new monarch to lodge before his coronation in the Tower, whence he rode in procession through the City to Westminster. In its day the Tower has also housed the Royal Mint and for centuries it was an arsenal for small-arms. It still is garrisoned today.

The present Resident-Governor of the Tower, Colonel Carkeet

James, O.B.E., M.C., a one-armed, veteran soldier of both world wars, has written the definitive history of this turreted landmark and from it he has resuscitated historically exact ceremonial, most of which revolves around the colourful Yeomen Warders of the Tower, whose Tudor uniforms—scarlet and black, and green velvet hats adorned with red, white and blue bows—are similar to but not identical with the Yeomen of the Guard.

The Yeomen Warders, also popularly known as "Beefeaters," can trace their predecessors back to a body of warders known to have existed as long ago as 1078, although the recorded history of the corps as it exists today began in 1543. There are 39 Yeomen Warders on the Tower's establishment strength today, and all of them dwell within its walls. Every man who applies for registration must be a serving warrant officer or colour sergeant in the services, and once sworn in they remain warders for life unless they voluntarily retire. They draw a basic wage of £5 16s. 6d. per week.[8]

Four times each year the company of warders march to their chapel, the Chief Warder at their head, followed by the Resident-Governor, with the Yeoman Gaoler bringing up the rear, when they parade outside the King's House, a beautifully-timbered structure built for Henry VIII, in which Anne Boleyn spent the last days of her life, and the adjoining house of the Yeoman Gaoler, from which the pathetic 17-year-old Lady Jane Grey, Queen for nine days, was led to her execution. Every fifth year the Queen must appoint a Constable of the Tower, a sinecure usually awarded a distinguished soldier or sailor on retirement, and this worthy is ceremoniously sworn in on Tower Green, the delightful grassy plot which was once a burial ground and scaffold-site, in the middle of the Tower. There the Lord Chamberlain, acting for the sovereign, presents the two golden keys to the fortress to the new Constable in the presence of the Yeomen Warders and the Tower garrison.

In the days of old the Yeomen Warders were primarily prison guards, as their name implies, but today—apart from their utilitarian function of guarding the crown jewels and their task of guiding visitors around the Tower—they survive mainly to provide cherished ceremonial links with the past. Chief among these is the nightly ceremony of the Keys, which has been performed continuously at the Tower for nearly 700 years. At precisely

seven minutes before 10 o'clock every night of the year the Chief
Warder takes up his ornate lantern and, accompanied by a patrol,
known as the Escort to the Keys, furnished by one of the five
regiments of the Brigade of Guards, locks the gates of the Tower.
On their return through the archway of the Bloody Tower (so
called after the murder of the two children, Edward V and
Richard, Duke of York, by their uncle, Richard III) they faithfully re-enact the ritual which has been followed for centuries.
The sentry on duty challenges: "Halt. Who goes there?" "The
Keys," announces the Chief Warder. . . . "Whose Keys?". . . .
"Queen Elizabeth's Keys," the Warder replies. . . . "Advance
Queen Elizabeth's Keys. All's Well," says the sentry. At the
guardroom the Chief Warder removes his Tudor hat and concludes with "God Preserve Queen Elizabeth," to which the guard
answer "Amen," and as the clock strikes 10 the nightly ceremony
concludes with the sounding of the Last Post. The keys are then
deposited with the Resident-Governor in the King's House.
Thereafter only those with the password can gain admittance
until the gates are opened to the public in the morning.

Of all the sights at the Tower probably none is more striking
to visitors than the big black ravens which croak and hop un-
gainly on the grass of Tower Green. According to legend, ravens
always enjoyed the sanctuary of the Tower and Charles II is reputed to have predicted that if no ravens occupied the fortress the
whole British Empire would collapse. With typical British regard
for the niceties of tradition, six "resident" ravens are now
maintained in feathered comfort at the Tower, and an allowance
of one shilling and sixpence per week per raven is duly made for
their food.

V

OFFICES OF THE MONARCHY

THE royal household is an ancient institution, as old as the monarchy itself, and its members today preserve the memories of past centuries in their strange and archaic titles.

In the misty beginnings of the monarchy, when the king's chamber consisted of his living quarters, his office and his storehouse, his chamberlains were his personal attendants, but as power concentrated in the hands of the sovereign and the government of the kingdom grew more complex the monarchs increasingly turned to their chamberlains for advice and gradually they became, in effect, the administrators of the realm. During the long, losing battle which successive sovereigns fought with their Parliaments from the twelfth to the seventeenth centuries one department after another—Parliament itself, the Exchequer and the judiciary among them—was taken from the monarch's chamber and transferred to the control of Parliament. When Parliament finally emerged victorious from the tug-of-war the chamber reverted to its original functions, responsible only for the sovereign's personal affairs and the domestic arrangements of his household.

In the early reigns the household appointees were usually the king's friends and favourites and they were frequently embroiled in the struggle for power between Parliament and the crown. When Parliament won the fight and party government came into fashion the party in office deemed it wise to place its own sympathizers in the posts closest to the monarch and so the household became a sort of "spoils system" and was replaced with fresh appointees whenever a new Government came into power. This practice continued until Queen Victoria, beset by a series of Government changes as Liberals and Conservatives alternated every few years, rose in imperious wrath and successfully protested against the inconvenience of having to change her ladies-in-waiting almost as soon as she got to know them, a constitutional set-to that became famed as the "Bedchamber incident."

Over the centuries the traditional functions of the household officials became obscure, until they often duplicated or overlapped each other. It is recounted that Victoria, deciding one day that she would like a fire in her dining room, called in the Master of the Household, only to be told that it was not his affair as it was the business of the Lord Steward to have it laid and the Lord Chamberlain's duty to see that it was lighted! Other ceremonial functions fell into disuse although their offices continued to be filled, and as recently as Edward VII's reign it was found that obscure officials who never set foot inside Buckingham Palace were still drawing salaries for non-existent jobs.

In the last three reigns the sinecurists, the court hangers-on and the unnecessary office holders have been weeded out and Elizabeth II is now served by a highly efficient household whose ornamental titles belie their well-defined, workaday responsibilities.

Altogether the Queen's household has ten departments, and a complete listing of the establishment fills nine pages of Debrett, but only four departments are permanent within Buckingham Palace and only one—the Chancery of Orders in Knighthood—is permanent outside the Palace. The others, which include the ecclesiastical and medical households, the members of which act in an advisory capacity that does not interfere with their professional careers, the household in Scotland and the Ascot Office, are either honorary or staffed from time to time on occasions of great ceremony such as the coronation or the funeral of a monarch.

Today the main members of the household are chosen personally by the sovereign and have no political connections, with the exception of four ceremonial officials—the Vice Chamberlain, the Treasurer of the Household, the Comptroller and the Lord-in-Waiting—who are by custom nominees of the political party in power. Connected to the household only in name, their duties and salaries are purely Parliamentary. The Government in power also fills, with the Queen's approval, the offices of the Captain of the Gentlemen-at-Arms and the Captain of the Yeomen of the Guard.

Although the financial rewards of the ceremonial and part-time offices are small they are eagerly sought after, partly because of the prestige that goes with them and partly because they provide a welcome addition to the income of many officials who enter court service after their pensioned retirement from government or military careers.

The ancient authority of the sovereign's chamber is symbolized today in the nine Great Officers of State, lineal descendants of the chamberlains of early reigns. Only three of them—The Lord High Chancellor, The Lord High Treasurer and the Lord Privy Seal— are now actively connected with the day-to-day business of running the state, however, and the others blossom into something of their historic importance only at times of high ceremonial. In their antiquated order of precedence they rank as follows: the Lord High Steward, the Lord High Chancellor, the Lord High Treasurer, the Lord President of the Council, the Lord Privy Seal, the Lord Great Chamberlain, the Lord High Constable, the Earl Marshal, and the Lord High Admiral.[1]

The office of Lord Chancellor—the High being generally omitted in ordinary usage—is probably the oldest and certainly the most anomalous of the high ministerial offices under the crown. It is the only one of the nine ancient offices which still functions actively with much of its old authority and importance, and in the absence of a permanent Lord High Steward the Lord Chancellor is the first lay subject of the crown, ranking in precedence immediately after the Archbishop of Canterbury. The office is known to have existed at the time of Edward the Confessor, and about the time of the Norman conquest the Lord Chancellor was apparently something of a secretary to the king and head of a body of scribes who prepared royal charters and documents. In time he became custodian of the sovereign's seal—and today the Lord Chancellor has custody of the Great Seal of England, a matrix of two heavy silver discs, about six inches in diameter, hinged together, into which is poured the wax to make the seals which are affixed to the most important treaties, commissions, public documents and regal papers. The Great Seal, the emblem of royal authority, is the Lord Chancellor's official badge of office and its delivery into his hands by the sovereign is all that is necessary to appoint him to the position. The Lord Chancellor may not leave the country without the express permission of the

87

monarch, who then deputes a commission, usually three peers appointed for the purpose, to take custody of the Great Seal so that the formal business of the office can continue in the Lord Chancellor's absence. Whenever a sovereign dies the Great Seal is formally defaced by his successor with a tap of a special hammer and a new seal is ordered. The defaced matrix is then presented to the Lord Chancellor as a souvenir of office.

Over the centuries when the houses of Lancaster, York and Tudor supplied the reigning monarchs the Lord Chancellors were invariably great ecclesiastical statesmen, such as Thomas à Becket, and in their hands the power of the office steadily grew. Henry VIII's Cardinal Wolsey was the last of the eminent ecclesiastical Chancellors and since the reign of Elizabeth I the office has been mainly filled by prominent lawyers, which accounts for the present nature of the Lord Chancellor's functions.

In the words of Viscount Jowitt, who held the office under the Labour Government, the Lord Chancellor is a "sort of combination of chief justice and a minister of justice." As the highest judicial officer of the crown he presides, when he can, over the Supreme Court of Appeal (a committee of the House of Lords) or over the Judicial Committee of the Privy Council. As the head of the judiciary, he personally appoints all justices of the peace (except in Lancashire) and recommends to the sovereign the judges for the Court of Appeal, the High Court and the county courts. His other duties are multifarious. He is the guardian of all minors in the care of the courts, and of idiots and lunatics; he supervises all royal foundations; and he has special jurisdiction in relation to charities and trusts. In addition, as a carry-over from the earlier churchmen who filled the office, he has a large ecclesiastical patronage to dispense, the church livings in the gift of the crown. At the same time the Lord Chancellor is an important political appointee. He is a member of the Government in power, one of its principal spokesmen in the House of Lords and usually a member of the Cabinet, and, of course, when the Government falls he leaves his office. By long tradition he also sits on the symbolic woolsack as Speaker of the House of Lords. Every day the upper house sits he is escorted to the chamber by his own dignified procession—first the serjeant-at-arms, carrying the mace, and then the purse-bearer carrying the Chancellor's purse, a silk satchel emblazoned with the royal arms, which is the receptacle of the Great Seal (the Seal itself, too valuable to carry into the chamber each day, is kept under lock and key), and finally the Lord Chancellor followed by his train-bearer.

The combination of these apparently conflicting duties in the same office and the same person demonstrates the historic British genius for compromise. As Speaker of the Lords, the Lord Chancellor is recognized as the presiding officer, but he has no power to keep order—the peers are responsible for keeping order among themselves. The Lord Chancellor simply asks for the votes and proclaims the results. When he wishes to shed his non-party role and speak for the Government he simply takes one step to the left of the woolsack and becomes a member of the chamber.

Among the ancient titles carried by his unique office is that of Keeper of the King's Conscience—dating from the time when the ecclesiastics who held the office acted as the King's confessor—but this is no longer considered an active responsibility. "The King's conscience is much easier to keep than my own," Lord Jowitt once joked.

The Lord President of the Council is chairman of the Privy Council and in the days when the monarch ruled through his Council the Lord President's powers were great. Nowadays the office is practically a sinecure which is given to an important member of the Government, enabling the holder to carry out assignments without being tied down by departmental duties. The Lord Privy Seal is another practically sinecure office and the holder functions, in effect, as a Minister without portfolio. As his title implies he is custodian of the sovereign's Privy Seal, which must be affixed on royal warrants, charters, pardons, etc. before they are presented for the Great Seal.

The office of Earl Marshal, also one of great power in early reigns, is now confined to purely ceremonial duties. As titular head of the English College of Arms, which is the final authority on the medieval traditions surrounding the crown, the Earl Marshal is responsible for organizing the complicated ceremonial which accompanies the funeral of a sovereign and the coronation of his successor. In addition, it is he who arranges all details and order of procedure at all royal marriages and state processions. He also attends the sovereign at the state opening of Parliament and throughout the year assists at the introduction of newly-created peers to the House of Lords. For all this he draws an annual fee of £20, fixed upon the office back in 1483, which is paid from the rent of a farm in Ipswich.

Like the Lord Great Chamberlain, the Earl Marshal is an hereditary post. In early reigns it went from family to family at the whim of the ruling monarch but in 1672 Charles II bestowed the office on the great house of Howard, the Dukes of Norfolk, and it has been passed down in the male line ever since. By a curious twist of fate, it is one of the few high court or state offices in Britain to be held by a Roman Catholic. The Dukes of Norfolk are heads of one of the few great families which did not follow Henry VIII when he left the Church of Rome and have always remained Roman Catholics. The present Earl Marshal is the 44-year-old Duke of Norfolk, who has held the office for some 17 years. In his crowded span of service he has been called upon to organize the state funerals of George V and George VI and the coronation of George VI and to arrange the coronation of Elizabeth II.

Technically, the two houses of Parliament today occupy what is properly called the Queen's Palace of Westminster, a historic convenience that goes back to the days when Parliaments were summoned by the sovereign to give him guidance and provided with accommodation while they were sitting, and the royal link between the monarch and the Palace of Westminster is still preserved in the person of the Lord Great Chamberlain.

As the direct representative of the Queen at Westminster the Lord Great Chamberlain is theoretically responsible for the accommodation arrangements, the cleaning, the repairs and the general management of the Palace (except for the provision of food for the members, which is in the hands of a catering committee of members themselves). Even when the members are in session the Lord Great Chamberlain's authority is exercised in the precincts outside the chambers by the serjeant-at-arms and when Parliament stands adjourned the Lord Great Chamberlain's department has authority over the whole building. In fact, the maintenance of Parliament is carried out by the Minister of Works, but the Lord Great Chamberlain is personally responsible for arranging the procedure inside Westminster on all royal occasions, particularly the state openings of Parliament, when he wears his full ceremonial robes and carries the symbol of his office, a key to the Palace of Westminster. The two-handed sword of state is in his keeping and he selects a peer, usually a member of the Government, to carry it before the Queen in royal processions. He also assists at the introduction of new peers into the House of Lords. Formerly the Lord Great Chamberlain played a leading role in the coronation, but many of his duties have been taken over by the Earl Marshal.

The Lord Great Chamberlain's office is one of two Great Officerships which are still hereditary, and it has been continuously filled by a nobleman since early Norman times. It was created in 1133 by Henry I and the Lord Great Chamberlain of those early reigns was charged with the duty of handing the monarch his shirt, stockings and underwear before the coronation. For his fee he was allowed to take away some of the king's bedroom furniture.

Successive Earls of Oxford held this hereditary post until 1387, when the ninth earl was disgraced and deprived of all his offices. His successor, the Earl of Huntingdon, was beheaded in 1400 and after a lapse of 85 years the Earls of Oxford regained their hereditary right to serve as Lord Great Chamberlains. In 1902, after three centuries of dispute because of a confusion in the line of succession, the House of Lords ruled that the office should be jointly vested in three families—the Lords Cholmondeley, Ancaster and Lincolnshire and their heirs—which should discharge its duties in turn during separate reigns. The present Lord Great Chamberlain is the Marquess of Cholmondeley.

The routine functions once performed by the chamberlains are now carried out by permanent officials within the royal household. Thus the Master of the Household supervises Elizabeth II's domestic household, the Keeper of the Privy Purse handles her finances, and her private secretary's office transacts her official business.

By long tradition the senior official of the Queen's household is the Lord Chamberlain, at present the 75-year-old sixth Earl of Clarendon, the son and nephew of previous Lord Chamberlains. The post is extremely ancient. A roll of its holders exists from the year 1360, but there were Lord Chamberlains in Anglo-Saxon times. Then the Lord Chamberlain was the head domestic official within the King's chamber—in token of which he still carries a golden key on his hip on ceremonial occasions—but by the reign of Athelstan early in the tenth century he had added to his domestic duties the witnessing of royal charters. Ever since his functions have been multifarious. He no longer performs any domestic duties in the household, but he supervises all ceremonial connected with the royal family other than state functions such as the coronation, the state opening of Parliament and the funeral of the sovereign. He is the organizer of courts and levées and the reception and entertainment of visiting foreign dignitaries. It is his office which sends out the invitations to garden parties, scans the list of debutantes who seek admission to the court, arranges the closely-timed procedure of investitures and sorts out the black sheep from the social elite who apply for admission to the royal enclosure at Ascot racecourse. On state occasions the Lord Chamberlain himself conducts Her Majesty to and from her carriage.

Among his many secondary duties are the appointment, on the Queen's behalf, of the royal chaplains, the royal physicians and surgeons, the Poet Laureate, and the Queen's Bargemaster and Watermen, and under his special eye come such officers as the Master of the Queen's Musick, the Keeper of the Swans on the Thames, the Shower of State Apartments at Windsor Castle, the Serjeants-at-Arms, the Gentleman Usher of the Black Rod, the Lords- and Grooms-in-Waiting as well as the pages of the back-stairs, the chamber and the presence. He is also the superintendent of the royal collection of art and antiques.

By a historical accident, the Lord Chamberlain is also respons-ible for censoring British drama, a duty for which he is frequently criticised. His office has been connected with the theatre in England at least since 1574. In those days the royal house pro-vided the chief sponsorship for plays and actors, usually against fierce Puritan opposition, and the Lord Chamberlain became the monarch's principal agent through whom the dramatic art was encouraged, although his powers were usually delegated to a Master of the Revels. The Lord Chamberlain's office continued to control both plays and players and when Parliament passed a Licensing Act in 1739 the Lord Chamberlain was made dictator of the drama. This invidious post was wished on him because it was presumed that the Lord Chamberlain, appointed by the sovereign and not by Parliament, would be a non-political, noncontroversial public figure whose cultural and moral judgments would remain above reproach. Nowadays, either Lord Clarendon or one of his two assistants, Sir Terence Nugent, his Comptroller, and Brigadier Norman Gwatkin, the assistant Comptroller, read the manuscript of each new play submitted for presentation on a public stage in the United Kingdom. They have absolute authority to decide which is fit to be shown. No play may be publicly performed in the country without the Lord Chamberlain's licence, and in this century he has banned, among others, works of Shaw, Ibsen and Maeterlinck. Parliament has frequently debated his role as censor but has never been able to agree on the larger issue of censorship of the theatre and so the Lord Chamberlain has retained his anomalous prerogative.

The Lord Chamberlain, who is by custom always a member of the Privy Council, is required to carry his symbol of authority, a white staff of office, whenever he attends the sovereign on ceremonial occasions. In olden days it was customary to break the staves in half on dismissal from office, but in modern times they have been made to unscrew so that the retiring official may keep half as a memento of his high office. Likewise, with the death of a monarch the Lord Chamberlain's appointment (and most of the others in the household) comes to an end, although in practice these officials remain in office for at least six months of the new reign, but the tradition of an abrupt break in service is retained and at the funeral of a monarch his Lord Chamberlain unscrews his white staff and places half upon the coffin as a final gesture of farewell.

Despite their titles, the Vice Chamberlain, the Treasurer of the Household, the Comptroller and the Lord-in-Waiting have only a ceremonial connection with the royal household and take no part in its internal affairs. These posts are customarily filled by the Government of the day, and by recent tradition the holders of the first three are usually members of the House of Commons who serve in some administrations as Government whips, or party floor managers. The Vice Chamberlain does have the royal duty of writing for the Queen every day a summary of the proceedings in Parliament. The Treasurer of the Household and the Comptroller are required to attend the Queen in the House of Lords when she opens Parliament and the Vice Chamberlain, by custom, remains at Buckingham Palace to receive her on her return from the Lords. When they wear their full ceremonial dress, the ornate and heavily gold-braided uniform of their household offices, the Vice Chamberlain carries a large gilt key in his belt as a token of his authority. Like those worn by the Lord Chamberlain and the Lord Great Chamberlain, it opens no known door and its precise origin is lost in the past.

To attend her on ceremonial occasions and accompany her on state drives through London the Queen is entitled to summon a number of part-time officers, who bear among them such ornamental titles as the Master of the Horse (the Duke of Beaufort), the Gold Stick in Waiting (a colonel of the Household Cavalry), the Field Officer in Brigade Waiting (a high officer of the Brigade of Guards), the Silver Stick in Waiting (an officer of the Household Cavalry) and the Vice Admiral of the United Kingdom (usually a distinguished admiral).

The preservation of the medieval pageantry which surrounds the monarch today is the special responsibility of the College of Arms, or Herald's College as it is sometimes called. The supreme head of the College is the Earl Marshal, but it is actively administered by the Garter King of Arms in his capacity as the principal King of Arms in England. The College, incorporated by Richard III, has its own offices in London in a handsome old building tucked away in the shadow of St. Pauls' Cathedral and consists of the three Kings of Arms (Garter King of Arms, Clarenceux King of Arms, and Norroy and Ulster King of Arms), six Heralds (Lancaster Herald, Somerset Herald, Chester Herald, York Herald, Richmond Herald and Windsor Herald) and four beautifully-titled Pursuivants, one-time attendants who rank just below the Heralds (Bluemantle Pursuivant, Rouge Dragon Pursuivant, Rouge Croix Pursuivant and Portcullis Pursuivant).

The main public function of this unique survival from the Middle Ages is to assist the Earl Marshal on occasions of royal ceremony, and on most such occasions the officers of the College are present in person, attired in their magnificent medieval tabards of velvet, emblazoned with the royal arms embroidered in gold thread. As custodians of many of the customs of the past, the officials of the College are frequently called in to arbitrate disputed details of pageantry and state ceremonial and to decide ticklish precedential problems of who walks before whom at ceremonial and social functions. They also assist the special Court of Claims, which is set up before each coronation, under the presidency of the Lord High Steward, assisted by the Lord High Chancellor and the Earl Marshal, in order to adjudicate the claims of individuals who assert their hereditary rights to participate in the ceremony.

In its other important function the College of Arms serves as a genealogical records office. It has sole charge of armorial bearings except in Scotland, and the Kings of Arms, acting for the sovereign through the Earl Marshal, have the right to grant arms to all persons privileged to bear them. This privilege is granted through letters patent which are given to those who can present proof of direct male descent from a bearer of arms shown in the College records and to newly-created peers who have the right to apply for a grant of arms. Although the original purpose of the pictorial art of heraldry dates from the days when few could read or write and armorial bearings provided evidence of identity, there is still a surprisingly continuous demand for coats of arms. The College handles an average of some 2,000 inquiries each year from people who think they are entitled to them. It is a revealing sidelight on Britain's Labour Party that its members who were raised to the peerage, while they may have disdained inherited privilege as commoners, were generally first in the queue for family escutcheons.

These claims for armorial bearings involve the College of Arms in a painstaking search of pedigree, for which it is equipped with the finest collection of genealogical documents in the world.[2] Once a claim has been established, the officials of the College design a suitable armorial bearing, drawing on their vast collection of heraldic emblems to make sure that no two heraldic symbols are exactly alike. Several resident craftsmen-artists, known as Herald Painters to the Queen, are maintained by the College to paint crests, banners, book plates and other armorial insignia.

As the principal officer of the College, the Garter King of Arms has special rights and duties. When appointed Garter he receives his sceptre of office from the sovereign and at the coronation he is entitled to wear a coronet. At the burial of royal personages it is his duty to recite the royal style and titles.

The Garter King of Arms, in his role as keeper of the nation's pedigrees, formally declares who is entitled to sit in the hereditary House of Lords and personally introduces all newly-created peers to the upper chamber, a precaution taken in former times to forestall the possibility of impersonation. On the first day of the sitting of each new session of Parliament the Garter King presents to the Lord Chancellor, who represents the crown in the Lords, a parchment roll inscribed with the titles of the peers, in order of their precedence, who are entitled to sit in the upper House [3]—first the royal princes, then the Archbishop of Canterbury, the Lord Chancellor, the Archbishop of York, the Lord President of the Council and the Lord Privy Seal, and after them the dukes, the marquesses, the earls (headed by the Master of the Horse), the viscounts, the bishops and, lastly, the barons. When a newly-created peer takes his seat he is traditionally accompanied by two sponsors of his own rank who are supposed to know his identity, another precaution against impersonation. They are formally led into the Parliament Chamber, as the House of Lords is officially called, by the premier duke of England, in his hereditary position of Earl Marshal, accompanied by the Gentleman Usher of the Black Rod and the Garter King of Arms. On arrival at the woolsack, the great crimson hassock stuffed with wool from every part of the Commonwealth to symbolize Britain's early dependence on the trade, the Garter King, on bended knee, presents the roll of the peers and the patent of nobility of the newcomer to the Lord Chancellor. The documents are read out to the House by a clerk, and then the new peer takes the oath and signs the roll, after which the Garter King shows the fledgling to his seat among other peers of his same rank along the red morocco benches of the chamber. The peer and his two supporters seat themselves but immediately rise and bow deeply to the Lord Chancellor, who acknowledges the courtesy by removing his three-cornered hat. Twice more these salutes are exchanged. The new peer then leaves the House, stopping en route to be introduced personally to the Lord Chancellor, after which he retires to remove his robes before returning to the chamber to take his seat officially. When the new peer is the Lord Chancellor himself, the same procedure is followed except that, as there is no representative of the crown present, the railed-off throne itself is uncovered. After his patent has been read to the House, the Lord Chancellor bows to the throne and his patent is then de-

22. The colourful pageantry of the historic Order of the Garter: the royal family leaves the 1948 service at which Princess Elizabeth and the Duke of Edinburgh were installed as a Lady and Knight of the Garter

23. *Elizabeth II takes part in annual Maundy ceremony*

24. *The Queen reviews her Brigade of Guards at Trooping of the Colour*

posited upon it, where it remains on the empty seat until the end of the day's sitting.

The patents of nobility, prepared by the College of Arms, are the most prized possessions of the peers of Britain, for they are considered the only legal proof of their owners' rank. They are handed down from father to son, and when the son of a peer takes his seat in the Lords on the assumption of his father's title he must bring his father's patent of nobility along with his own as proof of his identity.

Scotland proudly retains its own counterpart of the College of Arms, the Lyon Court, complete with Scottish Heralds and Pursuivants, an inheritance which survived the union of the kingdoms.

The Lyon Court, the only court of chivalry in the world, is presided over by the Lord Lyon King of Arms of Scotland, who derives his name from the lion rampant, the armorial bearing of the Scottish kings. Armorial bearings are protected by statute in Scotland, and the Lyon King of Arms has authority to inspect all arms and armorial ensigns of Scottish noblemen and gentlemen, to issue proper arms to those entitled to bear them, and to fine those who bear unauthorized arms. Like the College of Arms, the Lyon Court is the final authority on genealogy in Scotland and the Lord Lyon is often called on to rule on disputed claims to succession within the numerous Scottish clans and septs.

When the Lyon Court sits as a court of chivalry, the Lyon King of Arms is assisted by two hereditary Assessors, traditionally the holders of the two premier titles of Scotland, at present the Countess of Erroll and the Duke of Hamilton. The Countess of Erroll, the twenty-seventh of her line to be hereditary High Constable of Scotland, an office conferred upon her ancestor by Robert the Bruce at Bannockburn in 1314, is recognized as the head of the Scottish feudal nobility and first subject by birth in Scotland after the blood royal. Her ancient office carries with it the duty of guarding the sovereign's person when he is in Scotland as well as his Parliament house, and of judging any cases of assault that occur within the verge of the royal court, that is, within four miles of the monarch's person when he is in Scotland. In observance of the old custom, the Countess appoints a skilled Scottish lawyer to act as her Constable Depute at Holyroodhouse, the sovereign's Edinburgh palace, and holds her court of the High Constable there when the Queen is in residence. During the reigns of the Scottish kings the High Constable was also the keeper of the sword of state and in commemoration of this ancient function is still entitled to walk in the British coronation procession. No woman may officiate at a British coronation, however. The present Countess of Erroll had not succeeded to her title when George VI was crowned and the only other Lady Erroll to have been High Constable in her own right had to appoint a male deputy to walk in her place at the coronation of George II.

The Duke of Hamilton, on whose estates Rudolf Hess intended to land when he made his dramatic flight from Nazi Germany (Hess claimed to have met the Duke at the Olympic Games in Berlin), is the fourteenth of his line to hold the dual title of Hereditary Keeper of the Palace of Holyroodhouse and Lord Steward of Her Majesty's Household in Scotland. The second subject of the Queen in Scotland, it is his job to receive the sovereign when she makes state visits to the country.

VI

MONARCHIC TRADITIONS

UNTIL the reign of George VI an official of His Majesty's Government, usually the Secretary of State for Home Affairs, attended at the birth of all heirs to the throne. This invasion of royal privacy went back two and a half centuries, when Britain was swept by an ugly political rumour which made out that the son born to Queen Mary of Modena and her arrogant, Catholic husband, James II, was in fact a changeling which had been surreptitiously slipped into the royal childbed in a warming-pan. The rumour was later proved false, but for a time it was exploited to bolster the claim to the throne of James's Protestant daughter Mary, a claim she later realized anyway when she ascended the throne as co-sovereign with her husband, William of Orange.

From that day, right up to 1948, the ruling family observed the precaution of having a Government official present in the royal bedchamber to witness the births of royal heirs. During Queen Victoria's confinements Prince Albert strongly objected to this intimate custom and succeeded in banishing the representative of the state to an antechamber, but the official was always called in to view the new baby at its first gasps.

In November, 1948, with the birth of Princess Elizabeth's first baby near at hand, her father decided to spare his daughter the indignity of a witness. "The attendance of a Minister of the crown at a birth in the royal family is not a statutory requirement," said a brief announcement from Buckingham Palace. " . . . It is merely the survival of an archaic custom and the King feels that it is unnecessary to continue (the) practice." The Home Secretary stayed at home and got the news of the royal birth by telephone.

This was one of the few archaic customs which George VI dared to do away with. Like a woman with a piece of cloth, the

99

British are loath to part with their old traditions and ceremonies, even though many are relics of feudalism.

The role of the monarchy is of such antiquity that almost every function connected with it is naturally steeped in tradition and ancient custom.

For instance, many of the so-called "quit" or "service" rents paid today on properties held from the crown trace directly back to feudal days when kings made grants of land for services and demanded from the tenants only a token recognition of the crown's prime ownership. Some of these "services," though they make small demands on the pockets of the respective owners, entail a certain amount of ingenuity for their proper fulfilment.[1]

Many of the crown lands were given on strange conditions of tenure, which are still ritually filled today. When George VI visited the Marquis of Ailesbury in 1942 the host was required to celebrate the occasion by blowing a twelfth-century silver-mounted ivory horn, the condition under which he is allowed to own the great Savernake Forest, the only forest in England possessed by a subject. Sir George Clarke, a Scottish baronet, holds his property on condition that he blows three blasts from a bugle whenever the monarch hunts stags on the moors nearby, and a farm near Edinburgh pays its rent by keeping handy a silver basin and ewer and a damask napkin, which must be proferred for the washing of the royal hands whenever the monarch passes by. The origin of this ceremony goes back to the time when the original owner reputedly saved King James V from assassination and afterwards washed the monarch's wounds, for which he was given his land on condition that he and his successors paid the sovereign this token service. Kidwelly Castle, one of the oldest in Wales, is held on condition that the monarch, when in the vicinity, is furnished with the services of a knight in full armour, and the condition on which the post of hereditary keeper of ancient derelict Dunstaffnage Castle in Scotland is retained is that the owners of the title shall spend a night once each year within the roofless and ruined castle walls.

But the strangest tenure of all was imposed by a monarch who wished some utilitarian as well as token return for his land. The owner of a manor house known as Archer's Court, in Kent, is by tradition required to accompany the monarch, carrying a silver bowl, whenever the sovereign crosses the Channel, in case His Majesty should be seasick. George VI, who considered himself a sailor-king, never availed himself of this service.

Once each year, on the anniversary of the battle of Waterloo—June 18—the Duke of Wellington goes to Windsor Castle before twelve noon and, on bended knee, hands to the Queen a miniature French tricolour flag as "quit" rent for his Hampshire estate of Strathfieldsaye, which a grateful nation bought for £263,000 and presented to the Iron Duke, the conqueror of Napoleon. On the anniversary of the battle of Blenheim —August 2—the Duke of Marlborough also pays the rent on his great ducal estate with a flag, a small white satin banner emblazoned with three *fleur de lis* and fringed with gold bullion, which was the "quit" rent Parliament decreed should be paid by the first Duke of Marlborough and his successors when the magnificent Blenheim Palace (in which Winston Churchill was born), the largest private house in Britain, and its estate, valued at least £2,000,000 today, was given to the first Duke for winning the great victory at Blenheim. The Duke of Marlborough does not present his flag personally to the Queen: it is mailed direct by the manufacturers to the superintendent of Windsor Castle, who presents it to the Garter King of Arms. Both flags hang throughout the year in the great, manorial guard room at Windsor Castle.

The guard room itself is dominated by a life-sized equestrian statue of a knight in full armour, one arm raised in the act of throwing down a gauntlet. This commemorates the King's Champion, an office which is still filled though its main ceremonial function has fallen into disuse. The post of King's Champion has been in existence since the time of William of Normandy, first being filled by the Lords Marmion and now by their descendants, the family of Dymoke. At each of the coronation banquets in the spacious Westminster Hall to mark the accession of a new sovereign, the King's Champion, wearing the King's second-best suit of armour and mounted on the King's second-best horse, rode into the hall to the end of the table where the newly-crowned sovereign sat, and hurled his steel gauntlet to the floor while a herald proclaimed his challenge: "If any person, of what degree soever, high or low, shall deny or gainsay our Sovereign Lord . . . to be the rightful heir to the Crown of the United Kingdom or that he ought not to enjoy the same, here is his Champion, who

101

saith he lieth sore and is a false traitor, being ready in person to combat with him." When no reply was forthcoming, the King drank his Champion's health in a silver cup and proffered it to him. The Champion took the cup, pledged his King in it, and retained it as his fee and then finally backed his horse out the full length of the great hall. Up to the reign of George IV this chivalric touch was retained, but in modern times, when the state banquets have been omitted, the King's Champion attends the coronation on foot, dressed in a tabard like a Herald, and generally carries the standard of England in the procession.

By ancient law, the monarch still enjoys many rights and privileges that were his by right as the first lord of a feudal society.

Thus swans were once royal birds, and of the 800 or so which today inhabit the Thames some 600 still belong to Queen Elizabeth, while the remainder are divided between the Worshipful Company of Dyers and the Worshipful Company of Vintners, on whom the crown bestowed gifts of the birds in the fourteenth century. Poaching of these swans still draws a heavy fine. Every summer on the Thames there takes place a delightful ceremony known as swan upping, in which crews of punters, decked in colourful jerseys and caps to represent the Queen and the Dyers' and Vintners', round up and mark the swans on the river. The records of swan upping go back to 1363, but the custom of marking the royal birds goes back even before this. Deer were at one time royal animals, and the penalty for unauthorized killing of them was severe. The sturgeon is still a royal fish, and every sturgeon taken in British waters—a comparatively rare event—is, by ancient law, the property of the sovereign. By a lucky omen, on the eve of Princess Elizabeth's wedding the crew of the Grimsby trawler *Mitre* hauled in a magnificent, 105-pound sturgeon, which they quickly dispatched to Buckingham Palace to grace the royal table. Technically, the king is entitled to any whale taken on the coast of Britain, and the queen is entitled to all whales' tails—to use in the boning of her corsets! All "treasure trove" found buried in the ground is technically the property of the crown, although modern monarchs pass on these finds and their proceeds direct to museums or the Treasury.

Some customs have been observed for so long that they are taken for granted in royal circles and their origins are obscure.

For example, no person is supposed to enter the monarch's presence while wearing gloves, a precautionary custom going back to the days when the king's enemies might conceal weapons or poisoned rings in their gloves. Hats are customarily removed in the presence of the monarch, but the heads of two old families still cling to their right to wear their hats in the sovereign's presence and have resisted the efforts of successive monarchs to abolish it. The Lords of Kingsale won this rare privilege more than 700 years ago. The King of France challenged Britain's King John to mortal combat, and, as was the custom, two champions were designated for the ordeal. King John nominated Lord Kingsale, one of the biggest men and bravest fighters in his kingdom, and when the French champion set eyes on him he declined battle. As a reward, John granted Lord Kingsale and his successors the right to remain covered in the royal presence. Some centuries later a commoner, William Forester, risked his life to protect Henry VIII during a hunting expedition, and he and his descendants, who bear the title of Lord Forester, were given the same privilege.

Until early in this century finger-bowls were never placed on the table when royalty was entertained. This was because in Georgian times those Jacobites who were secretly in sympathy with the banished Stuarts used to pass their glasses over the bowls before drinking a toast to the King, a covert allusion to "the royal exiles over the water." [2] Edward VII, feeling that his house was by then firmly established on the throne, abolished the custom on his accession.

Not long afterwards a foreign potentate being entertained at Edward's dinner table innocently lifted his finger-bowl and drank from it. Edward, who made a reputation as a diplomatic monarch by his friendly relations with his European neighbours, was equal to the occasion. Without a moment's hesitation he drank from his own finger-bowl, a precedent that all his guests followed for the remainder of that meal.

The custom of drinking the loyal toast to the health of the monarch and members of his or her family, which is still invariably observed at all public and official dinners and in the messes of the fighting services in Britain and overseas, is a complicated national ritual with many variants.[3]

Even toasts have a long-established order of precedence and

soon after her accession Elizabeth II approved that the future order of toasts in her reign should be: (1) the Queen; (2) Queen Elizabeth, the Queen Mother; (3) Queen Mary; (4) the Duke of Edinburgh; and (5) the other members of the royal family. By custom, no one smokes in a formal dining-room until the toast or toasts have been given.

Some years ago the suggestion was made that the toast could only be drunk in wine and that anything else was a tacit insult to the sovereign, which led the Lord Chamberlain's office to rule, solemnly, that "wine is most usual, but it can be tea, coffee or cocoa, according to the whim of the people concerned," and Edward VII, no teetotaller, let it be known that he nevertheless considered the toast to his health just as loyal if drunk in water.

The manufacture of money was originally the exclusive prerogative of the king—"the right of coining money is in the very bones of the Sovereign," proclaims the antiquated wording of the civil law—and though this right of the crown was long ago taken over by Parliament, Britain's metal coinage is still made at the Royal Mint, built in 1810 to replace the Mint which had operated for centuries under royal jurisdiction at the Tower of London, and the Chancellor of the Exchequer carries in addition the royal title of Master of the Mint, a title that has existed since the reign of Henry I. The overburdened Chancellor delegates his Mint duties to a Deputy Master. Periodically specimens of all denominations of coins made at the Mint are tested officially at an elaborate ceremony known as the Trial of the Pyx—first instituted in the time of Henry III, when the makers of the King's money were not above suspicion—which is conducted by the Freemen of the Goldsmiths' Company, with the Queen's Remembrancer, the Deputy Master, officials of the Mint and the Board of Trade looking on.

New coins and stamps, bearing the profile of the monarch, are traditionally issued for each reign. By long custom, each new sovereign's face is opposite to that of his predecessor. George V looked to the left in his coins and stamps, but when Edward VIII was shown the new designs of himself looking to the right he protested vehemently that his left profile was his better side (he likes the parting of his hair to be shown). His stubbornness eventually broke down the tradition, but comparatively few of the new stamps were printed and the coins were never issued. After his abdication the Royal Mint and Post Office authorities simply pretended that Edward VIII had adhered to the tradition: on his stamps and coins George VI looked to the left, and Elizabeth II looks to the right.

Theatre-goers attending London's Drury Lane Theatre are usually surprised when they come face to face with bewigged and breeches-clad footmen in royal livery, looking as if they had stepped from the wings of a Restoration drama. This apparent anachronism is quite in order, for Charles II made Drury Lane the first royal theatre in the world when he gave its charter to a family friend who served as his groom of the bedchamber. Its charter is still held direct from the monarch and, unlike its competitors, it needs no licence from the Lord Chamberlain. Charles, incidentally, conferred a great boon on the theatre when he insisted that Drury Lane's female parts should be played by women, not by boys as had been the custom, and thus legalized the profession of actress. All members of the first company were sworn in as court officials—Gentlemen of the Great Chamber, they were called—and given the right to wear the royal livery. This right still exists, but "the Lane" is content to show off its royal pedigree only in the dress of its footmen.

Most picturesque of the age-old customs kept alive by yearly repetition is the ceremony of the Royal Maund, the annual distribution of Easter alms by the king or queen to the poor, which takes place at Westminster Abbey on Maundy Thursday, the day before Good Friday. This ancient and colourful ritual, which symbolizes the function of royalty as the foundation of all Christian charity and the humility of the sovereign before the poorest subjects in the land, commemorates Christ's symbolic washing of the feet of His disciples on the Thursday before the Last Supper. The Maundy service is supposed to derive its name through the old French corruption of the Latin word *mandatum*, meaning a commandment—the service traditionally begins with the exhortation from St. John: "A new Commandment have I given unto you, that ye love one another; as I have loved you, that ye also love one another"—although some authorities argue that it stems from the word *maund*, meaning basket, a reference to the olden days when religious orders, before beginning their fasts, placed foodstuffs in maunds for distribution to the poor.

Whatever the origins, the Royal Maund is without doubt one of Britain's oldest rituals. Its beginnings can be traced back with certainty to the twelfth century and there are continuous records of Maundy Thursday alms distributions dating from the reign of Edward I. In early reigns the monarchs or their designated representatives emulated Christ by washing the feet of the poor—it is recorded that in 1300 the Westminster Abbot washed the feet of 13 poor men and gave them money, food and drink—but the last monarch to perform the full washing ceremony was James II and it was finally dropped in 1737 in the reign of the second George. Today, however, the Bishop of Lichfield, who officiates at the ceremony as Lord High Almoner to the Queen, and the principals at the service are still wrapped around with white towels as a reminder of the Maund's significance.

Since the beginning of the fifteenth century it has been the custom to present alms on Maundy Thursday to as many old men and as many old women as the sovereign is years of age. The neediest recipients are carefully screened by the Bishop of Lichfield and the Royal Almonry Office and although most of those chosen are too aged or infirm to appear—only two score or so nominees manage to attend each year—there is never a lack of candidates for the honour.

The Abbey service still conjures up much of the ancient reverence of the occasion. According to tradition the procession is led by the beadle of the Abbey, bearing the mace, followed by the Cross of Westminster. Behind them walk the fresh-faced young choirboys of the Collegiate Church of St. Peter's, as Westminster Abbey is properly called, and then the Queen and members of the royal family, accompanied by the Dean of Westminster. Heading the Royal Almonry procession walk two of the Yeomen of the Guard, the first carrying the Maundy alms in bright-coloured Tudor purses laid out on a great silver platter, which he holds waist-high, the second bearing purses in a silver gilt dish held atop his head, and behind them come the partisan-carrying Yeomen of the Queen's Bodyguard. At the end of the procession walk the Lord High Almoner and Sub-Almoner in their dark crimson robes and the officers of the Royal Almonry, girt with their towels. The Queen and the participants of exalted rank in the ceremony each carry a pretty nosegay of sweet herbs or flowers, a colourful touch that was once thought necessary to ward off the plague and protect the royal nostrils from the stench of the unwashed poor.

During the short, simple service the Maundy money is distributed, by the Queen in person if she is present, by the Lord High Almoner if she is not. From the great alms dish each female recipient is first given a green purse containing £1 15s., and each male a white purse holding £2 5s. in lieu of the former gift of clothing. Then, in the second distribution, the Queen or the Almoner hands to each recipient a red purse with white thongs holding £1, representing part of the Maundy, and an allowance of £1 10s. in lieu of provisions formerly given in kind, and, finally, a white purse with red thongs containing "as many pence as the Queen is years of age," the balance of the Maundy money, made up of specially-minted silver pennies, twopences, threepences and fourpences, which are turned out for the occasion by the Royal Mint. These coins are actually legal tender, but because their rareness gives them far higher than face value, they are usually kept or sold as curios.[4]

A lesser known but similar ceremony commemorates the gifts of the three wise men of the New Testament. On the Feast of Epiphany it was customary for the reigning sovereign to present at the altar gold, frankincense and myrrh. The last monarch to do this in person was George III, however, and nowadays the Lord Chamberlain, representing the Queen at a special service at the Chapel Royal at St. James's Palace, and attended by the Yeomen of the Guard, ceremoniously deposits in the alms dish three purses symbolic of the wise men's gifts, which contain £30 for distribution to the poor of the parish.

VII

FOUNTAIN OF HONOURS

THE honours system, by which commoners are advanced to higher station and the high-born moved to more exalted rank through the conferment of titles, orders and awards in the name of the sovereign, is another time-honoured custom which it is found useful to preserve. No mere royal falbala, in an era when high taxation has cancelled out the money motive the prospect of receiving honours or a title remains a compelling incentive for hard work and good behaviour to more men and women in British business, political and public life than would care to admit it. In the case of hard-working civil servants, who reap the bulk of the awards on the way to the top of their profession, the grant of honours serves in part as compensation for their relatively poor pay.

Paradoxically, while retaining the ancient traditions of the system, in which honours flow from the fountainhead of all honours, the sovereign, the British have so altered its character that in its modern operation it serves to strengthen the democratic structure of their society. Originally confined to court officials and the aristocracy supporting the royal house (and, until the nineteenth century, flagrantly used by the ruling monarch as a means of bribing people to support the "king's party" in politics), the granting of honours has been gradually removed from royal hands and successively widened until today the bi-annual list of honours reads almost like a social cross-section of the nation. Military, political and diplomatic personages predominate in the higher ranks, but with every list actors and actresses and artists, poets and writers, musicians and medical men, farmers, engineers, scientists and those who spend their lives in the outposts of the Empire are entitled to append the coveted letters of some order to their names. Not overlooked,

108

particularly when the Labour Government was in office, are working class recipients, and railroad men, farm hands, miners and other workers who have set a sort of Stakhanovite example in long service and hard work are usually singled out for recognition.

From this it should not be inferred that every little Briton carries a title in his school satchel but it is at least true that most of the honours conferred in the name of the sovereign today are democratically open to people of all classes and backgrounds. Relatively few of them can be inherited; none of them can be bought; and most of them have to be earned.

The hierarchy of orders to which admission brings distinction and, in the higher ranks, a title is as carefully graded as the Masonic degrees or the castes of the Hindus (for instance, there are five ranks in the peerage—barons, viscounts, earls, marquesses and dukes, in ascending order—and five classes of peers, five classes of baronets and ten different classes of knights) and the selection and investigation of nominees for honours is a carefully administered procedure to which Elizabeth II, like her father before her, is compelled to give much of her time. Although nowadays most honours are dispensed through the Prime Minister's office, many of them as obvious political rewards—only the 600-year-old Most Noble Order of the Garter, the Royal Victorian Order and the Order of Merit remain as the absolute gift of the sovereign—all of them are awarded in the Queen's name and most of them are personally presented by her.

Honours are announced twice each year, in the Queen's birthday list around the time of her official birth-date, and in the New Year's list. In addition, there is generally a Dissolution list of honours granted after the dissolution of a Government. Honours and titles awarded by the Queen to distinguished citizens of her Dominions (some of which do not accept honours at all) are awarded solely on the advice of her Dominion Ministers but they are published in supplements to the British lists.

In Britain nominees for honours and titles are put forward by various departments like the Foreign Office, the Treasury, the armed services and by the Prime Minister himself, but the final selection of proposed recipients, even for minor honours, is made by the Prime Minister personally except for those orders which are reserved to the sovereign. The Prime Minister's list of nominees is first put before the Political Honours Scrutiny

Committee at the Treasury, a watch-dog tribunal composed of one Conservative peer, a Labour peer and a non-political Law Lord which was set up after a 1922 scandal aired charges of trafficking in honours. By discreet inquiry, this body then examines the fitness of each nominee on the list to receive the honour proposed. How these inquiries are made remains a Committee secret, but it is thought that Ministry of Health inspectors or their deputies around the country are called on to investigate the background of each recipient. If it is discovered that any candidate had a criminal past, or had been found dishonourably bankrupt, or had a grave blemish on his private life he is dropped from the list. At one time divorce was regarded as a serious blot on a person's character, but George VI was more broadminded about divorces than his predecessors and seldom regarded them as a bar against the award of honours. If the candidates survive this personal examination the party whips are called in on each case to assure the Committee that "no payment or expectation of payment to any party or political fund was directly or indirectly associated with the Prime Minister's recommendation." The Prime Minister then submits the complete list to Buckingham Palace for the Queen's informal approval. He is not obliged to accept the Committee's findings about the candidates, but he is, by tradition, obligated to inform Her Majesty what the Committee thinks about dubious cases. Once the list has passed this stage, the recipients are then informed secretly about their proposed honour, before the list is published, to give them a chance to refuse it. No person is forced to accept an honour against his will, and occasionally someone refuses. John Galsworthy, for example, refused a knighthood in 1918. He was erroneously awarded the rank in the published list when his letter declining the honour went astray, but he was never given the accolade and the honour was later withdrawn.

Comparatively few titles awarded in recent years have been hereditary. The Labour Party is antipathetic to hereditary titles and Clement Attlee as Prime Minister confined his recommendations largely to barons, who sit as peers in the House of Lords. As peerages have political uses the Labour Government was not backward about recommending them, but it drew the line at awarding hereditary baronetcies, one of the oldest honours, ranking between the peerage and non-hereditary holders. From 1945 to 1951 the solitary baronetcy accorded each year (except for one

granted in 1947 to the secretary to the Speaker of the Commons)
was to the retiring Lord Mayor of London, who by long tradition
is offered this honour after his one-year term of office. In 1945,
when Winston Churchill last drew up a list of honours before his
party's electoral defeat, he created 17 baronetcies and in his first
grant of honours after returning to the Prime Minister's post in
1951 he restored the rank to favour and created four new
baronetcies. Even if few new baronetcies are created, however,
there is little danger of the rank dying out for a long time to come,
for on the official roll there are still some 1,500 baronets. The
baronetage as it exists today was founded by James I in 1611—
earlier baronetcies had been created as far back as the fourteenth
century, but they were not regularly hereditary and had practically disappeared—and the first title-holders enjoyed the privileges
of a place near the royal standard in battle and a funeral ceremony
"meane betwixt that of a baron and a knight."

The various gradations of orders and titles [1] are carefully supervised jointly by the Lord Chamberlain's office, the Central
Chancery of the Orders of Knighthood and the College of Arms,
but the honours system was not always as scrupulously administered as it is today. In fact, when James I founded the baronetage
as one of the most exclusive hereditary degrees in the world he
did it to raise badly-needed funds for supressing rebellion in
Ulster and for cultivating that province. Although it was pro-
scribed that the first members should be of gentle birth and good
reputation, with an annual revenue of at least £1,000, each
baronet had to "maintaine thirty foot (soldiers) for three yeares
for the defence of Ireland, and especially for the plantacion of
Ulster," and contribute a sum of not less than £1,000 to the
Exchequer to finance the undertaking. Charles II reversed the
process and remitted all fees when he used the baronetage as a
means of rewarding those who suffered great losses in standing
by his father and himself during the Cromwellian interlude, but
it was not until 1938 that all fees payable on conferment of honours
were finally abolished. Until then you paid £730 in fees to be
created a duke, £630 to become a marquis, £530 an earl, £430
a viscount and £330 a baron. Today the British taxpayer meets
all expenses, but if a new peer wishes to own his own robe of
crimson velvet with ermine trimmings it will cost him £400 out
of his own pocket and a further £80 for a gilt coronet. Most peers

today are satisfied to inherit their finery or borrow from their colleagues.

In the days when monarchs had absolute power, titles were often awarded on the spot for personal services rendered. Charles II and the first two Georges bestowed life peerages on their mistresses, and there is a legendary account that James I, having been invited to dinner by one of his nobles, was so delighted by the loin of beef set before him that he drew his sword and knighted it, thus giving us the sir-loin cut!

With the exception of the Order of the Garter, honours and military awards are personally bestowed by the Queen periodically throughout the year at investitures, generally in the great State Ballroom of Buckingham Palace (although governors-general and other representatives of the sovereign can also confer the accolade of knighthood when empowered to do so). Each recipient advances in turn to the royal dais and receives from the Queen's hand his medal, his riband or badge of his order, or his accolade of knighthood. Although it may well have taken a lifetime to earn, the ceremonial "dubbing" by which a knighthood is conferred takes only a few seconds. Each candidate advances before the Queen, bows, and kneels before his sovereign on a small red plush stool. The Queen then takes her ceremonial sword from her equerry, touches the kneeling figure with it on each shoulder and bids him to "Rise, Sir ———."

As befits the senior order of chivalry, the installation of new Knights of the Garter takes place during the unique annual service of the order in St. George's Chapel in Windsor Castle, where the turreted battlements form a medieval backdrop for the majestic pageantry of the occasion.

How such an article as a garter came to be the insignia of this premier British order has long titillated historians. One legend is that while dancing at a state ball at the court of Edward III Joan, the Countess of Salisbury and one of the King's favourites, dropped her garter. The nobles tittered when the sovereign himself stooped to pick it up and Edward, noting his Queen's displeasure, reputedly rebuked them with the famed remark, *"Honi soit qui mal y pense"*—literally translated "disgraced be he who thinks ill of it." Some historians doubt this frivolous origin, but most agree that some such incident took place, though it has never been ascertained whose garter was dropped. One version is that it was the Queen's garter which Edward found when following her to the state apartments after a ball and the famous words were the Queen's rejoinder when he rebuked her for losing it.

What has been established is that Edward III, a martial monarch, desired to band the warrior nobles who gathered about him into a chivalric fraternity like King Arthur's Round Table and when he founded the order in 1348 he adopted a blue garter adorned with the words as its emblem.

The Garter carries no special privilege, but the sheer magnificence of its robes and regalia set it apart as Britain's highest honour. Each Garter Knight wears a loose, heavy mantle of dark blue velvet lined with white taffeta and emblazoned with a red cross, which sweeps almost to the ground like a cavalryman's cloak, a hood and surcoat of crimson velvet, and a large dark velvet hat surmounted with a plume of ostrich feathers, fastened by a band of diamonds. The regalia includes a finely-worked, 30-ounce gold collar, into which is worked the garter device and from which dangles a gold and enamel pendant figure of St. George fighting the dragon; a gold enamelled star of the order, worn on the left breast; the broad blue ribbon of the Garter, from which hangs another medal replica of St. George and the dragon, known as the "lesser George"; and the Garter itself, a heavy, unfeminine band of dark blue velvet, with the motto and its edgings picked out in gold. Male Garter Knights wear it upon the left leg, just below the knee, while the ladies of the order wear it on their left arm, above the elbow. When not wearing full regalia, Knights of the Garter wear the broad ribbon of Garter blue across their chests, from which they suspend the badge of the order.

Before the last war the robes alone cost around £250 and the regalia, particularly if the stars and garters were set with precious stones, often cost £2,000, but in these years of post-war austerity new Knights usually borrow the finery for their installations. On the death of a Garter Knight his heir is expected to hand back his robes and insignia to the sovereign in person, and the Garter King of Arms receives the deceased Knight's crest as a perquisite of his office.

For a long time it was customary to award the Garter to reigning monarchs and their heirs, but as each Garter Knight swears on oath never to take up arms against the British King this custom

8   113

became an embarrassing mockery during the two world wars. When the First World War began there were no fewer than seven Garter Knights among Britain's enemies, including the German Kaiser and crown prince, the Austrian Emperor and high German nobles. Their banners were removed and they were expelled from the order at a solemn service in St. George's Chapel in 1915. When the Second World War broke out there were no German Knights of the Garter, but Italy's King Victor Emmanuel was a member, and in August, 1940, when George VI decreed that all German and Italian holders of British orders of chivalry should be expelled, his banner was taken down from its Chapel stall. The banner of the Emperor of Japan was likewise removed in 1941. Today this royal courtesy is more sparingly extended, and the foreign members of the order number only four monarchs —the kings of Norway, Sweden, Denmark and Greece—and two ex-kings, Carol of Rumania and Leopold of Belgium, one ex-queen, Wilhelmena of the Netherlands, and the exiled Prince Paul of Yugoslavia, brother-in-law of the Duchess of Kent.

As his wedding present, George VI gave the Order of the Garter to his daughter and the Duke of Edinburgh, making Elizabeth a lady of the Garter and Philip the youngest of its Knights. It was a gift that only he could bestow and when the King, using the ancient form of words prescribed for this highest honour ("Be bold not only strongly to fight, but also to offer yourself to shed your blood for Christ's faith, the liberties of the Church and the just and necessary defence of them that be oppressed and needy"), called for the installation of his daughter and son-in-law during the service there was a hint of family pride in his voice that added a new note to the old ceremony.

St. George's Chapel, in Windsor Castle, where the picturesquely-named officers of the Garter—the Chancellor of the Order (Lord Halifax), the Garter King of Arms (Sir George Bellew), the Prelate of the Order (the Bishop of Winchester) and the Gentleman Usher of the Black Rod (Lieutenant-General Sir Brian Horrocks)—conduct the annual service, is claimed to be the only chapel in the world that is owned by an order of chivalry, a privilege the Garter has enjoyed since its foundation more than 600 years ago. Also attached to the Garter are the Military Knights of Windsor, ceremonial survivors of the oldest military body still in existence in Britain. Many of the knights and barons who gathered round Edward III achieved deathless fame in the battle of Crecy and the French wars of that period. Many were captured by the French and by the tradition of their time were able to regain their freedom only after paying enormous ransoms, which often meant the sale of their estates and the sacrifice of their wealth. To show his gratitude for their services Edward III created them Military Knights, allowed them to live with him in Windsor Castle and in 1350 incorporated their foundation in the Order of the Garter. Today's Military Knights—twelve of them and a Governor—are all senior officers of the fighting services who have given long and brilliant service to the crown. They are allowed to live within the precincts of the Castle, for which they perform certain duties, chief of which are attending the annual Garter service and the Sunday services in St. George's Chapel, when they wear their colourful, historic uniforms of scarlet tail-coats, blue trousers with broad stripes, and cocked hats with red and white plumes.

The royal cachet is not only given to individuals who have won merit or distinction. On the theory that royal patronage is good for trade a special honour, known as the royal warrant, is sparingly awarded to stores or firms or businesses that have, at one time or another, supplied the royal households with high quality goods. Visitors to Britain are frequently intrigued by shop windows which display the royal coat of arms and the lettering "By appointment." During the reign of George VI one prominent London bookseller headed even bills with the legend, "Booksellers to His Majesty The King."

The issuance of royal warrants is as carefully administered as the honours system. Only the Queen, the Queen Mother and Queen Mary are now entitled to grant them, and tradesmen, who compete fiercely for the privilege, must sell their wares to a royal household for three consecutive years before they can even apply for consideration as royal warrant holders. When a warrant is granted the firm or store is then entitled to display the royal arms of the person granting the warrant "over their wares." Periodically the lists of those awarded the royal seal of approval are revised and enlarged. In 1951 George VI added to his list of some 200 firms nine new tradespeople, including a dog-food manu-facturer, a garden contractor and a famed Dublin hosier who makes racing colours. Queen Mary, with a nice feminine touch, extended her warrant to a British firm famed for its nylons and another which has for long supplied her favourite delicacy, potted shrimps. When the then Princess Elizabeth and her husband moved into Clarence House, their first London home, there was keen competition among tradesmen to supply the household with food and drink in the hope that George VI would give his daughter the right to issue her own warrants, but both Elizabeth and the shopkeepers were disappointed until she became Queen in her own right.

All told, there are now about 1,000 holders of the royal warrant from this and previous reigns. Through their own trade organization—the Warrant Holders' Association—they are enjoined to avoid publicity in their royal dealings and refrain from boasting about their sales to royalty.

More rare though less valuable than the royal warrants are the royal licences held by five "pubs" in the vicinity of Whitehall. Their privilege of royal licence—as distinct from the police-supervised licences granted by the local authorities to their competitors —dates back to the days when they were "on the verge of the Palace of Whitehall" and for almost 400 years they have remained under the jurisdiction of the sovereign. Once each year the five publicans appear before the Board of Green Cloth, a green baize-covered table in Buckingham Palace, where the Master of the Household traditionally says "satisfied and agreed" when each in turn applies for a renewal of his licence for another year.

As the first family of Britain, the royal family heads the social life of the nation and the distinction of being admitted, however momentarily, to the court circle or even being permitted within the confines of Buckingham Palace is eagerly sought after by dowager and debutante alike.

Prior to the Second World War the high spots of what was known as the London season were the evening courts at Buckingham Palace—generally four each year—when selected debutantes from the year's crop were presented to the King and Queen amid all the pomp and splendour of a full dress occasion. The King and Queen wore their crowns and occupied their thrones in the Throne Room, the male guests wore the official court dress of black velvet tailcoat and knee breeches, black silk stockings and pumps, while the women being presented wore full evening dress

116

in the old-fashioned court style, complete with five-foot trains, three curled ostrich feathers in their hair and a long, white tulle veil hanging down behind. While a string band played softly in the gallery, those being presented passed in front of the King and Queen and made their curtsies when their names were called out by the Lord Chamberlain. Ushers with long rods swept up each lady's train and deftly threw it over her arm as the curtsy finished.

To have been presented at court gave a certain social standing, as well as the right of entrée to courts abroad, and this coveted distinction was governed by an elaborate, traditional procedure. Invitations to the courts were personally issued by the King and Queen. The chosen debutantes had to be presented either by their mothers or by someone who already had the entrée. Each girl had to be presented again on her marriage, under her new name, and could in turn present to the King and Queen her own children, or others of her acquaintance for whom she took social responsibility.

The male equivalent of the evening presentation courts were the royal levées, which the King himself conducted four times each year, usually at the odd hour of 11.30 a.m., in the Throne Room at St. James's Palace.

Courts and levées were abandoned as unseemly and unnecessary during the years of the Second World War and it was with little regret that George VI, who disliked social ostentation in any form, decided that they would be equally out of place amid the austerity which his nation has had to endure in its post-war struggle for recovery. To meet the desires of the nation's debutantes for formal presentations to royalty and yet avoid the expensive layout of the pre-war courts, George VI and his consort devised an austerity presentation party which they held once each year, generally on a summer afternoon in the great garden of Buckingham Palace. In 1951 the late King reinstated the formal, individual presentations when some 700 selected debutantes stepped forward to "Pass the Presence" in the great Ballroom of Buckingham Palace and dropped their slow curtsies to the King and Queen.

In addition to the presentation parties, Queen Elizabeth, like her father, plays host at less select, annual garden parties at Buckingham Palace. Her father held two each summer, usually in July, each attended by from 6,000 to 7,000 guests. Unlike the presentation parties, anyone can apply for an invitation to a garden party, though not all applications are granted.[2] The Queen personally scans each invitation list and selects those whom she wishes invited into the private royal enclosure, and if she spots the name of someone who has won recent distinction in his or her field she instructs the court officials to find them and bring them along for presentation.

Like most British ceremonial, the proceedings at these garden parties seldom vary from the established tradition. Long before the scarlet-liveried Palace footmen give the signal to enter, the first guests are waiting at the gates. Although they may enter through gates opening directly into the 40-acre garden at the rear of the Palace, most guests prefer to join the queue of cars—as many as 3,000 in line—along the Mall, leading to the main gate, so that they can be seen by the waiting crowds and get a quick peep at some of the Palace interior as they go through the Grand Hall and the Bow Room to the terraced garden. The expansive lawn is soon almost blotted out by a swirling, shifting mass of colours: dresses and gowns of every style in organdie, chiffon, tulle and voile, the military uniforms and grey toppers and tails of the males, with a sprinkling of lounge suits as a concession to austerity, and, standing out to the eye, the bright saris and longyis worn by female guests from the east.

About 4 o'clock one of the two bands that play alternately under the trees strikes up the national anthem, a signal that the royal family has emerged from the Palace, and a sign that the waitresses furnished by the London restaurant chain entrusted with the catering may begin serving tea. The royal family splits up at the edge of the crowd, the Queen and her husband moving off in one direction, the Queen Mother and Queen Mary, if she is present, in another, with lesser royalty following behind them. The crowd courteously falls back to make lanes through which they pass, stopping here and there to shake hands when they recognize an old friend or to exchange a few pleasantries with someone brought forward by a courtier. At the royal tea marquee, an ornate canopy once used for an Indian durbar, the royal family link up again and receive the more privileged guests who are presented to them. About 6 o'clock, provided rain has not cut short the ceremony, a band again plays the national anthem, and the royal family walks slowly back across the lawn through the crowd to the Palace. Their departure is a signal for the guests to go home.

THE ROYAL FAMILY

VIII

THE LIFE AND TIMES OF GEORGE VI

OVER much of the world kings and queens and the institution of monarchy are out of fashion. Great wars and the waves of egalitarianism that followed them have carried away the royal houses of the world—Christian Bourbon, Apostolic Hapsburg, martial, aggressive Hohenzollern, adventurous Karageorgevic, parvenu Savoy. In the year of George VI's birth a score of monarchs still ruled on the continent of Europe. The First World War and its aftermath knocked out of existence, in Europe alone, three great monarchies together with their royal houses—the Russian, German and Austro-Hungarian. The Second World War swept away the monarchies in five other European nations—Bulgaria, Rumania, Yugoslavia, Italy and Albania—leaving the surviving monarchies somewhat huddled together in the democratic nations of northern Europe: in Britain, in the three Scandinavian kingdoms and in Holland, with another rather precariously installed in Belgium, another in troubled Greece and one in abeyance in equally troubled Spain.

The capitals of Europe abound with throneless royalty, but in Britain, the only major nation where the monarchy survives, the house of Windsor stands today on solid foundations of extraordinary affection, higher than the crown has ever stood before. And, ancient as the institution is, it has never looked less likely to become obsolescent than it does today.

Britons are apt to hark back to the Victorian age as days in which their institutions stood stable and secure, and yet even in Queen Victoria's time republican sentiment was openly expressed. In the middle years of Victoria's reign frequent clashes between the crown and the people roused strong republicanism among her subjects. During the latter half of her rule some of the country's leading political figures, such as Joseph Chamberlain, publicly voiced their doubts about the value of the monarchy as a political institution, and Walter Bagehot, the great expert on the English constitution, in the last years of Victoria's reign referred to her and the Prince of Wales as "an elderly widow and an unemployed youth," language that would never be used about the royal family today. After the First World War there were Liberals and Socialists who talked openly of abolishing the monarchy as an outmoded and archaic institution, and more recently even the late Sir Stafford Cripps struck a republican pose in a rebellious moment in the early 1930's when he declared that a Socialist Government would have to "overcome opposition from Buckingham Palace."

It would be quite impossible in 1952 to find any responsible public figure in Britain speaking or even thinking about the possible advantages of a republic, as Joseph Chamberlain did three-quarters of a century ago. Today there is no republican sentiment in Britain worth reporting, among any class or income group.[1] In fact, it is noticeable that during the visits of the royal family around the country, the poorer the area toured the more vociferous is the welcome.

The popularity of the late King and his family is indisputable: it was, and is, general and widespread. Neither the election of a Labour Government nor the social revolution which followed detracted in any way from the high regard with which George VI and his family were held. They demonstrated simply, if proof were needed, that Britain could swing from right to left and back again and yet remain staunchly loyal to this symbolic family at the head of the nation.[2]

All this might not have been had a less kingly king and a less royal family occupied the throne.

The life story of George VI is a profile of royalty at its finest and best, just as his conduct on the throne, in the words of Winston Churchill, "may be a model and a guide to constitutional sovereigns throughout the world today, and also in future generations." But his life story is also a paradox—the story of a self-effacing man, ill-suited in physique, in outlook and in temperament for the role of kingship, thrust into a job he did not want.

That he became a good king, and possibly a great king, was due to the two strongest, overriding elements in his character—his indomitable courage, which he applied with unremitting effort and determination to overcome his physical handicaps and his shy, retiring nature, and his stern and uncompromising sense of duty, in the execution of which he died.

In order fully to understand the character of the late King one must trace back through the crowded, anxious years of his reign, through years of almost continuous illness as a young man to the days of his somewhat unhappy royal childhood.

Even his birth was inauspicious. The future George VI, the second son of the then Duke and Duchess of York, entered the world at York cottage on the Sandringham royal estate early in the morning (3.00 a.m.) of December 14, 1895, which happened to be the anniversary of the death of Victoria's beloved Prince Albert. Although that sad event had taken place 34 years earlier, time had not removed the black-edged grief which came over the old Queen as the "terrible anniversary" approached, and when her grandson, Prince George, telegraphed her at Windsor that he had added a second son to his family he appended his regret that the child should have been born on such a sad day. Victoria, who recorded this in her journal, magnanimously added that "I have a feeling that it may be a blessing for the dear little boy, and may be looked upon as a gift from God," but her grandson, who succeeded in time to her throne, used to say privately that the old lady to the end of her days took the birth of his offspring as "a personal affront." At any event, the note of apology on which the young prince entered the world seemed to stamp his character for the first 40 years of his life.

The new prince was named Albert (because of Victoria's express wish that all her male descendants bear the name of her consort) Frederick Arthur George and duly baptised with water brought from the River Jordan, a royal custom that originated during the Crusades. His early years were spent at a variety of royal residences. One was the homey, comfortable York cottage, built as bachelor quarters for overflow guests from the big house at Sandringham and given to the Duke of York as a wedding present by his father, the then Prince of Wales. Another was the more commodious White Lodge in Richmond Park, outside London, which was the home Victoria gave to the Duke and

Duchess of York. When the Prince of Wales ended his long apprenticeship and became Edward VII on the death of Victoria in 1901 he gave the Duke and Duchess the use of Frogmore, a Georgian house in Windsor Home Park and later, when he promoted his son and daughter-in-law to Prince and Princess of Wales, he gave them Marlborough House as their London residence, as well as Abergeldie Castle, a small Scottish house dignified by the name of castle, about three miles down the River Dee from Balmoral, as their holiday home.

Young Prince Albert spent an unsettling, migratory childhood shifting from one residence to another as his father and mother accompanied the court of Edward VII on its gay, annual swing about the country—to Sandringham for Christmas, to London for the social season, to Windsor during Ascot week, to Balmoral in the autumn and back to Sandringham at the year's end. For playmates he was usually limited to his brothers and sister—Prince Edward (the Duke of Windsor), known to the family as David, who was the eldest by almost 18 months; Princess Mary (the Princess Royal), born 18 months after Albert; Prince Henry (the Duke of Gloucester), born in 1900; Prince George (the late Duke of Kent), the family favourite, who was born in 1902; and Prince John, a sickly child born when Albert was 10, who died in 1919 at the age of 13. As children do, they had their family squabbles. Mary, the more gifted in her early years, flaunted her feminine prerogative and bossed her brothers. David, who grew up a spoiled youngster, good-looking, with an easy charm of manner, but early conscious of the limelight which reflected on him as eventual heir to the throne, used to taunt the shy, slow-moving Bertie, as Prince Albert was known, and the two frequently came to blows and had to be separated by royal aides.

As a boy and young man Prince Albert was subjected to numerous repressive influences, the chief of which was undoubtedly the overbearing and often arbitrary parental authority exercised by his father.

George V was a strange personality. In the middle and latter years of his reign he publicly exemplified most of the kingly and personal virtues which the British hold in high regard. He read his Bible daily and struck a responsive chord in the hearts of his people in his role as dutiful father to his own large family. George V was indeed a pious man and a good ruler to his people, but he was a tragic failure as a father. Contrary to popular belief, he was anything but mild-mannered. Possessed of a furious temper, when aroused he roared in the salty vocabulary of an old seadog, a trait which George VI inherited. A regular officer in the Royal Navy for much of his life, he was a domestic martinet who ran his household with time-table precision and expected the same obedience that he got on the quarter-deck. Although he dearly loved his children, he was one of those unlucky parents who lack completely the knack of showing affection, and to cover up his clumsy failure he so arranged his domestic routine that his children remained, as far as possible, remote from him, occupying small, fixed niches in the household. A stern upholder of the Victorian dictum that children should be seen and not heard, when he did concern himself with his children's upbringing his manner with them was usually punctilious and often severe and harsh. He always insisted that his sons call him "Sir" and before they could speak to him when he was in his study or private apartments they were required to send a page to ask permission. To venture into his presence unannounced was to risk a royal tongue-lashing, or worse, and the youngsters understandably avoided both procedures.

In this unnatural, repressive home life, young David resorted to the childish defensive mechanism of temper tantrums to get his way. As he grew older he became more rebellious and flouted his father's wishes in small, annoying ways. George V retaliated with biting criticism of David's dress and tastes, his deportment and his friends, and the gap between them widened until normal conversation between father and son became difficult and often impossible.

Young Bertie reacted in the opposite direction. A quiet, grave child, he allowed himself to be eclipsed by his more pushful older brother and his sister and grew up to be an inhibited and sensitive youngster, lonely and uncertain of himself. He had his rebellious moments—it is recorded that his German tutor once complained to his father that when Bertie had been scolded for being inattentive at lessons one day the youngster had pulled the tutor's beard—but for the most part he was a shy and effaceable child, reluctant to assert himself. He preferred to sit in a dark room rather than ask a servant to light the gas. The limited companionship of his early years was another reason for his painful timidity and it was not until he was thrust into the rough-and-tumble of a naval school that he began to overcome it.

Another cause of young Albert's early backwardness was that he was what psychologists today call a shifted sinistral. By nature left-handed, he was forced to change to the right by his parents, who had the Victorian belief that left-handedness was unorthodox, and as a result he developed a childhood speech impediment which grew into a nervous stammer that was to plague him for the rest of his life. His father, who was inclined to be contemptuous of fellow men who were less robust than he was, had little patience with his second son who stuttered agonizingly when he became excited. Under orders to stamp out his unorthodoxy, governesses and tutors taught Albert to write with his right hand but when he went off to school on his own he reverted to his natural "cack-handedness," particularly for games, and to the end of his life the King was a right-hander in some things, such as writing, and a left-hander in others.

George VI's memories of his father were decidedly mixed. At a royal film show a couple of years ago he apologized to a British film star, Trevor Howard, who had stood waiting in line for 20 minutes to be presented, and remarked, "I know what waiting on parade is like. I had to do it for my father."

In public, of course, he revealed nothing but respectful affection. Unveiling a memorial statue to George V in London's Westminster in 1947 the King eulogized his father in these words: "He was loyal, kindly and unselfish: he had the loftiest conception of honour and duty. All these qualities grew out of the experience and habits of his youth, from a happy and affectionate home life, from the practice of the Christian religion formed in childhood, and from his training as a sailor in discipline and teamwork."

It may be that George VI's memories of his unhappy childhood receded with the passing years. On the other hand, those who knew him in the intimacy of his family believed that he deliberately tried to create the happy home life and the close, personal relationship between himself and his daughters that he missed in his own upbringing.

With his brothers, young Albert learned to play football, cricket, golf and tennis, to shoot, fish and ride, not so much because he was a keen gamesman as because it was his father's wish that his boys should become proficient in sport. So diligently did Bertie apply himself that as a tennis player (left-handed) he became good enough to reach the top of the second class and make a brief appearance, playing with his close friend Louis Greig, in the doubles competition at Wimbledon in 1926. Middle age slowed down his tennis and the war years interrupted his golf, which he used to play (right-handed) consistently in the low 80's, but he retained his interest in shooting and ranked as one of the best and quickest guns in the kingdom.

The education of royal children is apt to be sketchy, due to the tradition that they must not mix competitively with other youngsters, and Prince Albert's was no exception. Exposed to the influence of a succession of governesses, David and Bertie were put in charge of a tutor, Henry Peter Hansell, a vintage Edwardian who gave them the rudiments of an education mixed with sound Norfolk common sense.

George V's great love was always the Royal Navy (although he was a bad sailor and was always miserably sick in rough weather) and for each of his sons, regardless of differences in temperament, he laid out the same curriculum: they went into the Navy, whether they liked it or not. He thought that the exclusive, so-called public schools, which most of the aristocrats of the day attended, would teach his sons bad habits. "The Navy will teach them all they need to know," he said. And so when the time came David and then, in 1909, young Bertie were packed off first to the Naval Training College at Osborne, on the Isle of Wight, and then on to the Royal Naval College at Dartmouth. "Treat them like cadets and make them realize their responsibilities," were George V's bluff orders to the officers at the schools.

Prince Albert enjoyed this phase of his early life most of all. Asking no favours, he submitted to schoolboy hazing, and went through the mill as a "snotty" (midshipman), taking his turns at coaling ship for the traditional supper of bread, beer, onions and cheese. A slow, plodding scholar, he was generally near the bottom on his exam lists. His frail physique was unsuited for the rigors of naval training and frequent bouts of illness—influenza, pneumonia and recurring gastric pains—set him back, but he persevered with a courage that was commendable to his officers and in 1913, when he was 17, he was assigned to H.M.S. *Cumberland*, a cruiser then employed as a training ship. Aboard *Cumberland* he visited the West Indies and Canada on a training cruise and discovered that even the second son of the King had to undergo the ordeal of public appearances before His Majesty's subjects. Later that same year he was assigned as a midshipman to H.M.S. *Collingwood,* then the flagship of the 1st battle cruiser squadron, on which he voyaged to the Mediterranean, where, under the name of Mr. Johnstone, he hid his royal identity from visitors who came aboard.

When the First World War began *Collingwood* and its Mr. Johnstone were confined to the great naval base of Scapa Flow, at the tip of Scotland, where they sat out the first year and a half of the war in boring inactivity. Twice during the long wait Prince Albert was carried ashore, prostrate with almost continual gastric pains, and on the second occasion he was operated on for a suspected inflamed appendix. He was back on his ship, a sub-lieutenant charged with supervising the firing of a 12-inch gun in the fore gun turret, when the fleet of 51 British vessels of the line sailed out to engage the German fleet in the epic battle of Jutland in May, 1916. *Collingwood* was in the thick of the action and although she was not hit during the battle an enemy shell struck the water and ricocheted over the ship, missing by inches the future King of Britain, who was sitting unconcernedly on the edge of his turret to get a better look. His superior officer, forgetting royal rank for the moment, yelled at Mr. Johnstone, "What the hell's the matter with you?" The Prince scrambled down. After the battle Albert wrote an artless letter to a friend: "The Jutland battle was a great thing to have been in, and it certainly was different from what I expected. We, of course, in *Collingwood* saw a great deal more than some of the other ships and we fired more than they did. We were not hit at all, which was very lucky, though we were straddled several times. One shell dropped over the foc's'le, missing us by inches. I was in the fore turret, second in command. During some of it, I was sitting on the top when they straddled us. I didn't remain up very long after that. The men were quite marvellous. Just as cheery as usual, and worked like demons." For this action, Prince Albert was mentioned in dispatches for his "coolness and courage."

The young Prince's naval career ended abruptly in November, 1917 when his recurrent abdominal trouble culminated in an operation for duodenal ulcers and he was invalided out of the service. Towards the end of the war George V decided that one of his sons should serve with the new air arm and when Prince Albert was fit again he sent him into the Royal Naval Air Service, which was soon incorporated with the Royal Flying Corps to become the Royal Air Force. Like his father, his first love was for the sea but the conquest of the new element caught his interest and Albert begged to be trained as a pilot, but neither the King nor the Government would allow the risk of an accident and so Prince Albert sweated out the last months of the great conflict in desk jobs, first at the air station at Cranwell, in Lincolnshire, then at Spa, in Belgium, on the staff of Viscount Trenchard, and finally on the staff of the naval commander-in-chief at Portsmouth. In November, 1918, he represented his father at the ceremonial liberation of Belgium and rode into Brussels with King Albert of the Belgians.

Bertie had already demonstrated that he was a young man of stubborn perseverance and when the desire to fly remained with him when peace came he persisted in his demands to earn his wings. Finally his father yielded. George V never looked kindly on flying and it was with grudging approval that he watched his son drive daily from Buckingham Palace to a little airfield on the outskirts of London, where he took his flying lessons. The venture was hedged around with special precautions. His instructor, now Air Chief Marshal Sir Alec Coryton, was one of the best in the R.A.F., and the spindly two-seater Avro trainer plane had to be tested in flight, on Government orders, each morning before the lesson commenced, but Prince Albert was an apt pupil and in a few months he was ready for his official examination. One of his officers at Dartmouth had already remarked that Albert had "a tremendous lot of guts" and the determination that kept him going through his naval service while enduring racking visitations from ulcers emerged again on the first day of his two-day test. The morning broke rainy and gusty, but when a companion urged Albert to postpone the flight he shrugged and replied, "If I don't fly today, I'll never do it." He did, taking an inspector up with him for the examination, and on the next day completed his 80-mile cross-country hop, buzzing Windsor Castle on the homeward route, to pass out a fully qualified air pilot. Having won his coveted wings, Prince Albert seldom piloted a plane afterwards,

9

but his accomplishment at least served years later in another war to create a deep bond of comradeship between himself as King and the young men of the R.A.F.

The broadening contacts of the war years finally convinced George V that the naval education he had provided for his sons was less than adequate to prepare them for the emerging problems of the post-war era. David had been given a fling at Oxford before the war, and so when Albert persuaded his father to let him resume his education in 1919 he had to go to the rival university at Cambridge, where, along with his younger brother, Prince Henry, he took a year's crammed courses in history, geography and civics at Trinity College. Then aged 24, Bertie applied himself diligently to his studies. He lived quietly in a private house with his friends, Louis Greig and his wife, rode to his lectures on a belt-driven motorcycle, and kept as much to himself as his station allowed. He was once caught and fined six shillings and eightpence for smoking in the street while wearing his cap and gown, but generally managed to sidestep the more devilish escapades of the disillusioned, irresponsible post-war student body.

All the while his father kept a watchful eye on him, and twice called him down from Cambridge to deputize for the King in welcoming foreign visitors to Britain, once to meet the Shah of Iran and again to greet the French President. Reports which George V requested on Bertie's behaviour on these occasions showed that he shaped well as a royal host and, in recognition of his son's growing stature, the King in 1920 created him Duke of York, the title that has usually been conferred on the second son of the monarch since the reign of Edward IV in the fifteenth century.

About this time an enlightened, go-ahead clergyman named Robert Hyde, who had worked during the war years in the Ministry of Munitions, conceived the Industrial Welfare Society, the intention of which was to pool the experience of employers and employees in encouraging the human element in industry. Hyde was struck by the fact that, although Britain was then the most highly industrialized nation in the world, in the four years before the First World War not more than a score of factories had been visited by George V and members of his family and he approached the King for royal patronage for his scheme.

George V, intent then on taking the crown to the people by using his sons and daughter as royal ambassadors, gave his consent and turned the chore over to Bertie. The new Duke of York, who had already absorbed some of his mother's concern for social problems, was offered and accepted the presidency of the new organization, though he still dreaded even the modest limelight that went with it. "I will do it," he told the Reverend Hyde. "But I don't want any of that damned red carpet." When the Duke went back to Cambridge to finish his course he added economics to his studies, and while still attending the university he began visiting factories in the vicinity, dropping in on short notice so that they would not be dressed up for his inspection. He talked to work people and employers and sat on committees that dealt with every sort of welfare problem from accident prevention, night shift fatigue, canteens, summer holidays to pension schemes and thrift funds. In 1921 he founded the first of the Duke of York's summer camps, a small-scale jamboree which annually brought together 200 boys from factories in various parts of the country and 200 public school boys for a week's summer holiday, a get-together which he personally attended almost every year until the outbreak of the Second World War. By the time he came home from Cambridge for good the Duke had visited so many industrial plants that his brother David nicknamed him "The Foreman," a handle which stuck to him within the family for years.

A self-effacing, highly-strung young man, the Duke of York was quite content to live in the shadow of his more gifted and colourful elder brother. While David, as Prince of Wales, was winning popularity in a series of tours of the Empire, Bertie, by preference, found satisfaction in going through greasy factories all over his country, diligently picking the brains of the men who operated them and worked in them, until he had acquired an expert's insight on British working conditions.

He was not too busy to escape romance, however, and soon after coming down from Cambridge he became the suitor of Lady Elizabeth Bowes-Lyon, a gentle-born Scottish commoner, five years younger than himself, who was a childhood friend of his sister Mary. There is a legend that the Duke of York first met her at a children's party in London when she was a golden-haired little girl of five and was so struck by her features that he instantly remembered her when they next met, at a London wedding, when Elizabeth was 13.

Lady Elizabeth, member of an ancient Scottish family whose lineage was almost as royal as the Duke's, was the ninth of the ten children of the Earl and Countess of Strathmore and Kinghorne. Most of each year the family spent at St. Paul's, Walden Bury, a mellowed Queen Anne house of rosy brick, covered with magnolia and honeysuckle, in Hertfordshire. Each autumn they moved for three months to the Scottish family seat, storied Glamis Castle, which has descended in the family in an unbroken male line for almost 600 years. Young Bertie, carefully attired in the tweed plus-fours and cloth cap that were fashionable in those days, became a frequent visitor to St. Paul's over a period of some 18 months and on a mild winter Sunday, while the couple walked in the beech wood around the estate, he conquered his shyness sufficiently to propose—but at the critical moment his nervous stammer intervened and he had to write out his offer of marriage on a pad.

A few days later the Court Circular announced the betrothal, "to which the King has gladly given his consent" (a necessary provision under the Royal Marriages Act of 1772, by which the sovereign must give consent before a descendant of George II can lawfully marry), and when old George V got to know his future daughter-in-law he added his personal approval. "She is a pretty and charming girl, and Bertie is a lucky fellow," he gallantly remarked.

The royal couple were married in regal splendour at Westminster Abbey on April 26, 1923, and the crowds that jammed London's streets for the procession to and from the Abbey testified to their popularity. The marriage itself was popular for several reasons. Albert was the first of George V's sons to marry, and it set a precedent in modern times in that it was obviously neither an arranged match nor a foreign marital alliance designed to strengthen the dynasty. Also, the new Duchess of York, despite her high-born background, was a homebody whose mother, the daughter of a country parson, had seen to it that she could cook, sew, knit and run a house. She never featured in the social gossip of the day and her pictures were seldom seen in the glossy-paged weeklies which recounted the doings of the smart set which surrounded the Prince of Wales. Noting this, Britons concluded that the Duke of York had set an admirable lead for his elder brother to follow.

Their honeymoon over, the Yorks straightaway retreated into as secluded a life as they could manage, first at the White Lodge in Richmond Park, which George V gave them, and then, when their royal duties required a house in London, at 145 Piccadilly, a private, white stone residence, tall and narrow, not far from Buckingham Palace. For their annual Scottish holiday, a tradition in the royal family, the King also allowed them to use Birkhall, an old-fashioned house on the Balmoral estate, about six miles from the Castle. Their domestic seclusion was frequently shattered, however, whenever George V insisted that Bertie share with David some of the more onerous duties of royal ambassadors.

In the year after their marriage the Duke and Duchess of York paid a state visit to Northern Ireland and then went to Kenya and Uganda on a visit that was half-mission, half-hunting trip, from which they returned through the Sudan and Egypt. George V, as Duke of Cornwall and York, had been sent out by his father to visit Australia for the inauguration of the Commonwealth in 1901, and when Australia got ready to open its new Parliament House in its brand-new federal capital, Canberra, the Dominion petitioned the King to send his own Duke of York to officiate on his behalf. Early in January, 1927, leaving Princess Elizabeth, then nine months old, in the charge of her two grandmothers, the Duke and his Duchess sailed aboard the battle cruiser *Renown* on what was to become a triumphal six-month tour of the world. They sailed by way of Jamaica and the Panama Canal to Fiji and New Zealand, visited the state capitals and the federal capital of Australia and returned by way of Mauritius and the Suez Canal.

This was Albert's last princely journey as an ambassador of the Empire. Thereafter he left foreign travel to the Prince of Wales and gave over his public life largely to industrial affairs. Elizabeth dutifully adopted her husband's intense interest in the welfare of working folk and it was characteristic of them that they commanded that a wedding gift of £2,500 should be used to provide entertainment for children in five industrial towns. Albert covered industrial Britain in a series of dreary tours, and opened and inspected so many factories that the newspapers dubbed him "The

Industrial Prince." His intensive interest in industrial relations was backed by an extensive and well-read library and his Piccadilly home was frequently turned into a sort of seminar in industrial relations when he brought together his acquaintances from both sides of industry—trade union leaders as well as managerial men—to discuss their mutual problems over the after-dinner port.

When the general strike paralysed Britain in 1926 George V was asked by friends to intervene. "That is not my province. That is the Duke of York's department," the King jestingly replied. In private, however, George V advised his sons to abstain from public or private comment on the strike, which they did, although the Prince of Wales secretly loaned his car and chauffeur to transport to Wales copies of the Government's newspaper, the *British Gazette*, which Churchill edited. The Duke of York had seen enough of working conditions in Britain not to be swept away by the public hysteria against the striking miners and their supporters. With his background of both sides of industry he would have been an ideal arbiter, but he knew his constitutional position and did not intervene, though he kept in touch with his labour and industrial contacts.

In the years that followed Albert put himself at the head of numerous worthy causes. He continued as president of the Industrial Welfare Society and put up the money for the Duke of York's camps. In addition, he became a patron of the Miners' Welfare Commission, the Dockland Settlements and the National Safety First Association and president of the National Playing Fields Association. In 1935 he took on the job of chairman of the administrative council of King George's Jubilee Trust, a fund used to provide clubs, workshops, gyms and other facilities for young people in areas hard hit by unemployment. Deeply concerned over the problem of unemployment, which was spreading like a blight over his nation, the Duke encouraged the opening of occupational clubs, where the out-of-work could meet to repair boots and furniture or do other odd jobs that might earn them a few pence, and there were 1,500 of these clubs in existence by 1939.

His connection with these and other causes entailed an endless round of public speeches, and it was a measure of Albert's uncommon will-power that he undertook them at all. His speech defect was a cruel burden for a man fated to appear constantly at public functions. More of a slight throat constriction than a stutter, it was seldom noticeable in normal conversation, but when nervous or excited he flustered easily and the nerve-wracking experience of speaking in public made him stammer painfully.

A series of embarrassing incidents occasioned by his impediment during his youth had left a permanent mark upon him. Once when he was a first-term cadet at Dartmouth a teacher, unaware of his disability, suddenly asked young Albert to stand up in class and answer the question: "What is the half of a half?" The youngster struggled to say "quarter," but the word froze in his throat. He stubbornly refused to compromise with himself and say "one fourth," which would have come more easily, and he sat down amid sarcastic comments and titters from his classmates, who thought him unable to solve a simple sum. He had great difficulty in articulating the words "King" and "Queen," and generally referred to his parents as "Their Majesties." According to court etiquette, a royal person is supposed to open the conversation whenever anyone is presented, but on ceremonial occasions the young Duke of York found that it was often embarrassingly impossible for him to do so. These painful experiences only made him more shy and nervous in public and there were gloomy moments when he confessed to friends that his impediment seemed to be an unconquerable curse which "God had put upon" him.

It was Elizabeth, sympathetic and understanding, who helped him through this difficult time. When Albert was going through the agonies of a public speech the Duchess could be seen literally suffering with him and there were many moving instances when those closest to the royal couple saw her hand reach out to give her husband a reassuring touch as he struggled to articulate a difficult word.

In his efforts to learn to talk like a normal person Albert had tried every known system of speech training and voice production. No fewer than nine specialists had treated him, but they all diagnosed his difficulty as a nervous mental condition and little progress was made. Just as an equerry was about to leave for the U.S. to search for an American speech expert who might be able to help the Duke he chanced to hear of a brilliant Australian, Lionel Logue, who had recently arrived in London and set up a practice in Harley Street. Logue, who had worked wonders curing children of speech defects by a system of diaphragm breathing while practising in Perth, Australia, agreed to examine the Duke but he insisted that Albert make the psychological effort of coming to his Harley Street consulting room. Two days later, on October 19, 1926, the Duke appeared at the specialist's office and at the end of an hour and a half of difficult conversation he heard the first encouraging news in his long fight.

"I can cure you," Logue assured him, "but it will need a tremendous effort by you. Without that effort it can't be done." Logue correctly diagnosed the trouble as the failure of the Duke's diaphragm to co-ordinate with his brain, but warned him that a long, tedious course, involving a complete re-education in the simplest sounds of speech, would be necessary. Albert's life to date had been a constant duel between a weak physique and his indomitable will, and so at the age of 30 he set to work with indefatigable industry to conquer his disability. He put himself in Logue's hands, spent an hour a day with the specialist for months on end, and put in another hour or two each day practising sounds and breathing exercises in private. After months of effort, Albert succeeded in conquering the few consonants which had formerly been tough for him and when he opened Australia's new Parliament at Canberra seven months after his first session with Logue, instead of a few hesitant words which a sympathetic audience had expected, he surprised his listeners with a set speech delivered with little hesitation.

For years the Duke continued his remedial schooling in the privacy of his home, and when he wrote out his speeches he often called Logue in to advise on difficult words to avoid, generally those beginning with *g*, *k*, *q* or *n*. By the time he became King he had succeeded in conquering much of his nervousness, and speech-making had lost some of its terrors for him.

At the time of his accession he stood up proudly and slowly and deliberately, but without making a mistake, repeated the archaic accession declaration: "I do solemnly and sincerely in the presence of God profess, testify and declare that I am a faithful Protestant; and that I will, according to the true intent of the enactments which secure the Protestant Succession to the Throne of my Realm, uphold and maintain the said enactments to the best of my powers according to law." Few knew at that time that he and

Logue had worked for hours on this formalized paragraph, breaking down the words which gave the new King trouble, until he could repeat it without faltering even at a moment of high emotion. And then, a few months later, came the greatest ordeal of all, the coronation ceremony, in which the King had to give his responses throughout the long service in an ancient, stylized language that would trip many a person blessed with normal speech. Again patient and specialist spent hours in practice, but when the great day came, with the world listening, at the end of the microphone (and Logue sitting in the royal box to throw his patient encouraging glances) the King went through his responses with hardly a falter. It was the proudest triumph of his long fight.

For several years after he took the throne the King insisted on having Logue beside him whenever he broadcast (on the historic broadcast on the night of the coronation it was Logue who stage-whispered just before George VI began to speak, "Now take it quietly, Sir") but in the last years of his reign he was content to broadcast alone, proof that he had completed the cure he embarked upon in 1926. In the last years of his life he had so overcome his difficulty that it seldom troubled him among his family or friends, and only when he was under great nervous strain on a public occasion could he be seen constantly to work the back of his jaws. In private speech he did not pronounce his r's, but, strangely enough, when reading aloud to his family even this slight disability disappeared.

Among the smart socialites of the 1930's the Yorks, as they were known, acquired the reputation as a dull couple because they seldom entertained and were almost never seen in the smart night clubs frequented by the Prince of Wales. In fact, they found that Albert's allowance as Duke of York did not permit expensive entertainment, and in any event the Duke and Duchess really preferred to dine quietly at home and perhaps slip round the corner to a neighbouring cinema when their children were safely abed. On the rare occasions when the Duke went out alone in the evening to some convivial affair it was not unusual for the Duchess to telephone him a wifely reminder of the hour if he had not returned home by midnight.

Their unpretentious Piccadilly home, which was to be shattered by a bomb early in the Second World War, was a domestic haven, deliberately shut off from court routine. Their two daughters—Princess Margaret Rose had been born at Glamis on August 21, 1930—were often in the public eye, particularly when their proud royal grandmother showed them off, and for years the top-deck passengers in the buses passing 145 Piccadilly used to crane upwards in the hope of seeing the royal youngsters at their nursery windows, but Albert and Elizabeth guarded against childish pretensions and brought the two girls up as much as possible like normal, ordinary children. When Margaret was added to the family they felt the need for a suitable country residence as well and in 1932 they took over a comfortable, rambling structure known as Royal Lodge, in the Great Park at Windsor, 21 miles west of London, which is still considered the family's real home.

Early in 1936 the long reign of George V drew to a close and on January 20 the old King passed away at the Sandringham home he loved. With his brothers, Albert emerged from his seclusion to participate in the impressive ceremonial funeral, but for the next eleven months, while the spotlight played continuously on the new Edward VIII, he retired gratefully to his domesticity and his comparatively obscure public duties. The absence of attention suited the development of his quiet, ordinary virtues. He became intrigued by the absence of records of Royal Lodge and pored over the archives at Windsor Castle and corresponded with scholars with the intention of writing a book of historical research about his house.

The events which culminated in Edward's abdication only 325 days after he took the throne surprised Albert and Elizabeth almost as much as they did the British people. Cut off from social gossip they knew almost as little of Mrs. Simpson as did most Britons, who were denied the news of the early stages of the crisis by the self-imposed conspiracy of silence on the part of the British press. When Albert was finally brought into the picture by his elder brother, only a few days before the crisis reached its climax, Edward's decision to abdicate was already irrevocable.

George VI's version of what passed between the two brothers at their last meetings before Edward sailed away from England was never revealed.

It has been suggested that Albert hesitated to take the throne from the modest fear that he would not be acceptable to the nation or that he was not fit to assume kingship, but this is not in keeping with his character and upbringing. Having been brought up in the monarchical tradition, he knew that it was his solemn duty to step into the place his brother had left, and he accepted his new role as inevitable. He regarded it as a cruel, unkind twist of fate because he felt himself physically and temperamentally unsuited for the ordeal ahead, but he knew what was expected of him. His main concern, however, was not for the burden of the crown that would rest on his shoulders, but the thought that he would one day have to pass on its great weight to his elder daughter. If he had any hesitation about taking the throne, it was out of consideration for Princess Elizabeth. He dreaded the certainty that he was sentencing her to a life of public service that would rob her of any chance of the quiet, domestic enjoyment to which he and his Duchess had looked forward.

It was therefore with heartfelt reluctance that he made his declaration to his Privy Council: "Now that the duties of Sovereignty have fallen to Me I declare to you My adherence to the strict principles of constitutional government and My resolve to work before all else for the welfare of the British Commonwealth of Nations. With My Wife as helpmeet by My side, I take up the heavy task which lies before Me. In it I look for the support of all My Peoples."

And so on December 12, 1936, in a raw, drizzling rain, the tabarded Heralds took up their appointed places in London and proclaimed "That the High and Mighty Prince Albert Frederick Arthur George is now become our only Lawful and Rightful Liege Lord, George the Sixth, by the Grace of God, of Great Britain, Ireland, and the British Dominions beyond the Seas King, Defender of the Faith, Emperor of India." There were few cheers from the listening knots of spectators.

To the new King and Queen the hardest blow was in giving up their Piccadilly home to move to the vast, impersonal spaces of Buckingham Palace. This was the end of much of the domestic privacy which both of them had guarded and cherished for 13 years. From then on their lives would be played out in the fierce glare of publicity and their daily doings and much of their intimate family life would be churned out by the press, for the lives and loves of their royal family has for long been Britain's favourite serial. This Bertie and Elizabeth found hard to accept as their new future. On their last night in 145 Piccadilly before they moved over to Buckingham Palace they slipped quietly out of their garden gate and, unescorted and unnoticed for the last time, went for a long walk in Hyde Park.

IX

WARTIME MONARCH

ON the day the Duke of York announced his willingness to take the throne vacated by his brother an elderly female cousin, Princess Helena Victoria, solicitously asked him whether he thought he could handle his new job. "I don't know," answered the Duke honestly, "but I am going to do my best."

The first of many changes the new King made was to change his name. Like his grandfather, Edward VII, who had also dropped his name of Albert on becoming King, the new King felt that Albert was still associated in the public mind with Victoria's husband and so he chose to be styled by the last of his four given names, becoming George VI, a choice which shrewdly emphasized the continuity from his father's reign. To the Queen and close members of his family, however, he continued to be known as Bertie.

For the first few months George VI was busy learning his new job. With the Queen he toured the British Isles to give his people a glimpse of their new sovereigns. Determined to be a good King, he devoted long days and nights to a study of the subtleties which govern the relationship between the sovereign and his Ministers. He learned to work closely with his own advisers, most of whom he inherited without change from Edward, and Buckingham Palace, which Edward disliked and avoided as much as possible, became again the punctilious headquarters of the monarchy as in the reign of George V. One of the advisers on whom the new King relied was Lord Wigram, who had served his father as private secretary. Edward had found the then 63-year-old courtier too elderly for his taste, but George VI leaned on his accumulated experience and judgment to guide him through the intricacies of constitutional monarchy.

When he stepped, unprepared, into the place his brother had

left George VI had the sympathy of his subjects. "Quiet sort of a bloke he is," his people said. "Wonder what sort of a job he'll make of it?" By the time of his coronation on May 12, 1937, George VI had obviously got the hang of his job and as he sweated through that exhausting, four-hour ritual the nation's mood changed to one of admiration and respect. Among the estimated 5,000,000 spectators who poured into the streets of London that morning to watch George VI and Queen Elizabeth and their two young daughters drive to and from the Abbey there were many who thought with satisfaction that the monarchy had been restored to its high level of quiet, family dignity.

Travel has always been in the kingly tradition, and the splendour of the coronation was hardly over before George and Elizabeth set out in 1938 for a four-day state visit to France. Early in 1939 they crossed the Atlantic for an 8,000-mile train tour of Canada and the United States. Their Atlantic crossing was a double first: it was the first occasion on which a reigning British sovereign had visited any of the Dominions, and it was the first time a King of Britain had set foot in the U.S.

Their U.S. visit was suggested by President Franklin Roosevelt (in a personal letter to George VI on August 25, 1938), who thought that "it would be an excellent thing for Anglo-American relations" if Their Majesties visited the U.S. during their projected Canadian tour, but the prospect of visiting the United States had long been in the back of the King's mind, ever since his elder brother had sung the praises of this great country after his visits there in the 1920's. The Prince of Wales had expressed the conviction that every Briton able to do so should visit the U.S. at least once every two or three years, although, ironically enough, it was the sensationalized reporting in the U.S. press of David's escapades that prevented the other members of his family from visiting America. George V had a high regard for Americans, based on his limited contacts with a series of dignified American ambassadors and his acquaintance with a few of the socialites who sought entrée to his court, but when the sensational headlines and uninhibited articles from American newspapers on the real and imagined doings of the Prince of Wales during his 1924 U.S. holiday found their way back to George V's desk the old King was so outraged at what he considered the "effrontery" of American editors in their flippant treatment of royalty that he privately broke off relations between the U.S. and members of his family.

"If this vulgarity represents the American attitude toward people in our position," he told David on his return to London, "little purpose would be served in exposing yourself again to this kind of treatment." He never actually banned further visits to the U.S., but whenever David or Bertie or their younger brothers tentatively suggested going there he found reasons why they should not.

George and Elizabeth saw little of the United States in their brief visit in June of 1939, but what they saw they liked, and it gave them a common ground on which to meet their growing circle of American official contacts during the war and post-war years. Having been forewarned that Americans were apt to regard royalty with a mixture of amused cynicism and romantic enthusiasm, they were somewhat taken aback by the frenzy of their welcome in Washington, their full ticker-tape treatment in New York and the crowds who lined the streets and shouted "Attaboy King! Attaboy Queen!" but they accepted it in the spirit of the New York *World-Telegram* editorial which said: "The King and Queen are greeted by the American people, not merely as representatives of another great democracy, or as Royalty, but as two great human beings who have won that distinction in their own right. We like them, and we hope they like us." They found an immediate affinity with President and Mrs. Roosevelt and with the President's aged mother, the late Sarah Delano Roosevelt, which formed the basis for an understanding exchange of letters and messages between the King and the President during the Second World War and a close personal friendship between the Queen and Eleanor Roosevelt, which is still kept up by personal correspondence. When Mrs. Roosevelt visited London during the war and again in 1948, to unveil a memorial statue to her husband in London's Grosvenor Square, she was a guest of the royal family.

On their return from Canada the King and Queen landed at Southampton on June 22. Ten and a half weeks later their nation was at war.

The foreign tours, when George emerged as a warm, gregarious individual and Elizabeth demonstrated her flair for wearing queenly clothes, killed the socialite suspicion that they were a dull, uninspiring couple, but it was not until the "phony war" came to an end with the glorious debacle of Dunkirk and the crash of bombs on Britain that the King and Queen really fulfilled their symbolic role as the first family of the land, at one with their people.

According to Herbert Morrison, the wartime Minister who kept close watch on Britain's morale, the King and Queen, by their example in the crucial months when the country stood in lonely desperation, did more to keep up the spirits of their people than any other single factor. When invasion and bombing were imminent they refused to send their children abroad to safety, as many of their well-to-do subjects did, although they did "evacuate" them. "The Princesses could never leave without me—and I could never leave without the King—and, of course, the King will never leave," the Queen stoutly told Harry Hopkins when Roosevelt's personal emissary visited Britain early in 1941. The two young girls remained for some months at Birkhall, on the Balmoral estate, where they had been on the outbreak of the war, and in May, 1940, they moved into Windsor Castle, which was their residence for the remainder of the war years.

During the worst of the *blitz* raids on London, the King kept his royal standard flying from the masthead at Buckingham Palace to show that he was in residence, a sight that cheered the capital on many a dreary morning after a night of bombs.

When a German *Luftwaffe* pilot swooped out of the clouds and dropped five bombs on the Palace on the morning of September 13 (a Friday), 1940, he unwittingly did more to bring the King and his people together than a battery of press agents. London's morale was sagging. The bombing until then had been concentrated largely on the dingy working-class areas of the east end and Thames side, arousing the defeatist suspicion that only the poor were in Britain's front-line, but that day the cockneys made a pilgrimage to the Palace, saw for themselves the King's bomb damage, and went back to their battered homes echoing His Majesty's words, "We're all in this together." One workman was killed in this attack on the Palace and two injured. The King and Queen, who had just arrived at the Palace from Windsor, were in a sitting room overlooking the quadrangle and actually saw the bombs falling before they had time to take cover. They

25. *George VI visiting Field-Marshal Montgomery's mobile H.Q. in 1944*

26. *Escorted by Herbert Morrison, His Majesty visits ordnance factory*

27. *The hour of triumph: acknowledging the cheers on V.E.-Day, 1945*

28. *George VI takes the salute at the Victory Parade on June 8, 1946*

made a quick tour of inspection of their own damage and then left for London's east end to comfort those who had been harder hit. In all, during the five and a half years of war, Buckingham Palace and its precincts were hit nine times, by orthodox bombs, flying bombs and rockets, until the King could boast to his friends, "There's not a window left in the whole blinking place." His old home at 145 Piccadilly was totally destroyed.

The tempering effect of the war years gave George VI a new toughness and gave his people a new conception of the nation's most devoted public servant. At the outbreak of the war the King changed into the uniforms of his fighting services, and thereafter made no public appearances in civilian clothes, which he wore only on his week-ends at Royal Lodge. A security blackout was clamped on his movements to keep the Germans in the dark as to his whereabouts. When invasion was likely and an airborne assault a possibility the King always kept a Sten gun handy in his briefcase whenever he travelled and his chauffeur and the Scotland Yard detective who rode with him in the splinter-proof and bullet-proof car he then used were also armed.

An elaborate master plan was drawn up by the Cabinet for spiriting the royal family to safety in the west of England if German paratroopers attacked London. A select band of officers and men from the Guards and Household Cavalry stood by, night and day, ready to carry out the plan. Officers familiarized themselves with the route to be used and cars were kept ready, marked with secret code signs that would give them absolute priority over all other traffic. A company of fighting troops was detailed to guard Queen Mary at her wartime home at Badminton—the Gloucestershire estate of the Duke and Duchess of Beaufort, her niece and nephew by marriage—and motorcycle dispatch riders stood by to guide her to safety if the Germans tried to capture her.

Once a week the King practised pistol shooting at targets in Buckingham Palace grounds and even the Queen learned to shoot with a rifle and pistol, which she was quite prepared to use if the German airborne troops assaulted the Palace. When fire bombs were added to the hazards of the *blitz* the King and the two Princesses formed a stirrup pump team and performed regular practice drills at Windsor.

Through all this the unending routine of kingship went on. The orders in Council by which the Coalition Government ruled

10   145

the nation were promulgated in thousands of documents which required the King's assent and signature, and the King made it a daily practice to read most of the dispatches coming in from his fighting commanders and all of the directives going out from his Cabinet. He further made it a point to meet or get a personal line on most of his top-ranking air, naval and army officers. When Harry Hopkins lunched with the King and Queen in 1941 he was somewhat surprised to find from the King's conversation that he had obviously read carefully most of the important official communications going in or out of Britain, including a dispatch to Washington which Hopkins had sent through the Foreign Office a few days previously. General Eisenhower, too, found George VI very much "in the know" as to current and prospective plans for Allied operations when he met the King for the first time in 1942 and at their subsequent meetings throughout the war. A meeting between the King and Eisenhower just before D-Day produced an apocryphal story which quickly went the rounds of the court. According to it, Eisenhower complained that his deputy commander, Britain's General Montgomery, seemed to be gunning for the Supreme Commander's job. "Don't be silly, Ike," the King was supposed to have replied. "It's my job he's after!"

When Winston Churchill moved into 10 Downing Street in May, 1940 there were some who wondered how the King and his first Minister would get along. Churchill had been a friend of the abdicated Edward and his champion in the Commons and was widely credited with writing Edward's "the-woman-I-love" abdication speech (although the Duke of Windsor later revealed that he had written it himself and asked Churchill to "touch it up"). These doubters failed to take into account the fact that George VI, who steadfastly refused to harbour any ill feelings towards his brother, had already come under the Churchill spell in the other war, when he was Mr. Johnstone in the Royal Navy and Churchill was First Lord of the Admiralty. From the beginning of their new relationship the King was aware of Churchill's great qualities as a war leader and when Hopkins talked to him in January, 1941, at the height of the bombing raids on Britain, he freely admitted that his country would be in great difficulties if anything happened to Churchill. Whenever they were in London the King invited Churchill to lunch privately with him at the Palace once each week, utilizing the necessary luncheon interval to avoid interrupting the Prime Minister's very full day. Even the Queen did not sit in on these private discussions. One of the King's telephones also connected him by direct wire to 10 Downing Street.

The developing intimacy between the monarch and his wartime Prime Minister was underscored at the war's end, when Churchill was given permission to publish letters written to him by the King in his personal history of the war, in itself an unusual dispensation, for letters signed by the King are made public only "in very exceptional circumstances." In 1940, just before Churchill took the premiership, the King addressed him as "My dear Mr. Churchill." In January, 1941 the King called him "My dear Prime Minister," but by the middle of the war he was addressing Churchill as "My dear Winston." Following court custom, Churchill always called the King "Your Majesty" when speaking to him for the first time and thereafter "Sir." In personal conversation, George VI usually called Churchill by his first name or referred to him as "P.M.," which Churchill liked.

Periodic investitures and presentations of medals took up a large share of the King's wartime life. George VI regarded this chore as one of his most important functions. As the representative of the people, he conceived it his duty personally to honour those who had served the state, and by successive enlargements or modifications in the traditional ceremony he sought to bring it more in line with the democratic opinions of his people. Previously it had been the practice that only officers of the fighting services received their medal decorations from the King's hand but early in 1940 George VI announced that he intended to decorate personally all n.c.o.'s of all the services who won medals for gallantry, and this privilege was afterwards extended to all ranks, to the women's services, and to the winners of civilian awards for valour. At the King's wish, the next of kin of those killed in action or dying on active service were brought to Buckingham Palace to receive the decorations their relatives had won.

Several investitures went on when London was under air attack and some honours in 1944 were conferred in the royal air raid shelter underneath Buckingham Palace while flying bombs fell on the capital. On two occasions in 1943, when the King was abroad visiting Allied forces, the Queen and the Duke of Gloucester deputized for him at investitures, but between 1940 and the early

147

months of 1945 the King at Buckingham Palace personally decorated more than 37,000 men and women of his own and the Allied fighting services, as well as hundreds of civilian award winners. Each of these was allowed to bring two relatives or friends to watch the ceremony, so that some 100,000 of the King's subjects saw him in his home.

Travelling about the country in his private, ten-coach train,[1] often with the Queen, the King spent nearly a third of the war years among his people. Instead of putting up at the country house of a local nobleman, which involved a certain amount of ceremonial formality, the King and Queen preferred to stay aboard the royal train, which became their mobile headquarters. Whenever it halted for the night, generally on a branch line or siding where the King and Queen could take a quiet after-dinner stroll undisturbed by crowds, it was hooked up to the telephone system, enabling the King to keep in touch with Buckingham Palace and the Cabinet. All told, the King made nearly 300 wartime rail journeys within Britain in the royal train, covering some 40,000 miles.

As the *Luftwaffe* extended its *blitz* bombing from London to hit most of the major cities of Britain the King visited each stricken city in turn, usually accompanied by his wife. On these morale-boosting visits, which often took place on the grim morning-after when the ruins were still smouldering from the night attack, the King and Queen seemed heedless of danger to themselves, either from German hit-and-run daylight bombers or unexploded bombs. After the King had visited badly-bombed Coventry it was discovered that more than 100 live, unexploded parachute mines lay among the ruins through which he had walked. At this stage of the war the Duke of Gloucester stood by constantly, ready to act as Regent for Princess Elizabeth in case her father was killed.

On these visits George VI was genuinely interested in learning about other people's problems, a carry-over from his earlier factory inspections. During these *blitz* years of 1940–1941 he showed such practical and sincere concern about municipal problems of his bombed cities, particularly hard-hit London, that Herbert Morrison, who had been head of the London County Council and often accompanied the King in his capacity as Minister for Home Security, was moved to remark: "What an excellent alderman of London the King would make."

A complete list of the factories visited by George and Elizabeth during the war years would read like an index to British industry. From his experiences as Duke of York the King regarded himself as something of an authority on industrial affairs and from the time of Dunkirk, when the British Army's losses had desperately to be made good by new production, to the end of the war he gave special attention to the nation's war plants. He was intensely interested in new weapons and war gadgets and whenever he heard of a factory making a new development he would go out of his way to visit it. Despite his urgent request that work should go on as usual, production invariably fell during the day of a royal visit as the workers crowded around to cheer, and for a time the King was tempted to cut out these royal inspections, but the Ministry of Supply produced a statistical survey of factories which he and the Queen had visited which showed that, while output figures dropped sharply on the day of the visit, the moral boost provided by the presence of the King and Queen invariably resulted in higher production for weeks afterwards.

It was popularly rumoured during the war years that His Majesty himself was setting his country's work force an example by secretly labouring in his spare time in an underground factory in London. This story had at least an element of truth in it, although it was not disclosed at the time. Privy to the fact that there was an acute shortage of parts for the 17-pound anti-tank guns needed to turn back Rommel's *Afrika Korps* the King flabbergasted his Ministry of Supply officials by suggesting that machines be installed at Windsor Castle so that he and his staff could turn out at least a few of the required parts in their off-duty hours. He knew from his factory tours that, once proper machinery had been installed, certain parts of the gun's breech block could be made by comparatively unskilled labour. When the startled officials recovered from their initial surprise, a battery of lathes and other machines were quickly set up in one of the Castle dungeons and one lathe was even installed in the King's private apartment. Whenever they could spare a free hour the King and his staff members set to work turning out the gun parts, which, after a routine checking for accuracy, were sent on to one of the royal ordnance factories for assembly.

Changing his uniforms to suit the occasion, George VI paid five wartime visits to the Home Fleet, which, to an ex-sailor, were probably the high spots of his wartime experience, during which he led the Fleet to sea for gunnery exercises, watched the tactical manœuvres of Fleet Air Arm pilots from the flight deck of the aircraft carrier *Victorious*, and went out in a destroyer on a dummy run after an imaginary U-boat. He devoted some 40 tours to the R.A.F., dropped in at almost every R.A.F. airfield in Britain and visited a good many fields operated by the U.S. Eighth and Ninth Air Forces. He visited every division of his Army before it embarked for the battle zones, including Dominion divisions trained in Britain. On these occasions he instituted a new routine for royal inspections. Breaking away from the spit-and-polish inspections, when men in the ranks sometimes never even saw the visitor after spending hours on preparation and parade, George VI directed that each division be lined up along the sides of a country road. Leaving his car at the head of the division, the King then walked for miles between the rows, giving each soldier a chance to see him. This thoughtful gesture, much appreciated by the men, was characteristic of him, as was his insistence that all cooks, orderlies and others not normally mustered on parade should be included on these informal reviews. The men also liked him because he had no hesitation in dressing down the top brass. He even ticked off General Montgomery in front of others one day for wearing two badges in his cap. On one occasion, inspecting a unit, he asked a corporal a question. A high-ranking officer hovering in the background broke in to give the answer. "Please keep quiet," snapped His Majesty. "I am asking this corporal a question, and I want *him* to give me the answer."

Despite the global spread of the war the King managed to see more of his fighting men in action than any sovereign since George II, who was the last King of England to lead his troops into battle (at Dettingen, in 1743). In all, George VI paid five visits to the battle zones.

In December, 1939, he crossed over to France, visited British and French troops and inspected the Maginot Line during the winter lull of the "phony war." In June, 1943, he flew in great secrecy to North Africa, where he inspected units of the British, American and Free French forces which had cleared the enemy from the continent, met General Alexander, General Montgomery and General Eisenhower, the last of whom he made an honorary

Grand Commander of the Bath,[2] and visited the long-embattled island of Malta, a strenuous journey of some 5,800 miles in all. Nine days after D-Day the King again crossed the Channel, this time to Normandy, and on a quick tour of the invasion bridgehead he saw the massively-building Allied armies that had dared and done what Philip of Spain and Napoleon failed to do and what Hitler never had the courage to try. The next month, after the fall of Rome, he flew to Italy where he visited units of the international army of British, Dominion, Empire, American and Allied troops doggedly fighting their way up the long peninsula. King Victor Emmanuel, who was then his co-belligerent, had not yet re-entered Rome and so George VI considerately refrained from visiting the Italian capital. Towards the close of 1944, when the headlong drive that liberated Europe had been temporarily halted, the King visited the British and Canadian divisions of Montgomery's 21st Army Group drawn up in battle line across Belgium and Holland and then went down to the Ardennes to meet Eisenhower and the American field commanders.

Like his father in the First World War, George VI expected every eligible member of the royal family to take part in war service and except for the very youngest each of them had his or her special function during the war years.

The Duke of Gloucester, who had made the Army his career, served in France in a liaison job during the "phony war" and was slightly wounded. His ambition was to be allowed to command a division in the field but after Dunkirk he was requested to remain in Britain, acting as understudy to his brother, in case he was required as Regent in the event of George VI's sudden death before Princess Elizabeth reached the age of 18 on April 21, 1944, but during these years he carried out an arduous round of royal inspections, mostly connected with the Army.

The Duke of Kent, the King's youngest brother, had been designated Governor-General of Australia just before the war's outbreak, but he postponed the assumption of this imperial office and went into the Royal Navy, in which he had been trained as a young man. Good-looking, affable and unassuming, he was almost as popular with the British people as the Prince of Wales had been and in 1940, after the collapse of France, shrewd old Ernest Bevin, who was Minister of Labour in Churchill's new Coalition Government, asked for the Duke's transfer to his ministry and sent him on industrial tours around the country to stimulate production and report on factory morale. Later, at the King's request, the Duke joined the R.A.F., dropping his titular rank of Air Vice-Marshal to serve as a Group Captain. He made welfare work and morale in the service his special concern, flew to Canada—becoming the first member of the royal family to fly the Atlantic—to investigate the great air training scheme in operation there, and achieved his ambition of a short visit to the U.S., where he stayed with President Roosevelt at the White House. While taking off from Scotland in 1942 for a welfare visit to R.A.F. units in Iceland the flying boat in which he was a passenger crashed in bad weather in the Scottish hills and the Duke was killed. A few days later the King made a pilgrimage from Balmoral to see the isolated spot where his favourite brother had died. The Duke's body was recovered and buried with royal and military honours at Windsor.

The Duchess of Kent, besides bringing up her three children, acted as head of the Women's Royal Naval Service and took a heavy part in the royal round of welfare visits to service and civilian organizations. The Duchess of Gloucester held a similar place in the Women's Auxiliary Air Force until late in 1944, when she and her husband went to Australia where the Duke took over the post of Governor-General left empty by his brother's death. The Princess Royal, whose elder son, Lieutenant Viscount Lascelles, was captured in Italy in June, 1944, and held by the Germans until the end of the war, acted as head of the Auxiliary Territorial Service, the women's army corps, and presided over the British Red Cross Society and the R.A.F. Nursing Service.

King George appointed his wife commandant-in-chief of the three women's services, but the Queen refused to wear a uniform for a number of personal reasons. She felt that her chief wartime duty was to run the King's household and appear at his side in public as often as possible. With her three sisters-in-law assigned to their respective services Her Majesty decided that royal patronage was adequately distributed. Also, she frankly conceded that uniforms did not flatter her appearance and she consoled herself with the theory that in a nation of uniforms she meant more to the women she reviewed if she remained feminine.

The two Princesses were too young to share the burden of royal visits and the King and Queen endeavoured to shield them from the direct impact of the war so that their education and up-bringing could continue as nearly normal as possible. At the age of 16 Princess Elizabeth, as required by wartime law, presented herself at the Labour Exchange at Windsor and filled in her registration form for national service, but when she became 18 the King announced that as her special training as heiress pre-sumptive and her public duties outweighed the claims of national service, she would not enter any of the women's auxiliary services. But the King underrated the determination of his daughter to play at least a token part in the wartime life of her nation. When her closest girl friends went off into one service or another Elizabeth chafed under her father's decision and eventually she persuaded him to revoke it. Her choice was the A.T.S. The King granted her an honorary commission as a second subaltern (by the end of the war, however, she wore the three stars of a junior com-mander) and she happily went through the ordinary n.c.o.'s train-ing course for drivers at a depot near Windsor, returning to the Castle each evening.

In the spring of 1945, when the Allied armies resumed their thunderous drive that was to carry them to a junction with the advancing Russians in the heart of Germany, the sense of victory was strong in the air. The dispatches which King George took with him in his leather "boxes" for his after-dinner reading at Windsor provided an exhilarating running commentary as the King's enemies were everywhere confounded, scattered and crushed.

The King and Queen were at Sandringham when the news came to them that Germany's unconditional surrender was imminent and they returned hurriedly to Windsor for the long-awaited day of victory. On Sunday, May 6, in response to an urgent call from 10 Downing Street, the King and Queen drove in to Buckingham Palace, from where the King kept in hourly touch with Mr. Churchill. That evening, although the public declaration of victory in the war in Europe had to be postponed until the next day, the people sensed what was coming and in London they flocked out into the streets, free from danger at last. Drawn by a common, spontaneous impulse they found their way not to Downing Street or Whitehall, where their country's contribution to the victory had been planned, but to Buckingham Palace, as they had on November 11, 1918.

In normal times Britons are drawn to the Palace for the spectacle, the ceremony, like grown-up Christopher Robins. On every ordinary day there is always a gathering of friendly gapers outside seeking nothing more than a momentary proximity to the royal family. But in times of great national rejoicing or sorrow Buckingham Palace almost mysteriously takes on a deeper meaning. It becomes the focal point for the nation's emotions and thousands upon thousands are drawn to it as one to express in their restrained and self-disciplined way the bond of affection that exists between the sovereign and his family and the people.

All through the night before V.E.-Day and throughout the great day itself rivers of Londoners flowed toward the great, grey building until by early evening, when they stood in packed silence to hear the King's own victory message over the loudspeakers, the roadway in front of the Palace and the parks and the Mall became a vast sea of faces. Again and again—eight times in all— the King and the Queen and their two daughters came out on to the famous balcony above the Palace forecourt that evening to acknowledge the roaring cheers of the crowd and the repeated singing of the national anthem. Once they brought Winston Churchill out with them and the architect of victory received his special acclaim from the grateful nation and then withdrew to leave the salutes to his sovereign. For this was not Mr. Churchill's hour. He had directed and inspired his nation to victory, but the people of Britain had fought and won the war in the name of the King and in their hour of deliverance the universal focus for their gratitude was their sovereign. Here, in action, was a demonstration of the constitutional truth—the King *is* Britain. Down below in the great dark mass of bodies stood the people of Britain; and their thunderous cheers which roared upward to the foodlighted balcony saluted the people of Britain, incarnate in the person of the sovereign.

Victory over Japan, which came unexpectedly three months later, brought an equally tumultuous emotional pilgrimage to Buckingham Palace and again the King, accompanied by his family, accepted the symbolic tribute from and for the people. As an English commentator afterwards described them, these victory salutes were moments of high and rare emotion such as come but seldom even in the lives of kings.

X

"THE PEOPLE'S KING"

THE post-war years brought fresh challenges to Britain—a
bloodless revolution in her social structure, a drastic drop in
her economic status in the world and a gradual evolution in the
form of her Commonwealth and Empire to accommodate the
rising aspirations of nationalism in the eastern half of the globe.
And yet, despite Britain's material weaknesses, the forced
austerity of Britons' daily living and the loosening of the bonds
in the modern Commonwealth of Nations, the monarchy remained above and apart from all challenge.

These post-war convulsions in the old order brought changes
into the life of George VI as well as in the lives of his subjects.
The 1945 general election, which swept a Labour Government
into power, brought him his fourth Prime Minister—first Stanley
Baldwin, then Neville Chamberlain, then Winston Churchill and
then Clement Attlee.

Like most observers who counted on Churchill's colourful personality to lead the Conservatives to victory, George VI was
surprised by the election result, but like his father in the parallel
circumstance when the first Labour Government took office in
1924 under J. Ramsay MacDonald the King held that it was no
cause for alarm. Many of the new Labour Cabinet Ministers were
no strangers to him. Attlee, Bevin, Morrison, Cripps, Dalton,
Greenwood and Jowitt, among others, had held key positions in
the wartime Coalition Government, and Attlee, as Deputy Prime
Minister, had frequently stood in for Churchill in dealings with
the King when Churchill was out of Britain.

George VI had a high regard for the quiet little leader of the
Labour Party and Attlee, on his part, came to look forward to
their customary weekly conferences when he could discuss affairs
of the state with a man who was above the political battle. "The

155

longer I served him the greater was my admiration, respect and affection," said Attlee in his Parliamentary tribute at the time of the King's death. "No Prime Minister had a kinder or more considerate master."

Very privately the King used to complain that Attlee as Prime Minister did not seem to tell him as much as Winston Churchill did during the war years, and while they got along well together their relationship was never as close as the wartime association between George VI and Churchill. Whereas the King affectionately called Churchill by his first name Clement Attlee was always addressed by the sovereign as Mr. Attlee. Even when Churchill was out of office, he and the King remained gay and intimate friends, though they could not have their regular meetings of the war years. As leader of His Majesty's Opposition, Churchill could constitutionally be consulted by the King at any time, but George VI could not call him in too often in this capacity without seeming to show favouritism, and so he contrived to see Churchill privately as often as possible. When Mrs. Roosevelt stayed with the King and Queen at Windsor Castle in 1948 after unveiling the London statue to her late husband, the King asked Mr. and Mrs. Churchill along to spend the week-end. Churchill remarked on the fact that neither Attlee nor any other Labour politician had been invited. "This is a private family party," said the King, stoutly, "and I saw no reason to invite any of those fellows."

In his official capacity, however, George VI's relations with his Socialist Ministers were faultless. Many of them he had met as trade union leaders when, as Duke of York, he had concerned himself with industrial relations, welfare problems and unemployment and when they became the King's Ministers they were already old friends or acquaintances. On his part, the human touch which he brought to their relationship, his readiness to entertain new ideas and his complete freedom from political prejudice served to deepen their regard for him as a man and remove any lingering doubts they had about the real value of the British monarchy. He had his likes and dislikes among them. Herbert Morrison, whom he respected as an administrator, used to upset him by the light-hearted way in which, as Lord President, he conducted the formalities of the Privy Council, and Aneurin Bevan, the Minister of Health and then Minister of Labour until he resigned dramatically from the Attlee Cabinet in 1951, used to baffle and occasionally irritate the King by what appeared to be studied informality in the royal presence.

At a London exhibition "Nye" Bevan once stood talking to the King and Queen and kept his hands stuffed into his overcoat pockets. Unwilling to regard this as a sign of wilful disrespect, the King said nothing—unlike his crusty father, who would have treated the offender to a royal tongue-lashing. Bevan, who once boasted that the coal miners in his Welsh constituency did not send him to Parliament to "dress up," consistently refused to wear formal dress at Palace functions. After a royal hint, Attlee once requested Bevan to don "white tie" for a "Buck House" reception. Bevan turned up with a white tie all right—but he wore it with a business suit! On another occasion, however, the King and Bevan hit it off amiably. Afflicted with a slight speech defect which he has never been able to correct, "Nye" boldly asked the King how he had managed to cure his stammer. The King, pleased to find at least one subject of common interest, cheerfully explained.

Under the concept that the monarch should reign but not rule, the royal family today is obliged to be not only politically neutral but, if possible, a-political. In public George VI was scrupulously non-political during the post-war years of partisan politics which bitterly, and almost evenly, divided his people, but in private he had political convictions like any ordinary man. Those closest to him, Conservatives by birth, breeding and bank balance, were happily convinced that if he had been a private citizen he would have voted Tory. This may have been so, but at least his earlier background and self-education when he was Duke of York and his genuine interest in the social and economic problems of his people would have labelled him as a very progressive-minded Conservative. His wife, who absorbed and shared much of his concern for the social problems of an industrial age when she was Duchess of York, leans even more toward the Socialist's conception of the welfare state than did her husband.[2] Thus it was with interest, if not with approval, that George VI from his detached position at the head of the state watched the efforts of the Labour Government to cope with many of the industrial and social problems which had concerned him when he was Duke of York—through such measures as the nationalization of the moribund coal industry, the re-location of industry in the once-depressed areas, the physical face-lifting of town and countryside with new factories, new towns and working-class housing, the national health programme (it was one of the royal doctors, the late Lord Dawson of Penn, who outlined the national health service), and the extension of the social services in which his country has long pioneered, even under Conservative governments.[3]

Soon after the Socialists came to power in 1945 the story circulated around the court that the King, when driving with a friend past Runnymede, scene of King John's surrender to the barons, pointed to the historic spot and cracked, "That is where all this bloody trouble started!" The story is no doubt apocryphal. At any rate, George VI privately believed that the Labour Government did a very creditable job in its almost six and a half years in office under most difficult circumstances.

The post-war years also wrought momentous changes in Britain's international responsibilities. The gradual and still-continuing transmutation of the Empire into the Commonwealth was speeded up under the Labour Government, but George VI was broadminded enough to realize that changes in his country's imperial status were inevitable, and with sure judgment, a grasp of essentials and a disregard for formalities he helped devise the political miracle by which the link of the crown proved strong enough to hold within the Commonwealth the Republic of India and the two great Asiatic Dominions of Pakistan and Ceylon.

When Indian demands for independence were finalized with the creation of the new states of India and Pakistan in 1947 Conservative circles implied that the King-Emperor had been compelled to stand by powerless while the Labour Government "threw away the Empire"—as if Indian independence depended solely on a decision from Whitehall. In fact, India's independence —which had been held out as bait by the Coalition Government in return for Indian support during the war—was as inevitable as tomorrow. Churchill inclined to the off-hand opinion that India could be held in the Empire by the dispatch of a couple of additional divisions of British troops, but George VI had no such illusions. He warmly approved the Labour Government's nomination of his second cousin, Lord Louis Mountbatten, whose versatility and ability he admired, as the 29th—and, as it turned out, the last—Viceroy of India [4] and from Mountbatten's reports to the Cabinet and Buckingham Palace it became increasingly clear that nothing less than the creation of two separate, independent states would satisfy the aspirations of the Indian people, a solution which Mountbatten was eventually ordered to implement. Along with the Labour Ministers, the King perceived that the Commonwealth would be immeasurably strengthened by the inclusion of India and Pakistan of their own free will. Pakistan chose to become a Dominion, but India, in her first pride of self-government, threw off her imperial allegiance while at the same time she expressed a desire to remain within the Commonwealth. It was in part due to a personal suggestion of George VI that the unique formula which made this possible was devised and adopted at the Commonwealth Conference in London in April, 1949. At the end of the historic session the Dominion and Indian Premiers, led by the late General Smuts, went to Buckingham Palace to thank the King for his wise counsel. "Do not thank me," replied George VI, deeply moved. "It is to Almighty God, who, I am sure, has led you, that all our thanks should now be given." [5]

Shortly before then the King made what might have been one of his few ventures into the borderland of politics which surrounds the throne. In his Christmas Day broadcast to his people in 1948 he pointedly remarked that, in his opinion, the extension of freedom and independence to the new nations of Asia had strengthened the world-wide Commonwealth organization.

"Our Commonwealth—the British Commonwealth—has been subject to the laws of evolution," His Majesty said. "We would not have it otherwise. But it is stronger, not weaker, as it fulfils its ancient mission of widening the bounds of freedom wherever our people live; and for myself, I am proud to fulfil my own appointed share in that mission." Not a few of his subjects interpreted this remark as a decisive rebuttal of Winston Churchill and those die-hard Tories who berated the Labour Government for "throwing away the Empire" by the extension of self-government to India, Pakistan and Ceylon.

In 1876 Queen Victoria had ordered Prime Minister Disraeli to introduce a Royal Titles Bill in the Commons creating her Empress of India, and on New Year's Day of 1877 she was proclaimed *Kaisar-i-Hind* on the great plain of Delhi. In 1948, in the twelfth year of his reign, her great-grandson issued a royal proclamation which formally dropped the imperial title of Emperor of India from his royal style and left him with a new signature of George R. instead of George R.I.[6]

Like most of his subjects, George VI hoped that the new United Nations organization would provide the world forum in which nation could work with nation in amity. He followed with close interest the reports of its embryo days at San Francisco and was particularly pleased when its first General Assembly was held in London in January, 1946 so that he could formally bless it on its way. He even ordered the belligerent, imperious second stanza of "God Save the King" rewritten to bring it more into the spirit of the brotherhood of nations.[7] He followed closely the reports from the British representatives at the U.N. Security Council and Assemblies but, like most of his subjects, he was disappointed when the organization's performance fell far short of the free world's hopes.

Even before the politicians on both sides of the Atlantic were ready to admit it, the King sensed that the Anglo-American partnership born of the war would have to continue in the shaping of the peace and he made a personal effort to strengthen the friendly relations between the two nations. The sudden death of President Roosevelt was a great blow to him, for he had looked forward to renewing their personal relations after the war, but he took the first opportunity to get to know Roosevelt's successor. When President Truman returned from the Potsdam conference in mid-summer of 1945 he was invited to stop over in Britain, but with the Japanese war still on in the east Truman apologized that the best he could do was to call in at Plymouth aboard the *Augusta* for a few hours on his way back across the Atlantic. Disregarding protocol, King George hurried down to Plymouth and in between the exchange of naval formalities managed to engage the new President in amiable discussion.

The King had grown to like the Americans he met during the war years. Their uninhibited friendliness and easy informality appealed to him and he and the Queen were always pleased to meet new Americans at small gatherings organized by David Bowes-Lyon, the Queen's brother, or the late Oliver Stanley, one of the King's long-time British friends. In time, this partiality for Americans began to show up at "Buck House" functions, where more and more Americans were included in the guest lists. The

29. *A civic welcome at Adelaide Town Hall during the 1927 Australian tour of the then Duke and Duchess of York*

30. *A 1939 visit with the Roosevelts at their New York home*

31. *Escorting the Australian cricketers around Balmoral Castle in 1948*

32. *Entertaining the Commonwealth Prime Ministers at Buckingham Palace*

King and Queen took a special interest in the trans-Atlantic
activities of the English-Speaking Union and made it a point to
meet the contingent of U.S. school-teachers who exchange jobs
with their British counterparts each year. The King also kept up
his contact with Eisenhower and when the general and his wife
and son visited Britain in 1946 they were invited to spend a week-
end with the King and Queen at Balmoral.

Much of the credit for this royal affinity for America goes to
Lewis Douglas, who served as U.S. Ambassador to Britain from
1947 to 1950. The King and Queen took an immediate liking to
Mr. and Mrs. Douglas, and their daughter, Sharman, became an
intimate friend and confidante of the two Princesses. Through
Lew Douglas George VI learned more about the U.S. than any
of his royal predecessors.

Early in 1947 George and Elizabeth and their two daughters
sailed aboard H.M.S. *Vanguard*, the pride of the Royal Navy, for
their first visit to what was then the youngest of the self-governing Dominions, South Africa. It was the first time the royal
family had made an official visit abroad since 1939, and the first
time the Princesses had been outside the British Isles. George VI
also became the first King of South Africa to set foot on its soil.

The tour had been suggested by the late Field Marshal Jan
Smuts, who thought that a royal visit would have a healing and
reconciling influence on the nationalist and racial differences
which unhappily beset his country. Not long afterwards Smuts
was out of office and the Boer nationalists were in power, bent on
pursuing a policy of racial discrimination and ardent nationalism
that put South Africa out of line with the rest of the democratic
nations and may carry it out of the Commonwealth altogether,
but at the time of the royal tour there was no doubt about
South Africa's vociferous welcome, which Smuts later confessed
"exceeded even my most optimistic expectations." Even the
most intransigent nationalists wilted before the royal family's
charm as the King and his wife and daughters, squired by Smuts
and the political leaders of each area, made their triumphal progress through the circular tour that took them some 6,000 miles
by land and air.

They visited all four provinces of the Union of South Africa,
venturing into the hotbeds of nationalist sentiment, and the King

opened his Parliament in Capetown and presided in person over the Executive Council of the Union. They toured the three High Commission Territories (British protectorates) of Basutoland, Swaziland and Bechuanaland. They visited Southern Rhodesia, where the King opened Parliament at Salisbury, and crossed the Zambesi River to Northern Rhodesia, where they twice saw the spectacular marvel of the Victoria Falls, by day and under the moon. Everywhere they went they were greeted by spontaneous and moving demonstrations of loyalty by English and Afrikaans-speaking South Africans, by the segregated coloured and Indian communities in the Union and by the native tribes in the territories.

On May 12, having been away from home just over three months, the royal family returned to England on *Vanguard*, completing a round-trip of some 19,000 miles.

In their absence Britain endured the worst winter weather in memory, which blocked the roads and railways, choked off coal supplies and brought on emergency shutdowns to conserve power, light and heating such as the people had not had to endure even in the worst days of the war. The King was constantly concerned about the sufferings of his people at home and even talked of cutting short his tour and going back to share them.

The newspapers carried daily stories of the royal family sweltering in the hottest South African summer in years and there were grouses and letters to editors from austerity-ridden Britons who thought that the royal tour was one long, luxurious holiday. Few critics realized that, far from a holiday, the tour was a gruelling ordeal that left the royal family fatigued and cost the King a loss of 14 pounds. The strain of the close-timed programme was so great that many times the King and his wife and daughters were on the verge of sheer exhaustion. Princess Margaret, not a strong youngster, was so worn out during the tour that she would often fall asleep even in the midst of the excitement before the family's next appearance.

Even the preparations for the tour were arduous and prolonged. They began early in 1946 when Smuts visited the King to extend the invitation and then in long conversations briefed him on the involved and touchy political-racial problems of South Africa. Later that year the King and Queen learned more about the Dominion when they invited South Africa's Governor-General,

Major Brand van Zyl, and his wife to stay with them at Balmoral, and almost every important visitor from South Africa was invited to "Buck House" for an audience with the King. Then the King and his secretariat and, to a lesser extent, the Queen and her daughters settled down to an intensive course of reading books about South Africa and the native protectorates, from which the King first-drafted some of the many speeches he would be called upon to make. All four members of the family learned some Afrikaans and a smattering of the native tongues, enough to enable them to say a few words in greeting, to return a salutation and to master the pronunciation of difficult names and places, which they consider important in their jobs. George and Elizabeth personally supervised the selection of an immense collection of gifts which they took to the native chiefs and others.

While the Queen concerned herself with the dresses which she and her daughters would wear on the tour, the King sweated out the details of the tour's time-table. The main programme was worked out by a committee in South Africa, which communicated the plans to the King's secretary, but the King had the final say in fitting in competing claims for the family's appearances on a crowded schedule. Then there were transport problems to be solved. Eight special rail coaches were built in England and sent out ahead in ships to form the main part of the royal White Train, which served as a mobile office and hotel during most of the tour, and a fleet of four dozen sleek new Daimler, Humber and Austin cars were sent out to carry the royal party on side trips. Four aircraft of the King's Flight were flown out to stand by for emergencies and convey the royal family on long hops around the vast area to be covered.

All during the ceaseless round of parades, presentations, garden parties, state balls, processions of welcome, tribal festivities and royal inspections and amid the strain of almost constant travel the King's work went on. The White Train was hitched up at each stop, even out on the veldt, to the telephone system, allowing the King to get in touch with London, and the dispatch cases containing state papers from his governments in Britain and the other Dominions were rushed to him every day. A special Foreign Office cipher clerk travelled with the party to code and decode messages that demanded the King's attention.

Throughout the long tour the royal family had no real privacy, no time they could call their own. The royal party—including secretariat and personal staff—totalled 37 people and at each provincial or state border a new set of officials latched on to the tour. So many last-minute requests for the family's appearance came in, even when the tour was nearly over, that the King kept changing the programme to satisfy them and in the end they were left with only ten free days out of the whole tour. Even their rest days were free in theory only, for they were usually filled with unofficial engagements and the presentations of high local officials and their wives. The King had arranged to spend four rest days with his family in the Kruger National Park, quietly looking at the famed wild life in the reservation. The press was barred from this trip, but enough local snobs crowded along on the trip to make up a royal caravan of almost 40 cars.

During the remainder of 1947 Princess Elizabeth almost pushed the other members of her family off the front pages. She had come of age on April 21 during the South African tour, an event that was celebrated by a state ball at Capetown, and on her return she moved more conspicuously into the traditional position of heir to the throne. She sat at her father's right hand when he opened the new session of Parliament and rode with him when the pre-war ceremony of Trooping the Colour was resumed that year to mark his official birthday. Then on July 10, in phrases almost the same as had been used for his own engagement, the King confirmed the long rumoured romance between Elizabeth and the former Prince Philip of Greece, who had recently dropped his princely title and been naturalized a Briton under the surname of his uncle, Viscount Mountbatten. On November 20, Princess Elizabeth and Philip, raised that day to the peerage as the Duke of Edinburgh, were married in solemn state in Westminster Abbey and London celebrated the royal occasion with scenes of popular rejoicing unparalleled since V.J.-Day.

In the twelfth year of their reign, on April 26, 1948, George and Elizabeth celebrated another domestic milestone in their lives, their silver wedding anniversary. They drove in state for a thanksgiving service in St. Paul's, received loyal addresses of congratulations from the Lords and the Commons, and in the early evening drove in an open car through some 22 miles of London streets jammed with cheering subjects.

George VI was proudest of his sobriquet, "The People's King," and certainly he earned it. Never has a sovereign seen, met and talked with so many of his subjects or so fully shared their life.

The only reign that has rivalled his in popularity was that of his father's, and in the character of the two reigns there was much in common. Both monarchs were brought up in the comparative privacy of second sons, with no thought of being called to the throne. The death of George V's elder brother, the Duke of Clarence, in 1892 suddenly placed him in position as prospective heir to the throne just as the unexpected abdication of Edward VIII thrust George VI to the forefront of the royal line. Both were compelled to test their kingship in wartime within a few years of being crowned, and both had to re-establish the strength and dignity of the monarchy after interludes during which its steady reputation had been shaken.[8]

But George V, following the brief reign of his cosmopolitan father, had come to the throne in 1910 surrounded by almost contemptuous indifference that approached unpopularity. "He is not loved, he is not feared, the man with the receding beard," ran a jingle of that day. The holocaust that was the First World War fused king and country together, but it was not until the middle and latter years of his reign, when, with the aid of Queen Mary and their four sons and their daughter, he resumed the process of taking the crown to the people which had been interrupted during the long seclusion of bereaved Queen Victoria that George V achieved the degree of respect and affection that made his reign unique. George VI started with no such handicap: from the time he stepped hesitantly into the place left vacant by his brother he succeeded in identifying his personality with his high office, and vice versa, even more closely than did his father before him. Under George VI the symbol of the monarch became more human than ever before.[9]

The democratizing influence of two world wars stripped the monarchy of most of its earlier awe-inspiring magic and veneration. The eclipse of the aristocracy, an economic consequence of the two wars, which formerly acted as a social barrier between royalty and the public, has likewise brought the crown and the people closer together.[10]

Although he used to complain that he did not meet enough ordinary people—his own choice of secretaries and the possessive court officials who surrounded him, aristocrats schooled by court

etiquette to shield him from the public, was responsible for this—
George VI was more aware of life outside the palace walls than
any of his predecessors and he acquired a grasp of public sentiment and a knack of interpreting it that sometimes anticipated
the advice of his court officials and Ministers.[11]

In the early months of the Second World War, when his subjects
on the home front were under more severe attack than his troops
in the field, he quickly sensed the need for some recognition of
civilian gallantry and therefore created the George Cross and
Medal. In 1943, when the British people applauded the Russian
stand at beleaguered Stalingrad, it was the King's idea to express
their admiration by the presentation of a richly-jewelled sword
to the people of Stalingrad. When President Roosevelt died
early in 1945 George VI at once ordered a week of court mourning.
This was an unusual tribute to the head of a foreign republic, but
it reflected the universal sorrow of the British people when they
heard the news of Roosevelt's death.

Likewise the King's decision to permit a certain amount of
ceremony and public celebration at Elizabeth's wedding, although
his advisers counselled austerity, exactly met his people's wish
for colour and gaiety in their otherwise grim lives. On the other
hand, he refused to take a restful holiday on his return from
South Africa, although pressed to do so by his medical and
Cabinet advisers, because he sensed that the suggestion that
the King needed a holiday after escaping the rigorous winter
which his people endured might bring forth public complaints.

But it was not only on major issues that the King had the pulse
of his people. In the spring of 1951 Mrs. Margaret Johnson, a
young miner's wife and mother of two children, impulsively
picked three tulips from a public flower garden in her home
town of South Shields. She was kept in custody for the night and
the crusty local magistrates, determined to make an example of
her minor vandalism, fined her £5. There was an outcry of
protest from the press and the case of the stolen tulips got discussed in the Commons and commented on in the Lords and then
was dropped from the news. But George VI had not forgotten.
Acting through the Home Secretary, he invoked special powers
under the 1859 Remission of Penalties Act and some weeks later
a plain-clothes policeman appeared on Mrs. Johnson's doorstep
and, on orders from the King, remitted £4 of her fine.

XI

THE HAPPY FAMILY

IF, by some twist of fortune, George VI and his Queen had been transplanted from Buckingham Palace they could have settled down happily to an upper middle-class suburban existence anywhere as Mr. and Mrs. George Windsor. Their two daughters, especially Princess Margaret, were conscious of their royal stations as the first and second young ladies of Britain, but the King and his wife remained largely unaffected by their years of regal life. When Eisenhower lunched with them in their private apartments during the war he remarked afterwards with satisfied surprise that the informal, companionable atmosphere in the royal family's home was reminiscent of a meeting with friends in Tacoma, San Antonio, Washington or Abilene, Kansas.

This was mainly because George VI was above all a family man, subordinate only to his high sense of service to the state. Domesticated by preference, he was devoted to his home, his wife and his children, and it is probably true that no other British monarch, not even excepting his father, ever gave over so much time to his family circle. Characteristically, when he spoke of his family in his public addresses he preferred to call them "my wife and children," not "the Queen and the Princesses."

It is this domestic example, this glorification of the family as the unit from which any nation must draw its strength, that put the monarchy on its surest foundations during George VI's reign.

Because of the non-stop demands of their jobs "kings and queens are only secondarily fathers and mothers," as the Duke of Windsor has remarked. This was true of George VI's parents and was in large measure responsible for his own unhappy childhood. Mindful of his experience, the King managed to remain both a monarch and a father by drawing a sharp line between his official and his private, family life. His privacy was his most

167

treasured possession and he jealously guarded it against unwarranted and unwanted intrusions from the press and public.

"No family in these tumultuous years was happier, or loved one another more, than the royal family around the King," said Winston Churchill in his memorable broadcast after George VI's death. Perhaps because their public lives are so very public the members of the royal family are more tightly knit, more home-loving than most families. At home, surrounded by an atmosphere of quiet and contented domesticity, they have common interests, share family jokes and a family vocabulary of personal expressions which have meaning for them but not for outsiders.

Within the court circle, though a certain informality is permitted, even the highest court officials, men and women who were friends of the late King and his Queen for years, addressed Their Majesties with the formal "Sir" or "Ma'am." Within the family circle, however, all formality disappears. The King and his Queen used to address each other as "darling" in private. Within the family and to her closest friends his wife used to call the King "Bertie," the name by which he had been known to his family since boyhood, and he called her Elizabeth and sometimes "Peter" or "Peta," the childhood nicknames she invented for herself. Their daughters called the King "Papa" or sometimes "Dad" and the Queen Mother is still "Mummie" to them. Young Queen Elizabeth is still known in the family circle as "Lilibet," the result of her first babyish efforts to pronounce her name, but her husband dislikes this nursery affectation and has recently taken to calling her "Betty." In the family circle Princess Margaret sometimes refers to her sister as "Lil," but Elizabeth has never been called "Liz" or "Lizzie," diminutives her mother detested when she was young. Princess Margaret is always addressed as Margaret—never by her baptismal name of Margaret Rose, which she dislikes.

To all her royal grandchildren Queen Mary is "Granny," while the adult members of the family generally refer to her as "May," the name by which she was known as a young Princess. The Princess Royal is known within the family as Aunt Mary, the Duke and Duchess of Gloucester as Uncle Harry and Aunt Alice, and the Duchess of Kent as Aunt Marina. The Earl of Athlone, Queen Mary's brother, is known as "Uncle Algie," though his real name is Alexander. The Duke of Windsor, who used to be the special favourite of the younger members of the family, was known as Uncle David, though his name is not often mentioned within the royal family nowadays. The Duke of Edinburgh is Philip to his wife and the rest of the family. His uncle, Earl Mountbatten, is known to the family as "Uncle" Dickie, though his actual relationship is that of second cousin to the late King.

On most of their evenings at home George VI and his Queen slipped into their roles as husband and wife, father and mother. They seldom had more than two Buckingham Palace dinner parties a week. One reason was that George and Elizabeth had few close personal friends. Strangely enough, the members of the royal family visit one another very rarely. They seldom drop in on each other on casual visits and usually meet *en masse* only on such occasions as royal weddings, christenings or funerals or at state or ceremonial affairs. When his health began to decline George VI gave up many purely social engagements, which he never really liked. In the last years of his life whether he went out in the evenings depended on his mood, and he often threw society hostesses into a dither by not making up his mind to attend their parties until five—and sometimes later—in the evening.

In general, the royal family's taste in evening entertainment is inclined to be middle-brow. After dinner, if he had no urgent documents to read, the King and his wife would settle down in the sitting room they shared in the Palace's private apartments to listen to the radio or watch the B.B.C.'s television. George loved to tinker with early-model radio sets when he was Duke of York and he remained a keen T.V. fan since its modest beginnings in Britain. He kept a close watch on all programmes concerning his family. When he saw a T.V. newsreel of Princess Elizabeth's wedding procession he thought that the royal coach had come out too dark. He called in the B.B.C.'s television chief for an explanation and ended up in an involved conversation about electronic engineering. While he was confined to bed after his lung resection he had a T.V. set installed in his bedroom, and a page was kept standing by to tune it in for him. One day when the B.B.C. planned a 3.00 p.m. telecast from Ascot racecourse the King sent word that he would like to see his horse run in the

2.30 p.m. race. The B.B.C. obligingly moved the programme ahead by half an hour—and the King saw his horse win.

The Queen Mother and young Elizabeth II like to listen to opera and symphony broadcasts, but George VI's tastes ran more to comedy programmes. On Sundays, after church, he listened to a whole spate of them on the B.B.C. His sense of humour was not over-subtle and for radio listening he generally preferred the broad jokes and laboured puns of the B.B.C.'s comedy programmes to the fast-breaking wisecracks of American comedians. Until his death a few years ago Tommy Handley was the King's favourite comedian—His Majesty seldom missed a weekly broadcast of Handley's "ITMA" ("*It's That Man Again*") programme—but in his last years the King came to appreciate the zany antics of Danny Kaye. He was introduced to Kaye's records by his daughters, acquired a complete collection for himself, and then visited the London Palladium to watch Kaye's buffoonery. The King had an enormous collection of jazz records, and dance music from a gramophone or radio provided almost constant background music during the off-duty hours in the Palace.

Regular card players, George and Elizabeth were canasta fiends during the game's heyday. They were introduced to the game by ex-Ambassador and Mrs. Lewis Douglas, and when Douglas and his wife were in London the King and Queen occasionally popped into a Palace limousine and drove over to the American Ambassador's home alongside Hyde Park for a session. When their children were growing up, George and Elizabeth often joined in childish games of racing demon, fish or snap. The Queen Mother, who still plays a particularly fine hand at canasta, is also fond of playing solitaire in the evenings and likes to work out all sorts of very complicated forms of the game.

The King and his family were also fond of charades and other parlour pastimes. On holiday at Balmoral or Sandringham or during the house party season at Windsor Castle they kept their guests up until long past midnight every evening. At these friendly sessions, both George and Elizabeth were always gay and uninhibited, and those guests who were seeing her in the family circle for the first time were sometimes startled to see Her Majesty (now the Queen Mother), her skirts held high above her knees, skipping round the room.

Britain's ruling monarchs have always been regular patrons of the theatre. George VI and his Queen upheld the tradition, though they were apt to follow their own light tastes in the performances they chose to see. Whenever the King took his family out for the evening they were more likely to turn up at an old-fashioned music hall or vaudeville theatre. In 1950 he did take his wife and Princess Margaret across the Thames to the Old Vic to see a performance of "Twelfth Night." However, this was the first time that a sovereign had entered the famed, 132-year-old theatre.

George VI liked his humour broad and his stage entertainment knockabout. A few years ago, to celebrate his wife's birthday, he took her to their local theatre, the Victoria Palace, around the corner from Buckingham Palace, to see a rowdy, guffaw-raising review starring half a dozen top British funnymen known as the Crazy Gang. Gags are always especially cleaned up for a royal visit, but Margaret had seen the show without blue-pencilling a few weeks earlier and had told her parents all about it. At the interval the King asked, "Am I seeing the show my daughter saw?" He was told that some of the material had been censored.

"Put it all back again," said the King, and back it went for the rest of the performance. He was privately delighted when a top-line music hall artist at the Royal Variety show in 1950 deliberately strayed from his script, which had been specially vetted for royal ears, and indulged in some borderline jokes.

The King loved big musical stage spectacles, particularly importations of Broadway successes, a preference which is shared by his wife and her daughters. Their Majesties went twice to see the London performance of "Annie Get Your Gun" and their daughters saw it three times. To celebrate their last evening together before Elizabeth and Philip flew off for their Australian tour the King took his family to Drury Lane to see "South Pacific," an occasion made more eventful in that it was his first night out since his lung operation and the last but one of his public appearances.

Unlike a Mr. and Mrs. Windsor, the King and his wife could not pop around the corner to the neighbourhood cinema in the evening. They had their movies shown privately at home. A keen movie fan, the King used to put on at least one film a week, and sometimes several in a week when he was on holiday, in whatever home he was occupying. He paid commercial rental for

171

each film shown, and also paid the wages of the technicians who ran his sound projectors. There is no permanent projection equipment at "Buck House" and when George VI wanted to see a particular film for himself he used to go to his old home in Piccadilly, rebuilt into offices for British film-maker Sir Alexander Korda, and have it run off for him in a private studio.

Most of the films shown in the royal homes were personally chosen by the King on the basis of newspaper movie reviews, which he read avidly, or reports from a member of his family or his household. He was surprisingly highbrow in his cinematic choice. Although he ordered many of the first-run U.S. and British "A" pictures he also called for most of the outstanding foreign films that came to London ("To Live in Peace," the little Italian classic of a few years ago, was one of his favourites) and he particularly asked for all the good documentary films. In the autumn of 1951 he made a special request to have sent up to Balmoral Paul Rotha's vivid feature-length documentary, "No Resting Place," the drama of an Irish tinker's life. When any of the royal grandchildren were in the audience he usually put on a Mickey Mouse or another animated feature. At these private shows the King and his family sat together, with visitors and members of their official staff grouped around them, and the household and domestic staff members were generally asked in to fill up the room behind them.

George VI was a tireless dancer. Before his leg gave him trouble he danced at the parties he attended until the early hours of the morning and at his daughters' small dances at home he often ended up leading a hilarious conga line along the Palace corridors. His wife, extraordinarily light on her feet and as enthusiastic a dancer as was her husband, is a loyal exponent of the Scottish reel and is always ready to lead her house party guests through its fine points.

At state balls court protocol decreed that after the first dance with the King the Queen sent an equerry to summon the gentlemen with whom she wished to dance, but at small, private dances, where any of the guests could ask her to dance, she was usually the first to stir up the spirit of the party. She liked to dance to swingy, modern foxtrots with catchy, slightly suggestive lyrics, like "One of the Roving Kind," and "Baby, It's Cold Outside," and she was always willing to drop all royal decorum for the musical gymnastics of "The Lambeth Walk," one of her old favourites, "Boomps-A-Daisy," or "The Hokey-Cokey."

According to band leader Bert Ambrose, whose dance bands played for George VI's parties for almost 25 years, the King's favourite dance was a Viennese waltz. Once Ambrose and his band played a waltz that lasted a full 30 minutes. George and Elizabeth danced through it without stopping, and when it ended the King applauded for more. Queen Elizabeth II and her sister like their dance music tunefully pleasant and their lyrics somewhat sentimental. The Duke of Edinburgh likes his dance tunes hot, or at least jiggy.

George and Elizabeth could never dine out in public, but they encouraged their daughters to visit London's better restaurants and more exclusive night clubs, always accompanied by proper chaperons and impeccably aristocratic escorts. Privately, restaurant proprietors are inclined to regard these royal visits as nuisances, but the kudos resulting from royal patronage more than cancels out the inconvenience. The procedure by which a royal personage visits a restaurant or supper club for the first time is always elaborate. A day or two beforehand a Palace secretary telephones and reserves a table for the party. Usually on the day of the visit a brace of Scotland Yard men call at the restaurant and give it a thorough look-over from kitchen to powder room. When the royal party arrives two more Yard men are in attendance and they remain throughout the evening, having a discreet dinner close by the royal table. The waiters are expected to carry on as usual, serving royalty the same as the ordinary diners. When the party is ready to leave either one member asks that the bill be sent to Buckingham Palace or else nothing is said about paying and a day or so later a Palace secretary phones and requests the bill for the meal.

Although one member of the household, the Keeper of the Royal Cellars, has the job of providing an all-round stock of choice wines, liqueurs and cigars for guests, neither George VI nor his wife had expensive tastes. The Queen Mother seldom drinks, except for an occasional gin-based cocktail, and at dinner her only indulgence is a glass of very light claret or sometimes a glass of sweet Bordeaux white wine. The King's taste in wines ran toward hocks and moselles. Before dinner he was often content with a glass of sherry, but in the evening, particularly when the strain of his job began to tell on him, he averaged about four whiskies and water a night, occasionally varied with a brandy and soda.

As Defender of the Faith, the sovereign is head of the established Church of England and as one of his multifarious royal duties George VI gave conscientious attention to its affairs. It is the monarch who appoints all Archbishops and Bishops—on the recommendation of the Prime Minister—but the King did not consider this a mere formality, as are some royal appointments. He knew most of the top churchmen in Britain, kept himself well posted on their qualifications, and if he felt insufficiently informed about a nominee would call for more background details about him before ratifying the nomination.

As was expected of him, George VI was a regular churchgoer, and except through illness he never missed a Sunday morning service from one year to the next. The private chapel in Buckingham Palace, bombed early in the war, is still unusable and so whenever members of the royal family remain in London over the week-end, an infrequent event, they go either to the Chapel Royal at St. James's Palace or to the chapel at Wellington Barracks, itself gutted by a flying bomb but temporarily repaired. At Royal Lodge the members of the family attend service at a small chapel nestled in the heart of Windsor Great Park, and when they stay at Sandringham they worship at the little estate church. When the court is in residence at Holyroodhouse at Edinburgh the royal place of worship is St. Giles' Cathedral, but at Balmoral the family worships at a little Presbyterian church on a hillside at Crathie, a mile or so from the royal residence, continuing a custom started by Victoria and Prince Albert.

Victoria's preference for the Presbyterian Scottish kirk while on her visits to Scotland touched off a sectarian squabble among churchmen that still raises an occasional echo in church assemblies today. As an individual Queen Victoria was a member of the Church of England and was expected to attend services of the Scottish Episcopal Church while in Scotland. But the Episcopal Church is a minority body in Scotland: the established state church is the Presbyterian Church of Scotland, and Victoria argued that as head of the state in Scotland she was entitled to worship at Presbyterian Crathie—which also happened to be the nearest to Balmoral Castle. Against the strongest objections from the Archbishop of Canterbury she once took the sacrament in the kirk, a happening that was hushed up and kept out of the newspapers of that day. Although they try not to show partiality, the new Queen, the Queen Mother and Princess Margaret all have a liking for the simplicity of the Scottish form of service and it was the Scottish metrical psalm, "The Lord's my Shepherd, I'll not want," set to the tune of Crimond, that Princess Elizabeth chose for her wedding.

Apart from a conventional show of devotion, George VI was quietly and sincerely religious. His religion was a deep, personal matter and his beliefs guided his actions. Like his father, he was prepared to admit that much religious doctrine went over his head, but he did not regard public worship or thanksgiving services as mere formalities. He was an active participant in every service, listened to the sermon with an informed mind, and afterwards liked to discuss it and the parts of the service that impressed him. His favourite hymns, which he sang with robust enthusiasm, were those he had sung in the choir at Dartmouth.

As a practising Christian, George VI was continually seeking ways in which he, from his position as head of the nation, could direct all churches and sects toward the common aim of re-establishing the Christian faith as a way of life. A little more than three years ago, when it came to his attention that a new college based on the Christian faith and philosophy of life, a religious project that promised to be a spearhead in the movement for Christian unity, was to be established in England, he offered it premises in Cumberland Lodge in Windsor Great Park and provided the principal with living quarters in Windsor Castle.

Among his many private interests one which attracted little public attention was his long attachment to the order of Freemasonry. From his initiation in 1919 in the Navy Lodge, No. 2612, to which many of his service companions belonged, he took a close interest in the order. He mastered its complicated ritual and studied its dignified ceremonial and symbolism and it was as much due to his ability as his princely rank that he moved up through the higher offices of the Order to head the Masonic Province of Middlesex in 1924, a post he retained until his accession. In 1936 he was installed as Grand Master Mason of the Grand Lodge of Scotland, but when he took the throne a short time afterwards he terminated the holding of all active Masonic offices. However, as King he came more and more to believe in the spiritual and moral principles of the fraternity. In 1937 he accepted the rank of Past Grand Master in the Grand Lodge of England, and periodically he took part in the great Masonic assemblies. In 1939 he installed his brother, the late Duke of Kent, as Grand Master; in 1943 his brother-in-law, the late Lord Harewood; and in 1947 the late Duke of Devonshire.

Although the British people are far more broadminded and tolerant than they were in Victoria's day, when her fun-loving son, the Prince of Wales, was savagely attacked in the press and pulpit because he was involved in a divorce case and a gambling suit, the members of the royal family are still subjected to tiresome attacks by minority groups who would impose their puritan, non-conformist conscience as a standard for royal behaviour. Thus when Elizabeth and Philip, on their official visit to Paris in 1948, followed the continental custom and attended the races on a Sunday afternoon they were berated by blue-noses who thought they should adhere, wherever they were, to the quiet, pious Sabbath of eighteenth century Britain. And in 1949 when Princess Margaret, and, in 1951, Elizabeth and Philip paid courtesy calls on the Pope—in his role as head of the Vatican state—during their visits to Italy their action was roundly condemned by Protestant fanatics, particularly by free churchmen in Scotland, who saw in the visits a sinister attempt to re-establish papal influence in the British reigning house.[1]

These minority protests are trifling pinpricks to the royal family's popularity, but when the influential Church of England asserts its pervasive authority the royal house takes heed. After all, it was an Archbishop of Canterbury, primus of the Church of England, who was one of the behind-the-scenes figures during the abdication of Edward VIII.[2]

As a king, George VI suffered from the peculiar occupational trouble of having no equal, no little group of cronies with whom he could talk over the day's affairs. He could unburden himself only in the privacy of his family, and shop talk can be boring even to royal families.

In the late years of his life he had no real hobbies because he was too nervous to concentrate for long. While he was Duke of

York he took a keen interest in unusual clocks and watches. He became quite an expert at tapestry work (his brother, as Prince of Wales, found solace in crocheting) and some years ago completed a set of a dozen dining room chair covers in *petit point* for Royal Lodge. When the Princesses were growing up he enjoyed taking still and movie pictures of them and their mother, though he remained strictly amateur in technique. When Cecil Beaton photographed the Queen one day against the sun, with the light filtering through the trees behind her, she chuckled and remarked: "How the King will laugh when I tell him you photograph me always directly against the sun. We always have to spend our time running around to face the sun for the King's snapshots." Even the relaxation which most males find in driving their own cars about the countryside was denied him most days of the year because of the demands of royal dignity. However, he occasionally drove himself in his sports-model Daimler or his new, green Ford Zephyr around his Sandringham and Balmoral estates.

George V used to shut himself up in the stamp room at Buckingham Palace every Thursday afternoon and nothing short of a declaration of war or the death of his Prime Minister would budge him from his stamp albums. George VI inherited the tremendous collection, which now numbers close to 250,000 stamps displayed in some 330 large red albums and is valued at around £1,000,000 (although some of its rarities are priceless), but the pressure of his job compelled him to leave its upkeep to Sir John Wilson, who holds the title of Keeper of the Philatelic Collection. The vast collection has now been passed down to Elizabeth II, who has been interested in stamps since childhood.

The one hobby which held George VI's interest even in his last years was his collection of campaign medals of the British Army. In time he built up a collection of important historical interest, and although he left its upkeep to Sir Owen Morshead, the librarian at Windsor Castle, the King became something of an expert on medal design. When he created the George Cross and George Medal the designs adopted were largely his own work. With his expert's eye he once spotted on the beribboned chest of a distinguished general two decorations which seemed to indicate that he had served simultaneously in China and South Africa. Fortunately for the general, he was able to substantiate his claim to both.

Ever since the earliest kings and queens rode out to the chase with their hawks and hounds the royal family has traditionally participated in the national sports and pastimes—sometimes at the expense of state affairs. George VI as a youngster and a young man promised to be the most proficient all-rounder the royal line has yet produced, but the constant demands of his desk work as king gradually forced him to abandon most of his outdoor relaxations. His wife does not like most sports, even as a spectator, except perhaps steeplechasing, and as the King preferred to spend his limited free time with her this was another factor in causing him to give up many of the games in which he excelled.

As a youngster he was a cricketer of some promise and in family cricket games on the royal estates displayed ability as a hard-hitting left-handed batter and a slow left-arm bowler. He retained a spectator-interest in cricket and followed closely the scores of the periodic Test Matches. When Sir Don Bradman and his crack Australian team played the Scottish cricket eleven in 1948 the King asked both teams over to Balmoral for a day's visit and showed them around the Castle. As a young man, the future George VI showed a natural ability for games and with application and time to practice might have become outstanding in many of them. He was a good squash player and once did himself proud during an ice hockey match at a London club. He was a capable swimmer, but though there are pools at "Buck House" and at Royal Lodge he seldom got an opportunity to swim in his late years.

As a polo player he played the game with more courage than skill, but he was good on a horse, an aptitude which he inherited from his father. Determined to master everything he tackled, the King persisted in his riding until he had acquired a seat that was nearly perfect, a gift never granted his elder brother, the Prince of Wales. As youngsters both boys got their early education in horsemanship with the West Norfolk Hounds, and after the First World War, when they rode frequently with the famed Pytchley, the Quorn, the Fernie and the Beaufort packs, the King as Duke of York matched his elder brother's interest in hunting, though he never got the publicity which accompanied the Prince of Wales's ventures in the field.

British royal patronage helped make horse-racing the sport of kings, and George VI was an enthusiastic race-goer and owner in the recent tradition of his grandfather and father. He was neither as spectacularly successful as Edward VII nor as excellent a judge of thoroughbreds as George V, but he had a sound knowledge of breeding and raced a sizeable string of horses in his own royal colours (gold-braided purple and scarlet jacket, black cap). He had his own stud and leased other horses from the National Stud, a patronage which helped promote the British bloodstock industry. The two Princesses used to joke that their father was the Bing Crosby of British racing, but the taunt did not stand up when the year's prizes were counted. George VI's horses never won the Derby, which was a great disappointment to him, but he carried off more top-rank classic races than did his father and in 1942 he headed the list of winning owners. In one three-year period (1946–1949) his horses earned £37,150 in prize money. The King liked to put a small bet on his own horses, never more than £5, but when he won he invariably sent the money to a charity.

A left-hander with a strong service and backhand, the King was once good enough at lawn tennis to reach the top of the second class when he was Duke of York and with more tournament practice might have become a very good player. Partnered by his friend Louis Greig he won the doubles championship of the R.A.F. in 1920 and in 1926 the pair entered as competitors at Wimbledon, the first time a member of the reigning family had entered this top tournament. In their first match they unluckily came up against two veteran Davis Cup players and were beaten in straight sets, but not before the royal entry and his partner had shown some first-class tennis.

The Prince of Wales was the first member of his family to achieve a modest distinction as a golfer but when he was Duke of York the King could generally play his elder brother on even terms. A right-hander at golf, he played down to an eight handicap in the early 1930's, and when he played himself in as Captain of the Royal and Ancient Golf Club of St. Andrews in 1930 by driving the traditional ball from the first tee in full view of the assembled spectators he cracked out a 200-yard drive, a creditable performance on this nerve-wracking occasion. After a bout with a poisoned left hand soon after he came to the throne he had to give up his regular games, and although he maintained a nine-hole course in the park at Windsor, first laid out by Edward VII, he seldom found time to play. The course which Edward VII had constructed at Sandringham when he first took up the game was ploughed up for agricultural use, and the short, nine-hole course which George VI laid out for his own use in the garden of Buckingham Palace just after his coronation is no longer kept in shape. The King, however, remained a member of the Royal and Ancient at St. Andrews until his death. In the summer of 1948, when visiting Edinburgh, he joined the spectators watching the second round of the British Open Championship at the famed Muirfield course and a few days later he returned to play the course himself, playing from a handicap of ten, which showed that he had lost little of his skill.

Throughout his life George VI's great love was shooting, and in his last years it was the one sport he would always find time for. "Even if the British Empire were crumbling all around him, I doubt whether you could get His Majesty to come off the moors," grumbled one of his aides. When Princess Elizabeth gave birth to her second child, Princess Anne, the King was out shooting and it took a Scottish ghillie an hour to find him and tell him the news.

George VI may not have been as good a marksman as his father, who was not surpassed by the most hawk-eyed of his subjects in an era of really good shots, but there were experts who thought him a more stylish shot than George V and in his adult years he certainly ranked among the top half-dozen outstanding small game shots in Britain. The late King got pleasure in all forms of the sport—rough shooting, wildfowling and organized shoots with beaters—but, like his father, he rated the least comfortable, wildfowling, ahead of all the others. Before his legs gave him trouble he actually enjoyed getting up in the middle of the night at Sandringham so he could go out alone and wait for the dawn flight of wild duck and geese winging in to the bleak saltings along the Norfolk coast. Fast and accurate with his guns, he frequently bagged from 30 to 50 wild duck before breakfast-time. An excellent shot with a sporting rifle and a tireless walker before his leg ailment struck him, he used to spend long days climbing and stalking the red deer in the hills around Balmoral, an arduous pursuit that was often rewarded with perhaps only one difficult shot at a stag all day.

Despite his sieges of ill health, George VI adamantly refused to give up his shooting, though he condescended to ride out to the Balmoral shooting butts (dugouts) aboard a "Land Rover," the British equivalent of a jeep, which is about the only vehicle that can negotiate the rough tracks up into the hills.

In his normal year the King was invariably on hand at Balmoral Castle for the "glorious twelfth" of August, opening of the grouse season, and for deer-stalking from mid-September onwards. In the autumn he took part in rough shoots over the estates of friends near London and then visited Sandringham for partridge and early pheasant shooting.

In the days of Edward VII pheasant shooting at Sandringham was a social occasion, in which the King and his guests indulged in wholesale decimation of birds that had been carefully raised in the pheasantry during the year. A day's kill for Edward VII and his party often totalled 2,000 birds.

George VI had no love for this sort of slaughter, although the grouse shoots which he ran at Balmoral during the season were highly organized affairs. Scottish soldiers on guard and household duties around the Castle acted as beaters—for five shillings extra pay per day—to flush the birds and the King took out his friends and visitors in parties of six guns. In a bad season they would bag 1,700 brace and in a good season 2,500 brace and more. The daily bag used to be packed in wooden crates marked with the royal cypher and hustled aboard express trains for delivery to Buckingham Palace, where some of it was consigned to other royal households and the bulk of it put into cold storage, where it lasted throughout the year. This arrangement helped King George cut down on his housekeeping bills, though it did not always suit his guests or the staff and households at the royal palaces, where the game appeared too often—and too aged—on their menus. As one guest complained after visiting Balmoral: "It was grouse, grouse and grouse all the day long."

XII

THE KING WHO WORKED
LIKE A MAN

"EVERYONE likes flattery; and when you come to Royalty you should lay it on with a trowel," Disraeli confided to Matthew Arnold. This may have been the basis of the semi-courtly, semi-familiar relationship between Queen Victoria and her favourite Prime Minister, but "Dizzy's" unctuous approach would not have found favour with George VI.

The late King, who had a sharp eye for character, had an intense dislike for insincerity, artificiality and pomposity in any form, and nothing annoyed him more than to suspect that he had been given an inadequate or inaccurate explanation of an unpleasant situation because of his exalted position. When he was Duke of York he told a man who joined his staff and later became his close friend: "Promise me you will always tell me the truth about things, even if you think I won't like it."

Like his father, George VI was particularly annoyed by un-punctuality in anyone except his wife, whose failing this is, or by a sudden, unexpected change in his plans. His ideas of kingship and much of the routine of his job were founded on precepts and principles handed down from his father, and when they were transgressed or ignored by members of his staff or officials he was capable of swift, blistering reprimands. In public at least he conquered the family legacy of a quick temper which, when he, was a young man, caused him to break up the furniture at Osborne or kick the paint off cabin doors aboard ship, and when he was Duke of York caused him to hurl books at the head of erring members of his staff, but in his private moments of un-repressed anger he could and did swear like a trooper, a faculty inherited from George V. Whenever his wife was present a quiet, "Bertie, Bertie," from her always stopped him.

The King's own service career and upbringing in the marine tradition of his family gave him the rather limited outlook of professional naval men. He regarded himself as essentially a blue-water sailor, and was happiest when he could sit down with his naval pals and swap gossip. He made no claims to intellectual brilliance and tended to shun intellectuals among his acquaintances. His limited circle of friends was drawn mainly from the services and he was always happy to attend military and naval reunions or regimental dinners of the units in which he held honorary rank.[1] When called upon to speak at these occasions he talked extemporaneously, with hardly a trace of stammer, and indulged in light banter and humorous jibes which his listeners appreciated. Once after listening to an effusive speech from a pompous old colonel who presented him with a sword, George VI rose and straightaway cracked, "I always thought that a sword was an obsolete weapon."

Like most seafarers, he was direct-minded, almost to the point of bluntness, which often made him sound ungracious. On a visit to a university centre an architect proudly showed him the model for a great new church. "Mmm," said His Majesty, "it looks more like an air raid shelter." A few years ago the Queen commissioned John Piper, a British painter with an abstract style, to do some water colour and chalk drawings of Windsor Castle. The King took one look at them and dryly remarked, "What bad weather you must have had, Mr. Piper."

Despite a rather forbidding solemnity in appearance, the King's manner in his informal moments was easy and comradely. He displayed an almost boyish enthusiasm for simple pleasures. When he met President Truman aboard the *Augusta* in 1945 the first thing he did was to whip out an autograph book and request the President to sign it. "My wife and daughters would like it," the King engagingly explained.

He took a great delight in practical gags. Once when the royal family were on a seaside holiday he gravely presented Miss Marion Crawford, the Princesses' governess, with a gift, which turned out to be a matchbox stuffed with green sand worms, her pet hate. While showing his personal movie films to his family, a Sunday night treat at Royal Lodge, he used to get a great kick from such simple tricks as running the film backward or stopping the action at a critical moment. On his public visits, he was always tickled when some carefully-planned programme went wrong, or when a visitor, even more nervous at meeting the King than the King was at receiving him, boggled his set speech or muddled his delivery. George VI remembered such incidents for years and recalled them again with a chuckle when he met the man concerned. Philip Mountbatten's schoolboyish pranks made him a firm favourite with the King during Philip's courtship of Elizabeth.

In his public moments, George VI's jocularity was apt to be obvious rather than original. When he went to Oxford in 1946 to open an extension to the famed Bodleian Library, soon after the successful "Britain Can Make It" exhibition, the silver key with which he was about to open the door broke in two in his hand. "Dear me," commented the King, "it looks as if Britain can break it, too." When the late, great comedian Sid Field was presented to him after a London performance of "Harvey," the King made the inevitable joke about the imaginary rabbit: "Where is he?" During the South African tour, when his ubiquitous personal detectives temporarily dropped out of sight on a walk in the Natal National Park, the King cracked, "We've lost the Gestapo!"

In private George VI enjoyed locker-room stories, of which he remembered a great many, and at private parties he generally manœuvred his male friends into a corner to swap ribaldries. Occasionally his own humour took on a ribald note. According to one story which went the rounds of the R.A.F. early in the Battle of Britain days the King noted with surprise when reviewing a crack squadron of fighter pilots that the airmen had not done up the top button of their R.A.F. tunics. It was explained to him that this was the current R.A.F. fashion to distinguish the battle-blooded day fighter pilots from the beginners. Moving down the line, the King suddenly spotted one airman who had inadvertently left a button open on his trouser fly. "I suppose that indicates that he's a night fighter," was His Majesty's comment.

He diligently learned all the verses of "Doin' What Comes Natur'lly" from "Annie Get Your Gun," and at family dinner parties, when he was in high spirits, he would break out and sing them, sometimes adding a few ribald touches of his own—despite the efforts of his wife to hush him up if there were guests present.

From his father George VI inherited the rare royal gift of making each person presented to him feel that he was the one man the King wished to meet. Often highly-strung and nervous at meeting new people, he could not radiate his father's affable geniality, but he was genuinely interested in hearing about other people's problems and he succeeded in drawing all sorts of different people to him by his obvious sincerity.

When Jamaica's William Bustamante called at Buckingham Palace in 1948 court observers predicted a somewhat stormy exchange between the King and this wild man of West Indian politics, but when Bustamante emerged from the interview he announced, with his usual histrionics: "What transpired in conversation between my King and me is sacred, for ever." During his South African tour the King engaged in a long conversation with a native Basuto chief. At the end of their talk the chief remarked: "When a South African comes to talk with me it's a white man talking to a black. When you talk to me it's a man talking to a man." After George VI died the Begum Liaquat Ali Khan, widow of the assassinated Pakistani statesman, told of her first meeting with the King. "With great temerity I remarked to His Majesty the first time I met him that he certainly belied my storybook idea of a king," she reported, "for talking to him I felt I was talking to a man rather than a king. With a slight smile he said: 'Have no fear. That is the greatest compliment you could have paid me and I thank you!'"

While insistent on the punctilious observance of the royal prerogatives that go with his high office, the King was thoughtful of the rights of others and frequently went out of his way to make certain they were respected. When W. E. Tucker, a London orthopædic and manipulative surgeon, was called to Buckingham Palace in 1948 to treat Princess Margaret for fibrositis of the neck the King learned that these visits cut into the specialist's busy day, already crowded with his own patients and those of an absent colleague. On the King's instructions the Palace visits were cancelled and thereafter Margaret took her turn with other patients at Tucker's Grosvenor Square clinic. When the late Mackenzie King, then Canadian Prime Minister, came to London in 1948 for a Dominion conference he was stricken ill on arrival and confined to his rooms at the Dorchester Hotel. Knowing that Mackenzie King had counted on a session with him, the King waved protocol aside, called on him at his hotel and added a homey touch by having tea brought in for the two of them.

Harry Butcher, General Eisenhower's wartime Man Friday, recounted an amusing story which highlighted this facet of the King's character. When Eisenhower had his first audience with the King in 1942 His Majesty, with great glee, told him of an incident which had occurred at Windsor Castle some six weeks previously. It seems that Lord Wigram, the King's old adviser and then Lieutenant-Governor of the Castle, asked permission to show two high-ranking U.S. officers around the Castle grounds on a certain Sunday afternoon. The Castle was then closed to visitors, but the King and his wife volunteered to remain indoors in their own quarters so as to give Lord Wigram a free hand with his guests. However, when that Sunday came it was such a fine afternoon that Their Majesties forgot their promise and wandered out into the garden to relax. They were sitting enjoying the sunshine when suddenly they heard Lord Wigram's voice conducting his visitors along the garden. Mindful of their promise and fearful that their presence, if discovered, would embarrass Lord Wigram and cause him to retreat with his guests, the King and Queen stooped down behind a hedge and quickly made their undignified exit from the garden by crawling on their hands and knees through a low hole in the garden wall. Eisenhower capped the King's story by revealing that the two American officers were General Mark Clark and himself!

Buckingham Palace, around which the monarchy revolves, has a triple function: it is the centre of court ceremonial, the headquarters of the sovereign's public and constitutional duties, and the London home of the royal family. Thus, like the business executive who lives in a penthouse atop his office, George VI lived "on the job" and could never entirely escape the atmosphere of duty.

To cope with his arduous labours, the late King attempted to keep his London daily routine as regular and unvarying as possible. When his health began to decline his public functions were somewhat curtailed, but right up to the day before his lung operation in 1951 he still insisted on putting in a ten-hour working day. Even when faced with the necessity for an operation his first concern was for his work. According to Clement Attlee, then his Prime Minister, the King's attitude was: "It's a nuisance. shall be off duty for a week or so."

His normal day began at 8 a.m. with his only indulgence, a morning cup of tea in bed, a black Indian blend brought in to him by Thomas Lawrence Jerram, his valet for some 24 years, or by James Macdonald, his assistant valet. The King's bedroom was a large, airy room at the end of the north wing of "Buck House," overlooking the Palace garden at an angle. A connecting dressing room, in which his wardrobe was kept, separated his suite from his wife's apartments. While drinking his tea, the King used to listen attentively to the eight o'clock news bulletins on the B.B.C. Afterwards he consulted with the valet on duty about the clothes required for the day's engagements, which often necessitated three or four changes of clothes.

George VI was fastidious about his clothes and prided himself on being one of the best-dressed men in his kingdom. His extensive wardrobe, an accumulation of more than 500 suits and uniforms, was kept in shape for him by Richard Howlett, a qualified tailor who carried the title of Superintendent of the King's Wardrobe. The King liked to wear uniforms, particularly naval rig, because they made him look a taller, more imposing figure than he really was. Slightly-built and somewhat stoop-shouldered, he was just average height (five feet eight inches) and only came up to the chins of many of his "Beefeaters." He bought about twelve new suits each year, preferring buff and grey lounge suits, from his London tailor, Benson & Clegg, unless he was going abroad on tour, when he usually bought an extra dozen. For shooting in Scotland he wore a specially-woven tweed material, a neutral colour that blended into the background of the moors. For country wear his taste generally ran to tweeds, often in such extreme checks that they would have turned heads even on Broadway. His shirts were made for him by Izod, a London firm of shirtmakers. The King's shoes, which invariably turned up at the toes, were usually the old-fashioned "blacking leather" type which had to be polished with liquid blacking and rubbed vigorously with a bone in order to give them their authentic lustre. On more informal moments, however, he wore suede shoes.

The King liked to shave himself every morning—using a tricky Wilkinson seven-day razor—although he had one of his

187

valets clean and strop the blades for him each day. Once a fortnight the court hairdresser called at the Palace to trim his thick,
wavy hair. If he had to go out on a public appearance he always
put on a heavy tan make-up to hide his naturally pallid complexion.

Before his breakfast, brought in on a tray to his bedroom at
8.15 precisely, a Palace page used to bring in the first of the day's
mail, usually letters marked "Personal to H.M. The King,"
which George insisted on opening himself. While he was eating
breakfast, the King's piper paraded below his window in full
Highland dress and played the bagpipes, a custom started by
Victoria's German-born consort, who actually enjoyed the skirl
of the pipes at any time of day.

Soon after nine each morning the King, followed by a blue-
coated servant, known as the Page of the Presence, who stands
on duty outside whichever room the sovereign occupies, entered
his office-study and began his day's work. His first chore was to
work his way conscientiously through the London morning
papers. He read *The Times* religiously from cover to cover and if
Parliament was sitting paid particular attention to the paper's
concise summary of the previous day's debates, and then scanned
all the others, including the *Daily Worker*, to see if his secretaries had marked articles for his special attention. All the national
newspapers, including such influential provincial papers as the
Manchester Guardian and the *Yorkshire Post*, are delivered to the
Palace, and although the King paid little attention to the tabloids
among them he never seemed to overlook anything of importance
in them. He kept a practised eye out for photographs of the royal
family, which he insisted on inspecting before publication. He
was most particular about photographs of himself, and adamantly
refused to be photographed wearing the half-lens glasses which
he used for reading.

George VI's first session each day was generally with his
principal private secretary, the Right Honourable Sir Alan
Lascelles, K.C.B., K.C.V.O., C.M.G., M.C., a tall, polished
aristocrat who has been 32 years in royal service and served as
assistant secretary to Edward VIII when he was Prince of Wales.
Sir Alan, whom the King called "Tommy," was one of the few
men with whom George VI was on intimate terms. They were
cousins by marriage: Sir Alan's cousin, the then Lord Lascelles,
married the Princess Royal, the King's sister.

After the principal secretary had received his instructions for the day, one of the two assistant secretaries then came in to deal with the day's mail, a formidable chore that takes up the full time of several underlings in the Palace secretariat. To most of the letters from personal friends the King liked to dictate a short answer which was typed out for him to sign later, but for most of the communications addressed to him he was able to indicate by a scribbled note or a few words to a secretary the answer to be drafted in his name.

The mail disposed of, another secretary would then bring in the King's "boxes," which His Majesty would open with the solid gold-barrelled Bramah key he kept on his pocket watch chain. These leather-covered, steel-lined dispatch cases, the red leather ones containing the most urgent state papers and the brown and black-covered ones the less important documents, are the bane of a monarch's life and from them there is no escape. During the war years aides even hammered on George VI's bathroom door when urgent "boxes" arrived. With the aid of the secretary on duty, the King each morning sorted out the documents submitted to him. The formal instruments requiring the sovereign's signature have a history of centuries behind them and are generally couched in the archaic language of the old courts. George VI, who insisted on the most punctilious observance of the minutiæ of the old forms, knew even better than his secretaries and Ministers how they should be expressed and frequently corrected the drafts submitted to him. Urgent documents requiring the King's signature were kept out for immediate attention each morning. He also made it a point to read all Cabinet minutes, cables and confidential messages from his ambassadors abroad within an hour or two of their arrival. The more lengthy reports he set aside for reading later in the day and in the evening. Business-like in his methods, he disliked to see work accumulate on his desk and he frequently returned to his office in the evening to work until his desk was clear or took his papers to bed to read.[2] Not a quick reader, he none the less refused to scan any reports. Meticulously minded, he slowly worked his way through a minimum of 30 to 40 state papers a day, some of them statistic-crammed Government reports that required an hour and more to read. When Parliament was in session he also got a daily summary of its proceedings, prepared for him by a member of the

Commons who bears the honorary title of Vice-Chamberlain of the Household, and at some time during the day the King also squeezed in time to read Hansard, the verbatim official account of each day's parliamentary proceedings. George VI insisted on being on the distribution list for most of the official memos circulated in Whitehall and his secretaries were quick to protest if "Buck House" was overlooked.

The King liked to be completely informed, and was gleeful if he could trip up his Ministers or secretaries by knowing more facts than they did. Like his mother, from whom he inherited his squirrel-like ability to store up facts, he had a remarkable memory. When the late Gil Winant presented his credentials as American Ambassador in February, 1941 he was surprised to find that the King, whom Winant had once met when he was head of the International Labour Office, immediately picked up the conversation where they had left off more than two years before.

Each day the King was in London the period between 11 a.m. and 1 p.m. was set aside for audiences. Scheduled to last a strict 15 to 20 minutes, the audiences took place in his private audience chamber on the first floor of the Palace and if the visitor was of proper rank the King used to ask him to sit and talk in a green armchair at the fireside in winter or at the open window overlooking the garden in summer. If the guest was an old acquaintance or proved particularly interesting the audience might stretch to an hour, or as long as the timetable permitted, and if the caller was a close friend he might be asked to remain for luncheon. Even after thousands of audiences George VI felt completely at ease with only very few people, however. He was given an *aide-memoire* with details of his visitor's career and interests before each interview, but unless he knew his caller well he was nervy and on edge during these talks and stumbled jerkily in an effort to keep conversation going.

Sometimes the question of an audience with George VI assumed political importance. When the Argentine's late Senora Peron was gallivanting around Europe in 1947 she let it be known that if she visited London she expected to meet the King and be received by the royal family. The King, who abhorred unnecessary ostentation, made it clear that he did not propose to receive her, whatever His Majesty's Foreign Office advised, and relations between Argentina and Great Britain have been strained ever since.

The late King was a stickler for fixed meal times, and lunch was always served promptly at 1 o'clock. At lunch, most often a simple, buffet-style meal at which the King and his family and guests helped themselves from hotplates on the sideboards, the King usually met his wife and Princess Margaret for the first time in the day. Prior to his leg ailment the early afternoon was usually set aside for public engagements, and though these were curtailed after his operation in 1949, until his lung operation he still accepted enough outside engagements—from public organizations anxious for his presence and patronage—to cut heavily into his rigorous time-table.[3]

If not called elsewhere in the afternoon the King used to settle down in his office to wade through the longer state papers or work on his speeches. Most of his speeches he wrote himself, usually from rough drafts submitted by his secretaries. He spent considerable time polishing and practising these and often called his wife in to hear him rehearse. He liked to prepare himself far in advance for the ordeal of a public occasion. For a full two weeks prior to the annual Trooping the Colour ceremony his secretaries were never surprised when they found him at his desk wearing his heavy Guards bearskin headgear. He wore it for half an hour each morning for a fortnight to accustom himself "just so he won't feel top-heavy on the day," his aides once explained.

Like almost all his subjects in Britain, the King stopped work at 4 p.m. for his afternoon cup of tea. This was a family gathering. Princess Margaret usually joined her mother and father and about twice each week Princess Elizabeth came over from Clarence House. Between tea time and dinner the King again returned to his office. He generally saw one of his secretaries again, signed his personal mail and then, unless he had to have a late-afternoon conference with his Prime Minister or a member of the Cabinet, devoted himself to his private business affairs, his investments, the accounts of the Privy Purse or the management of the royal estates, farms and stud. Dinner, for which His Majesty changed into a dinner jacket even if dining *en famille*, was always punctually at 8 p.m. The King preferred to keep this a family affair, but twice each week he or his wife or their daughters invited guests to join them.

After dinner, if his daily volume of paper work had mounted, George VI returned to his study and worked until bedtime, which was seldom before 11 p.m. His last chore of the day was to make a brief notation in his diary, a habit he continued, unbroken, since he began keeping a diary during his tour of Australia in 1927, in which he recorded his travels, lists of people he met and any facts or snatches of information likely to prove of importance.

The strenuous South African tour, added to the strain and anxiety over the long years of the war, seriously undermined George VI's health. For several months in the autumn of 1948 he suffered increasing pain in his right leg and foot, but he blamed it on too much walking and standing and resolutely tried to carry on his public duties without betraying a sign of his trouble. He was determined not to distract public interest from the expected happy event in the royal family, the birth of Princess Elizabeth's first baby, and not until ten days before the birth of her son on November 14 did he consult any of the Palace doctors.

The flood of congratulations on the royal birth had hardly ceased before the King's subjects were shocked to learn that he was suffering from an obstruction to the circulation through the arteries of his legs (both legs were involved, the right more seriously than the left), a serious ailment which necessitated complete rest and the cancellation of all public engagements for some months. The royal tour of Australia and New Zealand, which the King, the Queen and Princess Margaret were to have made in the first half of 1949, had to be indefinitely postponed.

The first medical bulletins from the King's doctors were deliberately vague because the nature of the King's ailment was little known and the reference to "risk to a limb" in one bulletin immediately exaggerated his illness in the public mind. In time it became known that George VI was suffering from Buerger's disease (so called because it was first fully described in 1908 by Dr. Leo Buerger, a Viennese-born surgeon who practised in New York). Other, more sinister, names for it are thromboangiitis obliterans and presenile gangrene. In non-technical terms, what had happened was that the wall of the artery carrying the blood to the King's right leg had gradually narrowed, starving the foot

33. *Queen Victoria, in 1900, with four little Yorks: Prince Albert (the late King), seated; Princess Mary (Princess Royal); Prince Edward (Duke of Windsor), centre; Prince Henry (Duke of Gloucester), on the old Queen's lap*

34. *The future George V and Queen Mary, at Balmoral, with their six children: from right to left, Prince Albert, Prince Edward, Prince George (Duke of Kent), the infant Prince John, Prince Henry, seated, and Princess Mary*

35. *Three monarchs: George V with (left) the Prince of Wales, later Edward VIII, and Prince Albert, later King George VI*

and leg of blood. If the condition is not relieved the tissues die for lack of oxygen, gangrene sets in, and the affected leg has to be amputated.

The King's doctors, believing that they had caught the disease at an early stage, prescribed complete rest and electric treatment to stimulate circulation and the King had to spend hours sitting in an electrically-heated bath or lying in bed resting the limb, often in great pain. However, he insisted on continuing his routine office work and even while in bed dealt with the masses of state papers that make up the business of the monarchy and received important visitors as usual.

Throughout that winter the anxiety of his doctors increased as the ailment failed to respond to treatment. The King doggedly continued to work every day and on March 1, after a quiet period at Sandringham, insisted on going through with an investiture, but a few days later he yielded to the advice of his doctors that an operation would be necessary to give him relief from pain. On March 12 at Buckingham Palace a delicate operation, known as a lumbar sympathectomy, was performed by one of the world's experts on the surgery of blood vessels, Professor James R. Learmonth, at one time on the staff of the Mayo Clinic, whom the King later knighted for his services. The operation involved the cutting of some of the sympathetic nerves, on the right side of the back, near the spine, which control the contraction of the leg arteries. As an operation it was a complete success, but the King was warned that it was only a palliative, not a cure, for his disease. The operation which had saved his right leg from amputation could not be repeated and none of his medical men could assure him that the disease would not progress in the artery first affected or attack other arteries, including the coronary arteries which supply the muscles of the heart with arterial blood. Although the findings of the King's doctors remain professional secrets, it is now thought likely that at this time they made the tragic discovery that all his arteries were in fact hardening beyond his years, the condition which led to his death two years and eleven months later.

Whatever George VI thought privately about this sentence of suspended doom, his public behaviour indicated that he considered that the conscientious performance of his kingly duties required him to ignore it. Although he consented to use a wheel chair

13 193

during a brief period of convalescence, his operation enabled him to get around again almost as well as ever. He attended assiduously to the heavy routine of his desk work and by the autumn of 1949 he resumed the normal round of his outward life.

Although his health seemed to be restored, those closest to the King began to note the signs of strain in his face and bearing. His hair, formerly thick and brown, began to show streaks of silver and his step lost something of its old vigour, although he would still walk for an hour or more in Windsor Great Park whenever he could get out to Royal Lodge. And though the public detected no sign of it the strain under which he was labouring sometimes made him forget his royal manners when dealing with officialdom. When he turned up with his family for a ceremonial opening tour of the great Festival of Britain he shook hands perfunctorily with Gerald Barry, who welcomed him in the capacity of director of the exhibition, and snapped, "Let's get this over with!"

The King's consistent refusal to ease up in his job and his unwillingness to convalesce for an adequate time after his leg operation took toll of his stamina and left him an easy prey to other ailments. Like his father and grandfather, he had always been prone to colds and bronchial complaints and in May, 1951, when he insisted on attending the installation service of the Order of the Bath at Westminster Abbey—where his haggard, ill-looking features shocked those who saw him close up and alarmed those who saw his picture in the newspapers—it was discovered that he had gone through the ceremony with a temperature of 103 degrees. He was confined to "Buck House" with what was described as a mild attack of influenza, but a week later his doctors noted a small inflamed patch on the left lung. This subsided within a fortnight, but in view of the attacks of catarrhal infection he had suffered during the year his doctors advised a prolonged convalescence.

The King, who was not what doctors would call an ideal patient, convinced himself that grouse shooting on the moors around Balmoral would be the best tonic for his health and early in August he and his family departed for their annual Scottish holiday. It was his wife who first suspected that George VI was suffering from something more serious than catarrhal inflammation. Although his face had browned from exposure on the moors, he continued to lose weight despite the easy regime of his holiday and at her insistence he requested two London specialists to visit Balmoral and give him another examination. They carried out a preliminary examination at the Castle, and, in turn, requested the King to return to London for X-rays and further examination, which he did on September 8. Back again at Balmoral, the King made light of his new ailment. To one of his shooting companions he remarked, jocularly, "Now they say there's something wrong with me blowers!"

On September 18, after a conclave of nine eminent medical men including five outside specialists called in to supplement the royal family's regular physicians and surgeons—the King was told the grave news. The X-ray and bronchoscope examinations had revealed a malignant growth on the bronchus of the left lung and a major operation, technically known as a pneumonectomy, to remove the lung was immediately necessary to prevent the infected tissues from spreading. The King told his wife the bad news himself and then informed his aged mother.

That same evening Prime Minister Attlee called by previous arrangement to give His Majesty a review of his Government's activities during the King's absence at Balmoral. When Attlee neared the end of his survey George VI broke in and said that he wished to address the Prime Minister not as the sovereign but more as the father of Princess Elizabeth. The King told Attlee that his doctors had informed him that he must undergo a very critical operation and that even if he survived it, which was risky because of the shock to his already-weakened system, the doctors could not then assure him that he had long to live. Although his daughter was competent and learning fast the job of kingship, the King said, if he were to die and be succeeded by her he felt it would be better for her sake if she could count on a strong, stable Government at the helm to make up for her lack of experience at the outset of her reign. Whether that Government was Labour or Conservative was not his concern, the King went on, but he wished that the Prime Minister would consider holding a new election so that whichever party came to power it would govern with a more substantial majority than the slim margin of six seats which Labour then held. Attlee replied that he had called that evening specifically to discuss with the King the same problem because he, too, had come to the conclusion that it was time the country voted again. And so then and there it was agreed to dissolve Parliament and hold a general election, the date of which was later fixed for October 25.

The operation, the King's fifth (the others were an appendectomy, an operation for duodenal ulcers, an operation on a blood-poisoned hand and his lumbar sympathectomy), was performed on the morning of Sunday, September 23, in the rococo Buhl Room of Buckingham Palace, which is periodically converted into an operating theatre whenever required by a member of the royal family. It was performed by Clement Price Thomas, one of Britain's foremost chest surgeons and an expert in the surgical treatment of cancer and tuberculosis. The King was on the operating table for just under two hours. The malignant growth proved to be bronchial carcinoma, a fast-spreading type of lung cancer.[4] The entire left lung was safely removed, but during the operation the surgeons saw what they had feared most—that the King's other lung was already affected. The spread of the cancer meant that George VI's life expectation could be only two years at the most and might be only a few months.

Although he lost 21 pounds in all during his ordeal, the King's apparent rapid recovery amazed his doctors, his family and his friends alike. Those who were closest to him confessed that his comeback was a miracle. Most patients after a lung resection require special deep-breathing exercises to strengthen their sound lung for the additional burden placed upon it, but here His Majesty had an advantage in that he had never really ceased doing the rigorous breathing exercises he had learned years before in his battle to overcome his speech defect.

Each day as he gained strength he became more persistent that he should be back at work. A Council of State,[5] composed of the Queen, Princess Elizabeth, Princess Margaret, the Duke of Gloucester and the Princess Royal, was set up to relieve him of some of the royal paper work and he allowed his wife to deputize for him in receiving ambassadors and other important callers, but there were some functions the King doggedly refused to delegate. On the fourth day after his operation he signed the warrant appointing the Council of State and on October 5, twelve days after his operation, he sat propped up in bed and signed the royal proclamation dissolving Parliament while three Privy Councillors, as required by law, witnessed his act from the corridor outside his open bedroom door. He sat up late to hear the results of

Britain's general election and insisted on personally receiving the outgoing Ministers of Attlee's Cabinet and greeting the incoming Ministers of Churchill's Cabinet.

By mid-November George VI was strong enough to attend a Palace birthday party for his grandson, Prince Charles, and on the tenth week after his operation he was allowed to make his first outing, a stay at Royal Lodge. Apart from his desire to be back at work, the King's main grumble while confined to bed was that he had missed the best shooting of the year and as soon as he was well enough to be allowed outside he startled his doctors by proposing to go to Sandringham for shooting and the traditional Christmas gathering. "You have had your fun," he told his doctors, "now I will have mine." On December 22 the King and Queen, accompanied by Princess Elizabeth and Princess Margaret, left London for what proved to be their last Christmas at Sandringham and later the other members of the royal family, except Queen Mary, joined them to make the largest gathering of the family since the war's end.

That George VI knew he had not long to live there is no doubt. Faced with the terrible realization that he was suffering from two progressive diseases, either of which might prove fatal and from neither of which was recovery possible, he was under a double sentence of death, but it was characteristic of the grit and will-power with which he had fought ill-health throughout his life that he deliberately chose to live out his days as normally as possible. Not even to his closest friends and intimates in the family circle did he reveal that his life hung by a thread, and it was only occasionally, in off-hand remarks, that he hinted that he might be approaching his journey's end. He insisted on making his traditional Christmas broadcast to his people, though he consented to record the message, a painful, agonizing ordeal that required two days of recording, a phrase or so at a time, because of the paralysis of one of his vocal cords which persisted since his operation. When one of his staff suggested that he let his wife or Princess Elizabeth read his message, the King replied: "My daughter may have her opportunity next Christmas. I want to speak to my people myself." The resulting six-minute broadcast, in which the King's voice sounded harsh and throaty, alarmed rather than reassured his subjects about the state of his health. At Sandringham, when one of his local friends met the King,

197

hatless and coatless, out walking he said to His Majesty: "Sir, you should take care of yourself and rest more." The King smiled and replied, "I might not have so long to live and I want to get out while I can."

The royal Christmas party broke up during the first week of January, but the King and Queen remained at Sandringham so that he could shoot for a few weeks longer. It was what the locals called "King's weather," cold, dry and bright, the conditions he enjoyed best for shooting, and the King savoured to the full the simple pleasures of the country squire. He wore a new electrically-heated waistcoat and heated boots, operated by batteries, used specially-shortened cartridges to reduce the recoil and spare his weakened frame the repeated kick of his shotguns, and rode between shoots in a "Land Rover" or estate wagon, but otherwise refused to coddle himself. He was out with his guns almost every day and remained out while the light lasted. He even proposed going out into the wet marshes after ducks, but his doctors adamantly ruled against this. Life at Sandringham agreed with him, however, and by the end of January he had regained eight of his lost pounds, a recovery which his doctors regarded as the best indication of his progress.

On January 28 the King and his wife returned to London to join in the family send-off for Princess Elizabeth and the Duke of Edinburgh, who had taken on the royal tour of Australia and New Zealand which George VI and his Queen had long hoped to make, and on the last day of January the King, erect and hatless in the razor-sharp wind, stood on the apron at London airport and waved a cheery farewell to his eldest daughter and her husband. He did not know that death stood beside him, nor could Elizabeth know that six days later she would be flying back from Kenya as Queen in her own right.

Newsreels and news-photos taken that day starkly revealed the King's haggard features, his face lined and drawn from long-continued suffering, but to his subjects the royal tour itself was reassuring. It was reasoned that Princess Elizabeth would never have undertaken so long a trip unless her father was well on the road to recovery. However, one member of her entourage, more prescient than the others, was so certain that George VI would not live until Elizabeth's planned return in July, 1952 that he packed the royal standard in her luggage, ready to be flown the moment she became Queen.

The day after their send-off for Elizabeth and Philip the King, accompanied by his wife and Princess Margaret and a small household staff, left his capital for the last time and returned to Sandringham. Right to the last his sense of duty was over-riding, however. The previous day he had fulfilled eight engagements, including a Privy Council meeting and an investiture, his heaviest schedule since his lung operation. And outwardly, at least, he remained cheerfully optimistic about his health. When Prime Minister Churchill had called on him late that same afternoon for their customary chat the King told him that five of his doctors had examined him that day and pronounced themselves satisfied with his condition. With a chuckle, the King said he'd told his doctors that he was in better health than they and would probably outlive the lot of them.

Tuesday, February 5, was for George VI, as Mr. Churchill later described it, "a happy day of sunshine and sport," just the sort of day the King would have chosen had he known it was to be his last. With Lord Fermoy, an Irish peer who was his friend and next-door neighbour, and a party of five guns the King drove out to the Flitcham beat on the royal estate before 10 in the morning. For six hours, stopping only for a picnic lunch in the local village hall, the King and his guests tramped across the bare, frost-hardened fields that sparkled in the wintry sunshine. "The King was happy and looked as well as he had since his illness," said Lord Fermoy later. "He was a splendid shot, and his illness had not meant the loss of any of his skill." During the shoot the King bagged nine hares and then brought down a high pigeon, by no means an easy bird, perfectly cleanly with a remarkable 100-foot wing shot. At the end of the day, pulling off his boots, the King said contentedly to his companions: "Well, it's been a very good day's sport, gentlemen. I will expect you here at 9 o'clock on Thursday." The King arranged to go out on a shoot on his own on Wednesday.

Queen Elizabeth and Princess Margaret, who had spent the afternoon cruising on the nearby Norfolk Broads, joined the King for a family dinner and a quiet, fireside evening. Twice during the evening the King went out to the kennels to look at his golden retriever, Roddy, who had got a thorn in his paw, and then after a last walk in the grounds he loved he sat and listened to Margaret playing the piano for half an hour, tuned in to the 10 o'clock news bulletin to hear the latest news of Princess Elizabeth's tour and went up to bed. Footman Daniel Long, who took the King a cup of cocoa at 11 o'clock, found him propped up in bed reading a sportsman's magazine. The King wished his servant a cheerful goodnight.

At 7.30 the next morning assistant valet James Macdonald began to run the King's bath and then went in to the King's bedroom to wake his master with his usual early morning cup of tea. Expertly balancing the tea tray, Macdonald drew back the window curtains, but the King, ordinarily a light sleeper, did not stir. Moving closer to the bed, Macdonald made the tragic discovery that was to send a wave of sorrow surging round the world. He immediately informed an officer of the King's household and a lady-in-waiting was quickly sent to waken Queen Elizabeth and Princess Margaret. The royal family's local doctor, Dr. James Ansell, Apothecary-in-Ordinary to the King, was hurriedly summoned to Sandringham and confirmed that George VI had been dead for some hours, probably since soon after midnight. The cause of his death: coronary thrombosis. As he slept the blood had slowed and thickened in one of his hardened and narrowed coronary arteries until a large clot stopped his valiant heart. Death had come to the King as a quick and silent visitor. There had not been enough pain to waken him.

So King George VI died, as he had lived, quietly, without fuss, in the bosom of his family.

XIII

APPRENTICE SOVEREIGN

ALTHOUGH she was thrust up to the throne in tragic circumstances years sooner than she had expected, Queen Elizabeth II came to her job better prepared for her high responsibilities, more knowledgeable about world events, and better versed in the affairs and problems of her people than any sovereign in modern times. The only monarch in the last nine reigns at least who had a comparable background and training on his approach to the throne was Edward VIII, but even his much travelled apprenticeship as Prince of Wales did not always result in serious preparation for the job that was to be briefly his.

In contrast to Victoria, a demure little German princess who stepped out of a life circumscribed by a jealous and domineering mother to become Queen at the age of 18 (and regally demand the right to have a private bedroom for the first time in her life), Elizabeth II began her careful schooling for the throne at the age of ten and for the next 15 years served an apprenticeship for sovereignty, a preparation for the role she would one day be called upon to play.

As Elizabeth's upbringing was directed toward fitting her for service to the country as its future Queen, so her education was increasingly planned to reveal to her, and prepare her for, the great burden of her office. Overlapping this formal preparation was the most valuable training of all, the friendly guidance of her father. The court intrigues and jockeying for position around the throne which clouded the youth of Victoria and marred the relationship between almost every sovereign and heir back through the long history of the British monarchy were completely absent from Elizabeth's apprenticeship. Instead, between the late King and Elizabeth there was a rare bond of deep understanding and love such as never existed before between a sovereign and his

heir. On long walks and rides at Windsor George VI increasingly took his elder daughter into his confidence. From the time
she came constitutionally, though not legally, of age at 18 she
was initiated into the inner workings of the monarchy, introduced to the notables of British and Commonwealth public life
and encouraged to take her place in official functions as the
heiress presumptive to the throne.[1] At the King's request,
Parliament amended the Regency Act of 1937 to enable Elizabeth
to serve as one of the Counsellors of State after her eighteenth
birthday, the first step in her approach to queenship, and she
twice served on the Council when her father went overseas to
visit his troops in the last year of the Second World War. At
Buckingham Palace state dinners she took her place as an adult
alongside Cabinet Ministers and Commonwealth and foreign
statesmen. From them she learned, but she also astounded them
with her grasp of affairs. Queen Victoria kept her eldest son, the
Prince of Wales, in leading strings and it was not until he was in
his fifty-first year that he was allowed to see copies of the Prime
Minister's reports on Cabinet meetings. George VI allowed his
eldest daughter to read many of the secret state papers while she
was still in her teens. Cabinet minutes remained confidential
between the King and his Government, but after her marriage
Elizabeth was permitted to see copies of the confidential telegrams and messages passing in and out of the Foreign Office in
order to give her an insight into international affairs.

When Princess Elizabeth was married her father gave orders
that she be spared from as many royal chores as possible, and for
a time she was able to devote most of each day to her domestic
life, her husband and her new family, but the precipitate decline
of George VI's health from late 1948 onwards compelled her to
take on more and more of her father's public appearances, acting
as his deputy. George VI always marvelled at her poise and
apparent confidence on these ceremonial occasions. "I don't know
how they do it," he once said as he watched his two daughters
perform in public. "We were always so terribly shy and self-
conscious as children." When Elizabeth led his Brigade of Guards
back to "Buck House" after brilliantly deputizing for him at the
Trooping the Colour ceremony in the summer of 1951 he was the
proudest father in the land. By acting as her father's stand-in
on such ceremonial occasions Elizabeth was as well prepared for

the exacting role of the monarch on parade as any heir to the throne.

Although the record of her travels abroad is only a small fraction of the mileage logged by Edward VIII as Prince of Wales, Elizabeth has used every opportunity on her foreign visits to acquire the background and knowledge she would need in her job. Confined to the British Isles during the Second World War, she made up for her stay-at-home years in a hurry and between 1947 and her accession to the throne crowded in her visits to South Africa, France, Italy, Greece, Canada, the United States and East Africa.

The final, and in many ways the most important, step in Elizabeth's preparation for the throne was her union with Philip, the Duke of Edinburgh. A love match of the kind often denied to royalty, the marriage gave young Elizabeth a new confidence and revealed to her a whole new world, the existence of which she could only glimpse from behind the walls of her childhood royal homes.

The future Queen Victoria was 12 years of age when a carefully explained history lesson revealed to her that she would one day be sovereign. "I will be good," were her recorded words when her child's mind first grasped the responsibilities that lay ahead of her. There was no similar dedication when young Princess Elizabeth became aware of her inescapable fate (she was only nine years and nine months when her beloved grandfather died, leaving her second in line to the throne, and only 11 months older when the abdication of her Uncle David made her heiress presumptive) but in her brief quarter century of life to date she has already demonstrated those qualities that proclaim her a good Queen and a gracious Queen—and a glamorous one.

During her 15-year apprenticeship for sovereignty Elizabeth as Princess proved that she possessed most of the virtues and a good many of the attributes that go to make a successful sovereign in the modern British conception of the monarchy.

To those who shape their behaviour on the royal pattern the most important function of the sovereign is to provide a model of quiet and contented domesticity in the first family of the land. Through her own upbringing the new Queen is strongly imbued with the sense of family, and in her early marriage to the man of her choice, her creation of a family of her own before the demands of her job claimed all her time, her obvious pride in her husband, in motherhood and in a happy home, she has given proof to her subjects that she intends to follow the example of her father and grandfather, who, more than any of their predecessors, made the family unit the natural, homely setting for the monarchy.

"Be ye well assured," said Elizabeth I when she pledged herself to her people's service, "I will stand your good Queen." Some 390 years later the future Elizabeth II stepped to a microphone in South Africa on her twenty-first birthday and in her clear, girlish voice made her solemn pledge to her father's subjects. "I declare before you all," she said, "that my whole life, whether it be long or short, shall be devoted to your service and the service of our great imperial family to which we all belong. . . ." Though the words were not her own, this simply-spoken dedication to a life of service came from her heart. (When her father's private secretary, who wrote the speech, asked her what she thought of the first draft she said, "It has made me cry.") Brought up in the lofty, rigid concept of service which George VI made his ideal, the new Queen has inherited her father's unflagging devotion to the discipline, the duties and the details of the monarch's job. When she was suddenly called upon to enter her life of service sooner than she had expected on the death of her father she met without complaint or question the demands of her new position even at a time of great personal and family grief.

A year or two ago a shrewd "Buck House" courtier who had watched Elizabeth emerge from the chrysalis stage into the spot-lighted public role as heiress presumptive remarked: "The girl never does anything wrong." This is almost completely true. Partly as a result of watching her mother and father in their public engagements, partly because of her meticulous training she almost invariably does the right thing—as rightness is understood in Britain. For instance, on the royal tour of South Africa it was Elizabeth who spotted a bus full of coloured Girl Guides kept well apart from their colleagues during a Guide review in Basutoland. Despite anguished exclamations from officials, she promptly walked over to talk to them and learned that they were the Guide troop from a leper colony. Next day Elizabeth's gesture was the talk of South Africa.

When she began to carry out public engagements on her own Elizabeth consciously modelled herself on her mother. After one of her first lone appearances, when one of her staff complimented her on her performance, Elizabeth frowned and said, "Oh, my mother would have done it so much better." But her sense of what is appropriate is not only the result of training and long practice: it is her nature to be warm, friendly, thoughtful of others.

Even during the prolonged, tiring ordeal of a royal tour she carefully remembers to thank those who organize or participate in the programme. At a British Embassy reception in Washington during her U.S.-Canadian tour, after shaking hands with some 2,000 visitors who filed past in a steady stream for more than two hours, she suddenly walked over and thanked the band leader for his music. So unexpected was this gesture in hard-boiled Washington that the bandsman almost fell off his podium. In Kenya, after recovering from the first shock of the news of her father's death and while waiting for the aircraft to be readied for her flight back to Britain, she spent the afternoon conscientiously penning thank-you notes to her hosts and apologies to those whom she would have to disappoint and signing photographs for the staff at her holiday lodge. Back at London airport, after a sombre exchange of greetings with Churchill, Attlee, Eden and other political figures waiting to meet her, the new Queen noticed the crew of her aircraft lined up alongside the plane. Before getting into her car she shook hands with and thanked each member for her flight home.

Like her mother, Elizabeth is genuinely interested in meeting people and from her she has inherited the priceless knack of putting people at their ease, even under circumstances that are unexpectedly embarrassing. She is seldom at a loss for the quick flash of humour or the apt remark that saves an awkward situation. When she and her husband visited Rome in the spring of 1951 a British Embassy ball in their honour featured an eight-some reel, one of Elizabeth's favourite dances. The young Italian bluebloods invited to the function pitched into the intricacies of the reel with more enthusiasm than foreknowledge and one young man, in his eagerness to master the new steps, suddenly fell flat on the floor at Elizabeth's feet. The Princess was equal to the occasion. As the crestfallen young man picked himself up, she smiled at him and said, "Please don't apologize, because I thought I had tripped you, and it was *my* fault."

Although not born to be Queen, Elizabeth's life has been circumscribed by the gold circle of the crown ever since she became direct heiress to the throne, but amid the close-knit, devoted family circle which George VI and his wife maintained inside the Palace walls she was never encouraged to regard herself as a person set apart by destiny. Any childish inclinations to be carried away by her sense of importance were gently but firmly quashed by Queen Mary, by her mother and her governess. "Royalty has never been an excuse for bad manners," her mother would sometimes remind her. As the private darling of every household young "Lilibet's" growing up was freely reported in the press and in time fact mingled with fiction to produce legends of her childhood. Once she was reportedly caught testing her royal prerogative by making a playmate bow low in homage. On another occasion, when Queen Mary had taken her to a public function in London, young "Lilibet" tugged impatiently at her grandmother because there were crowds outside "waiting to see *me*." Queen Mary, who kept an ever-watchful eye on Elizabeth's character, promptly sent the proud Princess home—via the back door. Another time "Lilibet" was supposed to have commanded an aged subject at an agricultural show to answer one of her youthful queries with the words, "This is Royalty speaking!" Elizabeth's governess has taken pains to deny that her charge was ever guilty of such a breach in her well-schooled manners.

True or not, as a result of her early training Elizabeth as a young woman seldom made the mistake of confusing deference paid to her as a symbol with a tribute to her own person. However, from her father and mother she has absorbed a reverence for the dignity of the sovereign's office and even as heiress presumptive she insisted on proper deference to her position, if not to herself. Once when Princess Margaret visited Elizabeth and Philip at Malta Elizabeth was seen to rebuke her younger sister for preceding her down the corridor after a public dinner. Again, during the royal tour of Canada Elizabeth stood up in the front of a white jeep to review troops in Quebec. Philip, seated in back, started to stand up as well but was covertly but firmly told by his wife to sit down. He did.

Like her father, the new Queen is a stickler for court protocol and etiquette [2] and like George VI she can show the sharp edge of her tongue to offenders. At a Palace party one night she came upon one of her girl friends powdering her nose in a corridor. "This is not the cloakroom," snapped Elizabeth as she passed.

"She may not comment at the time if anything goes wrong," said a member of her household recently, "but she certainly tells us off afterwards." One Christmas when a member of her staff took it upon himself to remind her of the custom of giving presents to her household she gave them to everyone—except him. When reporters on the Canadian tour requested her to issue a bulletin describing the clothes she would wear each day Elizabeth archly sent back word that she was on a visit to Canada, not on a fashion parade, and she would wear what she felt like wearing the moment she dressed.

Because of the rigid standard imposed on herself, Elizabeth sometimes took her royal duties too seriously, particularly when carrying out her first public engagements on her own. Once when she was invited to review the graduating class at a famed officers' training school she walked down the ranks and promptly called attention to an unshined buckle on one cadet. Amid an embarrassed hush, the offender was called up and rebuked, but word was passed along to Buckingham Palace that the Princess need not be quite so gimlet-eyed in her formal inspections.

This streak of severity in her make-up (as a child she was inclined to be over-critical of those around her), added to her rigid sense of duty and discipline, was particularly noticeable during the tour of Canada and the United States, and among Americans and Canadians, who expect their public figures to be both demonstrative and accessible, there was some criticism that Elizabeth was too regal, too remote, too unyielding in her public appearances. One incident symptomatic of those which occasioned this comment took place at Hamilton, Ontario, where the royal procession circled around a stadium packed with 30,000 cheering, flag-waving children. One of the moppets dropped his flag, a tiny Union Jack, and by a curious swirl of wind currents it dropped straight into Elizabeth's lap in her open limousine. The democratic gesture, one in keeping with the spirit of the occasion and the one the crowd half-expected her to make, would have been to pick up the flag and gaily wave it back at the children, but

Elizabeth, with a fixed smile on her face, impatiently brushed it off her lap and continued her slow-motion hand-waving.

In retrospect, much of this kind of criticism is now seen as unfair, for Elizabeth was labouring under a far greater strain of personal worry over her father's health than anyone then imagined. Also, it was her first major tour on which she was the focus of public attention and she was not prepared for either the size or the warmth or the vociferousness of her welcome, or for a newly-experienced familiarity in the approach to royalty. (She was at first flabbergasted when tough American news photographers, in an effort to get her to look their way for a picture, shouted "Hi, Highness!" but she learned to take it in her stride and later, when she and Philip were alone, she gaily mocked the newsmen's antics when she took snapshots of her husband.)

If the criticism had any point, it was that Elizabeth is not seen at her best at large-scale, formal occasions. Although by the time her Canadian tour had reached the half-way point at Vancouver she had recovered from the shy, nervous tension which marked her early appearances she remained cautiously regal on her formal appearances throughout the tour and appeared completely relaxed only at small, informal or impromptu functions on the crowded programme. This is because the young Queen, like her mother, prefers the informal to the official, the individual to the mass, and she appears at her best advantage when she can add the little personal touch that shows that royalty is made of the same stuff as the rest of us.

Out of the many simple, friendly gestures which won Elizabeth friends across the breadth of the American continent one incident was typical of her. On her visit to a Toronto hospital a 16-year-old crippled lad, Paul Mitchell, was determined to take a picture of the Princess from his hospital bed. For hours before Elizabeth's arrival he had fiddled with his camera and flash-attachment, but when she appeared and obligingly posed for him the flash-gun failed to work at the critical moment. Sensing his disappointment Elizabeth walked over to his bed and said, "I will stop on my way back." Ten minutes later she did, and Paul got his picture.

Teachers and tutors all played their appointed parts in preparing young Elizabeth for her destiny but the dominating single

36. *George VI, Queen Elizabeth and their daughters in the King's study*

37. *The royal family on a wartime visit to Sandringham*

38. *A happy family gathering at Balmoral Castle in the autumn of 1951*

39. *The late King and Queen Elizabeth entertain their grand-children, Prince Charles and Princess Anne, at Buckingham Palace on Prince Charles's third birthday*

influence that moulded her character was the family life in which she was privileged to grow up. The family circle has been her main background, and her parents, her younger sister, and, later, her husband, have been her only close companions. Within this happy home life, a rare accompaniment to the childhood of princes and princesses, Elizabeth's early years were kept as free from the shadow of the crown as possible.

Conscious of the shortcomings of his own upbringing George VI insisted that his two daughters be brought up as nearly normal as their confined Palace existence permitted. From the time the two youngsters could toddle, when George and Elizabeth were Duke and Duchess of York, their day invariably began with a visit to their parents' bedrooms about nine o'clock each morning and the four of them would romp and play for a quarter of an hour, no matter how busy the day or how pressing the official schedule. There was often another session of rowdy horseplay to end the day between the children's bath hour and bedtime. Nothing except absence from home of the King and Queen was ever allowed to get in the way of these family sessions, which continued right up to the morning of Princess Elizabeth's wedding.

George VI obviously adored his daughters—so much so that his wife often protested that he was far too indulgent with them. When they wanted a favour they generally first asked their father. Though never censorious, their mother is more strict with them and the two girls still stand a little in awe of her.

"My chief claim to fame seems to be that I am the father of Princess Elizabeth," the late King once grumpily remarked in the days when he was the Duke of York, but he was secretly pleased that his eldest daughter was the public's favourite and the darling of the royal family. George VI lavished on her the love and understanding he had missed as a child and at times was piqued when he had to share her childish affection with someone outside the family. "Lilibet's" first crush was for a groom from the Palace stables, a man named Owen, who taught her to ride. For many months her conversation was sprinkled with "Owen says" and "Owen does" until one day when she asked her father for his opinion on a matter the King answered, somewhat peevishly, "Don't ask me, ask Owen. Who am I to make suggestions?"

14 209

Although she was spared much of the heavy formality and publicity which attends the heir to the throne, Elizabeth's childhood was pathetically confined behind the walls of her royal residences. She has never ridden in a bus, and her one and only subway ride in London was organized for her like an expedition. When she reached school age she was denied the competitive challenge of the schoolroom, partly because her parents felt that the adulation of her schoolmates might turn her head, and her education was restricted to her home, with Princess Margaret, four years her junior, as her only competitor and companion. When Elizabeth reached her teens a special Buckingham Palace troop of Girl Guides (the 7th Westminster Company) was organized to give her contacts with other girls, but they were carefully selected from among the daughters of "Buck House" officials and staff members. Margaret was signed up as a Brownie (Leprechaun division). In time Elizabeth worked her way up to be a patrol leader, "a distinction," Palace publicists were quick to point out, "achieved only through merit."

It was Queen Mary, perhaps the greatest single influence in Elizabeth's life, who took the lead in organizing ventures into the outside world, treats to which young Elizabeth and, later, when she became old enough to toddle along, Margaret, looked forward with eagerness. Periodically the old Queen shepherded her small grand-daughters on tours of London's landmarks and institutions—the Victoria and Albert Museum, the Tower of London, the Zoo, the South Kensington Science Museum, the Royal Mint, Westminster Abbey, the National Gallery and Madame Tussaud's. From her regal grandmother Elizabeth learned how a princess must behave on occasions when the eyes of the world are upon her—never to hide her face in public, to acknowledge readily the greetings of the crowds, to contrive to appear regal and democratic at the same time, preserving the glamour of royalty and yet seeming to share in the enthusiasm of the people for a royal occasion.

For all their high-born status, Elizabeth and Margaret remained surprisingly simple in many ways. Their pocket money was severely limited—one shilling a week to start with—and even when Elizabeth, at 18, came into her Civil List allowance of £6,000 yearly her weekly allowance was only £1. They were trained to keep their rooms tidy, to darn their stockings and take care of their clothes. Proudly and painstakingly they fashioned their own presents to give away at Christmas and birthdays—linoleum cuts, pen wipers, pictures—or bought inexpensive knicknacks on forays to the Woolworth branch at Aberdeen when they were at nearby Balmoral.

Buckingham Palace, with its institutional air and museum-like furnishings, was a gloomy place to live in after the happy home atmosphere of the Yorks' residence at 145 Piccadilly and the two little Princesses did their best to liven it up with pranks and tricks when they moved in early in 1937. Three times in one morning they used the nursery extension of the Palace's inter-phone system to send the King's secretary scurrying along to their father's study on imaginary summonses. Their favourite trick was to hide behind the draperies in the Palace corridors and yell "Boo" at startled passers-by.

In their growing-up days Princess Margaret was far the more mischievous of the two royal sisters. As a child she never liked her second place position. She dropped salt in Elizabeth's tea and tapioca in her bath water. Once she rowed out to the middle of a pond to attract attention—and refused to come back. On another occasion, just after Elizabeth had won a life-saving certificate, Margaret, not to be outdone, heaved her sister's pet corgi into the lake at Buckingham Palace on the afternoon of a garden party and then plunged in after him in her new party dress. A precocious youngster, Margaret tried hard to grow up fast and close the four-year gap that separated her from her sister. At the age of ten she raised eyebrows in the royal family by remarking that one of the Palace footmen was "very handsome." At 14 she was caught red-handed sampling her father's champagne. When George VI told her not to drink any more sherry at one party she retorted, "If you don't let me have another glass I won't launch your old ships for you." By the time she was 16 she was dabbing herself with Schiaparelli's "Shocking" and experimenting with lipstick, eyebrow pencil and mascara. A leggy youngster who found the opposite sex as fascinating as had her Uncle David, she cheerfully crashed Elizabeth's first mixed parties during their wartime years at Windsor—where her bubbling conversation, her impish talent for mimicry and her sharp wit often stole the stage centre from her shy, reserved sister. Once when Elizabeth tried to pull her rank Margaret snapped, "You can go and look

211

after your Empire!" She became adept in the use of slang, and when her father asked her where she had learned to use such words she quipped, "Oh, at my mother's knee—or some such low joint." Irrepressible, Margaret generally managed to turn aside parental wrath or the scoldings of her governess by a funny remark. Once when her father was giving her a stern talking-to she suddenly asked, "Papa, do you sing 'God Save My Gracious Me?'"

Burdened with the family trait of a flash-fire temper, young Margaret put on childish tantrums that gave her the reputation of a holy terror in the staid court circle. Elizabeth, too, has the fierce family temper, though she keeps it under better control, but when finally provoked by Margaret she would explode and the two youngsters frequently came to blows. None the less, the royal sisters have always been fast friends and their relations are cloudless. As she grew older Elizabeth came to regard Margaret with almost maternal affection, and Margaret, on her part, was quick to recognize and respect her sister's more solid, queenly qualities. On one occasion when her mother firmly chided her for her behaviour, Margaret philosophically remarked, "Isn't it lucky that Lilibet's the elder?"

The contrasts between the royal sisters became more apparent when they began their schooling. Elizabeth, industrious and con-scientious, was a painstaking, almost plodding scholar who worked diligently at her lessons: Margaret, carefree and mercurial, seemed to absorb rather than learn her lessons as they went along.

Elizabeth's mother supervised her first efforts at reading, writing and spelling and outside coaches were called in to guide her in the social graces—the art of deportment, piano playing and the first steps in dancing—but in the autumn of 1933, when Elizabeth was seven, a prim but practical Scot, Miss Marion ("Crawfie") Crawford, was added to the household as resident governess, a position she was to hold for the next 17 years. Under "Crawfie" Elizabeth, and, in time, young Margaret settled down to a more or less regular schoolroom routine (in-terrupted by frequent holidays and royal occasions) which in-cluded lessons in history, grammar, literature and arithmetic. To give them added regal polish both girls learned conversa-tional French (which they speak without much trace of accent) from a second governess, Vicomtesse de Bellaigue, while other teachers coached them in German, art and dancing. For their Bible instruction and Scriptural history both girls paid regular visits to Canon Crawley, a kindly cleric who was a member of the Chapter of St. George's Chapel at Windsor.

The education of Princess Elizabeth, as heiress presumptive, was a matter of Commonwealth importance and the British Cabinet had the right to be informed at regular intervals about her progress and to submit ideas of its own, but in her early years at least the Cabinet was content to leave Elizabeth's schooling to the King and Queen and they, in turn, seldom interfered with Miss Crawford's curriculum. Queen Mary, however, kept her old-fashioned, grandmotherly eye on her granddaughters' education. Periodically she examined their curriculum and sent her suggestions to "Crawfie"—more poetry-by-rote, an excellent memory training for the future, more history, which they would need, and less arithmetic, which they would not, and plenty of Bible.

When Elizabeth embarked on a five-year study of constitutional history she was placed under the tutelage of the late Sir Clarence Henry Kennett Marten, the then Vice Provost (later Provost) of Eton. An erudite but unprejudiced scholar, Marten led his royal pupil through a broad-ranging study in which no historic milestone was overlooked, from the French Revolution to the rise of the Labour Party in Britain, from the Magna Carta to the Declaration of Independence. A progressive-minded historian himself, Marten's textbooks for his pupil inclined to the liberal viewpoint—G. M. Trevelyan's "English Social History," Herbert Fisher's "History of Europe" and Lord Elton's "Imperial Commonwealth." For her background reading on the United States Elizabeth started out with Lord Bryce's famed work of long ago, "The American Commonwealth," which was roughly equivalent to studying modern France through reading Caesar, but she made up for this lapse by a later study of Muzzey's standard history of the United States. In her course with Marten and later when she added a weekly discussion of current affairs with him as part of her education Elizabeth was encouraged to take a free-thinking look at both sides of every question. Thus, she studied the American Revolution from the viewpoint of the American colonists as well as from the side of her great-great-

great-great-grandfather, George III; she learned about the Boer War from President Paul Kruger's side as well as from Cecil Rhodes's; and she knew of the arguments of Gandhi and Nehru for Indian independence as well as the British case for keeping India in the Empire.

As a result of this intensive early training, Elizabeth came to the throne with a sounder knowledge of the constitutional history of her position and the law that surrounds it than any previous royal personage had possessed, not excepting George V, who accumulated considerable constitutional experience, both domestic and imperial, during his reign.

Princess Margaret's education roughly paralleled that of her sister until Elizabeth's schooling passed into the specialized branches required by her position. Margaret persevered with a year's crammed course in constitutional history when she was 17, but her schooling was interrupted when she accompanied her parents and Elizabeth on their prolonged tour of South Africa in 1947 and the schoolroom routine was never resumed. "Crawfie" continued to attend regularly at "Buck House" to discuss with Margaret for an hour or two each day any subjects that interested her but after Elizabeth's wedding, when Margaret eagerly swept into her role as an adult member of the royal family by day and the nation's number one debutante at night, her formal education came to an end.

Had it not been for the war Elizabeth, at least, would have gone on to a university for further study. For security reasons— the fear of enemy attempts to kidnap or kill the Princesses—this was impossible, but it is one of Elizabeth's great disappointments. Last year, when she and her husband received the degrees of doctor of laws from London University, Elizabeth confessed: "There is one piece of fortune which we have never known. We have never known a university from within. . . ."

Elizabeth was barely in her teens when the Second World War began. With Margaret she was packed off to the solid safety of Windsor Castle, which their parents visited at the week-ends. Bombs fell nearby and once Elizabeth had the excitement of seeing the wreckage of a German aeroplane shot down in the vicinity, but except for the anti-aircraft guns in the grounds, the troops on guard duty and the discomfort of living through the fuel-rationed winter months in a stone-cold Castle the war brushed lightly over this royal backwater. At the age of 16 Elizabeth, as required by law, registered for national service, but when she reached the compulsory calling-up age of 18 the King and his Cabinet decided that her royal education was more important than the nation's woman-power shortage. Elizabeth decided otherwise. Determined to emulate her girl friends who were doing their bit in uniform, she persuaded her father to reverse his decision and in February, 1945, she took up his commission as No. 230873 Second Subaltern Windsor in the A.T.S. The extent of her service was a short course in vehicle maintenance at the nearby Camberley depot, from which she returned under chaperon to the Castle each night, but Elizabeth fulfilled one ambition by learning to drive, and to celebrate her accomplishment piloted an Army car right into London and up to the forecourt of Buckingham Palace. Apoplectic court and police officials, fearful of the risks (and loss of dignity) of driving in London traffic, insisted that the heir to the throne must never repeat her performance.

The war years postponed Elizabeth's official debut into the public life of the royal family. In honour of her sixteenth birthday her father appointed her colonel of the Grenadier Guards and to mark the occasion she reviewed a special parade of the regiment at Windsor,[3] but as her eighteenth birthday approached, when she would be constitutionally of age, able to assume the crown if her father died, her official introduction to the nation could no longer be postponed and in March, 1944, she accompanied her father and mother on a tour of the mills and factories and pit villages of South Wales. On her eighteenth birthday she was made eligible to serve on the Council of State and her father granted her armorial bearings of her own and her own standard. Gradually she began to take on more of the jobs that are expected of royalty. She went to Scotland and launched H.M.S. *Vanguard*, the battleship on which she and her family were to journey to South Africa and back, she assumed presidencies of charitable societies and worthy organizations, made speeches and received honorary degrees. When the war ended Elizabeth was no longer a child: she was a young woman.

As Britons buckled reluctantly down to their first years of post-war austerity the elaborate balls and presentation parties which marked the social debut of a royal princess in the past were out of the question for Princess Elizabeth, but George VI's daughter scarcely noticed their omission. She was radiantly happy in the possession of a secret which few people then guessed —she was in love.

The quest for Elizabeth's heart could hardly be called a competition—in her very limited circle of friends there were very few eligible young men who could dare to ask her hand in marriage—and in any event almost from the time she first began to notice the opposite sex her heart had belonged to Philip. In fact, Philip had the advantage of an inside track since their childhood.

By birth and breeding he was eminently suited to be the consort for a future Queen. Like Elizabeth, he is a great-great-grandchild of Queen Victoria and Prince Albert (which makes Elizabeth and Philip third cousins through the Hanoverian line). By ancestry a Dane of the royal Danish house of Schleswig-Holstein-Sonderburg-Glücksburg, a branch of the princely house of Oldenburg, by an accident of history he was born a Greek, sixth in line for the Greek throne, but in schooling, tongue and outlook he is as thoroughly British as any of Elizabeth's subjects.

In 1863 Philip's grandfather, Prince William of Denmark, son of Christian IX who became King of Denmark the same year, was installed through British, French and Russian influence as King of the Hellenes and took the title of George I of Greece. Philip was born on June 10, 1921, on the island of Corfu, the youngest child and only son of Prince Andrew, who was the fourth son of George I and brother of the reigning King Constantine. On the maternal side, the line which was to govern his future, the young Prince was a direct descendant of Victoria and Albert. His maternal great-grandparents were the Grand Duke Louis of Hesse and Princess Alice, Victoria's second daughter. Princess Victoria of Hesse, a daughter of this union, married her cousin, a German princeling named Prince Louis of Battenberg, who forsook his native land and became a British subject in order to carve out a naval career in the service of his grandmother, Queen Victoria. Prince Louis, a great sailor and an efficient administrator, overcame the Royal Navy's prejudice against foreigners and rose the hard way to be Admiral of the Fleet and then First Sea Lord in 1914, but public prejudice against his

German background prevented him from leading the fleet during the First World War. In 1917, when his good friend, George V, called on his kinsmen to renounce their German titles Prince Louis Anglicized the family name to Mountbatten and accepted a British peerage as the first Marquess of Milford Haven. His eldest daughter, Alice, married Prince Andrew of Greece, Philip's father.

Soon after Philip's birth the Greeks launched an ill-considered attack on the Turks and in the bloodthirsty slaughter that followed the Greek Army was smashed. Revolutionaries tossed King Constantine off his throne and Philip's father, who commanded a corps in the broken Army, was sentenced (after pressure for leniency had been exerted by the British and the Vatican) to banishment for life. Prince Andrew and his family, whisked out of Greece on a British cruiser, settled down amid the growing Paris colony of exiled princes and homeless aristocrats.

Philip's youth was spent visiting relatives. He attended for a time a fashionable school at St. Cloud, outside Paris, but as the family funds ran short (his mother ran an arts and crafts shop in Paris) he was sent to England and put in the care of his grandmother, Lady Milford Haven, and his uncle, Lord Louis Mountbatten, who was then one of the rising young officers in the Royal Navy. The dashing Uncle Dickie, as Mountbatten is known in the royal family, became Philip's boyhood idol and the young Prince determined to make the British Navy his own career, but first Lord Louis sent him to a preparatory school outside London and then, at the age of 12, to a progressive school which the famed educational reformer, Dr. Kurt Hahn, had established at Salem, in Germany, on the estate of Prince Maximilian of Baden, whose son, Prince Berthold, had married Theodora, second eldest of Philip's four good-looking sisters. After a year Philip's nervous German relatives sent him back to Britain—legend has it that he laughed uproariously every time he saw the Nazi salute—but when Dr. Hahn also fell into disfavour with the Nazis and in 1934 re-established his educational institution at Gordonstoun, on Scotland's Moray Firth, Philip rejoined the school. As a scholar he was only fair, but when he left school after almost four years he took with him the highest honour for seamanship. His scholastic record was good enough to get into Dartmouth Naval College, where he won the coveted King's dirk as the best cadet of his term, but before he had completed his course Britain was at war. Young Philip went to sea as a midshipman in January, 1940, and put in nearly five years of wartime salt-water service, asking no favours and receiving none. He served on the battleship *Valiant* in the night battle of Cape Matapan—and was mentioned in dispatches for good work—did dreary duty in the Indian Ocean and dirty patrols in the North Sea, and ended up as a first lieutenant on a destroyer in the Pacific, where he served briefly as aide-de-camp to his uncle, Lord Louis, who had risen to be Supreme Allied Commander in the South-East Asia Command.

The war was a personal tragedy for Philip. He was cut off from the members of his own family, all of whom remained in occupied Europe. His father, who lived apart from his mother, died in Monte Carlo in 1944. His mother, a wraith-like lady who now spends most of her time living the life of a nun on the Aegean island of Tinos, spent the war years in Greece doing Red Cross work. Philip's four sisters all married German princes. Princess Margarita, the eldest, married Prince Gottfried of Hohenlohe-Langenburg. Princess Theodora, next in line, married Prince Berthold, the Margrave of Baden, and Princess Sophie, the youngest sister, married Prince Christopher of Hesse, who was on Himmler's wartime staff and served as Minister in charge of the Reich Air Forces before being killed while flying with the *Luftwaffe*. The fourth sister, Princess Cecilia, married the Grand Duke of Hesse bei Rhein. She was killed with her husband and their two sons in a plane crash in Belgium in 1937.

The romance between Princess Elizabeth and the fair-haired good-looking lieutenant in His Majesty's Navy, who was still known as Prince Philip of Greece in royal circles, flowered during the last years of the war, but it might have begun at any time in their childhood. The two youngsters met frequently during their early years. They played together at Brook House, the Mountbattens' London penthouse in Park Lane. They met at the wedding of Princess Marina of Greece, Philip's cousin, to the Duke of Kent in 1934, when Elizabeth, then aged eight, served as a bridesmaid, and they met again when Elizabeth's father was crowned King in 1937, but these contacts left no discernible impact on either of them. The first time they saw each other in the boy-meets-girl sense was in 1939, but the results were not propitious.

Elizabeth's father took his family in the royal yacht to inspect the naval college at Dartmouth, and Philip, because of his royal connection, was detailed to entertain the two Princesses. Elizabeth thought him bumptious and inclined to show off and Philip, with his five years' seniority, thought her too young to be interesting.

Their real romance began during the war, when Philip, in London on brief leaves, met Elizabeth at Windsor parties or at small, intimate gatherings organized by the Duchess of Kent at her country home. They wrote to each other when Philip was at sea and his picture, inadequately disguised behind a bushy beard, took pride of place in Elizabeth's bedroom. At the war's end Philip luckily drew a shore assignment at Corsham, in Wiltshire, about 100 miles from London, and his visits to Elizabeth came so frequently that he became almost a family fixture at "Buck House."

Though Elizabeth and Philip tried to keep their romance secret the press of the world soon ferreted out Philip's identity and for months the newspapers freely discussed whether they were in love, whether Elizabeth would marry him, and whether she should marry him. Although Prince Philip had formally renounced his remote claim to the Greek throne back in 1944, he was still considered by some Britons to be a foreigner. Moreover, Greece was again involved in a civil war and the royal house of which Philip was a member was not popular with British Labourites and had been the subject of bitter debates in Parliament.

In the autumn of 1946 Prince Philip was invited by the King to join the family at Balmoral, where royal suitors are customarily looked over in the intimacy of the family circle. Elizabeth was then 20, Philip 25. It was there that Philip proposed and Elizabeth agreed to marry him, and it was there that Philip had his first heart-to-heart talk with his future father-in-law. The King and his wife, while they agreed in principle to an early marriage for Elizabeth in order to give her time for a family life before ascending the throne, were not anxious for her to rush into marriage. They wanted her to be sure of her decision—divorce was out of the question for a heiress presumptive—and like fathers and mothers of less exalted station they advised the young couple to wait. The coming tour of South Africa was proposed as a deliberate separation which would be a time for reflection.

During her four-month absence in South Africa Elizabeth

pined for Philip. They wrote to each other constantly, spoke frequently on the telephone, and Elizabeth carried Philip's picture with her everywhere. When *Vanguard* tied up at the end of the homeward journey Elizabeth danced a happy jig in anticipation. Her mind was made up. Two months after her return to London their betrothal was formally announced.

In the royal family's absence Prince Philip had removed the last obstacle to the match by becoming a naturalized British citizen, a step he would have taken years earlier but for the war. He thereby dropped his princely title and chose to be known by the surname of his uncle, becoming Lieutenant Philip Mountbatten. On the eve of his marriage, however, his father-in-law-to-be restored him to loftier rank by creating him a Knight of the Garter, Baron Greenwich, Earl of Merioneth and the Duke of Edinburgh. At the same time he was also granted the title of His Royal Highness.[4]

Until her marriage Elizabeth had only a vague, distorted idea of how people lived outside the walls of "Buck House." Though she had been carefully taught the value of money, in her sheltered existence she had neither the need nor the opportunity to measure it against the cost of living. Thus, when the staff at Buckingham Palace staged an unofficial strike for higher wages after the war's end she saw it not in economic terms but only as a disloyal act to her father. The cost of furnishing her new London home, Clarence House, appalled her, but it was not until she flew to Malta to stay with her husband as a "naval wife" overseas that she began to grasp how different was the life of an ordinary girl from her own.

Like most fathers, George VI hated to see his daughter get married. He grew to be very fond of Philip—they shared the same kind of simple, homely humour—and he and his wife would tell their friends that they could not have hoped for a better son-in-law. Though he was proud of the way Elizabeth grew to royal stature, able to deputize for him with sureness and confidence, the late King took a long time to adjust himself to the realization that she was a grown girl, with a household and children of her own. One day when driving past Elizabeth's home, which was bedecked with flags, including her own standard which he had given her, George VI turned to a friend and said testily: "What is she trying to do—set up an Empire of her own?"

XIV

ROYAL CONSORT

ANY picture of Queen Elizabeth II without the complementary figure of her consort is like a portrait in black and
white. It needs the easy charm, the spontaneous wit and the gregarious, informal, open personality of Philip to add warmth to
Elizabeth's graciousness and colour to her sedate and regal
manner.

Just as the Queen Mother complemented George VI in her
role as "helpmeet," so by the same standard the Duke of Edinburgh is the new Queen's perfect partner. Not content to play
an Albert to Elizabeth's Victoria, he has refused to subordinate
his personality to his wife's, but by the interplay of his personality
upon hers he has, perhaps unconsciously and almost impercept-
ibly, assisted in moulding a new Elizabeth. Slowly, and more
noticeably in the last year or so, his wife has grown into
womanhood, capable of making her own decisions (until long
after their marriage Elizabeth, by family habit, almost daily
consulted with her mother about even minor details of her engagements, her household and her clothes) and gradually he has helped
her acquire the general knowledge and worldly experience denied
her during her sheltered Palace life and the necessarily-limited
governess-education which seems to be the lot of princesses.

On their Canadian-U.S. tour it was Philip who took the major
role as a salesman of royalty in putting over his wife. With the
advantage of five years' seniority and the experience of a naval
career that has naturally entailed living shoulder to shoulder
with ordinary people, it was he who sensed the unconscious demands and expectations of the crowds and was ready with the
spontaneous gesture that made the royal couple a solid hit along
the route. And always, without ever edging into the centre spotlight that shone upon Elizabeth, he played the role of consort to

the hilt. Throughout the tour he was at his wife's side, one or two reassuring steps behind her, ready to smooth out occasional upsets in her programme or flash her an understanding smile or exchange a personal wisecrack that eased her tension and made her relax.

Like the Queen Mother, the Duke of Edinburgh believes that his role as consort permits him a certain amount of informality on public parade, and with his quick sense of humour he is always ready to respond to the mood of the crowd. In Victoria, B.C., a college girl on the sidelines pretended to swoon when she caught sight of the good-looking, debonair Duke. Philip smiled at her and said, "Steady now." At a Washington reception a good-looking young matron in the line of visitors took one look at him and murmured an appreciative "Mm." Philip overheard her. Glancing quickly down the line he looked *her* over and said "Mmmmmmm."

Tall (6 feet 2 inches), fair-haired, well-proportioned and carefully if casually tailored, the Duke is almost too strikingly handsome to be a man's man (the feminine viewpoint was put by one of America's female columnists, Inez Robb, who wrote at the time of the royal visit to Washington that Philip, in full evening kit, "is a reasonable facsimile of why big girls leave home"), but he offsets this with a smooth charm and an affable manner that would be the envy of a practised politician. Noting this, one newspaper in Canada predicted that the Duke could be elected to any Canadian office he chose to run for and an American reporter on the tour topped this by declaring that "Philip could run for Congress on the Republican ticket in Texas and win."

The Canadian-U.S. tour was deliberately undertaken as an educative step in the development of the constitutional personality of the heiress presumptive—it was Elizabeth's first major public appearance abroad on her own without the overshadowing presence of her parents—but it also projected the Duke of Edinburgh into sharper focus in the public eye. For the first time the British people, reading of the triumphal progress of the royal couple, became really aware of how well Philip was fulfilling his exacting role as consort.

The Duke of Edinburgh has been compared *ad nauseam* with his illustrious forbear, Victoria's Prince Albert, the only other man in recent British history to have trodden the same path as husband and consort of a Queen Regnant. Both were foreign princes before they married into the British royal line, but to carry further the parallel between Prince Albert and his great-great-grandson is neither correct nor complimentary to Philip. Prince Albert was decidedly unpopular with his adopted fellow countrymen during most of his life. A weedy German princeling from the house of Coburg, which Britons disliked, he had manifested no particular admiration for the British way of life when he came to London to marry Britain's girl-Queen. Among the insular, sports-loving aristocrats who made up the court he was suspect as a foreigner and, what was worse, an intellectual. His naturalization as an Englishman was made the subject of a controversy, his status and precedence in the realm were only reluctantly conceded, and a hostile Parliament grudgingly voted him an annuity-settlement of £30,000 yearly after slashing it from the suggested figure of £50,000. And it was not until Albert was 38 and had been 17 years beside the throne, the last 12 of them as King in all but name in his position as secretary and intimate political adviser to his wife, that Victoria overcame the last of her own hesitancies and granted him the style and title of Prince Consort ("This ought to have been done," wrote Albert, gloomily, to his brother in Coburg, ". . . at our wedding."). Britons took a long time getting used to Victoria's husband, and it was not until the last years of his short life that he won public approval and prestige.

The Duke of Edinburgh took up his role as consort with few of Prince Albert's drawbacks. Though there were some crusty Britons who still suspected him as a foreigner at the time of his marriage to Princess Elizabeth, Philip's family ties, his British public school education and his creditable war record, essentials in the making of the ideal English gentleman, enabled him quickly to live down that tag and in the short space of four years since his marriage he has succeeded in making a mark in British public life such as his great-great-grandfather achieved only after years of heart-breaking, prematurely-ageing efforts. Undoubtedly Philip has absorbed some reflected admiration from his wife and the family into which he married, but in the course of becoming a national figure he has also earned a place in the country's affection for his own considerable virtues.[1]

Chief among the qualities that have given him a special place in the regard and affection of his wife's peoples is his ability to retain the common touch without doing much damage to royal dignity. Uninhibited by pomp and circumstance, he is the most "un-royal" member of the royal family and his entry into the closed circle of the monarchy brought a breath of fresh air into what, over the tradition-forming years, had become a rather stuffy royal routine. More than any member of the royal family he speaks the language of the people—most royal persons, even in ordinary conversation, are apt to be a bit stilted in their choice of words, a mannerism picked up from the rarefied atmosphere of the court—and while his education and upbringing could hardly be called typical it was closer to the commoner's lot than anything experienced by any of the other members of the royal circle.

Philip is not quite as brainy as the British press, bowled over by the workmanlike presidential address he gave to the British Association for the Advancement of Science in 1951, is apt to make him, but he possesses an original and unconventional mind, an alert and keenly quizzical intelligence not usually found in royal princes.

Before they got to know him the grave and staid Palace courtiers who have spent their lives in the service of royalty put in many nail-chewing hours worrying about Philip. He was new to the royal business. He was practically unknown to the people of Britain and the Commonwealth. Soberly the aged court officials anticipated that his being in the limelight would expose him to criticism: they feared that he would be too unconventional in his ways and expressed the hope that he would shun what they regarded as some of his more Bohemian habits. Their plan for him was to spend several years getting to know the people and getting known by them in the ways expected of royalty, through a series of carefully-planned tours and visits and the patronage of the sort of worthy causes that would insure for him a favourable press.

But Philip had his own ideas on how to put himself across with the public. Right from the start he refused to conform to the standards expected of royal males. He put on the kilt in the privacy of Balmoral to conform with royal custom—and engagingly confessed that he felt a bit of a fool in one—but for a long time he refused to wear the traditional royal bowler hat with his lounge suits, though he now makes the concession of wearing one or carrying one in his hand on official occasions. Whereas the other members of the royal family feel that they must do what is expected of them, whether they like it or not, Philip is more apt to follow his own inclinations of the moment. A fast but competent driver (on one occasion his sports car skidded on a slippery cattle crossing and overturned, an unfortunate accident which gave him a reputation as a breakneck motorist), he likes to take the wheel of his own cars, to the despair of court officials. While he condescends to sit sedately behind a royal chauffeur in London he and the driver generally change places whenever the Palace limousines reach the capital's outskirts. It was typical of him that instead of choosing his first equerry from among the dwindling ranks of Britain's aristocrats he gave the job to one of his sea-faring cronies, Lieutenant-Commander Michael Parker, an Australian who had recently served with Philip in the Royal Navy.

When the Duke decided to establish himself as a public figure he went about it with characteristic directness. His uncle, Earl Mountbatten, conveniently stepped aside as president of the National Playing Fields Association and Philip was installed in his place in time to launch the organization's silver jubilee appeal for £500,000 to provide new playing fields around Britain. His presidency gave him the opportunity for informal visits to all parts of the country, and provided contacts with local authorities, youth organizations, financiers and do-gooders on a community level. Athletically-inclined himself, he found this new sphere of activity congenial and to it he has devoted much of his time. A hard worker when his heart is in a job, he has proved a quick and able chairman and an extremely successful wheedler of philanthropic funds.

In his brief career in the public eye the Duke has built a reputation as one of Britain's best young speakers and he is much in demand on the after-dinner circuit. Unlike most royal personages, Philip insists on writing his own speeches, and what is more, he is perfectly capable of doing so. He has mastered the difficult art of the extemporaneous speech, to which he has added an ability to get off a witty quip or calculated remark that is seldom indiscreet or tactless. At first, however, "Buck House" officials, who are never consulted beforehand or shown advance notes of Philip's speeches, used to spend sleepless nights worrying about what the Duke was liable to say. Quick-witted, he is seldom at a loss for something to say. Once while visiting Venice on one of his naval shore excursions he was caught up in a students' celebration and subjected to a mock trial, at which he had to defend himself against the double charge of having fair hair and invading the Doge's domain. Philip's reply was that his fair hair proved him a descendant of the Vandals and Goths who founded the original settlement at Venice, and instead of invading the Doge's domain he had come merely to see how the settlement was getting along. For his slick answer he was presented with an elegant hat and an honorary degree in modern languages from the University of Venice.

In his younger years Philip's sense of humour was decidedly schoolboyish but Elizabeth's natural reserve and Philip's growing responsibilities as a husband and family man have tempered his early effervescence. He and Elizabeth still laugh heartily at each other's jokes in private, but in public Philip has learned to tailor his humour to suit the occasion.

When he and Elizabeth attended the opera during their visit to Paris in 1948 the crowd of French socialites and officials gathered on the steps gave the Princess a tumultuous reception. Elizabeth turned at the top and waved to them and the French people, having no princess of their own to applaud, cheered her again and again. Philip took all this in and then with an amused twinkle in his eye turned to Jules Moch, the then Minister of Interior, and said, "Isn't it too bad that you sent your royal family to the guillotine?"

The Duke is forthright in private conversation and when annoyed or upset he has full command of a naval vocabulary of swearwords. Recently when he had flown hurriedly back from Helsinki to take part in a yacht race off Cowes he made his way to the starting line with seconds to spare and found his boat hemmed in by photographers in motor launches. Philip told them where to go in language that burned even the newsmen's hardened ears.

A cosmopolite in background and tastes, Philip's choice of friends ranges from former naval buddies to polo-playing bluebloods, from Hollywood types to American and British journalists and photographers. At the time of his marriage he raised a few eyebrows when he invited to the wedding as his guests some of his bachelor friends and night-club cronies, some of whom would not ordinarily have been allowed within a mile of the court. Last year the eyebrows were pushed higher when the Duke appeared to have been pally with Frank Sinatra and Ava Gardner, who, in the minds of some Britons, carry the double stigma of being both Hollywood characters and divorced persons. In fact, Sinatra and his new wife, on their visit to Britain, had been asked to help raise funds for the National Playing Fields Association and Philip did no more than his duty in his capacity as president of the organization when he welcomed and entertained them.

Philip shrugs off such criticism. He has grown used to the royal ordeal of having much of his private life regarded as public property. "I am completely stoic," he told a gathering of British newspaper owners a few years ago. "I now read about myself—especially the ruder remarks—as if I were an animal at the zoo." Broad-minded in his beliefs, catholic in his interests, he is burdened by few prejudices. Late in 1951 he visited the London synagogue of the Spanish and Portuguese Jews, founded by refugees from the Spanish Inquisition, and heard a special service commemorating its 250th anniversary. When a noisy group of female fanatics demonstrated outside against the presence of a member of the royal family the Duke prolonged his visit to an hour and a half. A few weeks earlier Philip, who is not a keen fight fan but dutifully attends most of London's charity boxing bills, had stepped into the ring at Harringay Arena to meet the boxers taking part in the programme. One boxer, a coloured American boy named Jim Slade, was left sitting quietly in his corner, however. As he was about to climb down from the ring Philip noticed that Slade had been left out. He turned back and shook hands with him, and the audience cheered his gesture.

When he first stepped into public life the Duke found that his specialized naval training had left him with great gaps in his general knowledge, but he has burned the midnight oil in an effort to make himself a well-rounded man. Before making his much-acclaimed speech to Britain's scientists he had boxes of scientific books and treatises sent out to him to his naval station in Malta, sent a 5,000-word first draft to scientific experts to have his facts and figures checked, and then startled the high-domed audience with seemingly learned references to "Lanchester's vortex theory," "Kipping's silicon chemistry" and other developments to which scientists are privy. Before going with his wife to Canada he took the precaution of reading all he could about the country and he surprised—and pleased—Canadians with his up-to-date knowledge of their post-war boom. In preparation for his aborted visit to Australia in 1952 he walked unannounced one day into the London Wool Exchange and fired a stream of extremely technical questions at the buyers. Said one surprised buyer: "It was obvious that he already knew a great deal about the wool industry. He must have been doing some fairly extensive study."

Philip likes to see things for himself, preferably without too much beforehand spit-and-polish such as usually dresses up a royal visit, and soon after his wife's accession to the throne he undertook a heavy schedule of background-gathering to equip himself for his new role as consort. In the course of one month, for instance, he dined at 10 Downing Street with Prime Minister Churchill and the chiefs of the fighting services, visited the R.A.F.'s scientific and research establishment at Farnborough, the De Havilland aircraft plant (where he flew in a new Comet jet plane), the South Kensington Geological Survey Museum, the East Greenwich Fuel Research Station, the Atomic Research Establishment at Harwell, and a group of modernized collieries near Manchester, and presided over the first meeting of the Royal Mint Advisory Committee charged with designing the new coinage for his wife's reign.

The Duke of Edinburgh has never made any secret of the fact that his personal preference was to continue his career in the Royal Navy. Until he married Elizabeth his consuming ambition was to achieve a naval career that would rival that of the two other great admirals in the Mountbatten family, his famous grandfather, Prince Louis of Battenberg, and his equally-famed uncle, Lord Louis Mountbatten (whom the British Navy fondly calls "Batty Mount Louis"). There are high naval officers who assert that Philip might have gone to the very top had he not married George VI's daughter. Officers with whom he has served rate him magnificent in seamanship, a brilliant technician and an able administrator and the lower deck considers him "a real good 'un," which is high praise indeed.

At the time of his marriage Philip was blithely confident that he could continue to double as a royal person and a serving officer. For a time he was given convenient shore duty in London, but the need to assist his wife and his ailing father-in-law with a host of royal duties compelled him to drop back to inactive (and half-pay) status. The round of public engagements bored Philip, and with his wife's consent he prevailed upon George VI to let him rejoin the Navy on active service. He went back to sea in October, 1949, after his three-year spell ashore and from then until July, 1951 he was either at sea or in Malta (except for short leaves in London), an experience capped by a year's command of his first ship, *Magpie*, a frigate.

Though he continued on half-pay status and advanced to the rank of commander in the ordinary course of naval promotion after his wife's accession to the throne, Philip will probably have to forgo further active service for the public duties that go with his princely rank. In his role as consort he is expected to don the uniforms of all three of Her Majesty's services and assume some of the honorary high titles and ceremonial duties ordinarily filled by a male sovereign.

Constitutionally, even when promoted to the status of Prince Consort, the Duke of Edinburgh's role is a vacuum: he has no other function than husband of the Queen. The duties of the Queen's husband have never been laid down, but Victoria's Albert, the only predecessor to whom Philip can look for guidance, formulated for history after ten years of unhappy experience the requirements of this awkward status.

"The position of Prince Consort," wrote Albert at Windsor, "requires that the husband should entirely sink his own individual existence in that of his wife; that he should aim at no power by himself or for himself; should shun all attention, assume no separate responsibility before the public but make his position entirely part of hers, fill up every gap which as a woman she would naturally leave in the exercise of her regal functions." The passage of 102 years since they were written have not invalidated these precepts.

Philip has read the speeches and writing of Prince Albert and delved deeply into the royal archives of the Prince Consort's time, but those who know the Duke intimately doubt that he will be able to follow the path carefully paced out for him by Albert the Good. Philip is determined to be neither a court ornament nor a glorified courtier. He is a man of fixed ideas, firmness of purpose and a natural leader, and though ready to accept the fact that his authority is subordinate to his wife's the moment they pass into public it would be difficult for him to accept second place in the privacy of his home.

Just how awkward this new role could be was brought home abruptly to the royal couple the first morning after their hurried return flight from Kenya at the time of George VI's death. The new Queen, followed at a discreet distance by Philip, walked along the garden path from Clarence House to St. James's Palace, where Elizabeth was to receive the homage of her Privy Council and sign her oath of accession. The Duke took his place with the other Privy Councillors in the room. Then the Queen, accompanied by her court officials, made her entry and at the end of the brief ceremony she retired through a door at the rear of the room. When Philip tried to follow his wife he found the door barred to him until he persuaded the official in charge to let him pass.

Awkward as the role of the Queen's husband may be, Prince Albert proved in his time that a consort can amount to something. A man of great common sense, strong character and far better taste than commonly credited with (certainly his two London memorials, the Albert Hall and the florid Albert Memorial, do not do him justice), he had a profound impact on British public life, and in many ways contributed more to the shaping of the monarchy during his wife's reign than Victoria herself. He regarded himself as boss of the family, superintendent of the Queen's household (he reorganized the chaotic and extravagant management of royal housekeeping and in a few years had saved £200,000, enough to buy Osborne House, Victoria's favourite retreat in the Isle of Wight), and functioned as Victoria's sole confidential adviser, her private secretary and permanent Minister. By patience, hard work and sheer political wisdom he guided and educated his wife—and a good many of her Cabinet Ministers—and succeeded in moulding a new pattern of constitutional monarchy, on which the present British model is based. He made himself the patron of the British Army and Navy (the great military training centre at Aldershot was largely his creation), superintended the building of London's first working-class flats complete with bathrooms (an amenity which his contemporaries viewed with alarm), and intervened frequently and usually wisely in the field of foreign affairs. It was largely through his intervention that Britain did not become involved in the U.S. Civil War. Almost his last act before his untimely death was to modify an arrogant letter sent by the British Foreign Minister to Washington protesting against the boarding of the *Trent* by American authorities and the removal of two ambassadors sent by the Confederate States. Only slowly and grudgingly did Parliament and Ministers recognize his abilities and his devotion to his adopted country, but before his death (when Victoria, in an orgy of grief, put herself and her court into mourning that lasted four full years) he had made himself a forceful and, if not popular, an admired and respected public figure.

Because of the curtailment of the sovereign's powers since Victoria's time Philip cannot emulate his great-great-grandfather's behind-the-scenes role, but there remains a large area of useful work which he expects to perform as an auxiliary to his wife. Most important, he serves as the eyes and ears of the Queen. It is part of the monarchic tradition that the Queen, as sovereign, must live a life of formality, cut off from the daily doings of her people, confined by the constitution and bound to act only on the advice of her Ministers or the senior courtiers in her entourage. Philip can move more widely among her people, mix more freely and speak his mind more frankly—to outsiders and to his wife. Secondly, Philip intends to take on more and more of the ceremonial duties and formal public functions—somewhat like Prince Bernhard does for his wife, Queen Juliana of the Netherlands—leaving Elizabeth more time for the continuing routine of state business.

How much influence the Duke will have on his wife as Queen will only emerge as the years pass. Because of his wider knowledge of the outside world she will probably accept his advice on the public relations side of the monarch's job and she will undoubtedly consult him about state affairs, but she may also hold back most of the confidential state documents from him as Victoria did from Albert ("Albert helped me with the blotting-paper when I signed," wrote Victoria).

Although they have had drilled into them the a-political role of the sovereign and the royal family both Elizabeth and Philip are intensely interested in politics and the personalities of political life. In her private beliefs Elizabeth, who does not share her mother's interest in social welfare or her father's concern with industrial problems, is inclined to be conservative, while Philip, partly due to his Mountbatten upbringing and partly to the broadening influences of his varied circle of friends, reflects views that are more liberal than those of his wife.

Ultra-conservative Conservatives are apt to become irrational when they reflect that, through Philip, the Earl and Countess Mountbatten have moved nearer to the throne. To right-wing Britons of wealth and title the Mountbattens are looked upon as traitors to their class because they have interested themselves, more academically than practically, in the social problems of the day, because they have extended their friendship to Labour politicians, and because Lord Mountbatten accepted and implemented the Labour Government's brief to wind up the long rule of the British *Raj* in India.

Those who fear that the elevation of Earl Mountbatten's nephew to be consort to the Queen makes the Mountbattens potentially the most powerful people in Britain overlook two important facts, apart from the elementary consideration that the remaining political power of the throne is hedged about with Parliamentary safeguards. One is that the Duke of Edinburgh, while he reveres his uncle, is a young man who is not lightly swayed. The other is that Queen Elizabeth II, even more than her husband, has a mind of her own.

That she did not intend to lean constantly on Philip for the routine business of her new job the Queen made clear to her Buckingham Palace staff almost from the first days of her reign. At the time of her father's funeral she agreed to receive each visiting head of a foreign state for a brief talk at "Buck House," and to spare her from too many visitors at that difficult time it was understood that each dignitary would come alone, without the usual accompanying staff. On the day of the presentations a Foreign Office representative informed the Palace that the President of Yugoslavia, Dr. Ivan Ribar, spoke only German and therefore proposed bringing with him the Yugoslav Ambassador to act as interpreter. Sir Alan Lascelles, the Queen's principal secretary, replied that while Her Majesty had studied German the obvious solution was to get Philip, who reputedly spoke fluent German, to attend the audience and interpret, and this proposal he undertook to put before the Queen. Some time later the Foreign Office received another message. It was: "The Queen does not trust Philip's German any more than she does her own. Please tell Dr. Ribar to bring his Ambassador."

XV

ELIZABETH THE QUEEN

QUEEN VICTORIA always contended that women were unsuited for sovereignty, that it was a task for men. "I am every day more convinced," she wrote, "that we women, if we are to be good women, feminine and amiable and domestic, are not fitted to reign: at least it is *contre gré* that they drive themselves to the work which it entails." Queen Elizabeth II, who has inherited most of Victoria's adamantine qualities, is not troubled by her great-great-grandmother's doubts about the frailties of her sex. A remarkably self-possessed young woman, she stepped into her exacting triple role as Queen, wife and mother with a confidence that has amazed her Ministers, her court advisers and her family and friends alike.

Elizabeth was as well prepared as any new sovereign could be on the ceremonial duties of the monarch. In mastering the official business of the crown, however, she had much to learn when she came to the throne and it is to this job that she now devotes the largest share of her heavy daily schedule. As nearly as possible, she has retained the working habits and daily timetable of her father.

Her working day begins at 7 a.m., a whole hour earlier than her rising time as Princess, when her morning cup of tea is brought to her by her longtime maid, Miss Margaret Mac-Donald, a shy, competent Scot who still answers to "Bobo," the nickname Elizabeth bestowed on her in childhood. The Queen reads the main London morning newspapers carefully over breakfast (and like any young girl in the public eye she reads with interest any accounts of her own doings) and is ready for her desk work just before 9 o'clock. On her desk each day is placed a summary of editorial comment and news stories from British newspapers, London and provincial, prepared by her private secretaries, and a second summary of the major Commonwealth papers, furnished for her by her Office of Commonwealth Relations. Elizabeth is an avid reader of books and current magazines, which are marked for her to call attention to subjects in which she is expected to be versed. People meeting her for the first time are invariably surprised by the extent of her knowledge. "Not only is she charming but she is equally intelligent," remarked shrewd old Dr. Konrad Adenauer, the West German Chancellor, after two audiences with the young Queen. At a Washington dinner party Charles E. Wilson, the former director of the U.S. Defence Mobilization programme, found himself seated next to the then Princess Elizabeth. Wilson began by making polite dinner-table small talk, but Elizabeth startled him by directing their conversation to technical details about Sabre jet engines. "She appeared to be thoroughly conversant with my job," said a surprised Mr. Wilson afterwards.

Like her father, Elizabeth has come to like the Americans she has met. She appreciated the homespun friendliness of President and Mrs. Truman during her formality-packed visit to Washington and had Margaret Truman in for lunch at the Palace when the President's daughter toured Britain in the summer of 1952. She is a warm admirer of General Eisenhower (she once taught him to dance the Highland fling) and followed with great interest his presidential campaign. She has absorbed some of her father's deep belief in Anglo-American unity—as Princess Elizabeth she served as president of the English-Speaking Union—and even before she came to the throne the comptroller of her household, Lieutenant-General Sir Frederick ("Boy") Browning, who had close wartime contacts with Americans in his capacity as commander of Britain's airborne troops, made certain that she understood the area of similarity as well as the points of difference between the two nations. She subscribes to U.S. news magazines and has an up-to-date awareness of how the American viewpoint differs from that of her Government and people on such current problems as Korea, the Middle East, Germany, rearmament and the role of the sterling area.

Soon after 9 each morning Prince Charles and Princess Anne are brought down to see their mother and father for a brief romp until it is time for their morning airing in the Palace gardens. Elizabeth's official duties have cut heavily into what little domestic life she has managed to retain for herself but, like her father and mother, she religiously sets aside two periods each day when the family comes first. By readjusting her afternoon schedule she is sometimes able to snatch an hour with the children after lunch, but, in addition to the morning session, every evening without fail between 5 and 6 o'clock she and her husband go up to the nursery to play with their youngsters and help the nurse bathe them and tuck them into bed.

The Queen's first meeting each day is usually with her principal private secretary, Sir Alan Lascelles, who served her father for almost 15 years. Sir Alan's main job is to co-ordinate Elizabeth's interviews (every caller has a word with him before going up-stairs to see Her Majesty), arrange her personal appearances and provide a liaison between "Buck House" and the outside world. Together they go over her diary for the weeks and months ahead, pencilling in the engagements—on the average about one in 50 of the requests for the Queen's presence—which Elizabeth agrees to fill. Their first meeting of the day may last only a few minutes, but if the Queen has been absent from London it may go on for an hour.

The next chore is to attend to the day's mail, which the Queen does with one of her assistant private secretaries in attendance. An average day brings in upwards of 500 letters, of which some 50 may be addressed personally to the Queen, plus 20 registered letters and some 60 packages. On Elizabeth's birthday she may get as many as 1,000 congratulatory letters and telegrams. All are read. On the death of George VI "Buck House" was flooded with 50,000 letters and 15,000 telegrams expressing sympathy. Every reply was addressed and signed personally by a member of the royal household.

Most of the letters addressed to the Queen are from personal friends, but many come from obvious crackpots who are con-vinced that the sovereign has only to lift a finger to solve their personal woes. Regardless of their contents, all are answered, for Elizabeth, as did her father, has a standing rule that all communications must be acknowledged, even if no more than formally, and if possible on the day they are received. Letters in unknown languages are sent to the Foreign Office for translation. It is a constitutional rule that all requests sent to the sovereign by strangers must be referred to her Ministers, the Home

Secretary dealing with those from her subjects and the Foreign Secretary with those from aliens.[1]

The Queen and members of the royal family rarely sign letters to other than personal friends, partly because of the tremendous volume of their correspondence, but also to prevent their signatures being exploited by autograph hunters. Their letters are sent free through the mails and the Queen's telegrams, which take automatic priority over everything else on the wires, also go free. Their personal mail all goes by registered post, the envelopes being initialled by the writer. "Buck House" has its own post office, staffed by the General Post Office, and there are branches at all the Queen's other homes. When Elizabeth is away from London her mail is sent to her in locked, leather cases enclosed in special chained-and-padlocked mailbags. The Palace telephone room also houses several teleprinters connected to the central telegraph office, over which pass royal telegrams and cables. At peak periods these number several thousand in a day. The Queen, according to royal tradition, sends out about 600 congratulatory telegrams a year to couples among her subjects who have reached their golden wedding anniversaries and about a dozen each year to those who have attained their diamond anniversary. She also sends greetings to those of her subjects who reach their hundredth birthdays (and in a recent three-year period there were more than 300 of them).

Once the mail is out of the way the Queen turns to the dispatch boxes containing the secret or confidential papers requiring her study and signature. Each day she reads the batch of inward and outward telegrams passing between the Foreign Secretary and Britain's representatives abroad, and her Governors-General in the Dominions, the governors in the chief colonies and all British ambassadors or ministers abroad report to her regularly, either by letter or in person. Copies of all state documents that go to the Prime Minister go also to the Queen, including top secret memos from the Defence Committee and the British chiefs-of-staff committee. The advance agenda of Cabinet meetings and the secret minutes of each session are sent to her in a special locked box, for which, at the "Buck House" end, only the Queen and her private secretary have keys.

Elizabeth tries to break up her rigorous routine each week by leaving London most Friday afternoons for week-ends at Royal

Lodge at Windsor, but even here the dispatch boxes pursue her and the papers she deals with are returned in batches to Buckingham Palace on Saturdays and Sundays. When she is away from London the boxes are flown to the nearest airport and then sped to her by courier.

On most days the period before lunch is set aside for audiences. An unending stream of official and semi-official callers, many from overseas, come before the Queen to explain their policies, take up commissions in her name, or merely to present their compliments. All ambassadors and ministers from foreign nations present their credentials personally to Her Majesty on their arrival at the Court of St. James's and refresh their contact with repeated audiences during their term of service in London. All British ambassadors and ministers, including those from the Dominions who visit London, must kiss the Queen's hand on their appointment, as do all Cabinet Ministers, in token of the fact that they derive their authority from Her Majesty. Elizabeth also tries periodically to see the commanders of her armed forces and she is generally available to high-ranking officers from the U.S. and other friendly countries who wish to call on her. She has to approve the appointment of all archbishops, bishops, deans and some canons of the Church of England and usually grants them an audience when they are in London.

Once each week, generally at 6.30 p.m. each Tuesday, and sometimes twice a week when Parliament is in session, Elizabeth receives Prime Minister Winston Churchill for an hour's discussion, continuing the practice started by her father. Elizabeth has been a Churchill fan since childhood. He once presented her with a specially-bound set of his four-volumned life of Marlborough, which she treasures, and during the war years the busy Prime Minister frequently found time to stop and chat seriously with the young Queen-to-be on his visits to Buckingham Palace. Constitutionally, Elizabeth is bound to take Churchill's advice, but their relationship is not at all like that which existed between the youthful and inexperienced Victoria and her first Prime Minister, the supple and charming Whig, Lord Melbourne. Elizabeth is not content with generalities—Churchill confessed to friends soon after her accession that he was surprised at her grip on both domestic and foreign affairs—and the Prime Minister responds by talking to her in the same man-to-man fashion in which he discussed state affairs with George VI. The young Queen is determined to know the details and the reasons behind Government decisions taken in her name—she will not allow anyone to by-pass her either because she is young or because she is a woman—and soon after her accession she called in her leading Cabinet Ministers, one by one, to enlighten her on the work of their departments.

In the afternoons, unless she has an outside engagement to occupy her, Elizabeth reads state papers, fits in personal appointments with dressmakers, her hairdresser, portrait painters and photographers, sees the members of her household, and works on her speeches. Whenever she makes an official speech the Secretary of State for Home Affairs must see that the sovereign says nothing in conflict with the Government's policies and so the Home Office usually submits a draft speech, generally couched in Whitehall officialese and safe platitudes. Her private speeches, in which she speaks as a symbol and not as the fount of authority, are prepared for her by her private secretaries. Until recently Elizabeth was content to take her speeches ready-made, but when Philip blossomed as a public speaker she began to take more interest and now she cuts and corrects her drafts until they come closer to what she herself would like to say.

"When I was a little boy," said President Harry Truman at a Washington state dinner party he gave for Elizabeth and Philip, "I read about a fairy princess." Then, with a gallant wave of his hand toward Elizabeth, looking resplendently regal in one of her grand-manner gowns, he added, "And there she is."

Having lost with maturity the plumpness of girlhood (at 19 she weighed a hefty 137 pounds), Elizabeth is both prettier and tinier than most people seeing her for the first time had guessed. She is not a great beauty but at night-time, transformed by one of the elaborately embroidered crinoline picture gowns which her mother made fashionable for queens, and aided by poise and grace of movement of her own that are truly regal, she looks like a fairy princess come to life. By day, were she not who and what she is, she would probably pass without much notice in a crowd.

She is of medium height (5 feet 4 inches), slim, trim-waisted (25 inches), full-bosomed, with a creamy, fresh complexion, soft brown hair, soft blue eyes and white teeth (slightly oversize). The full extent of her charm, like her mother's, does not always carry across in photographs: hastily shot newspaper photos, in particular, do not do justice to her delicate colouring, which comes out more as a blank brilliance, and her warm, flashing smile. Elizabeth has not yet mastered the frozen smile which seldom leaves her mother's face during a public appearance, and when the camera catches her unsmiling she is apt to appear severe and scowly. Her facial features are thicker than those of Princess Margaret, which often gives her pictures a falsely hefty look, and her legs and ankles are inclined to the thick side, like her mother's, a fault which she likes to offset by trim ankle-strap shoes.

Unlike her sister, who could hardly wait to grow up to have an elegant wardrobe, Elizabeth had none of the teenager's concern for clothes and until her marriage she seldom bothered about her appearance. She accepted her clothes as part of her royal duties and wore what she was told to when she was told to. She placidly took her mother's advice about the clothes to buy and wear, often with disastrous results. The fussy fashions preferred by her mother usually made Elizabeth appear over-dressed and unsophisticated, years older than her age. Both were guilty of the same fashion mistake of leaving nothing at home: for day wear they donned pearls, diamonds, furs and feathers, and the young Elizabeth often made the added error of wearing a bulky silver fox cape, which gave her a boxy, five-by-five look.[2] She clung to pastel colours, partly because they were favoured by her mother, partly because of the royal tradition that they offer better visibility in a public appearance, even though they made her figure look bulkier than it was. For evening wear her choice of material was often shiny satin, which emphasized her luxurious profile.

The turning point in Elizabeth's acquisition of a clothes sense came during her state visit to Paris with Philip in 1948. Intrigued by French comments on her clothes created for that trip (said designer Christian Dior: "I never knew from pictures that she could be so lovely or wear her clothes with such distinction") Elizabeth returned home determined to take her dressing seriously. Encouraged by her husband, by Princess Margaret, and by her aunt, the stylish Duchess of Kent, she gradually

40. *George VI formally opens his South African Parliament at Capetown in 1947*

41. *An off-duty moment in Natal National Park*

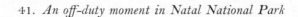

42. *King and Quee* *open a session o* *Southern Rhodesia* *Parliament*

43. *The late Fiel* *Marshal Smu* *photographs t* *royal family i* *Natal*

44. *Princess Eliz* *beth and the D* *of Edinburgh duri* *their honeymoon*

acquired a new, streamlined elegance. She adopted a simpler, shorter hair style, replaced her frilly, dressmakery clothes with expensively simple tailored dresses, suits and coats, and turned from pastels and light prints to darker shades of blue, lime green and grey, which made her appear slimmer and taller. Inclined to plumpness, she had a hard time losing all the weight gained during her second pregnancy, but early in 1951, spurred on by Philip, she went on a diet, cut out potatoes, bread and starchy foods, reduced her wine drinking and gave up chocolates, of which she had been particularly fond.

For her Canadian-U.S. trip Elizabeth again broke away from her mother's influence when she picked Hardy Amies, one of Britain's top couturiers, to share with designer Norman Hartnell the assignment of creating her trans-Atlantic wardrobe. Hartnell had enjoyed a virtual monopoly of the royal family's custom since he first designed state dresses for Elizabeth's mother in 1938. Amies, who made his name in tailored clothes, had never designed for the royal ladies, but Elizabeth had spotted his creations on one of her ladies-in-waiting and among her socialite circle of girl friends. Upwards of 80 dresses were created for that tour (the royal party carried 97 pieces of baggage, most of which held Elizabeth's clothes) and the admiration they earned across the Atlantic encouraged Elizabeth to give the same two designers a repeat command to create the even larger wardrobe she will take with her to Australia and New Zealand in 1953.

Hartnell and Amies, who know the value of royal publicity, take the major credit for Elizabeth's wardrobe, but in fact the young Queen does not confine her patronage only to the chic, expensive couturiers. Many of her dresses, including some for the Canadian and Australasian tours, are made for her by Miss Avis Ford, a little-known but top-flight London dressmaker, who has for years made clothes for Queen Mary and tweeds for Elizabeth's mother. Her show hats are generally the creations of London's top milliner, Aage Thaarup, but she also buys hats designed for her by the more modest millinery establishment of Miss Kate Day.

As befits a Queen, Elizabeth's jewel boxes look like Cartier showcases. For her Canadian-U.S. tour she took along as official jewellery to wear on public occasions the following eye-stopping items: a necklace of 21 graduated brilliant-cut diamonds

16   241

interspersed with baguettes, presented to her by the Union of South Africa on her twenty-first birthday; a diamond tiara, one of nine dazzling diamond heirlooms given her by Queen Mary at the time of her wedding; a floral diamond tiara, designed in the form of three large roses, given her as a wedding present by the fabulously-wealthy Nizam of Hyderabad; a sapphire and diamond necklace, with earrings to match, which was one of her wedding presents from her father; a diamond fringe necklace, a wedding present from the City of London; two diamond clips in the shape of maple leaves; and the diamond cypher brooch of the Grenadier Guards. Among her personal jewellery her favourites are an elaborate diamond necklace, with pendant, which was another wedding gift from the Nizam of Hyderabad; a diamond and ruby necklace, a twenty-first birthday present from her mother and father; a double row of pearls which her father gave her at her wedding; a tiny, diamond-studded wrist watch, another gift from her father; and an exquisitely designed diamond tiara, her favourite, which comes apart and becomes a necklace, two clips and a bracelet.

Despite the opulence which surrounds her, Elizabeth's private tastes remain simple and moderate. She does not like cocktails, but she enjoys a glass of sherry before meals. She often drinks white wine with her food, but usually toys with a single glass of champagne through a public dinner. A few years ago Britain's non-smokers went into a mild tizzy when a picture of Elizabeth's desk showed an ash-tray and matches. Until then the Princess had never been seen with a cigarette at a public or semi-private function and newspapers speculated on whether she was a smoker. Elizabeth *does* smoke, but only occasionally at home and never in public. Her husband has cut down on his public smoking since his marriage.

In her choice of food Elizabeth is apt to follow the family preference for game. Like George VI and his wife, Elizabeth and Philip enjoy the informality of eating by themselves, without the ministrations of servants, and one of the innovations they made at Clarence House was to add a hot plate near the service hatch so that they could help themselves. At Clarence House the young couple entertained simply and informally—their guests were usually relatives or young aristocratic couples from Elizabeth's limited circle of friends—and their idea of a perfect climax to an evening was to slip out with their party to one of London's smarter night clubs. Elizabeth is a gifted and tireless dancer and seldom sits out a dance at a party. She has decided views about the merits of old-fashioned dances (one of the official tips sent ahead to her hosts in Australia and New Zealand is that they had better brush up on their reels and folk dances) and has encouraged the reintroduction of Scottish reels at fashionable balls. Before her marriage she organized a weekly practice session of reel dancing at Buckingham Palace for her friends. Elizabeth was a hard task-master, but she used to dance every dance while her companions, no older than herself, had to beg off a turn to rest and recover.

Elizabeth has a wide and lively interest in the theatre, in the opera and the ballet. She is fond of music, both heavy and light, and had built up a sizeable collection of records, now added to the enormous record library inherited from her father. Both she and Princess Margaret like American popular music and there is great competition in their circle to see who can acquire the latest album of tunes from a current American musical. Elizabeth is a competent pianist—she had piano lessons from the age of five—but she lacks Margaret's imagination and ability to improvise on the keyboard. Although she read most of the English and a few French classics in her schooldays her taste in literature is middle-brow: in fiction she prefers to read Somerset Maugham, J. B. Priestley, Ernest Hemingway, John Steinbeck, P. G. Wodehouse and H. G. Wells. For bedtime reading she often chooses an Agatha Christie thriller.

Both Elizabeth and Philip are keen television viewers, with a professional interest in the medium. They frequently watch T.V. newsreels or telefilms of state events to check up on their cere-monial appearance as the public sees it. Elizabeth, like her father, is a persevering amateur photographer. She makes her own 16-mm. films and on less formal public appearances, such as at Ascot races, often takes her movie camera with her. One of her wedding presents was a 16-mm. sound projector, which she and Philip installed in a miniature cinema in the basement of Clarence House, where they delighted to run off movie shows for their friends. Like their T.V. set it has a utilitarian value as well, for they have been able to look at short educational films and docu-mentaries about Australia and New Zealand, a painless way of acquiring the feel of the countries they plan to visit.

The young Queen shares the average Briton's passion for domesticated animals. She has been surrounded by pets all her life. Her father presented her with her first dog, a Welsh corgi, in 1933 and Elizabeth's preference for this low-slung breed (two corgis slept in her room at "Buck House" and one went on her honeymoon with her) has boosted its popularity in the doggy world, according to the British Kennel Club, from eighth place in 1949 to fourth in 1951. Elizabeth was given a pair of budgerigars as a present when she was nine and now has a collection of more than 50 birds in an aviary at Royal Lodge, an interest she inherited from her grandfather, George V, who was so fond of feathered friends that he had an aviary opening out from his dressing-room. Prince Charles and Princess Anne have caged canaries in their nursery, a musical touch which also brightened Elizabeth's and Margaret's childhood.

For all her outdoor upbringing, Elizabeth, like her mother, avoids all sports that involve physical exertion. Years ago her father hired an expert to teach her tennis, but Elizabeth had no enthusiasm for the game and refused to try for a ball that did not return to her feet. She played an occasional and indifferent round of golf with her father but soon gave up the game. She is a competent swimmer but seldom swims. Under her father's tutelage she became a capable shot but she did not absorb his consuming enthusiasm for the sport. She stalked and shot her first stag (and brought down three, one a ten-pointer, in her first day's stalk) when she was still in her teens, but she was put off by the reproachful cluck-clucking of those who did not approve of her achievement. "My committee greatly regrets your action in shooting a stag for sport," wrote the secretary of the League Against Cruel Sports, "particularly in view of your connection with the Girl Guide Movement, whose sixth law states that a Guide is a friend to animals." At Balmoral she prefers to leave the shooting parties to the Duke of Gloucester and her husband and their male guests. On her first visit there after her accession she put on waders and went out for a quiet session of salmon fishing in the River Dee.

The new Queen is a superb horsewoman—she had her own pony at the age of four—with a natural seat and easy hands, and her mastery of a horse, astride or side-saddle, even in the excitement of a ceremonial occasion is nearly perfect. She takes a keen spectator interest in polo, which her husband (handicapped at two) and a band of fellow bluebloods have surprisingly succeeded in reintroducing as a growing public attraction in post-war austerity Britain. Philip has tried hard to interest her in his other favourite sport, sailing. They were given a racing yacht for a wedding present and Elizabeth, like a dutiful wife, has gone along with her husband for a few trials, but rough weather has always upset her and she has never conquered her childish dislike of the sea and ships.

It is likely that horse-racing will prove to be for Queen Elizabeth II what shooting was for George VI. Passionately fond of horses, before her father's death she became joint owner with her mother of three capable steeplechasers, kept sharp track of their progress and visited the tracks to see them jump. On her father's death she inherited his string of 14 horses and as soon as court mourning ended announced that she would continue racing in the royal colours (purple, gold-braided jacket with scarlet sleeves, black velvet cap) that have been used by Edward VII, George V, Edward VIII and George VI. On her first visit to Ascot after court mourning ended she made a beeline for the paddock to inspect one of her horses due to run in the first race, much to the confusion of the top-hatted brigade in the royal enclosure who were waiting expectantly for her to appear in the royal box. Her knowledge of horses is almost expert and the breeding and performance of her bloodstock is a happy task to which she gives up some of her limited leisure. Her target is to win the Derby, a feat which her father could not pull off, and beat the royal record set up by her gadabout great-grandfather, Edward VII, whose horses won the Derby on three occasions (in 1896, 1900 and 1909) and the Grand National steeplechase (in 1900).

XVI

THE QUEEN MOTHER (I)

ON the royal tour of South Africa in 1947 Their Majesties King George VI and Queen Elizabeth halted for a solemn, ceremonial moment in Durban to open the Gate of Remembrance which had been added to the city's Cenotaph in memory of the men of Natal who had fallen in the Second World War. As the final melancholy bugle notes of the Last Post echoed over the crowd, the King turned the key in the Gate, opened one leaf of its double door, and passed through with his wife at his side. When they had gone a few steps the Queen noticed that the other side of the door was still closed. Turning back, she gently swung it open herself. Her Majesty's gesture appealed to the crowd and was greeted by subdued cheering that did not detract from the solemnity of the occasion.

This little incident, trivial in itself, highlighted the complementary partnership of the royal couple who occupied the thrones of the British Commonwealth of Nations. Watching George and Elizabeth carry out a round of public duties together a royal aide once observed, "Without her he would be only half a King." With this judgment George VI would have been the first to agree.

"With My Wife as helpmeet by My side, I take up the heavy task which lies before Me," he told his Privy Council on his accession, and it is not too much to suggest that without the love and support of Elizabeth, calm and reassuring in her temperament, the nervous, highly-strung, embarrassingly self-conscious new monarch would have found the burdens of kingship as impossible to bear as had his brother before him.

Elizabeth was her husband's mainstay. When they were the Duke and Duchess of York it was she who urged him to battle against his stammer and conquer his painful shyness in public, and she was constantly at his side to give him encouragement and

246

an understanding smile. Conceiving the first of her duties to be those of a wife and mother she strove in their 29 years of happily-married life to create for her husband a serene home life and a close family circle, the "matchless blessing," as the Duke of Windsor called it in his farewell broadcast as sovereign, that has proved to be the strongest of the symbolic foundations on which the monarchy rests. And as Queen Consort during the 15 years of her husband's reign Elizabeth's companionship helped to ease the unique burden of the King's position, which Tennyson described in his somewhat high-flown remark to Queen Victoria ("You are so alone on that terrible height."). Whenever George VI was away from home without her Elizabeth sent him a letter in her own hand every single day.

But the Queen Mother [1] has made contributions in her own right to the idea of monarchy, and it may be that the understanding historian of the future will grant her a measure of service to Great Britain that is second only to the late King's.

During the war years, and particularly when her embattled country stood in lonely desperation under enemy air attacks, Elizabeth's example, her obvious interest in the welfare of her husband's subjects, her genuine expressions of sympathy, and her ready, infectious smile—all of which she displayed on her visits to the stricken cities—had a tonic effect on morale that was surpassed only by the symbolic figure of the King in person. Like her husband, she has a high regard for the public duties which have accumulated around the monarchy and is immensely energetic in carrying out those which fall to her. Since the war's end she has gradually taken on more and more of Queen Mary's duties as the ageing Queen Dowager has been forced to relinquish them, and when her husband was incapacitated with his illnesses she deliberately shouldered many of his public duties because she knew that the surest way to lessen his worries was to make up for his absence from public life.

Although these public engagements cut heavily into her time, her intimates at Buckingham Palace admit that she never complained beyond an occasional remark to her lady-in-waiting that "there seems a lot to do today." She was never bored in her round of office because she is genuinely interested in meeting new people in every walk of life. Unlike her husband, who preferred his public appearances well organized and was flustered if plans were altered, the Queen Mother regards time as flexible and is happy to allow informalities to upset her public programme, particularly if they bring pleasure to others.

For instance, when 50 Canadian schoolgirls visited Britain on a good-will tour in the summer of 1951 Elizabeth invited them to see Buckingham Palace. They were not V.I.P.'s and would have been thrilled by a distant glimpse of Her Majesty or the King or Princess Margaret as they passed through the state apartments. But when the girls arrived the Queen took time to shake hands and chat with each of them, much to their delight.

From her own family background, Elizabeth has inherited a deep reverence for the symbolic meaning and dignity of the monarchical institution and on ceremonial and public occasions she and her daughters were careful to pay the King the respect and homage which was due his office. For her own role as Consort Elizabeth felt that her chief function was to make a more intimate appeal to the hearts of the King's people by emphasizing the comparative informality and ease of manner which she thought was permissible to a Consort though not to a sovereign. This gave their joint public appearances a distinct quality of unison, which often succeeded in transforming otherwise dull, routine ceremonies into occasions of warm, human contact between Their Majesties and their people.

Uneasy at meeting new people in public, George VI's efforts at conversation on their tours often sounded abrupt and brusque, but this failing was more than counteracted by his wife, who has a natural ability to talk to anyone and to appear completely at ease in any circumstances. On most of their appearances together the King was the chief performer and was usually preoccupied with the formal proceedings. Sitting quietly at his side, Elizabeth, who has a sharp eye for detail, used to take in the whole scene and was usually the first to suggest to the King a variant in the programme that added a nice human touch. With a word to her husband when the ceremony ended she would lead him over to talk to some group in which they had a special interest or a little knot of people that appeared to have been overlooked while anxious officials fussed in the background over the interrupted details of the official timetable.

The importance of the Queen Mother's informal interventions, which were almost commonplace to Britons, was illustrated by an incident which took place at the outset of their South African tour. At their official welcome in Capetown the royal family stood for almost 40 minutes in blazing heat shaking hands with local dignitaries and listening to loyal addresses, to which the King replied. At the end of the ceremony, glad to escape from the sun, the King led the way down the steps of the dais to their car. The Queen paused a moment, spoke to her husband, and then both of them walked across the roadway to greet a party of war-wounded lined up in their invalid chairs. The crowd closed in around them, cutting them off from the royal party and the civic officials, and for the next quarter of an hour Their Majesties stood chatting with the wounded. This impromptu gesture, widely publicized throughout the Union, stamped the tour a success from the beginning, for it demonstrated to their subjects in South Africa what the British people already knew—that Their Majesties, for all their ceremonial surroundings, were genuine, human individuals who knew how to break with formality when the occasion offered.

Not all of Elizabeth's efforts to insert informality passed off so smoothly, however. On their timed-to-the-minute royal visits she frequently forgot the clock in her deep interest in people and places until the King gave her a pointed look that reminded her of their carefully-arranged schedule. Almost the only minor quarrels George and Elizabeth had were over her habit of ignoring time, for the late King was an extremely punctual person. He disliked being kept waiting more than anything else and would tolerate it from no one but his wife. Even in her personal life Elizabeth is far from prompt. She usually manages to remember some last-minute task which she must do in the Palace before rushing off to an appointment.

Although Elizabeth, like her husband, was careful never to overstep the bounds of her constitutional position she did influence British policy in a quiet, indirect way. She never hesitated to express her decided views to the King or to the few Ministers and public men whom Their Majesties liked sufficiently to invite to the Palace for a meal. She reads the newspapers thoroughly each day and keeps herself up-to-date on all public issues. Those who have her confidence say that she is shrewd in her judgment of British politicians and politics.

Like her husband, she is a great admirer of Winston Churchill, both as a person and as a political leader, though she does not share his views. When one of George VI's equerries told her that he was tempted to take up painting to fill in his off-duty hours the Queen immediately sent him a copy of Churchill's book, "Painting as a Pastime," and she sent out scores of other copies as gifts to her friends.

Elizabeth has always preferred to work by persuasion rather than by command, and with the King's approval she often called in departmental officials of the Government to discuss projects which interested her. During the war years, when she made the welfare of the people under air attack her special concern, she frequently sent for the Minister of Health to find out what was being done for them and to make suggestions based on what she had seen during her tours of damaged districts.

During the first months of her husband's reign anxious court and Government officials, still jumpy from Edward VIII's explosive remarks in the depressed areas of Britain, eavesdropped on the Queen's conversations on royal visits, but after a few experiences they were convinced that Elizabeth had a skilful knack of avoiding the expression of political views. Although few people now notice it, she is continually on guard against any slip of conversation that might be twisted into a partisan comment on a political issue.

One day when she visited air raid shelters in London early in the war years a would-be clever official asked, "Don't you think that deep shelters are best, ma'am?" Whatever Her Majesty thought privately, the question of providing deep shelters was a ticklish one which had frequently stirred the House of Commons. An opinion from the Queen might have provided a political advantage in the next debate, but Elizabeth was equal to the occasion. "I think the protection *all* shelters give is perfectly marvellous," she purred.

When the wartime evacuation of children from cities that were bomb targets was being discussed in Parliament, the Queen privately favoured making evacuation compulsory if persuasion failed, but she could not air her views in public. During another tour a woman councillor asked: "Don't you think it terrible, Your Majesty, to see all these little children left here in the danger areas? I'm sure you feel as I do that they should all be made to move out."

The royal reply was classically non-committal: "I think it is terrible that children anywhere should be in danger," said Elizabeth.

At the time of the South African visit the story circulated that a grumpy old Afrikander conquered his traditional dislike of the British sufficiently to tell Her Majesty that he was delighted to greet her, but that he still hated the power of Whitehall. To this the Queen was supposed to have replied, "I understand perfectly. We feel the same in Scotland." This anecdote sounds like a newspaperman's invention, but if it had any substance in fact it was one of the few times that Elizabeth's wit ran away with her caution.

The Queen Mother, who was born on August 4, 1900, at her family's English home, St. Paul's, Walden Bury, five miles from the town of Hitchin, in Hertfordshire, was the youngest but one of the ten children and the fourth and youngest daughter of the Earl and Countess of Strathmore and Kinghorne. To her family name of Bowes-Lyon, one of the most ancient noble families of Scotland, were added the given names of Elizabeth, Angela, Marguerite. The courtesy title of Lady was accorded her out of respect for her father's rank.

A commoner in that she is not of the blood royal, she can claim a proud descent and royal lineage from the ancient kings of Scotland, and with her husband shared a common ancestor in Robert the Bruce of Scotland.[2]

For some 580 years the Scottish seat of the Bowes-Lyon family has been ancient, turreted Glamis (pronounced Glaams) Castle, one of the oldest inhabited houses in the British Isles, which sits grandly on a windswept hill in Forfarshire, near Scotland's east coast. It came into the family in 1372 when the adventurous young Sir John Lyon received the thanedom of Glamis when he married the widowed daughter of Robert II of Scotland (1316–1390), Lady Jean Stewart, who brought Glamis Castle as her dower.

Although the present structure, a castellated, greystone building in the Scottish baronial style, dates mainly from the seventeenth century, the original parts were built in the eleventh century and for hundreds of years the thick-walled mansion played a central part in Scotland's bloody history. Its recorded story goes back to 1034, when King Malcolm II was murdered in its central tower and it was there, according to shadowy legend, that another eleventh-century Thane of Glamis, Shakespeare's Macbeth, murdered Duncan. One of the Queen Mother's ancestors, the young and beautiful widow of the sixth Lord Glamis, was burned at the stake in Edinburgh in the sixteenth century on a charge of witchcraft and conspiracy against James V, an accusation later proved false. Bonnie Prince Charlie halted in his wanderings at Glamis and on one occasion in 1746 he had to flee in such a hurry that he left his watch under the pillow. It is still at the Castle.[3]

When they were youngsters Princess Elizabeth and Princess Margaret, the latter of whom was born at Glamis, were often reminded by their mother of their Scottish blood, and their favourite school lessons were those in which they traced out their long and involved ancestral connections with English and Scottish history.

Scots are fond of proclaiming that the Queen Mother is Scotland's greatest gift to the Empire, even though relatively little Scots blood flows in Her Majesty's veins. Her mother was pure English, and the Earls of Strathmore, in the direct line, have married Englishwomen for the last seven generations, which made Elizabeth about the most English Consort, by blood, since the reign of Henry VIII.

The Queen Mother is proud of her ancestral link to Robert the Bruce, but she resents over-emphasis on the Scottish side of her origin. Thus, at the time of the coronation, when she and her husband attended a music-hall show and every turn went Scotch and wore kilts or talked with a Glasgow accent, there were no smiles when the performers turned expectantly to the royal box. "I am proud to be a Scotswoman," Her Majesty later said, "but I was born in England, and I am Queen of England."

Brought up in the homey atmosphere of a large, happy and warmhearted family, Elizabeth spent most of her childhood and youth in the lovely, rose-brick, Queen Anne manor house at St. Paul's, Walden Bury, with her brother David as her inseparable companion. A precocious youngster with a well-developed appetite for mischief, she delighted in devising such names as "The Bounding Butler" for the statue of the Discus Thrower which stood in the grounds of the house. One day during the First World War she dressed 15-year-old David in a hat, veil and dress and took him visiting soldiers in a Glasgow hospital. David played the part so perfectly that the joke was not discovered until the end of their tour through the wards.

According to David, he and his sister were once greatly attached to two pet pigs named Lucifer and Emma. One day Lucifer was taken away and donated for a charity raffle at Hitchin. The children broke open their banks and managed to buy half the tickets. They failed to buy the winning one, however, and the pig passed out of their possession.

For their holidays Elizabeth's family often went to Streatlam Castle, in Durham county, another property which came into the family when the ninth Earl of Strathmore and Kinghorne married the heiress of the Durham family of Bowes, but for three months every autumn they moved in a body to Glamis. David and Elizabeth delighted in employing all the spooky facilities of the old castle—secret staircases, trapdoors, chambers-in-the-wall— for scaring their visitors. Their favourite trick was to lay out a dummy ghost in the bed of a guest just before he retired. Once Elizabeth climbed on the roof and poured water down on guests as they arrived. Part of her upbringing was the task of showing tourists around Glamis, and once she dressed up as a maid and gravely escorted a party of visitors around her home. When tips were offered she accepted them.

Elizabeth's family was not wealthy—when her father died in 1944 he left an estate valued at £67,159 but much of it was in property—and with ten children to rear the Earl of Strathmore had neither the money nor the inclination to provide lavishly for his offspring. As a teen-ager Lady Elizabeth knew what it meant to be short of pocket money and, with her girl friends, often queued for the galleries at London theatres because she could not afford more expensive seats. Her mother, daughter of a rural minister, insisted that her daughters master the domestic arts and Elizabeth was taught to cook, sew and run a house.

Elizabeth was educated at home by her mother and a succession of governesses and instructors who taught her to paint, dance, play the piano and the harp, to speak excellent French and passable German. She spent two terms at a private London school when she was nine but did not like it, which in turn influenced her own later decision that her two daughters should be educated within the privacy of their homes.

After she moved into Buckingham Palace Elizabeth often recalled a day at Ascot racecourse in 1921, when an old gypsy
fortune teller read her palm and told her, "You will be a great
queen and mother of another queen." Her family laughed when
"Lizzie," as (to her annoyance) she was called, told them of the
prophecy and they did not even take it seriously when she became
Duchess of York two years later.

Until 1922, when she served as a bridesmaid at the wedding of
the Princess Royal, who has been her friend since childhood, Lady
Elizabeth's name had been scarcely mentioned even in the society
columns of the newspapers. Content to divide her social life
between the quiet, parochial society around Walden Bury and
Glamis, she was not accounted one of the smart set which took
its standards from the Prince of Wales. This, however, commended her to Queen Mary and when she reached marriageable
age Lady Elizabeth's name, unknown to her, was on George V's
and Queen Mary's approved list of eligible girls for the Prince
of Wales.

But it was Prince Albert, the Duke of York—Bertie to his
family—who fell in love with her. They had met as children—
Elizabeth is supposed to have met Prince Albert at a children's
party when she was a little girl of five and he a lad of eleven and
to have made such an impression that he immediately recognized
her when they next met eight years later—and they attended
some of the same social functions which gradually came back to
London after the First World War. In the summer of 1920
Prince Albert and his sister joined a house party at Glamis. The
Countess of Strathmore was unwell and Lady Elizabeth took over
as chatelaine. It was then that the young Prince fell firmly in love
with his competent young hostess.

Their match was not arranged, although Albert is supposed to
have had great difficulty in persuading her at first that he had not
"been sent." Under close scrutiny from Elizabeth's family the
pair had few opportunities for hand-holding tête-à-têtes. In an
unusual interview before her marriage Lady Elizabeth disclosed
that she twice rejected Bertie's proposal before she accepted him.
"I said to him I was afraid," she admitted, ". . . as royalty never,
never again to be free to think or speak or act as I really feel I
ought to think, or speak or act." But Prince Albert was a persistent suitor for almost two years. Once when he had plucked up

nerve to propose his courage failed him at the last moment and he is reputed to have sent one of his best friends to make a formal declaration. Elizabeth is supposed to have replied: "No. Not until he comes and asks me himself." His offer of marriage was finally accepted in January, 1923, when the pair went for a Sunday afternoon walk in the woods around Elizabeth's Walden Bury home. Even then the young suitor's nervous speech impediment intervened, but he tore a leaf from his notebook, scribbled his important message and handed it to her. There was at least one other competitor for Lady Elizabeth's hand, but she confessed to a friend a few years after her wedding: "It was my duty to marry Bertie and I fell in love with him afterwards."

George V and Queen Mary gave their blessing to the betrothal, and Queen Mary wrote approvingly, "She is not one of these modern girls, thank goodness." On April 23, 1923, when Elizabeth was raised to the rank of a Royal Princess, with the title of H.R.H., the young couple were married in the regal setting of Westminster Abbey. Elizabeth forgot her gloves— one of the few things she has ever forgotten.

The new Duchess of York was taken in hand by Queen Mary, who inducted her into the routine of royal duties and Palace functions. Determined to be a help to her husband—who was then acquiring his tag of "The Industrial Prince" because of his absorbing interest in industry and factory welfare—Elizabeth worked long and hard at dreary public tours and displayed such obvious enthusiasm for all she saw that the newspapers dubbed her "The Smiling Duchess." The Duke and Duchess deliberately took on the most onerous and least conspicuous of the royal family's public duties and contentedly left most of the limelight to the heir to the throne.

Although they had their share of foreign good-will tours—to East Africa in 1924 and around the world to Australia and New Zealand in 1927—the public life of the Yorks, as they were known, was overshadowed by the free and easy Prince of Wales. In socialite circles they were regarded as a dull couple because they preferred to devote themselves to such obscure but worthy causes as boys' camps and welfare societies, and because they were seldom seen in London's swank nightclubs. In fact, their money was short in those days and in any event they preferred their own company or their limited circle of friends to café society. As second son of the sovereign, the Duke of York was permitted a certain measure of privacy and in their comfortable, unostentatious homes—their London home at 145 Piccadilly, at Hyde Park corner, and their week-end home at Royal Lodge, in Windsor Great Park—the Duke and Duchess jealously guarded their intimate, domestic life from the invasions of privacy which accompanied their high stations.

The sudden turn of events which culminated in the abdication of Edward VIII and advanced the Duke of York to the throne was accepted by Elizabeth as a cruel turn of fate. Moving to the centre of the stage in Buckingham Palace meant an end to the domestic seclusion which she and her husband had hoped to find in their role as minor royalty, but in her almost 14 years as a member of the royal family she had absorbed enough of the monarchical tradition to know that neither she nor her husband could escape the call to serve.

"We must take what is coming to us, and make the best of it," she told her intimates as she closed up 145 Piccadilly and moved across the park to the Palace.

45. *On the Canadian tour Elizabeth and Philip watch a rodeo at Calgary*

46. *Greeting the crowd at Winnipeg after a visit to Parliament Building*

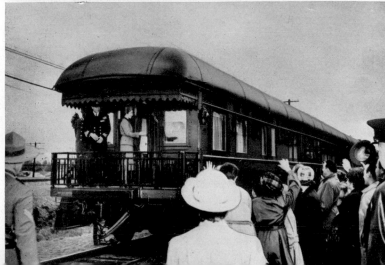

47. *Elizabeth and Philip aboard the royal train during the Canadian visit*

48. *Her Majesty Queen Elizabeth II*

XVII

THE QUEEN MOTHER (II)

COMFORTABLY plump in figure, matronly in appearance and moderately conservative in her tastes and interests, Queen Elizabeth, the Queen Mother, except for the fact that she is entitled to sign herself Elizabeth Regina, could fit happily into any upper middle-class community in Britain.

The secrets of her universal popularity with the people of her daughter's realms are her unerring instinct for the right behaviour, the correct gesture and the apt remark, her rare gift for putting people instantly at ease, her insatiable curiosity about everything she sees, and her gracious, infectious smile which seems to radiate happiness. As one admirer remarked, "To catch her smile is to become smiling oneself." Or as a French officer once enthused: "You enjoy yourself to see her."

But behind her sweet smile and charming manner there is a steely character and firmness of purpose that has stamped itself on her family. "The Queen rules the roost, make no mistake about that," one of her friends remarked while George VI was still alive. She had the main say in the upbringing of the two Princesses and her husband leaned heavily on her.

Quick-witted and resourceful, she is seldom taken by surprise. On a tour of the gold workings around Johannesburg one morning an excited Zulu came charging up to the royal car as it moved at a walking pace along the ranks of spectators. With her smile still on her lips, but determination in her eyes, the Queen calmly fended him off with the point of her parasol until the security officers discovered that his only desire was to press a ten-shilling note into the hand of Princess Elizabeth.

The Queen Mother is undoubtedly equipped with an exceptional intelligence rarely surpassed by a royal lady. As a young girl she began keeping a diary, a habit she has continued ever since, and every night before retiring she adds the day's entry. The few people privileged to open the diaries she has written since ascending the throne declare that she has set down a remarkable contemporary royal history, complete with pertinent comments, that will provide a better picture of her times—if they are ever published—than the personal journals penned by Queen Victoria. Elizabeth also insisted that her two daughters keep diaries of their own from the time they were first able to write.

The Queen Mother's wit is quick and responsive, her sense of humour sharp and sometimes dry. Once she asked a little Londoner where she lived. "Back o' 'arrods, mum," said the moppet, proudly. "And where do you live?" With scarcely a moment for reflection Elizabeth replied, "Oh, I live just at the back of Gorringes." Gorringes, of course, is the big store located on Buckingham Palace Road.

Elizabeth's fixed ideas have always been apparent in the problem of her wardrobe, for which she follows her own individual taste, not always with the best results. Whenever the press criticizes her clothes the Queen Mother asks one of her friends for advice, but as her friends are usually more tactful than honest Her Majesty generally concludes that the papers must be wrong.

From her first days as a debutante she has never bothered with a French maid but has always relied on the faithful, loyal but somewhat stolid services of a Scottish "dresser," first Catherine ("Katta") Maclean, who served as her personal maid for some 30 years until she went on indefinite sick leave, and then "Katta's" assistant, Miss Christine Willox, her present maid.

Unwilling to experiment with clothes for her small (5 foot 2 inches), square figure, she rationalized her wardrobe difficulties some years ago by declaring, "Some clothes like me and some don't," and when she ascended the throne she served notice that she did not intend to compete as a fashion-plate with her sisters-in-law, the Duchess of Kent and the Duchess of Windsor. "I have no desire to be a leader of fashion," she announced.

Comparatively uninterested in clothes as a debutante, Elizabeth remained faithful for years to Handley-Seymour, the conservative British house which made both her "coming out" dress when she was presented at court and her wedding dress, but in the 1930's she became a patron of Norman Hartnell, then an up-and-coming young designer who had made the Duchess of Gloucester's trousseau. Hartnell had little influence on Elizabeth's wardrobe until she came to the throne—for the coronation his assignment was to make the train-bearers' robes—but the wardrobe he designed for her state visit to Paris in 1938 aroused such comments that she sent for him again to create the clothes for her U.S.-Canadian tour in 1939. She wore his creations as they were meant to be worn, with an air, and although American style experts didn't exactly call her a leader of fashion they agreed that she wore her clothes like a queen. Back in Britain, however, Elizabeth shied away from Hartnell's more elaborate creations except for public and state occasions and clung to the conservative, almost timeless styles which she had adopted as her own.

For daytime public appearances she prefers ensembles, dresses and matching redingotes or edge-to-edge coats, either full or three-quarters length, and often trimmed with fur. Until she went into mourning on the death of her husband these were almost invariably in soft, pastel shades. Light powder blue, which matches her vivid, clear blue eyes, is her favourite colour, but other shades she likes are biscuit-beige, pearl grey, turquoise blue and a light, dusty pink that was once known as Margaret Rose pink in honour of her daughter, all of which complement her striking peaches-and-cream complexion. She rarely wears a fur coat in daytime, though she often carries fox furs and likes to have touches of fur about her ensembles.

Sleek, close-fitting evening dresses did not suit her dumpy figure and so, in conspiracy with Hartnell, who creates most of her evening gowns, she brought back into fashion the sweeping, drifting picture gown, which gives to most of her evening appearances a distinctly theatrical touch. For evening gowns she prefers pale-coloured satins, chiffons and fluffy tulle, usually bedecked with beads or sequins, but for more elaborate state occasions or banquets she usually appears in jewel-encrusted *robes-de-style*, richly-embroidered crinolines or picture gowns of rich satins or stiff brocades and damask specially woven for her. When going out for the evening she almost always wears furs, and prefers ermine to mink when dressed *en grand toilette*.

For week-ends or holidays in the country the Queen Mother is happiest in tweeds, usually a short skirt with a simple, tailored coat. She has never worn slacks. When they were on holiday

Elizabeth and her husband often wore suits cut from the same length of tweed. When they are at Balmoral the royal family follows the Scottish custom, adopted first by Victoria and Prince Albert, of wearing tartans, not so much because tartans suit them as because they are eligible to wear them.

During the war and the first post-war years of austerity, when Britons' clothing was severely rationed, the royal family made it a point to remain strictly within their coupon allowance, although they were given a diplomatic allowance of 60 additional coupons each year. This was no real hardship for the Queen Mother, who was well stocked with clothes from her French and Canadian-U.S. tours, most of which her people had never seen, and by a royal system of make-do-and-mend many of her elaborate state dresses were handed on to Princess Elizabeth when she grew up. Princess Margaret has her own ideas about the clothes that suit her and adamantly refuses to wear any more of these hand-me-downs.

The Queen Mother's hair is dark and naturally curly, and although she sported bangs when she was married she has resisted all suggestions that she follow the current fashion. For the past 20 years at least she has retained her own hair style—softly waved and parted in the centre—partly because she believes it suits a queen and partly because she discovered that it is the coiffure best able to support a tiara or a crown.

Her hats, most of which are made for her by milliner Aage Thaarup, are almost invariably the off-the-face style. The reason for this is not so much that they suit her but because the royal family long ago agreed that if people are eager to line the streets to watch royalty pass the royal ladies must wear hats that expose the face, with small brims or none at all and without full veils, and the Queen Mother has insisted that this rule apply to her hats and those of her daughters. Occasionally she varies the style by having her hats trimmed with feathers to make a becoming frame swept down on one side.

Catty critics have said that Elizabeth's *penchant* for pastel ensembles, furs and feathers made her look more like a retired actress than a queen, but when she was Consort Elizabeth felt that it was her duty to remain above fashion. Like her mother-in-law, who is also gifted with a sense of personal showmanship, Elizabeth believed that she had created a queenly style that was all her own, and she deliberately chose her clothes, particularly her evening gowns, to suggest majesty and to provide a background on state occasions for the stunning spread of jewels which she was entitled to wear. However, it was noticeable almost immediately after George VI's death that Elizabeth's taste in clothes had undergone a change. No longer under the compulsion to dress the way she thought a Queen should look because the people expected it, she now dresses more to suit herself and her clothes tend to be plainer and simpler—and more becoming—than during her years on the throne.

Apart from the state jewels which she was allowed to wear on ceremonial occasions, the Queen Mother is not as well-provided with jewellery as her position might indicate. Once when photographer Cecil Beaton asked her to wear as much of her jewellery as possible for a picture she apologized by saying, "The choice isn't very great, you know." For more formal occasions her jewel boxes include three complete sets of tiaras, necklaces, earrings and bracelets of diamonds and rubies and a tiara parure, necklace, earrings and bracelet of Persian turquoises given to her by George V because, he said, they matched the colour of her eyes. None of these tiaras are particularly eye-catching, however, and for her tour of South Africa Elizabeth borrowed a magnificent diamond tiara from Queen Mary. From among the family heirlooms the Queen Mother frequently wears four ropes of perfectly graded and matched pearls, the largest string of which belonged to Queen Anne, which are worth around £125,000 today. Aware that real pearls dry out unless they absorb oil from the skin, Elizabeth refused to store them away even during the war years and wore them on most of her public appearances.

Whatever the critics said, King George admired his wife's taste in clothes. He disliked what he called "hearty women," the tweedy, horsey types of British provincial society, and always encouraged the Queen and his growing daughters to be as completely feminine as possible. Whenever the royal family attends a formal function, there is a tradition at the Palace that the staff and servants may see them when they are dressed. The family assembles in the ground-floor Bow Room while the maids and household servants file in. The late King enjoyed this informal little touch and was always pleased when his wife was admired. One evening Princess Margaret waltzed in to the drawing-room to show her mother and father a new dress. George VI admired it affectionately and then said: "You are a lot like your mummy. Don't forget you have a very pretty mother."

Disliking colour clashes and over-vividness, Elizabeth carried her preference for pastels into her house decorating. Before the war she had the exterior of Royal Lodge painted in her favourite shade of pale pink and at Buckingham Palace she had the private apartments decorated in colour schemes of her own choosing— duck-egg blue or cream walls, with soft, pastel furnishings that were a welcome contrast to the dark walls and antiquated, uncomfortable furniture of earlier reigns. Even the wartime air raid shelter in the dungeons of Windsor Castle was done up with hangings of pale hyacinth blue.

The Queen Mother's fondness for pastels comes from her passion for flowers. Both she and the King were enthusiastic gardeners on their week-end visits to Royal Lodge, and Her Majesty delighted in arranging the masses of blooms which fill the rooms of the royal residences most of the year round. She also chose the plants that fill the flower beds at the head of the Mall, which she could see from her bow-windowed sitting-room in the north wing of the Palace. Her favourite flowers are roses, lilies, violets and carnations, and on every anniversary of their wedding her husband sent a bridal bouquet of white carnations to her room as soon as she wakened.

The British royal house has never been noted for its recondite tastes. The Queen Mother is something of an exception, though her tastes are tempered by her natural moderation.

Before the Second World War she purchased several paintings and hung them in Royal Lodge as the nucleus of a collection, mainly the works of Augustus John, Duncan Grant, Wilson Steer and Walter Sickert. After the war she bought a Monet sea-scape which came from Clemenceau's collection, and she has since made some notable additions to the royal pictures, particularly of modern English painting, including one very advanced canvas by Paul Nash and works by Matthew Smith and John Piper.

Though no highbrow, Elizabeth loves the ballet and has staunchly supported the Sadler's Wells venture with her patronage from the beginning. Since opera returned to Covent Garden in the post-war years she and her daughters have been frequent visitors to the royal box. Occasionally she persuaded her husband to accompany her, but opera was not to George VI's taste. When an aide once suggested that it would be diplomatic if the King patronized the opera George threw a book at him.

As a youngster literature was Elizabeth's favourite subject— she carried off the English literature prize during her short stay at a London day school—although she recalls with amusement the only effort that has survived her childhood. It is an essay, scribbled in a copybook, entitled "The Sea." It begins: "Some governesses are nice and some *are not.*" Her favourite authors are the classic oldtimers—Jane Austen, the Brontë sisters, Hardy, Conrad and Kipling. Nowadays she requires spectacles for reading or writing, but, like her husband, she is shy of wearing them and will not be photographed with them on.

One of her intimate friends, Sir Osbert Sitwell, is a frequent luncheon guest at the Palace, when he advises her on the newest books and latest plays to read and see. Having been trained in elocution as a girl, the Queen Mother is a pleasant public speaker and a good broadcaster. Like her husband, she prefers to work over drafts of speeches written for her, adding touches of her own personality. She speaks fluent French, with only a slight English intonation, as the result of being compelled to speak only French one day each week in her childhood nursery.

The Queen Mother has a good ear for music. She plays with competent feeling and expression and often played for the King on a walnut baby grand during their week-ends at Windsor. Her selections are usually Bach, Beethoven, Chopin, Schubert and Purcell, with an occasional bit from Ravel and Debussy. Like her daughters, she loves popular dance music and is always well versed in the hit tunes from the latest American and British shows and movies. Radios and gramophones provide constant background music for their off-duty hours.

Very fond of dancing, Elizabeth prefers waltzes and Scottish reels to any of the modern steps, although as a young woman she did teach the Charleston to the officers aboard a cruiser and on the South African journey, when the officers on *Vanguard* toasted her as "the life of the party," she led a conga line around the decks one evening. When she became Queen she insisted that professional dance bands play for Palace balls and parties instead of the customary military string bands.

Though she played tennis and rode horseback as a young

woman, the Queen Mother has never been keen on outdoor sports and the demands of her job as Queen gave her a good excuse to forgo the more strenuous forms of exercise. About the only outdoor activity she excels in is fresh-water fishing—the late Neville Chamberlain, a devoted angler, thought so much of her ability that he used to lend her his books on the subject—but her interest in this lazy pastime was partly defensive. The King did not like women in his shooting parties, so when His Majesty was out on the moors around Balmoral the Queen often took her rod down to the banks of the River Dee that borders the estate. Elizabeth is a moderate shot with a rifle, but she shoots best from a sitting position, with her legs crossed, Buddha-fashion, in front of her.

Through their friendship with the late Lord Mildmay, an outstanding amateur rider, the Queen and the then Princess Elizabeth were persuaded to become joint owners of Monaveen, a crack, nine-year-old jumper. Monaveen, which cost the royal partners £1,000, won some £3,000 in prizes and ran—unsuccessfully—in the Grand National steeplechase before it met with an accident and was killed. After Lord Mildmay was drowned, the Queen Mother bought two more horses from his stable and they now run in her own colours (blue, buff-striped jacket, blue sleeves, black cap with gold tassel).

Resigned to her middle-aged plumpness, Elizabeth resolutely refuses to take regular exercise and prefers to ride in a car rather than walk whenever possible. About the only walking she now does is to take the family's many dogs for strolls—and then only because she doesn't trust the servants to take them much beyond the front door. She gets around in London in one of several Palace limousines. She learned to drive when she was a girl, but has not taken the wheel herself for more than 20 years. Once en route to a country engagement for which she was late she told the chauffeur to hurry. He did, and just as he was about to turn out to pass a trailer truck Elizabeth became frightened and shouted "Stop! Stop!" The driver paid no attention, passed the truck, and then turned around and said: "I am sorry to disobey Your Majesty, but there can only be one in charge of the car." The Queen smiled and forgave him and has never done any more back-seat driving.

She is not fond of speed, however, and it is not until recent years that she has accepted the royal innovation of travel by air.

On her first air journey, accompanying her husband to Brussels in 1936, she became air-sick. But her quick sense of humour saved the situation. "It's lucky this is not a procession," she said, as she excused herself. Fascinated by her son-in-law's account of his flight in one of Britain's record-breaking Comet jet airliners, the Queen Mother accompanied Princess Margaret on a four-hour, 1,850-mile cruise over southern Europe in May, 1952, and during the flight exercised her queenly prerogative by taking over the controls (with the manufacturer's chief test pilot in the second pilot's seat) of the giant airliner as it zipped along at a speed of more than 450 m.p.h.

The Queen Mother has a good appetite and is fond of substantial, simply-cooked British food. She shuns white bread and potatoes, but otherwise eats what she fancies on the theory that her healthy appetite accounts for her flawless complexion. A year or so ago, in a half-hearted attempt to reduce from a heavy 160 pounds, she cut down on her large breakfasts and her consumption of tea cakes and sandwiches. During her husband's last illness the strain and anxiety under which she laboured caused her to lose 14 pounds. She has made one attempt at a rigid diet, just before sailing for Canada in 1939, and lost 14 pounds, but she did not like the ordeal and seized her chance to give it up when a female subject wrote to the newspapers saying: "It's not nice. We want to think of our Queen as a mother and none of us would like to hear that our mothers were losing weight."

Elizabeth smokes infrequently, and never during the daytime. She often lighted a cigarette after dinner when she was sitting with her husband, and at state banquets guests appreciated her gesture in lighting up immediately after the meal so that they could follow suit. Alcohol is a ticklish matter for royalty, who must not seem to be blue-stockings nor yet scandalize strictly temperate subjects. In drink, as in all her other characteristics, the Queen Mother's demands are moderate. She likes an occasional glass of claret with dinner and before dinner she occasionally asks for a mild gin and orange squash cocktail.

Elizabeth's health is excellent. She is rarely ill, beyond an occasional cold, and about the only thing she suffered from while on the throne was a fatiguing weariness from her non-stop round of public duties. The births of her daughters were difficult and Cæsarean section was necessary in both cases.

The Queen Mother is devoted to her relatives, and she seldom gave a party without inviting one or more of her many nephews and nieces. She still sees a good deal of her brother, David Bowes-Lyon, who has been her crony since childhood. David, who is married to a niece of Viscount Astor, is a director of *The Times* and inherited the Bowes-Lyon manor house at Walden Bury. In 1950 his royal brother-in-law bestowed on him the sinecure, ceremonial post of High Sheriff for Hertfordshire.

Despite her easy charm, the Queen Mother does not make friends easily, and apart from her royal relatives and her own family she has few intimates. The two woman friends who were closest to her are both now dead. One was Lady Helen Graham, daughter of the Duke of Montrose, whom George V chose as Elizabeth's first lady-in-waiting and secretary and who guided her through her first difficult years as Queen. The other was Mrs. Ronald Greville, a close friend of Edward VII and a famous hostess of Edwardian days, at whose house in the Surrey hills George and Elizabeth spent their honeymoon

Warm-hearted and generous, the Queen Mother is always considerate of the problems of people less fortunate than herself. During the war years she was often seen to cry openly when making her way through the rubble-strewn streets of the bombed cities. One winter day she noticed that the sentries who stand outside St. George's gate at Windsor Castle were suffering because their sentry boxes were in an exposed position. Elizabeth promptly ordered them moved into shelter. Even though personally affected by the mistakes of others she treats them with compassion and understanding. Some time ago one of her personal maids, after many years in Her Majesty's service, took to drink. The Queen hushed up the case, paid for the woman's treatment in a home, and supported her until she died a few years ago.

Because of the nature of her position as Consort, Elizabeth had to spread her time fairly and evenly over the various national bodies that claimed her interest—among them the three women's services, of which she was commandant-in-chief, the ancient university seats of learning, distinctively feminine organizations like the Women's Voluntary Services and the Mothers' Union and a host of professional bodies which had her patronage—but with her preference for the human over the formal she has always harboured a soft spot for one London institution, St. Mary's

Hospital at Paddington. It was at this drab, 100-year-old hospital that Sir Alexander Fleming discovered penicillin. Tucked away in its Dickensian corridors is the criminal laboratory of Dr. Roche Lynch, senior analyst for the Home Office and the man who knows more about murder and murderers than anyone else in Britain.

Sometimes when she has a free afternoon the Queen Mother visits St. Mary's. Perched on one of Dr. Lynch's high laboratory stools, Her Majesty will listen while the criminologist recounts the famed murder cases he has handled and shows her the gruesome evidence in his collection. Her curiosity satisfied, Elizabeth will then wander off and make a thorough round, visiting the poor and ailing in the wards.

One day the hospital's house governor remarked that it was a miracle that St. Mary's was never hit by bombs during the war. "A miracle?" said the Queen. "That may be so. You know, I include St. Mary's in my prayers every night."

Non-sectarian and broad-minded in her beliefs, Elizabeth holds her religion in deep and sincere conviction. Neither she nor her daughters miss a single Sunday morning service from one year to another except when they are ill. When the two Princesses were little girls Elizabeth loved to read Bible stories to them every Sunday. She also taught them their collects and psalms, but in the Scottish versions she had learned as a child. Both the late King and his wife found consolation in the Bible, and in their public speeches they continually put forward Biblical precepts as the best guide for today's troubled world.

"I can truly say that the King and I long to see the Bible back where it ought to be, as a guide and comfort in the homes and lives of our people," Elizabeth said in a message opening a London exhibition of the World's Evangelical Alliance in September, 1951. "From our own experience we know what the Bible can mean for personal life."

Like most people who have a careless regard for time, the Queen Mother is not an early riser. She has breakfast around 9, either in her room alone or with Margaret. Once the morning papers are read, however, she is capable of going through a great deal of work in a short time and with her lady-in-waiting and secretary she deals rapidly with her voluminous correspondence. When George VI was alive she had an office in the Palace next door to his and carried out a daily routine that was similar to though naturally less strenuous than that of her husband. Though no longer required to perform such official chores as receiving the wives of new ambassadors after their husbands have presented their credentials, she still has a steady stream of callers to fill up her days—representatives of charitable organizations seeking her support, local officials hoping to persuade her to visit their towns, dress designers and photographers.

As Queen Mother she is entitled to her own household and she has retained most of the officials who served her as Consort. The head of her household is the Earl of Airlie, a Scot who fills the ceremonial post of Lord Chamberlain to the Queen. Her two most important household aides are Major Oliver Dawnay, her private secretary, and Major Sir Arthur Penn, her treasurer, who budgets her personal spending, allocates her charity contributions in accordance with her wishes and settles her personal bills. Jack Crisp, who served as a Page of the Presence to George VI, has been appointed to control the domestic staff in her own establishment.

Like the late King the Queen Mother has always kept a sharp eye on all press coverage and news pictures of her family's activities. When her children were growing up she sorely resented newspaper efforts to report intimate details of their lives. The two girls were closely guarded from the press and as a result most of the anecdotes of their childhood were either garbled or fictionalized. At first Elizabeth was so infuriated about these legends that she had her staff ring up the editors and point out errors, but she soon gave this up and instead started a scrapbook of erroneous stories, which is still the source of many a royal family joke.

The Queen Mother is not photogenic, and even the most carefully posed pictures of her fail to convey her flawless pink-and-white complexion and the full charm of her personality. In the flesh she is prettier than any portrait has ever shown her. As a cameraman once remarked, "That little woman has grounds for a libel suit every time her picture is taken."

Elizabeth is not vain, but she feels that she has a duty as a Queen to show herself to her best advantage. Just before the outbreak of the Second World War, having noticed photographer Cecil Beaton's successes in glamorizing the society beauties of the day, Her Majesty summoned him to the Palace to photograph her in her handsomest dresses. "It is so distressing to me," she told Beaton, "that I always photograph so badly." The Queen was delighted with the posed, somewhat precious results and ever since Beaton has been rewarded with the cream of the Palace's photographic assignments, an honour which he has had to share in the last few years with another British photographer, Baron Nahum, one of the Duke of Edinburgh's friends.

Although her face is still unlined and no grey streaks her hair, the Queen Mother is well aware that she has passed her mid-century mark. When Beaton sent her the finished proofs of the pictures he had taken to celebrate her fiftieth birthday, Elizabeth sent them back to have some of the retouching removed! Her private secretary informed Beaton that Her Majesty felt that, since she had battled her way through a number of years, she could not have come through completely unscathed. This was the first time any of Beaton's sitters had suggested that his pictures were too flattering.

Hastily-shot press pictures seldom show the Queen Mother at her best, but news photographers like her because she has developed enough news sense to realize where the best pictures are to be had during royal tours and visits. Usually she led the King to some point of extra interest and waited there until the photographers got their pictures. Often His Majesty did not know what his wife was up to, but the photographers were grateful and repaid the favour by shooting Elizabeth from her best angles.

Having completed the main part of her life work—the moulding of the character of her daughter who is now Queen Regnant and the upbringing of Princess Margaret—the Queen Mother has earned a respite from the ceaseless, onerous round of public duties that go to make up the life of royalty. As Queen Mary did for her, she retired to the background immediately after her husband's funeral so that she would in no way overshadow her daughter's new position on the centre of the stage. As Queen Mother she has more freedom and more time for herself—she is no longer expected to attend every formal royal function—but Elizabeth still considers herself a main supporting pillar for the royal house and she has no intention of shirking her public duties. In the short, gracious message of thanks which she issued to the nation after George VI's death she said: "Throughout our married life we have tried, the King and I, to fulfil with all our hearts and all our strength the great task of service that was laid upon us. My only wish now is that I may be allowed to continue the work we sought to do together." Like the indefatigable Queen Mary, Elizabeth as Queen Mother can be expected to shoulder her share of the family's duties until illness or old age slows her down.

She is sustained in her royal duties by a remarkable common-sense philosophy, which she often passed on to her daughters when they chafed under the routine of royalty. "Your work," says the Queen Mother, "is the rent you pay for the room you occupy on earth."

XVIII

DOWAGER QUEEN (I)

HER MAJESTY the Dowager Queen Mary, the venerable and venerated matriarch of Britain's royal family, who passed the eighty-fifth milestone in her long life on May 26, 1952, symbolizes and personifies the continuity of the British monarchic institution. Like Winston Churchill, her younger but nearest contemporary in public life, she provides a visible, living link between six reigns and two centuries, between the gas-lit days of the mid-Victorian era and the beginnings of the atomic age.

In the year of her birth the American Civil War had freshly ended, Britain was engaged in a now-forgotten war with King Theodore of Abyssinia, Napoleon III and his Empress Eugénie, who was later to become a friend of Queen Mary's during her exile in England, still ruled in France and the Franco-Prussian War was still in the offing. In London, a horse-drawn city where women dressed in crinolines and men wore stovepipe hats and ornate chin-whiskers, Queen Victoria laid the foundation stone for the Albert Hall to commemorate her beloved Prince, Benjamin Disraeli (Conservative) and William Ewart Gladstone (Liberal) were beginning to dominate the political stage (though neither had yet reached the goal of Prime Minister), and John Stuart Mill, a reforming M.P., advocated votes for women and was laughed at in the House of Commons.[1]

Born near the half-way mark of Victoria's long reign, Queen Mary is one of the few adult survivors of those who stood by the deathbed of the old Queen. George III, the last King of the United States, was her great-grandfather and her grand-uncles included both George IV and William IV.

For the last half-century Queen Mary has been an international figure in her own right, and for the past 40 years the symbol of British royalty the world over has been her towering, ramrod-backed silhouette, every inch of which is so obviously a Queen. Her stately nineteenth-century air, her imposing, statuesque presence, as solid and unchanging as the high-button coats, the narrow, pointed shoes, the parasol clutched firmly as a sceptre and the characteristic toques which she long ago adopted as her fashion trademark, have combined to make her a symbol of all that is best in royalty and give her the permanency of a landmark in the public eye.

At any gathering of the dwindling ranks of the kings and queens of Europe, most of whom are her relatives, it is Queen Mary who stands out, not only because of her advanced years but because few of her younger colleagues wear their royalty nearly so well as this remarkable royal octogenarian.

Queen Mary's whole life has been devoted to an exacting double standard which she regards as the inescapable lot of royal persons: the conscientious acceptance of the duties and responsibilities of her position, and the meticulous observance of the traditional precepts that guide royal behaviour.

During the First World War when one of her relatives, due to visit a hospital, wearily complained, "I'm tired and I hate hospitals," Queen Mary snapped at her: "You are a member of the British royal family. We are *never* tired—and we all *love* hospitals."

Not even in her mellowing years has she relaxed her rigorous royal code. She has never been known to lose her regal poise, nor does she ever cut the corners on royal protocol. Even in the bosom of her family she pays strict attention to the niceties of royal behaviour, and in return she expects to receive the respect due her own station. When the Princess Royal heard the shocking news of the death of her brother, George VI, she rushed into her mother's apartment in a distraught state, with her hair askew. "Please do your hair properly when you come before the Queen," her mother sternly reprimanded.

Queen Mary's fine photogenic personality, the epitome of regal demeanour, has been achieved only at the cost of sacrificing some of her private life, however. Reserved by temperament, from childhood onward she has had to fight against a painful shyness, a family trait she shared with Victoria and George VI. She has no small talk, and a ready stream of polite conversation is foreign to her nature. She still refuses to make public speeches and even now when she is the centre of attraction at a public ceremony a blush rises easily to her cheeks. Her deep, natural reserve reflects itself in her features, which nowadays are nearly always set in a stern but kind mask.

On any public or ceremonial occasion in which she appears with members of her family there is always a personal cheer, a special ovation from the crowd, for Queen Mary alone. The special place which she holds in the hearts and affections of the British people is not due to her longevity or her links with history. It is a tribute to herself, a recognition in the public mind that in the transformation of the British monarchy from a dynastic to a real national institution which has occurred within her lifetime— the gradual broadening of the monarchic system to bring it closer to the needs of the people in a modern democratic society —Queen Mary has rendered her own considerable service to her country. More than that, by the sheer force of her personal example and her rigid insistence on high standards of royal family behaviour which set a model for every family in the land, she has done much to preserve the mould of British character.

In her own long reign as Consort to George V, from 1910 to 1936, Queen Mary combined with her husband to give the throne a new personal meaning. Their coming to the throne provided welcome sobriety after the gay nine-year-reign of Edward VII, but by making their own family circle the setting for the monarchy they also established a pattern for their successors to follow. They were the first royal couple to concern themselves seriously with tours of factories and visits to working-class areas, an offshoot of Queen Mary's girlhood interest in welfare and social problems (which she later passed on to George VI), and in doing so they began the democratizing process of taking the crown to the people.

During the constitutional crisis which the abdication of her eldest son precipitated—when the very future of the monarchy hung in the balance—it was Queen Mary who provided the unifying, stabilizing influence while the crown passed shakily from Edward VIII to George VI. She was consulted by the then Prime Minister, Stanley Baldwin, and both her sons came to her for counsel, the eldest to seek approval for his irrevocable decision to give up his throne, the next in line for courage and guidance in the new role which he accepted as his inescapable duty.

18   273

For the first few months of the new reign Queen Mary was prominently in the foreground, ready with advice and experience. She had already inducted her daughter-in-law, the new Queen, into the royal routine when Elizabeth was Duchess of York, and once she saw that Bertie and Elizabeth could handle their new jobs she gradually edged out of the spotlight. Remembering how her own mother-in-law, handsome, enamelled Queen Alexandra, remained in the limelight as Queen Mother during much of her own reign, Queen Mary refused to use that title and characteristically retired into the background after her son's coronation.

But perhaps Queen Mary's greatest contribution to the royal story has been her service in training the younger generations of her family, passing on to them—and drilling into them—the principles and standards she absorbed during her nineteenth-century upbringing, when manners, virtues and morals were held in higher regard than they are today.

In her role as "Granny" Queen she keeps her benevolent eye on her whole royal brood, but it was to the upbringing and development of Elizabeth II that she naturally gave her continuing attention. Without seeming to override young Elizabeth's parents or interfere with the necessary Cabinet supervision of the education of the heiress presumptive, the old Queen, working directly with Princess Elizabeth's governess, oversaw the whole of her grand-daughter's schooling and frequently suggested strengthening or filling in gaps in Elizabeth's education. She saw to it that Elizabeth read good books and every Christmas sent Elizabeth and her sister beautifully-bound sets of the classics of English literature. For her training as a "royal person" Queen Mary took the young Princess personally in hand, invited her on eagerly-anticipated outings beyond the walls of Buckingham Palace and gradually introduced her to the ordeal of being stared at and sought after, which makes almost every appearance of royalty a public occasion. Between the old Queen and the young girl who was destined one day to rule there developed a rare bond of affection and respect. They have the same facial features —there is a striking similarity between young Queen Elizabeth and Queen Mary when she was a young Princess—and in many ways they think alike. So close is the parallel, in fact, that young Elizabeth is almost a modern version of Queen Mary.

Even though she was heiress presumptive, Elizabeth as

Princess was taught to curtsy to Queen Mary and when "Granny" Queen came to visit she and her sister would politely escort their grandmother to her car. When Elizabeth was hurriedly summoned home from Kenya as Queen, Queen Mary, who is more punctilious than any other member of her family, was waiting at Clarence House, ready to curtsy to the new sovereign, but officials who watched the two Queens meet were surprised to see that it was Elizabeth who curtsied, probably for the first and last time in her reign. In Elizabeth's mind, the grand old lady still came first. Even now the young Queen frequently seeks out her grandmother's ready ear and consults her on personal matters.

Queen Mary has never obtruded herself upon her children or their offspring, but she is always ready with advice and counsel, which she gives firmly and freely, and in moments of difficulty or sadness it is generally to her that they turn.

When the young Duke of Kent came to her in 1934 and confessed his great love for the beauteous Princess Marina of Greece it was Queen Mary who promptly wrote to Princess Paul of Yugoslavia, Marina's sister, and tactfully hinted at a meeting of the two at a Balkan hunting lodge. Five days after the young couple met there they were engaged. When the handsome, charming young Duke, with whom she had more in common than with any of her sons, was tragically killed in an air crash in 1942 Queen Mary was deeply shocked, but her first thought when she heard the sudden, unexpected news was not for herself but for her son's wife. "I shall go to see Marina tomorrow," she stoutly announced, and next day drove across from her wartime Gloucestershire retreat to the Kent's home outside London to comfort the Duchess. For many weeks afterwards the grieving Duchess, numbed with shock at her great loss, remained gravely ill and to her doctors she seemed to lack the will to recover. Then Queen Mary took a hand. She spoke with mother-in-law directness to the still-young widow, impressed on her how much her children needed her and convinced her that she still had a part to play, if she chose, in the life of the royal family and the nation, and gradually the Duchess of Kent recovered something of her old zest for life and capacity for service.

Though she has no constitutional part to play, Queen Mary is vitally interested in national affairs. During the 1947 royal tour of South Africa, when George VI, Queen Elizabeth and their two daughters were absent from Britain, as the senior member of the royal family she made it a point to receive Prime Minister Attlee every week and discuss with him the winter fuel crisis through which Britain passed. She quickly sensed the growing peevishness of Britons caught in the icy grip of winter who complained, on the basis of tour broadcasts which stressed the gaiety and sunshine of South Africa, that the royal family had escaped on a long, pleasant holiday, and on her suggestion the B.B.C. subsequently emphasized in its broadcast reports the enormous amount of hard work involved in the royal tour. Later, when Queen Mary had been briefed on the intricacies of the balance-of-payments problem which beset her country she wrote Attlee and offered to help with a personal contribution to Britain's dollar drive, a gesture she backed up by donating her now-famous hand-made carpet to be sold for dollars. It ultimately netted $119,651.86 (£35,354 18s.).[2]

In her happy role as the nation's grandma, Queen Mary receives a steady stream of personal letters. Most of them are from well-wishers or ordinary folk who feel that they would like to share their joys and sorrows with a sympathetic, even if symbolic, old friend, but if they contain a complaint which she considers worth investigating she passes on a note to whatever Government department is involved—and then follows up to see that the complaint is not overlooked.

Not even George V, to whom she was devoted, escaped Queen Mary's occasional censure. Whenever her husband got too long-winded in conversation or swore at the wrong time she would prod him surreptitiously with her parasol and say, "Now, George!" Nor is it only upon the living royalty of the present that she keeps a supervisory eye. Once she happened to overhear a sniggering remark that the statue of Queen Victoria (erected by public subscription in 1911) which sits placidly at the head of the broad avenue of the Mall had no wedding ring. Queen Mary promptly dispatched a man to investigate, and to her chagrin learned that it was true, but soon afterwards a marital band was chiselled on to Victoria's pudgy stone hand.

While watching a whole epoch pass with the years into history Queen Mary has retained a majestic indifference to the technical miracles which have transformed the world around her. She has never made a radio address (and only spoken over the air briefly on a handful of occasions), never flown in an aeroplane (and worries whenever any members of her family fly), and does not use the telephone ("That instrument," she says, "is not meant for royalty").

She has become so enduring a fixture in British life that few people under 40 today remember that she once passed through youth and middle age.

Although she was not born to be Queen, she entered the world —at one minute before midnight on May 26, 1867—appropriately enough in the same room at London's Kensington Palace in which Queen Victoria had been born. As a lesser royal princess the future Queen Mary had her place down the line of succession, although her family was accounted not very considerable royalty. Her mother was the vivacious and talented Duchess of Teck, who, as Princess Mary of Cambridge, had been the most popular English princess of the day. The daughter of Adolphus, the Duke of Cambridge, who was a son of George III, she made an impecunious love match somewhat late in life, after declining the hands of several European princes, with Franz, Duke of Teck. Queen Mary's father was the only son of Duke Alexander of the former South German kingdom of Württemberg and his morganatic wife, the beauteous Claudine, Comtesse de Rhédey, who was descended from the ancient Hungarian house of Arpad, which traces its ancestry back to the year 1001.

The Duchess of Teck, as Queen Victoria's cousin, occupied a minor place in the royal hierarchy—in state processions she had to ride with her back to the horses—but at a time when the widowed Queen's court was openly referred to as a "mourning warehouse" her dashing, ebullient personality made her the darling of the crowds and she invariably drew more cheers than the Queen herself. On the day of her daughter's birth more than a thousand visitors called at Kensington Palace to leave their congratulations. Victoria herself, who made a point of inspecting all royal babies, paid a call a month later when she returned to London from Balmoral and put her stamp of approval on the newcomer. "A very fine baby," she recorded in her journal, "with pretty little features and a quantity of hair." The youngster was duly christened Victoria (after the Queen, who was one of her godmothers) Mary Augusta Louisa Olga Pauline Claudine

277

Agnes, which her mother promptly shortened to "my little May-flower," after the month of her birth, and then to "May." (To-day only the present Queen Mother and a few of Queen Mary's aged and intimate contemporaries call her "May." Her two remaining sons and her daughter call her "Mamma" and within the family circle she is referred to as "Granny." Others address her formally as "Your Majesty" for the first time and there-after as "Ma'am.")

With her three brothers who followed her in quick succession, May Teck, as she was then known, spent her childhood and early girlhood in a large, uncomfortable suite of apartments at Ken-sington Palace and then at the commodious White Lodge in Richmond Park (built by George I as "a place of refreshment after the fatigues of the chase"), both homes given to her parents by Victoria. No royal allowance went with them, and the generous, open-handed Duchess of Teck, whose own fortune was slender, spent and gave away money—mainly to charities—in a style that was so truly royal that when Princess May reached her sixteenth birthday her parents were obliged to give up their White Lodge residence and live abroad for almost two years in order to retrench. Those two years of economic exile, mainly spent in Italy, with side trips to Switzerland and France, had two lasting consequences for the future Queen. First, she learned the penalties of too-lavish expenditure, with the result that for the rest of her life she has been economical, even frugal, in her own household. She uses up old envelopes, saves her own and her family's Christmas cards (which she pastes into scrapbooks to give to hospitals) and has no patience with any form of waste. Second, as a result of a staggering programme of sight-seeing and cultural study, accompanied by her mother or her governess, she received such a grounding in the arts, architecture and the antiquities that she now qualifies as something of an authority in those fields.

On her return to London at the age of 19 Princess May simul-taneously made her entrée to Victoria's court, her formal debut into society and the discovery, as she later said, that she "was not educated." Her education, like that of most royal princesses, had been confined to her home. Her mother had given her her first lessons, heard her dates, taught her to sew and grounded her in the Scriptures, and a succession of governesses followed

278

on. When she began to hunger for a deeper educational background than was customary for young girls of her time and class,
Princess May had the good fortune to be under the charge of a
volatile French Alsatian governess known as Madame Bricka,
who was to have a major mental influence on the future Queen.
"Be thorough," Madame Bricka advised the Princess, and together they undertook a long course of study, in which May read
for six hours daily—mainly the works of the nineteenth-century
historians and philosophers—until the time of her marriage seven
years later.

The other formative influence on Princess May's keen young
mind was her Aunt "Gussy," the Princess Augusta Caroline,
Grand Duchess of Mecklenburg-Strelitz, who was the Duchess of
Teck's elder sister. "Gussy" was a level-headed old lady with a
radical turn of mind who took a passionate interest in political
matters and wasn't afraid to voice her opinions. From the old
Duchess the young Princess learned of new trends and movements then in the air—Darwinism, the Socialism of William
Morris, votes for women, the inquiries of a Select Committee
into sweated labour conditions in London's east end—the very
existence of which was unknown to most of her socialite friends.

Princess May was horrified by newspaper accounts of the
Select Committee's findings. She pumped more information from
one of the committee members who was a frequent visitor to
White Lodge, read the Blue Book of the committee's report, and
on the strength of its evidence became something of a crusader.
When she went in to the royal shoemaker's shop to order a pair
of boots she boldly asked, "What do you pay your work-
people?" The bootmaker estimated that they were paid eight
shillings a week on the average. "I will not buy boots made
by sweated labour," announced the Princess. "I don't mind paying more, but unless those wages are increased I shall go elsewhere and persuade my friends to do the same." The workers got
their increase. Years later when she had become Queen Consort
Queen Mary continued to crusade quietly on behalf of the poor,
particularly to get them better housing conditions, and her
astringent comments often produced results. Once a committee
of society people, to whom she had given her support, tried to
steer her away from some slum property they owned and show
her only some model flats they had erected. "It will never be

279

beneath my dignity to visit the homes in which the King's subjects have to live," said Queen Mary and marched off to inspect the slums. When she saw them she exploded: "These houses are a disgrace to the country and an outrage to the poor souls who live in them! I shall come here again—and, if nothing is done, I shall withdraw my name from your list of patrons." Two months later the houses had been rebuilt.

"I don't know how May does it!" George V often said of his wife in later years when Queen Mary came up with some surprising bit of information on a subject about which he expected her to know nothing. The explanation lay in her earlier interests. For years after becoming Queen and Consort she continued to wade through Government reports and private surveys on social and welfare problems. In the course of her studies she came into contact with many of the emerging women leaders in the trade union movement, and in 1924, when it fell to George V to receive the first Labour Government to take office in Britain, it was Queen Mary who astonished the new Cabinet Ministers with her deep knowledge of the social questions of the day, an understanding which further helped to bridge the gap between the monarchy and the people.

While Princess May busily educated herself old Queen Victoria busied herself with her favourite occupation, matchmaking. Young May, intelligent and strikingly beautiful, had long been marked out in the old Queen's mind as a future Queen Consort. She was the most eligible princess of British birth and in 1891, when Princess May was 24, she found herself engaged to Prince Albert Victor, Duke of Clarence, eldest son of the Prince of Wales and heir presumptive to the throne. Queen Victoria was delighted at the prospect of uniting the Cambridge branch of her large family with the ruling line, and press and public were equally pleased. Even on the day after Princess May's birth the newspapers had remarked that she was a cousin— "though not too near a cousin"—to the sons of the Prince of Wales.

Five weeks before the date set for their marriage the Duke of Clarence died of pneumonia during an influenza epidemic. Princess May went into seclusion in France, but on her return to London Prince George, the Duke of York and the new heir presumptive, having been encouraged by Victoria to speak up for himself, began to pay court to his cousin. On July 6, 1893, they were married in the Chapel Royal at St. James's Palace.[3] "I am indeed lucky to have got such a darling and charming wife," the Duke of York confided to his journal after their wedding. Queen Victoria, an indomitable diarist, entered her satisfaction in her own journal. "Thank God!" she wrote. "Georgie has got such an excellent, useful and good wife."

The first home of the Duke and his Duchess was York Cottage, a cramped little house on the Prince of Wales's Sandringham estate, and there, between 1894 and 1905, five of their six children were born (their first-born, Prince Edward, now the Duke of Windsor, entered the world at the White Lodge home of his maternal grandparents, the Duke and Duchess of Teck).

The 17 years' apprenticeship which she and her husband served before they reached the throne were not the happiest in Queen Mary's long life. Shy and serious-minded, devoted to her husband, home and children, and already settled in her dowdy fashions, she felt out of place among the stylish beauties who made up the court of Edward VII, who finally ended his apprenticeship of nearly 50 years as Prince of Wales and succeeded his mother on the old Queen's death in 1901. Like most royal couples, the Duke and Duchess of York were called upon to make long foreign tours, which meant leaving their children for months at a time. They spent nearly eight months on a world-wide expedition that took them to Gibraltar, Egypt, Aden, Ceylon, Australia, New Zealand, South Africa and Canada. Later they went to India, Austria, Spain and Paris. Like Elizabeth II, Queen Mary is a bad sailor, but she endured the agony of long sea voyages as part of her duty. Methodically she kept a detailed record of souvenirs she was given on the way, which she still keeps up to this day. She began keeping a diary, a useful habit she passed on to George VI, and started the first of her many photograph albums, in which she pastes prints of all the royal family photographs she can lay hands on.

Edward VII created them Prince and Princess of Wales at the conclusion of their world tour, but when they came to the throne in 1910 George V and Queen Mary were still comparatively unknown to the public and not really popular. The First World War was under way before King and people were united, but at the end of those four terrible years George and Mary emerged as respected public characters. Queen Mary undertook a massive amount of war work—organizing committees, collecting funds, inspecting troops and hospitals in Britain and France. Her vast Central Committee, which she had initiated in 1906 to provide work for women, had virtual charge of all paid female labour in Britain and transferred millions of women from peace to war work and back again. It was during these parlous years that Queen Mary's hair turned white.

Through the giddy decade of the 1920's and the troubled years of the 1930's their place in the people's affection grew steadily higher, and when George V and Queen Mary celebrated the Silver Jubilee of their reign in 1935 it brought forth a demonstration of popular affection probably unparalleled in history and unequalled since except for the emotional response aroused by the passing of their son, George VI.

The abdication of Edward VIII after eleven brief months on the throne was the deepest disappointment of Queen Mary's life. Having sacrificed much of her private life for her royal responsibilities, she could not understand how a man destined for the highest responsibility of all could put his personal inclinations, however strong, above the clear course of his duty. Although she did not publicly betray her real feelings, the personal message which she penned for the nation and the Commonwealth—in itself an unusual gesture—carried a faint sting of reproach. "I need not speak to you," she wrote, "of the distress which fills a mother's heart when I think that my dear son has deemed it his duty to lay down his charge, and that the reign which had begun with so much hope and promise has so suddenly ended."

After the abdication the Duke of Windsor did not see his mother again until 1945. Queen Mary does not talk much about him, but they write to each other regularly and the Duke calls on her and sometimes stays with her on his visits to Britain. Except for one brief moment at a pre-abdication party, Queen Mary has never seen the woman for whom Edward left his throne, and even to her intimates she has never mentioned the name of the Duchess of Windsor. Queen Mary regally refuses to receive a divorced person and this royal taboo is sufficient to bar her American-born daughter-in-law from her presence. Once the Duke of Windsor left the former Mrs. Simpson fretting in his car outside Marlborough House while he chatted with his mother.

When the Second World War began Queen Mary, then aged 72, reluctantly left her home and interests in London and went to live at Badminton, the Gloucestershire manor house of her niece, the Duchess of Beaufort. Even in this rural retreat the old Queen insisted on playing her part in the war effort. She visited every war plant and service camp within reach, including many U.S. installations and hospitals, led her own working party which produced 432 articles for the troops, personally knitted more than 100 scarves for the officers of her regiment, the Queen's Own, and in her spare time joined a wood-cutting party, taking her turn at wielding a double-handed saw, that cleared a 111-acre tract on the Duke of Beaufort's estate. She "adopted" the nearby village of Badminton and knew almost every resident by name.

In her long life Queen Mary has endured more than her share of grief and anxieties. She has seen one son go into virtual exile and three have been taken from her by death (her youngest son, Prince John, who was never strong, died in 1919 at the age of 13). When the news came of George VI's sudden death there were fears among her friends that it would prove the final blow to the old lady, but Queen Mary heard the sad message with stoic, iron-willed composure. Not since she conquered her childish outbursts has she ever been known to cry, and the only time when she ever showed signs of great emotion in public was at the coronation of George VI, when tears filled her eyes as the ceremony reached its magnificent climax. On the day of his death her household understandingly left her alone in her suite, where she sat, pale but composed, surrounded by the pictures of her loved ones. It took the combined pleas of her family to persuade her that at her age she should not ride in his funeral procession or stand throughout the poignant burial service at Windsor.

XIX

DOWAGER QUEEN (II)

ALTHOUGH she retired from public life in 1936 Queen Mary's retirement during her years of royal widowhood has been characteristically active and vigorous. Shunning waste, she regards waste of time as one fault she cannot condone in herself or others and never allows herself an idle moment. She still approaches each new day with the eagerness of a young bride, and her daily engagement book would dismay most women half her years.

London born and bred, Queen Mary likes to consider herself a Cockney (although Kensington Palace, her birthplace, was well beyond earshot of the old Bow Bells) and is happiest when she is in the nation's capital. When she left Buckingham Palace to make room for Edward VIII she happily moved over to Marlborough House, the stately, red-brick mansion that stands across the street from St. James's Palace (although it is technically within its bounds). Built by Sir Christopher Wren for the famous Sarah, Duchess of Marlborough, the old house has been home to a succession of royal occupants. Queen Adelaide lived there as the widow of William IV, Queen Alexandra made it her first London home, and George V was born there. Queen Mary and her husband lived in it briefly as Princess and Prince of Wales.

Within its ornate, richly-furnished, deeply-carpeted rooms the Dowager Queen still contrives to live in as queenly a state as her £70,000 yearly allowance will permit. Brought up in an age when servants were both cheap and numerous, she still employs a small army of 47, each of whom has a designated duty, such as the "boot boy," the "knife boy," and the page who stands on constant vigil outside her door to answer her ring. A kindly but firm mistress, she runs her home on Victorian lines, keeps her finger on her house-keeping bills, arranges the duties of her staff and supervises the spring cleaning.

Though she now plays only an infrequent part in the public life of the royal family Queen Mary, in keeping with her regal style and grand manner, still maintains a household that is second in size and activity only to Elizabeth II's. Her feminine household consists of her Mistress of the Robes, the Dowager Duchess of Devonshire, an old personal friend who does duty only on occasions of great ceremony, and, under her, 11 other ladies- and women-of-the-bedchamber. Only three of these ladies-in-waiting, whom Queen Mary insists on calling by their old title of women-of-the-bedchamber, attend her regularly, taking it in turn to do a fortnight on duty, during which time they live and sleep at Marlborough House or wherever the old Queen may be residing. At the head of her male household should be a Lord Chamberlain to the Queen, but inasmuch as she seldom participates in ceremonial functions nowadays Queen Mary has not filled this post since the death of the Marquis of Anglesey in 1947. The overall supervision of her household is the responsibility of her Comptroller (Lord Claud Hamilton), and her private secretary (Major "Jack" Wickham) heads her secretariat. In addition she is served by one equerry, and two extra equerries stand by to undertake occasional duties.

The ground floor of Marlborough House is mainly given over to the splendid grandeur of heavily-ornamented state rooms and imposing corridors, into which are jammed Queen Mary's collection of art and antiques, probably one of the most valuable private collections in the country. Also on the ground floor are most of the offices and domestic rooms. The Queen's personal apartments—a suite of rooms consisting of her bedroom, her boudoir, where she does most of her work, and her private dining-room—are on the first floor, overlooking the Mall. Also on the first floor are two rooms peculiar to Queen Mary, her children's gift room, in which she hoards gifts to be given throughout the year to her royal brood, and her bazaar room, where she stores stocks of purchases for presentation to bazaars and charity fetes, the organizers of which are forever asking her for contributions.

There is an unwritten rule at Marlborough House that visitors and staff acknowledge Queen Mary's presence only when she chooses to recognize them first. Sometimes the testy old Queen remembers these instructions, sometimes she doesn't. A few years ago one of her visitors, forewarned of the rule, making his way to the drawing-room where he was supposed to wait her formal summons, chanced to meet her in the corridor. Carefully averting his eyes, he passed the old lady as though she weren't there. Just as he thought himself safely past he received a smart blow on the head. Forgetting her own rule, Queen Mary had turned and bopped him with her cane.

Queen Mary's day begins at 7.15 a.m. if she is to be busy, at 7.30 or 7.45 if she is not. There is no running water in her old-fashioned suite, so her maids carry up cans of water which she pours into a silver sink for her morning ablutions. She dresses completely and punctiliously and does up her towering hair-do before breakfasting alone in her dining-room. In getting herself ready for the day Queen Mary is assisted by two or three maids, called dressers, and it is at this time that the testiness that comes with old age shows itself. To the dresser who laces her stays she says no word but "Pull," but by the time her old-fashioned, high-collared, many-buttoned dresses are arranged there is apt to be some foot-tapping and heavy breathing that precedes a royal explosion. She makes up with old-fashioned taste, using powder and rouge sparingly and a faint touch of lipstick, but beyond a dab of eau-de-Cologne she will not use perfume. Her nails are always highly polished, but she regards nail varnish as an abomination.

Between 9 and 9.30 Queen Mary is back in her boudoir, ready to deal with the day's mail. Every letter she receives is read to her, but she replies personally only to those from her family and close friends. To the others she indicates the reply to be sent out by her lady-in-waiting or her secretary. The only letters she refuses to answer are from crackpots and professional beggars. She can spot both instantly.

Part of each day she devotes to her personal finances and business affairs, either with her Comptroller, who acts as her treasurer, or her private secretary. She has the shrewdest big-business head in the royal family and her investments and financial interests have helped maintain through years of high taxation the private family fortune passed down by George V. According to the Civil List which covered her husband's reign she receives a yearly grant from Parliament of £70,000, out of which she is expected to pay her household expenses and the internal upkeep of Marlborough House. Comparatively frugal in her personal spending, she is at the same time extremely generous with her money. She helps out hard-up minor members of her family and donates large sums, mostly anonymously, to worthy charities.

Queen Mary is easily the richest member of the royal family. Royal wills remain state secrets, being outside the jurisdiction of any court, but at the time of George V's death it was reported that he had passed to his wife a fortune that was then assessed at £2,000,000, and Queen Mary has probably been able to add to that from the £1,190,000 she has drawn from the state in annuities since 1936.[1] When Queen Mary dies she will probably leave the bulk of her money to Elizabeth II, although the greater part of her fortune that remains at the time of her death will be drained off by the Exchequer in death duties, which are paid by all royalty except the sovereign.

At noon each day the lady-in-waiting on duty reads *The Times* aloud to Queen Mary, beginning with the editorial page and then the news columns, while the Queen busies her fingers with her ever-present embroidery.

Luncheon is punctually at 1.15, and she often has one or two friends or a member of her household to lunch with her. Her luncheon parties are famous, if not for her food at least for their conversation. Her wit is keen, her taste catholic, her knowledge encyclopædic, and the talk at her table ranges over a wide field. Recently her doctors attempted to put her on a diet. A trencher-woman all her life, Queen Mary promptly ignored it. She has few fads, but she will never touch any food with her fingers, and spears her toast and muffins with a fork. She generally eats a one-course meal—cold roast beef and hard-boiled eggs served together is one of her favourites, roast partridge another—but she wastes no time about it and members of her household, who are expected to keep pace with her and finish when she does, have been known to fill up beforehand in their rooms.

George V liked his cup, but Queen Mary never touches spirits. However, she often has a glass or two of Chablis, her favourite white wine, at lunch and sometimes drinks a pint of sparkling Moselle for dinner. In the days when she went out for dinner she was so particular about her wines that she used to send two bottles of her favourite vintage ahead for her hosts to serve her, and if any was left over she took it frugally home. When an American writer published this royal titbit in an article about her some years ago the old Queen reportedly called him in and rebuked him. "Of course it's true," she candidly admitted, "but I don't want it written about."

If she has guests for lunch Queen Mary usually produces a bottle of George V's port when the meal is over. If she is in the mood to obey her doctors' injunction to rest after lunch she will take leave of her guests, nod towards the port bottle and remark, "Let me see a 'dead man' before I come down."

Until recent months, when her outside activities have been curtailed, Queen Mary's afternoon was almost always devoted to one of her excursions around her beloved London. With her wide-ranging interests she was just as likely to turn up at an antique show or an agricultural exhibition, or to embark on a spontaneous shopping expedition. These outings, fewer in number nowadays, invariably cause a cheerful traffic jam, for a small crowd always gathers when the presence of one of her big, high-backed, box-like motor cars indicates that Queen Mary is about. In the spring and summer months she drives to one or another of London's many parks to see the flowers, usually making her stately way through the streets in her favourite auto, a 27-year-old Daimler limousine, which is fitted with spare instruments in the back seat so that she can check on her chauffeur's driving. Knowing that people want to see her when she is out she generally obliges by sitting upright on a raised jump seat but she is so determined not to waste a waking hour that she often has her lady-in-waiting read to her from a newspaper while they are driving.

Queen Mary seldom accompanies the rest of her family on their inevitable summer holiday at Balmoral and generally contents herself with a quiet six weeks or so at Sandringham, which was her husband's favourite royal home and with which she has many intimate associations. She used to be an energetic gardener and when she went to Sandringham took her own set of gardening tools with her. Ivy is her pet hate. Not a leaf of it is allowed on Marlborough House and when she comes across it elsewhere she has been known to give it a fierce jab with her parasol. Like her daughter-in-law, the Queen Mother, Queen Mary is a flower addict. When Britain's great lupin specialist, the late George Russell, managed to crown his life's work at the age of 74 by producing a multicoloured lupin he clung jealously to his secret for five years. George V sent his own gardener to Russell's cottage at York with instructions to offer "any sum within reason" for seeds or plants of the new lupin, but Russell refused to part with them. Then Queen Mary took a hand. She sent Russell a personal message—and that same autumn seeds and plants, the first Russell had parted with, arrived at Buckingham Palace.

In the course of her long life Queen Mary has accumulated an enormous collection of *objets d'art* and historical souvenirs of the royal family. London's antique dealers and jewellers recognize her as a connoisseur gifted with an uncanny knowledge of the fine arts and a remarkable memory and few of them would question her judgment on a piece about which they had any doubts. A tireless, acquisitive collector, she will spend hours prowling around the shops, poking into odd corners with her parasol and asking, "Well, what's under here?" Her own rich, individual collections are chiefly of Chinese porcelain and jade, which she began acquiring on her visit to India, Georgian silverware and furniture, on which she is an accepted expert, and nineteenth-century furniture, particularly Victorian *papier-mâché* tables and chairs.

As Queen Consort she put her artistic tastes and knowledge to good use by restoring and rearranging the state rooms at the royal palaces, particularly at Windsor Castle, an exhausting job that involved separating and styling in hundreds of rooms the furnishings, pictures, period pieces and knicknacks which time and Queen Victoria (who generously allowed her large family to take away what they needed from the royal homes) had allowed to fall into a hopeless muddle. Relentlessly Queen Mary searched through the royal palaces and poked around the homes of her relatives until she found a missing piece of furniture, a matching vase or a chair lost from a set. Sometimes on her rounds of the antique shops she came across pieces which, from old royal records, she recognized as having been lost, strayed or stolen from a royal home and she bought them in at once for the royal collection. In the jam-packed lumber rooms at "Buck House,"

St. James's Palace and Windsor she unearthed treasurers from other days that had been stored away and forgotten. At Windsor she used her knowledge of the period to recreate the state suites in Regency style and she did the same at Buckingham Palace, ruthlessly stripping away the dark draperies, patterned wall-paper and Victorian embellishments that made the place a gloomy mausoleum.

In recent years Queen Mary has added to her many other interests a passion for archæology. "Let anything interesting be dug up anywhere—and Her Majesty is off at once to see it," say her staff.

At some time each afternoon she indulges in what her staff calls "Queen's rest," but this is no more than a brief relaxation period when the old lady sits bolt upright with a cushion behind her back, her feet up on the sofa, stitching on her *gros point* embroidery while her lady-in-waiting reads to her. Her favourite books are Georgian diaries, historical novels, recent memoirs or biographies. She is currently working her way through Winston Churchill's many-volumed story of the Second World War (Churchill presents her with a specially-bound copy of each volume as it comes out). Neatly arranged in bookcases through-out Marlborough House are some 5,000 beautifully-bound volumes that make up Queen Mary's personal library. Methodical in her methods, every one of them has been catalogued in a filing cabinet system which enables her to have any volume produced at a moment's notice. Very infrequently she reads a thriller to herself at night, and when she does it is generally an Agatha Christie "whodunit" that she chooses.

Queen Mary seldom misses her tea, and when she takes it away from Marlborough House a chauffeur is sent ahead with a package of the special China tea she always drinks. She invari-ably dresses for dinner, even if she is merely going to sit down for a quick meal with her lady-in-waiting. After dinner, when her household members are ready to call it a day, the old Queen looks forward to a full evening. The death of George VI noticeably slowed down the tempo of Queen Mary's life—even after the end of court mourning she continued to lead a sort of semi-retirement—but until that sad event she was a great gadabout in the evenings. An ardent theatre- and movie-goer, she liked to turn up for stage and screen first nights, and she frequently pursued a movie she had heard about out into the suburbs if she had missed seeing it in London's west end.

Despite her Victorian moral standards and her deep religious feelings, Queen Mary is no prude. Her taste in stage and film entertainment is catholic and her sense of humour is on the earthy, robust side. When music hall comedians appeared on the wartime shows she arranged for the troops around her Badminton home she told them, "Don't cut out any jokes just to please me. I'm broad-minded." When she expressed her intention of attending the première of a sexy film called "The Wicked Lady," which the J. Arthur Rank organization turned out soon after the end of the Second World War, there was consternation in the film world and during the showing an operator in the projection box stood by to turn down the sound and make inaudible some of the earthiest dialogue. At the end of the film, however, Queen Mary marched straight up to the British film tycoon and said, "A very good film, Mr. Rank, and a fine moral." When she learned that parts of the dialogue had been discreetly toned down the old Queen alertly dispatched a lady-in-waiting the next day to see the film and report what she had missed, and later she went to see it again herself.

A few years ago when an old friend, the Earl of Clarendon, who doubles as Lord Chamberlain of the royal household and chief censor of the British stage, banned a topical play called "Pick-up Girl," which dealt with venereal disease, Queen Mary went to see it at a private club theatre and let it be known that she considered it a highly moral play about juvenile delinquency. (So seriously did she take its message that at the end, when she met the girls who played in it, she wagged a finger at them and said, "Let this be a lesson to you!") After Queen Mary's visit the censor changed his mind and licensed the production for a major theatre in London's west end.

Nowadays most of Queen Mary's evenings are spent quietly at home writing personal letters or working on her embroidery while being read to. When she is alone she sometimes smokes a cigarette, using a holder, but she will never smoke in public. She has a radio and a T.V. set in her apartments. Invariably, whether guests are present or not, she listens to the B.B.C.'s news round-up at 9 each evening, and she sometimes tunes in to serious musical programmes or talks on special subjects which interest her, but otherwise her radio set stands idle. She is not a T.V. enthusiast either, and sits down to view only when there are telecasts of outstanding interest, such as a royal procession or the annual tournament at Wimbledon. Never a tennis player, she gave Wimbledon her patronage years ago and religiously attended the championships each season until a year or so ago.

Queen Mary's day normally ends at 10.45 p.m.—never before —and reluctantly she goes off to bed, looking forward to to-morrow.

Britons are apt to look upon Queen Mary as ageless, and until recently she was inclined to agree with them. For many years of her widowhood she steadfastly refused to use the title of Queen Mother because she thought it implied advancing years and she had only began to accustom herself to that style when the death of George VI made her the Dowager Queen.

Queen Mary told her friends that she wanted to live to see the Festival of Britain, but after she toured the 1951 London exhibition she confessed that she had been disappointed. "It is all very interesting, but I am afraid it is too modern for me. Perhaps I am too old-fashioned," she said, which was a rare and sensational admission for her. Now she is determined to witness the coronation of her grand-daughter as Elizabeth II, the fourth coronation in which Queen Mary will have participated as a member of the royal family.

Although her doctors have tried to persuade her that even a royal octogenarian should rest and be thankful, her health is surprisingly good. Throughout her long life she has been troubled by no more than an occasional cold, and except for a prolonged attack of sciatica in the 1950 winter which weakened her she has suffered none of the usual infirmities of old age. Her eyesight is good, although she wears spectacles for reading and embroidering, and her hearing, always remarkably acute, is still keen enough for her to overhear remarks not meant for her ears. She still stands as erectly as she did 50 years ago and her carriage, which she uncompromisingly says is as a result of being made to rest on a hard floor when she was a child, should be the envy of many young ladies.

However, after a life span of more than 85 years, the Dowager Queen is more inclined to tolerate reminders of her old age.

When her staff decided she could use a wheel chair they were fearful of provoking her royal wrath when they first confronted her with it, but Queen Mary merely poked at the chair, studied its shiny chrome, soft upholstery and pneumatic tyres, and then sat in it. "It is quite comfortable," she announced, approvingly, much to her staff's surprise. Now she uses it in the privacy of her apartments (although she often ignores the Marlborough House elevator and walks downstairs) and she consented to use it publicly for her tiring tour of the Festival of Britain.

But, with the indomitable will which has sustained her for the better part of a century, the grand old lady of the royal family still refuses to submit meekly to her advancing years. When a friend wrote to congratulate her on attaining her eighty-fourth birthday, Queen Mary sent back a note of thanks in her firm longhand. "I am growing old," she appended, *"and I don't like it!"*

XX

ROYAL RELATIVES

AS the burden of the monarchy is shared by other members of the royal family besides Queen Elizabeth II and the Duke of Edinburgh Parliament grants five of them annual allowances which total £177,000. Of this sum Queen Elizabeth, the Queen Mother, receives £70,000 yearly, according to the provisions of George VI's Civil List which were to become operative on his death, and Queen Mary also draws an annuity of £70,000.

From August 21, 1951, when she reached the age of 21, Princess Margaret has drawn the £6,000 yearly provided for her in the 1937 Civil List as George VI's second daughter. Until then she had to depend on an allowance from her father and the interest from her own private fortune—a sum of £20,000, tax-free, left to her by the late Mrs. Ronald Greville, a close friend of her parents—to pay for her clothes, her gifts and her personal expenses. Under the new Civil List voted for Elizabeth II's reign Princess Margaret continues to draw an annuity of £6,000 until her marriage, when the annual grant increases to £15,000.

With the exception of the sovereign's monies, the annuities paid to the members of the royal family are subject to Britain's stiff rate of income tax. However, in view of the fact that the major share of their grants are spent in the public interest in the performance of their duties and the upkeep of their homes, they are given substantial allowances for expenses on their tax returns.[1]

The Duke of Gloucester receives a yearly allowance of £25,000, which is the annuity granted him as a younger son of George V. (During the minority of Princess Elizabeth he was granted a supplement of £10,000 yearly because he had to assume additional functions on her behalf.) On this he has to maintain his official position, his London home, York House, the main residential part of St. James's Palace, which served Edward VIII as a bachelor establishment when he was Prince of Wales, and his private home, a rambling country house, Barnwell Manor, in Northamptonshire. The Duchess of Gloucester, a shy, plain-featured, dark-complexioned little woman, who was Lady Alice Montague-Douglas-Scott before her marriage, came from an ancient and wealthy family. Her father, the seventh Duke of Buccleuch and Queensberry, left £974,482 when he died in 1935, just before her marriage to the Duke.

Henry, Duke of Gloucester, known to the family as Harry, as George VI's only surviving younger brother constitutionally occupies the position as the first of the Lords Temporal, the lay peerage, until such time as Prince Charles, the heir to the throne, takes his seat in the Lords.[2] The Duke of Gloucester also held the same premier position during the reign of George VI because Princess Elizabeth, as a woman, was not allowed to sit in the Lords.

On ceremonial occasions, such as the state openings of Parliament, the Duke of Gloucester sits at the head of the front bench to the left of the throne, opposite the Archbishop of Canterbury, who sits on the right at the head of the Spiritual Lords. In the day-to-day routine of royalty, however, the Duke served as his brother's principal male understudy since 1937, a role he later shared with the Duke of Edinburgh after Princess Elizabeth's marriage, and the royal chores he has undertaken have been many and varied.

It is a tradition in the royal family that at least one male member makes the British Army his career and young Prince Henry was selected for this role by George V. Born in 1900, he was too young for active service in the First World War but in the years between the wars he set out to become a professional soldier, first in the infantry and then in the cavalry, and during his father's reign his concentration on his military career allowed him to escape some of the public duties that fell to his three surviving brothers, although he was called upon to represent his father at the centenary celebrations of the Australian state of Victoria in 1934.

His military activities were interrupted when his elder brothers, first David and then Albert, ascended the throne. Along with his younger brother George, the late Duke of Kent, the Duke of Gloucester had to put his services at the sovereign's disposal for the discharge of general royal duties, but at the outbreak of the Second World War he returned to the Army as a major-general and was assigned as chief liaison officer to Lord Gort, the commander-in-chief of the British Forces in France. Slightly wounded in France, the Duke returned to England and served in a similar capacity with the home forces during the period of rearming that followed Dunkirk. On behalf of the King he carried out an extensive air tour in 1942 to investigate the welfare of British troops serving on remote fronts in the Middle East, Africa and India.

The Duke's ambition was to command a division in the field, but in view of the possibility of George VI's sudden death before Elizabeth reached the age of 18 he was required to stand by to act as Regent for her, and in the latter stages of the war his military work was confined to liaison missions, mainly with troops stationed in Britain.

At the end of 1944, when Princess Elizabeth had begun to assume some public duties as her father's understudy, George VI appointed the Duke Governor-General of Australia, at the request of the Australian Government. This post, the sovereign's personal representative in the Commonwealth, was intended for the Duke of Kent, who had accepted it and then postponed his acceptance because of the outbreak of the Second World War, but his untimely death cut off his career before he could fulfil it. The Gloucesters were popular in Australia and in their two years of royal duties in that vast country they covered over 76,500 miles. The Duke's term of office was cut short in 1947 when he was requested to return to Britain to act as senior member of the Council of State while the King and Queen and their daughters journeyed to South Africa and back.

In the post-war years the Duke of Gloucester deputized for his brother as the monarch's representative at important Commonwealth occasions—he attended the celebrations when Nairobi, the capital of Kenya, was raised to the status of a city, visited Malta for the inauguration of its new constitution, and opened the first sovereign Parliament in the new Dominion of Ceylon—but after Princess Elizabeth's marriage he gradually turned over his main duties as royal deputy to the heiress to the throne and her husband. Like George VI when he was Duke of York, the Duke of Gloucester takes a real interest in Britain's youth movements—he is president of the National Association of Boys' Clubs and of the Boy Scouts Association and the active chairman of the administrative council of King George V's Jubilee Trust, which grants funds to organizations concerned with the bodily and spiritual welfare of young people—but much of his private time is now spent at his farm at Barnwell, where he specializes in cattle breeding. His Duchess, who served as honorary head of the W.A.A.F. during the wartime division of duties among the royal ladies, continues to serve as air chief commandant of the post-war Women's Royal Air Force. Retiring by nature, she devotes much of her time to her homes and the upbringing of their two children, Prince William, born in 1941, and Prince Richard, born in 1944. An accomplished watercolourist, she turns out delicate little paintings in her spare moments.

George VI's only sister, Victoria Alexandra Alice Mary, who bears the honorific title of Princess Royal, draws the same annual allowance from the state as Princess Margaret, £6,000. However, as the Dowager Countess of Harewood she is also a member of one of the great land-owning families of England.

The title of Princess Royal, implying a higher rank than that of other princesses of the realm, is misleading. First introduced in the reign of George II, it is ordinarily given to the king's eldest daughter, but since it is held for life it sometimes happens, as in the reign of George VI, that the king's sister holds a higher-sounding title than his daughter, even though ranking far below her in the right of succession. The present Princess Royal, outranked by Elizabeth II's children, by her brothers and their children and grandchildren, ranks only tenth in the line of succession to the throne.

It was in 1922 that Princess Mary, as she was then known, married Henry George Charles Lascelles, who then bore the title of Viscount Lascelles and was heir to the earldom of Harewood (pronounced Harwood). The Lascelles family has had its roots in England for almost 900 years, ever since the first member of the family, Picotus de Lassels, fought for William the Conqueror at Hastings and was rewarded with a Yorkshire manor for his services. Living like feudal princes in their Yorkshire domain, succeeding generations of the family added to their holdings until in the early years of this century the Lascelles were reputed to own nearly 100,000 acres of land in the United Kingdom as well as great sugar plantations in Barbados. The title of Baron of Harewood was first created for the head of the family back in 1790, and when the vast pile of Harewood House was erected as the family seat, where kings and queens were entertained in sumptuous splendour, the title was raised to an earldom.

Shortly before Lord Lascelles took George V's daughter as his bride the family's fortunes had begun to shrink, but they were revived by the timely acquisition of land holdings in Ireland and a vast money inheritance, the fortuitous result of a meeting between Lord Lascelles and a great-uncle, the Marquis of Clanricarde.[3]

At her first Yorkshire home, Goldsborough Hall, and later at the ancestral Harewood House, to which they moved when Lord Lascelles succeeded to the family title and estate (£300,000, plus 30,000 acres of land in Yorkshire) on the death of his father in 1929, the Princess Royal so identified herself with the public life of her area that the people of the county proudly called her "our own Yorkshire Princess," and until Princess Elizabeth and Princess Margaret grew up to share the national spotlight her popularity in the north of England was second only to George VI's.

Indefatigable in her public work, the Princess Royal has carried a heavy share of the minor royal duties since her brother came to the throne as George VI. Somewhat stern of feature and unfeminine in bearing, she does not shun the wearing of uniforms like her royal sisters-in-law. She chose the British Army as her special royal province, serves as colonel-in-chief of several corps and regiments, and seldom misses an opportunity to visit a unit in which she is interested. She was the first royal lady to visit troops serving overseas after the war when she toured the military welfare establishments of the British Army of the Rhine in the spring of 1948. During the war years she served as honorary head of the women's branch of the Army, then called the Auxiliary Territorial Service, and when its members were given full military rank when it became the Women's Royal Army Corps after the war the Princess Royal became the first female major-general in British history. A trained V.A.D. nurse herself, she headed the wartime R.A.F. nursing service and presided over the multifarious activities of the British Red Cross Society, of which she is still commandant-in-chief.

The Princess Royal was left a widow when her husband, 15 years her senior, died early in 1947, leaving an estate valued at £549,000. Her elder son, George, who had been captured in Italy in 1944 and held prisoner by the Nazis until the end of the war, succeeded to the title as the seventh Earl of Harewood. The young Earl, who was born in 1923, is an exceptionally brainy, accomplished individual and with the possible exception of Princess Margaret and the Duke of Edinburgh he is probably the only member of the present royal family who could have won recognition in a competitive society where brains count more than breeding. Passionately interested in all forms of classical music—he has a collection of some 6,000 gramophone records—he wrote occasional opera reviews for the left-wing *New States-man and Nation*, still writes a column of long-haired criticism for the right-wing *Daily Mail* and is co-editor of a British periodical, *Ballet and Opera*. As a prisoner-of-war he read through all the volumes of Grove's "Musical Dictionary."

Having broken the family tradition in the choice of a career the young Earl set yet another precedent in his choice of a bride. Instead of picking a wife from among the daughters of the landed aristocracy, as generations of his predecessors had done, he proposed to a pretty, dark-complexioned, Viennese-born musican, Miss Marion Donata Stein, daughter of a London music pub-lisher, who became the new Countess of Harewood on their marriage in 1949. Their infant son, who bears the title of Viscount Lascelles, is twelfth in line for the throne, ranking just behind his father.

The Princess Royal's younger son, the Honourable Gerald Lascelles, born in 1924, is thirteenth in the line of succession to the throne.[4] A rugged, outdoor type, Gerry, as he is known to his friends, is also a music enthusiast, though his taste is in violent conflict with that of his brother. He is a jazz fan and a jitterbug and owns one of the biggest libraries of jazz records in Britain. At the age of 21 he inherited the family's sugar plantations in Barbados but he lives modestly in London, where he works for an automobile firm. Like his brother, he broke with the family tradition when he took as his bride in July, 1952, a former show-girl-actress, Angela Dowding.

The imposition of two substantial death duties within a score of years (in 1929 and again in 1947) has drained away much of the Harewood family fortune. Most of their land in Ireland has been sold, Goldsborough Hall has been sold and turned into a school, and in a series of auctions from 1950 to 1952 the family disposed of more than 32,000 acres of property, including farm-lands, houses and whole villages, which brought in £591,810, in order to keep ahead of the tax collector. As a further sacrifice the Princess Royal was compelled to auction a treasured collection of rare porcelain objects of art, eighteenth- and nineteenth-century silver plate, Adam and Chippendale furniture and old paintings, many by seventeenth-century Dutch masters, from Harewood House, a sale which brought in another £55,000. However, the family's 1,100-acre sugar plantations are still thriving enterprises, and some 30,000 acres of Yorkshire land as well as Harewood House and its 2,000-acre estate remain in the family's possession.

In an effort to stave off the euthanasia of the rich, a consequence of the bloodless social revolution which has been going on in Britain since the turn of the century, the Princess Royal has joined the growing band of embattled aristocrats who have turned their stately, ancestral homes into tourist show-places in order to help pay for the upkeep and repair of their great man-sions. The imposing, box-like structure of Harewood House is opened to the public twice weekly during the summer months and for a charge of two shillings and sixpence tourists can rubber-neck through the magnificent state apartments and gawk at the treasury of paintings by Vandyck, Reynolds, Turner and other celebrated artists, and the fine Sèvres and Celadon china, one of the most valuable private collections in the world.

Though she regards Yorkshire as her home, the Princess Royal is generally on hand for royal family events in the capital. She divides her time between Harewood House and the 13-roomed apartment allotted to her by George VI in St. James's Palace. She shares her elder son's passion for music and spends much of her leisure attending concerts and opera. Her other great interest is the breeding and racing of horses. She inherited her husband's string and frequently attends one or another of Britain's many racecourses to see them run. Until the Queen Mother and Elizabeth II acquired their own horses the Princess Royal was the first royal lady since the days of Queen Anne to race her own horses.

Financially the worst-off among the front-rank members of the royal family is the Duchess of Kent. Although in her widowhood she has carried on the greater part of the Duke of Kent's public work as well as her own share in the royal duties she gets no allowance from the state, apart from a pension of £398 per annum, which is the meagre sum given to the widow of an R.A.F. air commodore with three children. Her only income derives from the £157,735 left by the Duke when he died on active service in 1942. Most of this capital is held in trust for her eldest son, the second Duke of Kent, who was born in 1935. To help cover the cost of her official engagements and the private expenses for herself, her children and her small household Queen Mary occasionally aids her financially and the late King contributed a certain amount for the education of her children. Occasionally and quietly, however, the Duchess sells some of her possessions. A few years ago the sale of pictures and antiques belonging to her husband brought her some £92,000.

She still possesses some magnificent jewels, gifts from her husband and his family and from her own relatives, who belonged to the royal houses of Russia, Greece and Denmark, as well as her comfortable, moderately-sized home, Coppins, at Iver, in Buckinghamshire, which the Duke inherited from his aunt, Princess Victoria. The Duchess has no London home and uses a suite at Queen Mary's Marlborough House as her official headquarters.

At the age of 45 the Duchess still retains the slim figure (she measures 36 inches, 26 inches and 38 inches in the usual places), the striking features and the flawless complexion that made her one of the world's most beautiful women when, as the 28-year-old Princess Marina of Greece, she married the Duke of Kent at Westminster Abbey in 1934, and without spending lavishly on clothes she still ranks high in any list of the world's best-dressed women. Style experts say that she instinctively knows what goes with what in the matter of dress and accessories. For years her clothes were made in Paris by Molyneux. During the Second World War years Madame Bianca Mosca took over but after the war, when Molyneux retired from business, she extended her custom to Norman Hartnell and Hardy Amies. She is the style-setter for the royal family and whenever the members are assembled for a public function she is the one figure women always crane to see.

Although she came from a foreign royal house—her father, Prince Nicholas of Greece, who lived for years in exile in comparative poverty in Paris, was the son of King George I of Greece, and her mother and her grandmother were Grand Duchesses of the Russian imperial dynasty of Romanov—Princess Marina's marriage to the Duke of Kent, whom she had known since childhood, was obviously an unarranged love match, and it was almost as popular with the British people as the earlier union of the Duke of York and Lady Elizabeth Bowes-Lyon had been. The Duke, who called his wife "Mara," and the Duchess were devoted to each other and her grief at his tragic death was deep and black-edged. Week after week she would slip quietly into the royal vault in the chapel attached to Windsor Castle and leave a sheaf of flowers on his unburied coffin. It was a gloomy resting place and the Duchess finally persuaded George VI to bury his brother's remains in an outdoor grave, an inconspicuous burial ground which the Duchess still carefully tends, in Windsor Park, close to the mausoleum of Victoria. When she recovered from the shock of her personal loss, the Duchess did not retire into the obscurity of a private citizen. Throughout the war years she served as chief of the Women's Royal Naval Service and took an active interest in service and welfare clubs throughout the nation.

Her home life now revolves around her three children, Prince Edward, the new Duke of Kent, who now attends a private school in Switzerland, Princess Alexandra, born in 1936, an attractive youngster who is destined to be as beautiful as her mother, and her second son, Prince Michael George Charles Franklin, born on July 4, 1942, who had the late President Roosevelt as one of his godfathers.

Aside from the Duke of Windsor, who was always close to Marina and her husband, and the Duke of Edinburgh, her first cousin, the Duchess of Kent is the only cosmopolite in the royal family—she speaks seven languages—and her tastes are correspondingly catholic. Her mother, Princess Nicholas, now lives near Athens—her father died in 1938—and her two sisters married into foreign noble houses, one becoming Princess Paul of Yugoslavia, the other Countess Elizabeth von Toerring-Jettenbach of Bavaria. The Duchess herself is Parisian by upbringing. From her father, who struggled to make a living in exile by painting, she has inherited some talent as a portraitist. Her taste in music is modern. She is reputed to have the most complete collection of calypso records in Britain, an interest that began when she and the Duke had a song-story composed for them while on their honeymoon in Trinidad. She is an ardent theatre-goer and Noel Coward, whom the Duke also knew, is her frequent escort to first nights and theatre parties. Conductor Sir Malcolm Sargent is one of her close friends, as are Sir Laurence and Lady Olivier. Danny Kaye is also one of her friends and it was the Duchess who first introduced Elizabeth and Margaret to Kaye's crazy records.

The Duchess of Kent has probably had more influence in the development of Princess Margaret and Queen Elizabeth II than any other member of the royal family except Queen Mary and their parents. Elizabeth and Margaret regard their Aunt Marina as almost a member of their generation and they have frequently turned to the young widow for companionship and advice. When Elizabeth fell in love with Philip the Duchess naturally encouraged the match and her home outside London was one place where the young couple could meet in private before their engagement was announced. When Elizabeth was expecting her first child she turned to Marina, whose youngest child, Prince Michael, was then only six, for advice on the problems of motherhood and child care and later, when Elizabeth and Philip set up their own home at Clarence House, they drew on the Duchess of Kent's experience in running her small household on economical lines. Elizabeth even took over Marina's cook. Princess Margaret has always regarded Aunt Marina as a glamorous figure ("I am going to dress just like Aunt Marina when I grow up," announced Margaret when she was still a child) and when she staged her family battle for the right to wear clothes of her own choosing it was the Duchess who came along to back her up.

Like the Duchess of Kent, the Duke of Windsor receives no allowance from the state and since he gave up his job as Governor of the Bahamas, one of the lesser plums of the Colonial Service, he has not received an official salary from the British Government or any British possession. He got no financial recompense when he renounced the throne. The royal estates of Sandringham and Balmoral were his by inheritance from his father, but because they had become an inseparable part of the monarchy in the eyes of the British people he voluntarily turned them over to his brother, a precedent that George VI followed in passing them on to his daughter. By a purely personal arrangement between them, George VI reputedly paid the Duke of Windsor a yearly allowance of £25,000, which ceased on the late King's death, but it is thought likely in court circles that Elizabeth II has agreed to continue this family arrangement.

Even for a royal D.P., however, the 57-year-old Duke of Windsor is still able to live in a fairly lavish style, dividing his time between New York and Paris. As the Duke of Cornwall, to which rank he advanced in 1910, he was entitled to the income from the Duchy of Cornwall for some 25 years at a time when taxes were low and the Duchy's estates were yielding around £70,000 a year—out of which he paid his own and his household expenses until he ascended the throne—and when he left Britain in 1936 it was estimated that his personal wealth then ran into hundreds of thousands of pounds. Publication of his life story in magazines and newspapers alone—apart from the sale of his memoirs in book form in 1951—reputedly brought him nearly £180,000.

George VI never wavered in his affection for his elder brother. "I have suffered a very real loss," he told his Privy Councillors, "by the decision of my brother (to abdicate), for by his going I am deprived of a friendship which I valued highly." One of his first acts was to create the dukedom of Windsor for his brother and a few months after his accession George VI announced his wish that his brother should continue to enjoy the style of His Royal Highness. Letters patent were subsequently issued confining the use of that style to the Duke of Windsor personally. This became a point of soreness to the Windsors and although the Duke purposely but erroneously refers to his wife in private as "Her Royal Highness" he could never persuade the late King, despite repeated requests, to grant the Duchess of Windsor the regal style that would have made her, in fact if not in the public mind, a member of the royal family. George VI, more tolerant than his father in his attitude to divorce and broader-minded in his moral standards, had nothing against the Duchess of Windsor personally, but Queen Mary regally refuses to receive her as a divorced person and his wife, the present Queen Mother, adamantly refuses to accept the Duchess as a member of the royal family.

Another sore point has been the Duke of Windsor's failure to land an official job commensurate with what he believes are his talent and experience. Though he said quite clearly in his abdication broadcast that "I now quit altogether public affairs" this was apparently a rhetorical touch and almost from the time of his marriage he has been avid for some public function. Except for the minor governorship none has been put his way. It is no secret in British political circles that the Duke would like a high state appointment. When Ernest Bevin was Foreign Secretary the Duke reportedly approached him for a diplomatic assignment (he was supposed to have angled for the British ambassadorship to Washington) and he has frequently discussed the matter with his old friend Winston Churchill (who helped him polish his abdication broadcast), both while Churchill was out of power and after his return to office.

The death of George VI temporarily healed the breach in the royal family, at least on the surface. The Duke of Windsor left his Duchess in New York and hastened back to England by five-day boat (he is supposed to have taken a dislike to flying) to comfort his mother. Queen Elizabeth, the Queen Mother, agreeing with Queen Mary's wish that the royal family should be reunited at a time of great sorrow, invited the Duke to Buckingham Palace for tea, their first meeting in 15 years—a historic moment in which Elizabeth II and the Duke of Edinburgh also participated. Later the new Queen again received her uncle before his return to the U.S.

There is no barrier against the Windsors returning to Britain to live—their exile is voluntary—except the blunt, uncomfortable truth that the Duchess could not hope for the same degree of respect and affection which the public extends to her royal relatives. Fort Belvedere, the Duke of Windsor's favourite residence, could again be made available as their home but it is not likely that Queen Elizabeth II, whose attitude towards divorce is more strait-laced than was her father's, would grant her American aunt the coveted style of "H.R.H." or accept her as a member of the royal family.

Except as a private person, however, the Duke of Windsor has no foreseeable future in Britain. While the bitter feelings of the abdication have been largely forgotten—except when the Duke deliberately brought them flooding briefly back with the publication of his memoirs—there is still an implacable and sizeable minority who cannot forgive him for placing the throne in jeopardy in 1936 for his own personal reasons.

THE APPARATUS OF MAJESTY

XXI

THE ROYAL HOUSEHOLD

THE domestic side of the royal household, the personal entourage of the sovereign as distinct from the court and ceremonial household officers, consists of a number of departments and offices, each under a principal household officer.

A new monarch usually means a clean sweep of the household office-holders at "Buck House," although it has been customary for the new sovereign to make no major changes in personnel for the first six months of the reign. Queen Elizabeth II, who was served by a devoted though inexperienced household of her own when she was Princess, has for the present incorporated her Clarence House entourage into the old guard at Buckingham Palace, the inner circle of household officials who served George VI during most of his reign, but as most of these practised courtiers inherited from her father are getting on in years it is to be expected that they will one by one be replaced in time by household appointees of the new Queen's choosing.

Titular head of the Queen's domestic household is the Lord Steward, a ceremonial appointee who still carries a white staff as emblem and warrant of his authority on state occasions.[1] For several centuries he was responsible for the below-stairs management of the royal palace, but nowadays his role as major domo is filled by a permanent officer who resides at the court, the Master of the Household, 61-year-old Lieutenant Colonel the Honourable Sir Piers ("Joey") Legh. Assisted by the Deputy Master of the Household, 38-year-old Group Captain Peter Townsend, an ex-R.A.F. fighter ace who doubles as an equerry, he is responsible for the routine internal administration of Buckingham Palace, the catering for state banquets and royal entertainment, the hiring and firing of the domestic staff and the payment of all household expenses. Under his authority come such specialists as the Keeper of the Royal Cellars, who is responsible for stocking the royal vaults with choice wines, liqueurs and cigars.

The Treasurer of the Household and the Comptroller of the Household are by tradition under the Lord Steward, though both are now political appointees, nominated by the Government in power, their main function being to act as party whips in Parliament. The Coroner of the Household, who exercises jurisdiction in the royal palaces and in any other place where the sovereign may be staying, is also under the Lord Steward.

The Keeper of the Privy Purse and Treasurer to the Queen is tall, dyspeptic Sir Ulick Alexander, a 63-year-old ex-Guards officer turned businessman who looked after the Duke of Kent's financial affairs and later served Edward VIII as Keeper of the Privy Purse. With the aid of an Assistant Treasurer, 45-year-old Brigadier Lord Tryon, Sir Ulick acts as a personal accountant for Her Majesty, allocates the Privy Purse budget, pays all Palace salaries and wages and manages the Queen's private finances.

The closest of all officials to the Queen is Sir Alan Lascelles, her principal private secretary. Sir Alan, whose cousin married the Princess Royal, has been in royal service on and off since he became assistant private secretary to the Prince of Wales, now the Duke of Windsor, at the age of 32. Now 64, he has behind him the rich experience of 15 years of service as confidant and adviser to George VI, first as assistant private secretary and then, from 1943, as principal secretary.

A figure of higher importance than his title implies, the monarch's principal secretary is one of the most influential men in any reign. In addition to heading the Palace secretariat, he serves as a pipeline of communication between the Queen and her Ministers. He must be on first-name terms with every member of the Cabinet, and with the leading politicians on the Opposition side. It is his duty to keep his royal mistress informed of political or constitutional developments in Whitehall that might not be apparent to the Queen even after the closest scrutiny of the official memos in her dispatch boxes—the arguments within the Cabinet, the jockeying for position within the parties, or the viewpoint and tactics of the Opposition. Beyond this, the private secretary sees to the smooth working of the Queen's

public life and is responsible for the good public relations of the
Queen and the royal family. As a link between Her Majesty and
her people, the private secretary must keep an ear cocked to the
world beyond Whitehall so that he can advise the sovereign on
the shaping of royal policy.

The post of private secretary, which lapsed in 1688, was revived by George III but in those days it was seldom a full-time
occupation and Queen Victoria even turned over her secretarial
chores to Prince Albert. As the direct powers of the monarchy
were whittled down the paper work increased, however, and nowa
days there is not only a principal private secretary and three
assistant private secretaries—Sir Michael Edward Adeane, a
personable, diminutive, 41-year-old whose grandfather, Lord
Stamfordham, was private secretary to George V; Major Edward
Ford, one-time tutor to Egypt's ex-King Farouk, who joined the
royal staff in 1946; and 38-year-old Lieutenant Colonel Martin
Charteris, a wartime intelligence officer and brother of the Earl
of Wemyss and March, who became private secretary to the
then Princess Elizabeth in 1950 and accompanied her into
Buckingham Palace—but there is a secretary to the private
secretary and an office full of female clerks and typists. The
Keeper of the Royal Archives is also attached to the private
secretary's office.

Queen Victoria handled her own press relations and in her
daily court circular, in which she recorded such trivial domestic
details as the fact that the royal children had been taken for an
airing in their prams, she kept the country informed of the doings
of herself and her large family. In keeping with the times Buckingham Palace now maintains a full-time press department,
presently headed by an ex-naval man, Commander Richard
Colville. In recognition of the widespread feminine interest in
the dress and doings of his wife and their two daughters, George
VI set a further precedent in 1947 and appointed a woman, red-
headed Diana Lyttelton, who had worked in Churchill's map room
during the war years, as assistant press secretary.

Unlike most press agencies, the press secretaries at "Buck
House" never have to sell their clients to the public; in fact, their
main function is to protect the royal family from the persistent
hounding of the world's press. They arrange the strictly-limited
press coverage of royal events and movements, issue the daily

court circular and other news bulletins from the Palace, answer queries about the royal family in carefully-measured, formula phrases, and occasionally provide the more insistent journalists with suitably-filtered details of the royal family's private life, but they are quick to protest if a publication oversteps the bounds of familiarity. "We are not publicity agents for the royal family," explains press secretary Colville. "We are here to tell the press how far they cannot go."

The third-ranking dignitary at court (after the Lord Chamberlain and the Lord Steward) is the Master of the Horse, at present the Duke of Beaufort. Formerly the holder of a powerful office, his jurisdiction is now limited to all matters relating to the sovereign's stables and he generally attends the Queen only on state occasions, when he is entitled to ride immediately behind the sovereign. His job is carried out for him by the Chief or Crown Equerry, Sir Dermot Kavanagh, who is responsible for the provision of horses, carriages and motor cars required by the royal family.

The Master of the Horse also has jurisdiction over all the equerries and pages in the Royal Mews department. Elizabeth II is served by a permanent equerry and several short-term equerries, promising young men selected from the armed services because of their intelligence, family background and social charm, who take it in turn to be continually on call for a fortnight at a stretch at "Buck House" or wherever the Queen is in residence. The duties of the equerries, who unobtrusively accompany Her Majesty on most of her public appearances, are multifarious and range from such chores as knowing the names and something of the background of the guests presented to the Queen at public functions to booking seats at the theatre.

On certain high ceremonial occasions the Queen is also accompanied by aides-de-camp, an honorary office usually confined to high-ranking officers of the armed services and, in the past, of the Indian Army. In 1949 George VI again broke with tradition and appointed the heads of the three women's services to be honorary aides-de-camp to the monarch.

A household officer primarily concerned with ceremonial is the Marshal of the Diplomatic Corps. Assisted by a Vice-Marshal and an Assistant Marshal, he is responsible for all foreign ambassadors and ministers attending court ceremonies. He arranges for their reception by the Queen, provides for their requirements when they are in Britain, and settles the touchy precedential problems of who comes before whom at diplomatic court functions.

When the ruling sovereign is a queen the composition of the female side of her household is somewhat different from when there is a king and a queen consort on the throne.

Though smaller in number than that of a king's, the female household of a queen consort is almost as ancient in its origins. The ladies who attended the queen in the old days were expected to keep their mistress entertained, to carry her messages and attend her when she went to bed and got up, when the woman-of-the-bedchamber would hand each garment to the lady-of-the-bedchamber, who passed it in turn to the queen.

As Queen Consort the present Queen Mother had a female household of ten members, four ladies-of-the-bedchamber, four women-of-the-bedchamber, and two extra women-of-the-bed-chamber who did not take one of the regular spells of duty. Queen Elizabeth II, with a full male household staff to serve her, may not require as large a female household as her mother had.

At the head of the Queen's female household is the Mistress of the Robes. She personally attends Her Majesty only on cere-monial occasions—when she is entitled to ride in a state carriage —and has nothing to do with the Queen's everyday wardrobe, although in earlier reigns the Mistress of the Robes was exactly what her title implies and for her services was entitled to a choice of the queen's cast-off clothing.[2]

The Mistress of the Robes supervises the Queen's female attendants and arranges the duty roster. The ladies-of-the-bedchamber generally attend Her Majesty only on ceremonial or important social occasions. The women-of-the-bedchamber, colloquially known as ladies-in-waiting, have the greatest burden. They take it in turn to be in waiting or on duty for a fortnight at a time at Buckingham Palace or wherever the Queen may be. Except for mealtimes and evenings the lady-in-waiting seldom leaves the Queen's side. She makes Her Majesty's phone calls, passes on her instructions and acts as a link between the outside world and the Palace. She accompanies the Queen when-ever she leaves the Palace, unless the Queen is on a purely private visit, and remains present when the Queen receives visitors, unless they are Elizabeth's intimate friends or relatives. For all this the ladies-in-waiting draw less than £500 per year, out of which they pay their own expenses.

The Duke of Edinburgh, as consort, is entitled to a small household staff of his own. When he moved into Buckingham Palace with his wife he appointed as Treasurer of his household Lieutenant-General Sir Frederick Browning, who served as Comptroller and Treasurer to the household of Princess Elizabeth. Smoothly charming, with a staccato yet informal manner, 55-year-old "Boy" Browning is the acknowledged leader of the new guard of court officials around Elizabeth II. Though very much to the manner born, he has not the traditional background of a palace courtier. Husband of novelist Daphne du Maurier, he served in both World Wars and in the Second rose to be commander of the British Airborne Corps and, later, chief of staff to Lord Louis Mountbatten in S.E.A.C. Self-dedicated to the courtier's role, he is said to have listened to the broadcast of Princess Elizabeth's twenty-first birthday pledge of service while she was in South Africa and to have declared, "I will serve that young woman." True or not, he applied for and got the key job in Elizabeth's household when she moved into Clarence House. As Treasurer to the Duke Browning remains in intimate contact with the Queen and her husband and it is likely that his present post is an interim appointment until the major household roles are reshuffled.

Private secretary to the Duke of Edinburgh is 31-year-old Lieutenant Commander Michael Parker, who served the Duke and Princess Elizabeth as equerry from 1948. Like Browning, Parker is also not out of the traditional mould of aristocrats who serve the court. An Australian who served in the Royal Navy— where he became friendly with Philip—he is the first Commonwealth-born man to be drafted into the royal entourage.

The royal household also includes a number of offices whose holders flash into brief or occasional prominence in the royal orbit.[3] There is Her Majesty's Representative at Ascot, a recently created office which supervises the administration of Royal Ascot racecourse and issues the coveted tickets for the royal enclosure. Under the Lord Chamberlain's department are such functionaries as the Constable and Deputy Constable of Windsor Castle, the Dean and sub-Dean of the Chapel Royal, the Keeper of the Jewel

House, the Master of the Queen's Musick, the Poet Laureate, the Shower of State Apartments at Windsor Castle, the Art Surveyors, the Queen's Bargemaster and the Keeper of the Queen's Swans. The Royal Almonry, under the Keeper of the Privy Purse, is in the charge of the High Almoner, an ecclesiastical appointment usually held by a bishop, who in olden days was responsible for the almsgiving of the kings and queens. Nowadays it comes into its own mainly on the occasion of the annual Maundy service.

The ecclesiastical household consists of the Clerk of the Closet, usually a bishop, whose traditional duty it was "to attend at the right hand of the sovereign in the Royal Closet during divine service, to resolve such doubts as may arise concerning spiritual matters"; the Deputy Clerk to the Closet; and a number of domestic chaplains and chaplains-in-ordinary. The chaplains-in-ordinary are not connected solely with the court. They take it in turns to conduct divine service and preach at royal chapels.

When George VI was operated on for his leg ailment a brash American reporter inquired of Buckingham Palace's press office whether His Majesty would get his medical treatment free under Britain's national health scheme and was icily told that this was a private matter between the King and his doctors. As a matter of fact, the royal family enjoyed a free health service long before their subjects did. By long tradition, the physicians and surgeons attached to the royal household have always given their services free of charge in return for the prestige that goes with their appointment. Outside specialists, when called in, are paid, but their fees are usually considerably reduced because of the honour attached to their service.[4]

In practice, only one doctor (71-year-old Sir John Weir, a genial, pawky Scot who is a top-flight pathologist and consultant at the London Homeopathic Hospital) looks after the health of the royal family, but in the case of serious illnesses or major events like royal births the half dozen or so doctors who hold medical appointments to the Queen and the household are usually consulted jointly, and in emergencies outside specialists are brought in. The Queen and her family have their own private dentist, to whom they make regular private visits.

Although it is not part of the royal household, a special unit of the R.A.F. exists exclusively to take care of the flying requirements of the royal family. Until the post-war years George VI and his family seldom used aircraft as a means of transport, but after their satisfying flights during the South African tour they increasingly relied on their special Flight of planes for their longer journeys within the United Kingdom and abroad.

Founded with one aircraft in 1936 by Edward VIII, the King's Flight, as it was then known, was disbanded during the war years but reformed again in 1946, and during the South African tour its four aeroplanes flew some 160,000 miles without incident. It now consists of five Vickers Viking twin-engined planes, four of which are fitted to carry passengers and the fifth as a freight-carrying workshop equipped with spare parts that may be required on tour. Under command of Air Commodore Edward H. ("Mouse") Fielden, Edward VIII's personal pilot who is now Captain of the Flight and Air Equerry to the Queen, the Flight functions as a self-contained R.A.F. unit from its home airfield near Oxford.

For obvious reasons, the operations of the Flight are hedged about with rigid safety precautions. Despite their wartime records and long hours of flying time, the chief pilot and his two assistant pilots must undergo severe flying tests every six months. No aircraft carrying a royal person is permitted to land at an airfield which it has not previously visited, and so before any flight into strange territory on a royal mission the pilot and crew make a preliminary inspection and landing trip.

During the wartime years George VI had no V.I.P. aircraft of his own and when he flew abroad to Africa and Italy he had to borrow Churchill's personal plane. On these occasions the strictest security measures were enforced to conceal the fact that the King was flying abroad and elaborate precautions were taken to cope with any emergencies. The Chief of the Air Staff personally instructed the plane's crew that if an emergency landing became necessary en route they were to try to reach neutral Lisbon, and warships were stationed across the Bay of Biscay to provide navigational checks and rescue units. But on one flight the precautions concealing the King's presence broke down. His Majesty's luggage was carefully tagged in the name of "T. Jerram," his valet, but George VI himself unthinkingly brought along one leather cabin case embossed with "The King" and another that carried the engraved legend, "The Privy Purse."

XXII

THE PRIVY PURSE

BRITAIN'S inclusive bill for the institution of the monarchy, the royal family and the apparatus of majesty averages close to £1,000,000 per year. This is somewhat more than the United States, with more than three times Britain's population, spends on maintaining the dignity of its presidency (£35,714 presidential salary, taxable, plus another £17,857 in tax-free expenses, and up to £14,285 for travel and entertaining), its White House staff and various executive offices connected with the presidency (£681,000) and the upkeep of the White House and its grounds (£149,767 in 1952), which adds up to £898,923 for the year.

To those Americans who feel that the U.S. foreign aid programme entitles them to scrutinize the spending of dependent nations in the manner of an official receiver examining the books of a bankrupt the upkeep of the British monarchy may seem a prodigal expenditure, but few Britons consider the cost excessive. It works out at a fraction over five cents a year to each Briton— or less than the price of two British cigarettes. Considering that it serves as a symbol to some 610,000,000 people all over the world, maintains no fewer than seven royal palaces and eight royal residences, supplies an almost ceaseless round of pomp and pageantry, and provides a livelihood for about 1,000 persons, ranging from Elizabeth II to the most junior chambermaid at Buckingham Palace, most Britons regard their monarchy as cheap at the price.

In one sense, the monarchy costs Britain nothing. This is the result of a historic bargain struck between the businesslike George III and Parliament by which the sovereign surrenders the income from the crown's hereditary property in return for

317

a fixed annual allowance, a deal in which the nation now comes out ahead due mainly to the rise in real estate values since Elizabeth II's great-great-great-great-grandfather occupied the throne.

In early reigns all expenses of government, civil as well as military (except for certain special levies for military purposes), were defrayed by revenues from crown lands and various hereditary rights and taxes. The crown lands, relics of the feudal properties of Britain's kings, made the sovereign the largest landowner in the kingdom.

At the restoration of the monarchy in 1660 Parliament took a tighter grip on the royal finances, distinguishing between the money to be used for military expenses and the cost of the civil establishments of the government, and with the accession of William and Mary Parliament passed the first Civil List act by which certain national revenues and part of the excise duties, estimated to yield some £600,000 a year, were passed on to the crown to defray the expenses of the civil service as well as the cost of the royal household and the monarch's personal expenditure, known as the Privy Purse. However, as the cost of government rose with the growth in Britain's population the sovereign's finances were increasingly strained and recurring deficits had to be made up by Parliament.

When George III came to the throne in 1760 the Civil List had grown to £1,030,000, out of which he was expected to pay the civil service, the judges, ambassadors and important officers of state. On his accession George III struck a sharp bargain with Parliament.[1] In return for a fixed Civil List of £800,000 yearly, a guaranteed, king-sized annuity for life, he surrendered to the state his revenue from the excise and the Post Office and his rights to most of the crown lands in England and Wales, property which then yielded a gross revenue of £89,000 a year and a net return of only £11,000. In effect he agreed to make the sovereign a salaried servant of the state, and the state, in turn, undertook to pay those officers, judges and ambassadors who had previously been dependent on the monarch for income.

The bargain in those days was all in the King's favour. George IV surrendered to Parliament all the hereditary revenues of England and Scotland, and his successor, William IV, was compelled to surrender the crown revenues from Ireland in addition, but it was not until Queen Victoria's accession that George III's bargain was finalized. Victoria surrendered all hereditary revenues from crown lands for life, except for personal properties belonging to the Duchy of Cornwall and the Duchy of Lancaster, and Parliament agreed to divest the crown of all governmental expenses and support the monarchy by means of a fixed annual payment known as the Civil List. The last governmental responsibility to be given up by Victoria was the secret service, then costing the monarch a mere £10,000 a year.

By law, the title to the crown lands remains in the sovereign's hands and one of the first acts of a new monarch on his accession must be to send Parliament a message formally surrendering their hereditary revenues and placing himself "at the disposal of the House of Commons with regard to the Civil List." Within six months of a new monarch taking the throne a select committee of members of Parliament drawn from all parties in the Commons, after consultation with the Keeper of the Privy Purse and various members of the royal household, must recommend to Parliament an amount adequate to maintain the royal establishment. The sum that is then voted by Parliament becomes the new sovereign's annual income for the duration of the reign.[2]

In June, 1952, the select committee set up to determine Elizabeth II's Civil List recommended payment of an annual £475,000 for her reign, a sum which the full House of Commons promptly approved with surprisingly little protest. The Duke of Edinburgh was voted an annuity of £40,000 a year for life.[3] Additional payments, now totalling £177,000 a year, are made as annual allowances to five other members of the royal family, and the Treasury also foots the bill for pensions paid to the household employees of Edward VII, George V, Edward VIII and George VI, which at present runs close to £44,000 per year. Maintenance and structural repair of the royal palaces and the state-provided royal homes and the services provided for the royal household by various Government departments (fuel, lighting, telephones, telegrams, etc.) work out at around £150,000 yearly. The cost of royal ceremonial (great royal occasions are expensive affairs: the coronation of George VI cost the Government £574,000 in direct expenses, apart from municipal expenditure, and a sum of £58,000 was needed to defray the expenses of his funeral) and the trappings of the monarchy bring the annual cost of the monarchy to roughly £1,000,000 (£931,503 in 1948, just over £1,000,000 in 1950).

Even at this substantial sum, the state now comes out well ahead on George III's bargain. The crown lands, administered by Crown Commissioners for the benefit of the Exchequer, cover some of the choicest real estate in Britain. Extending over some 320,000 acres, they include immensely valuable, high-rental sites in London's crowded west end (both sides of Regent Street, the south side of Piccadilly Circus, two theatres, three restaurants and a hotel), large blocks of property in north London, great estates in Dorset, Wiltshire and Somerset, more than 100,000 acres of farmland, miles of seashore in Cornwall and Devon (rented out to seaside towns for pleasure beaches), mineral rights in Wales, the entire forest of Dean, rents in the Isle of Man and stretches of salmon water in Scotland (the fishing rights to which were worth £6,000 alone in pre-war years).

The revenue from the crown property surrendered by the sovereign now yields the Treasury a gross return of some £2,350,000 a year (1951), and after paying for repairs, maintenance and administrative costs the net profit to the Exchequer during the 15 years of George VI's reign averaged £1,000,000 per year. In addition, the sovereign turns over to the Exchequer various hereditary fines and forfeitures, known as small branches of hereditary revenue, which in 1951 amounted to more than £350,000.

Another royal windfall picked up by the Exchequer is the surplus revenue from the vast estates of the Duchy of Cornwall, part of the crown lands withheld in the bargain with Parliament, which traditionally belongs to the sovereign's eldest son. Created six centuries ago for the Black Prince, the Duchy's holdings now range from some 160,000 acres scattered over the west of England, including the forest of Dartmoor, to warehouses, wharves and working-class blocks of flats and houses in London, the famed cricket Oval at Kennington and oyster beds in Cornwall's Helford River. The personal estate of the monarch's eldest son, who bears the title of Duke of Cornwall, its substantial revenues are diverted to pay for his household and provide his income when he comes of age until such time as he ascends the throne.[4]

When Edward VIII became King, there being no Duke of

Cornwall, he agreed to hand over the Duchy's revenues, which had provided his income until he succeeded to the throne, to the Exchequer to be offset against his Civil List, and George VI volunteered to continue the practice when he followed Edward, with the proviso that the £10,000 yearly supplement paid to the Duke of Gloucester during Princess Elizabeth's minority and the £6,000 yearly allowance paid to Princess Elizabeth from the age of 11 (increased to £15,000 annually from the time she came of age at 21 until her marriage) should be paid out of the Duchy's revenues, which during the years of George VI's reign averaged just over £100,000 a year net.

Under Elizabeth II's Civil List a similar arrangement has been made. Prince Charles, the four-year-old Duke of Cornwall, is to receive a yearly sum of some £10,000 (one-ninth of the yearly net revenues from the Duchy, which have averaged £90,000 a year since the war's end) until he reaches the age of 18, partly for his maintenance and education and partly to provide the heir to the throne with a comfortable nest-egg of capital. During the last three years of his minority, from the age of 18 to 21, this is to be increased to £30,000 a year, after which he will be entitled to draw the Duchy's full revenues.[5] In the meantime the bulk of the Duchy's surplus each year will revert to the Treasury and, by a book-keeping transaction, be used to help pay for the Civil List.

At a rough calculation, therefore, the Exchequer can count on a yearly revenue from royal sources of some £1,430,000 to off-set the yearly £1,000,000 cost of the monarchy.

Unlike a top business executive, Britain's number one civil servant does not receive her salary by monthly cheque. Elizabeth II is paid by a unique system of "negotiable receipts" drawn on the national Exchequer. Every three months the Keeper of the Privy Purse and Treasurer to the Queen receives from the assistant Paymaster-General chits to the value of £118,750, one quarter of the Civil List, to be used as a drawing account to cover the Queen's personal expenses, the salaries of her household officials and domestic staff and the running expenses and upkeep of her homes. The Duke of Edinburgh, the Queen Mother, Queen Mary and other royal relatives who receive allowances from the state are paid separately by the

Treasury. Parenthetically, any personal cheques drawn by the Queen are on the Bank of England or Coutts & Company, private bankers, where she keeps her ready cash, but she seldom signs cheques herself. Most of them are signed for her by the Keeper of the Privy Purse.

The Civil List, a term now restricted to legislation providing finance to maintain the sovereign and the royal household (but not other members of the royal family), includes five classes of royal expenditure.

The first is Her Majesty's Privy (or private) Purse, which is fixed at £60,000 per year. This is £50,000 less than the Privy Purse provided for George V and George VI, who had Queen Consorts to keep, but Elizabeth's reduction is partly offset by the £40,000 a year for life granted to the Duke of Edinburgh. The Privy Purse is the Queen's personal income (and need not be accounted for to the select committee determining the Civil List at the outset of each reign), out of which she pays her private expenses, such as her clothing bills, her racing stable and stud, and makes her contributions to charities and the lesser members of her family.

Unlike the President of the U.S., who currently pays back in taxes some £21,400 of his £35,714 yearly salary and is left with a weekly take-home pay of some £270, Elizabeth II pays no income tax at all on her Privy Purse, which works out at a cool £1,153, 16s. 11d. per week, or on any of her public income paid by the nation. This has not always been so. When income tax was reintroduced in Britain in 1842 there was a public outcry over the "crippling rate" of sevenpence in the pound sterling and to encourage the public to face this terrible imposition Queen Victoria nobly submitted the whole of her income to tax. Edward VII followed his mother's practice, but as taxes rose with the First World War George V prudently reclaimed the royal privilege of exemption from tax, and his successors have enjoyed the same dispensation. The privilege of paying no income tax on her Privy Purse is more than cancelled out for Elizabeth, however, because it comes out of the royal pocket in the first place—being more than covered by the surplus revenues handed over to the Treasury each year by the Duchy of Cornwall.

The second class of Civil List expenditure covers salaries paid to members of the Queen's household, including the heralds, ecclesiastics and royal functionaries in the Lord Chamberlain's department and the equerries and pages in the Royal Mews department. This is fixed at an annual sum of £185,000. This is £51,000 more than was provided yearly for the salaries and retired allowances paid to the households of George VI and his wife, an increase mainly due to the discovery by the select committee which examined the finances of George VI's reign prior to settling Elizabeth's Civil List that about 100 senior members of the household had for some years accepted salaries lower than appropriate for their duties in order to help the late King live within his income.

The third category of Civil List expenditure provides for the running expenses of the Queen's homes—the food bills, the royal cellars, wages of the domestic staff, travel costs, garden and presentation parties, the upkeep of Sandringham and Balmoral, liveries for the servants, purchase of horses, forage and farriery, the purchase and upkeep of coaches and motor cars, and all the apparatus that makes the monarchy a self-contained community behind the palace walls.

To cover these expenses an annual sum of £121,800 is allocated by Parliament. This is £31,000 less than was given to Elizabeth's father, but in the meantime Parliament has agreed to take over certain services and costs from the Civil List—such as the salaries of the Gentlemen-at-Arms and the Yeomen of the Guard (£9,000 per year in all), the upkeep of Buckingham Palace's gardens (£2,000 per annum), certain supplies of fuel and light, the charges for telephones and telegrams, now borne by the Post Office, and the wages of the industrial staff engaged on the maintenance of the royal palaces—which has relieved the royal purse of the expenditure of more than £75,000 a year. The accounts for royal household expenditure are scrupulously audited by the Treasury and disbursed under the supervision of the Keeper of the Privy Purse.

Contrary to popular belief, the Queen and her husband pay as private citizens for almost everything they require. They may accept nothing free. They pay all their travel costs except when they journey by naval vessel or by an aeroplane of the R.A.F.'s special Royal Flight. Travel by royal train is an expensive luxury. The Queen is charged for its use at a special rate of around ten shillings per mile, plus first-class rail fares for every member of the party. Ponies, horses and dogs belonging to the family are generally shipped on ahead, while the royal cars are shipped in freight cars attached to the royal train. Chartering the train for the 566-mile journey from London to Balmoral costs the Queen some £325 for the single journey for herself, her husband and a staff of two—which is one reason why Elizabeth and her family increasingly use their free aircraft.

Entertaining something like 30,000 official guests each year makes another big hole in Elizabeth II's Civil List allowances. The structural repair of the royal palaces and their maintenance as administrative or ceremonial buildings is now the responsibility of the state, provided for by grants additional to the Civil List, and over years of discussion the Keeper of the Privy Purse and the representatives of the Treasury have settled the involved problems of who pays for what. For instance, at "Buck House" the Queen pays the utility bills for gas and water, but the state pays for lighting the courtyard and the water to wash it down. At Windsor Castle the state foots the bill for all the water used —even for the royal baths—and since 1951 it also pays for all the light bulbs for Windsor and Buckingham Palace.

George VI used to tell his friends that he was the most underpaid monarch in the business.[6] Although the cost of living has approximately trebled over the first half of the century his Civil List was £60,000 less than the annual £470,000 granted Edward VII in 1901. And as rather more than half of the increase in the cost of living since the turn of the century was concentrated into the 15 years of George VI's reign the late King fought a losing battle against inflation. Although he was able to live well within his income until 1945 (in 1947 he voluntarily contributed to the Treasury £100,000 which he had saved on curtailed expenditure during the war years and he had previously handed back £20,000 in interest payments on £200,000 worth of Government securities bought with money saved from his Civil List during the war), from 1946 onwards, due to steeply-rising post-war costs and wages, he ran into the red at an average of £31,800 a year on his Civil List, a deficit he had to make up from his Privy Purse or his private fortune. In order to ease his burden Parliament in 1947 and again in 1951 agreed to relieve the Civil List of costs and charges amounting to around £50,000 a year and in 1948, to meet the increased costs of labour and material, he was given an additional grant of £33,000 yearly towards the care of the royal family's private suites in the royal palaces.

The royal household accounts from her father's reign which Elizabeth II submitted to the select committee in the summer of 1952 provided both a graphic illustration of inflation and a fascinating peek into the economics of kingship. George VI's housekeeping bill went from a low of £126,428 in the mid-war year of 1943 to a high of £196,604 in 1950. Only during the first years of his reign and the wartime period was he able to stay within his Civil List housekeeping allowance of £152,800 a year. In spite of rationing and kitchen economies, his food bills rose more than 50 per cent., from £18,365 in 1937 to £28,096 in 1951. Despite the fact that the staff of the royal establishments had been reduced by more than 100, his board and wage bill rose from £34,656 in 1937 to £63,130 in 1951 (his Palace servants, almost solidly organized in a branch of the Civil Servants union since 1946, demanded and received several post-war pay increases). Similarly, though the number of the King's horses had been reduced in the same period from 86 to 35 the cost of horses, forage and farriery remained virtually the same—£5,581 in 1937, £5,472 in 1951. Bills for the purchase and repair of household goods soared more than 100 per cent., from £10,282 in 1937 to £21,500 in 1951.[7]

Anticipating a further rise in costs and wages during Elizabeth II's reign the select committee prudently provided a new class of Civil List expenditure, a supplementary provision of £95,000 a year to be held in reserve as a contingency margin to make up any future deficits in the second and third categories of the Civil List. The supplementary allowance is also intended to provide financial aid to minor members of the royal family, not provided for by Parliamentary payments, who assist the Queen in the carrying out of royal duties. These family hand-outs are at the discretion of Elizabeth II, subject only to an upper limit of £25,000 a year.

The final class of Civil List allowances is known as the Royal Bounty, Alms and Special Services, for which £13,200 (the same as in George VI's reign) is allocated each year. Alms are distributed by the Queen in the form of Maundy money and other gifts. Each Christmas, for example, 100 poor subjects are chosen

325

by their parishes to receive a gift of ten shillings each from the Queen. It is also customary for the Queen to greet parents of triplets born in her reign with a gift of £3 in each case, paid from her Privy Purse.

Apart from the Civil List, Parliament also votes a separate expenditure for Civil List pensions. These grants, which are administered by the Financial Secretary to the Treasury on behalf of both the Queen and Parliament, are payable to famous men of letters, artists, actors, scientists or their dependants who have fallen on hard times. There are currently about 220 Civil List pensioners and in the course of a year (during which only £5,000 in new pensions may be granted) they receive a total of some £30,000 from public funds. One of these is the Poet Laureate (John Masefield), who receives £70 per year from the Civil List and an allowance of £27 in lieu of the traditional butt of sack, for which he is expected to compose special odes on great occasions.

Aside from those members of the family who draw allowances from the state, the Queen provides from her own pocket small living allowances or pensions to a host of lesser royal relatives, old court officials and family retainers who are wholly or partly dependent on Her Majesty's bounty. George V provided for some 150 such dependants during his reign, and George VI paid out compassionate pensions amounting to £1,300 yearly, the payment of which has now been taken over by the Treasury. In addition, the Queen provides rent-free for her relatives, friends and court officials more than 50 private residences—known as "grace-and-favour" houses—ranging from great mansions like Marlborough House to small cottages in the royal parks and estates.

In her private capacity Elizabeth II is the head of a vast estate business. The hereditary Duchy of Lancaster, dating from the time of Henry IV, who was Duke of Lancaster, is the personal property of the sovereign and its 53,000 acres of land in the north of England and in London produces a yearly revenue of between £90,000 and £100,000, which helps replenish the royal coffers.[8]

The Queen's Balmoral estate, bought for the family by Victoria and Albert and considerably added to by George VI, now encloses some 80,000 acres, mostly moorland and forests, and is valued at £500,000. George VI also increased the monarch's holdings at Sandringham to 17,000 acres and its 15 tenant farms are run on a sound commercial basis. The house and its great estate, probably Elizabeth's most paying proposition, thanks to her father's management, are valued locally at £1,000,000. In addition, George VI also ran a small 540-acre mixed farm in the grounds of Windsor Park, which his daughter has inherited.[9]

The monarch has the right of exemption from tax on all private, as well as state, income, but Elizabeth II, like her father, waives this exemption and pays tax on all her property income and un-earned investment income on the same scale as her subjects, which on her rate of earnings runs to a confiscatory nineteen shillings and sixpence out of every twenty shillings. George VI was particularly hard hit by the Labour Government's "capital levy" in 1947, which took a large bite out of his investment income. Much of young Elizabeth's capital, inherited from her father, is invested in real estate and railroad stocks, and her holdings reputedly include large blocks of stock in American companies, the result of far-sighted investment by her royal ancestors. Chief financial adviser to the Queen and her family on matters concerning their private money is 81-year-old Sir Edward Peacock, a sagacious old Canadian who is the head of Barings, one of the great banking houses of the City of London. Sir Edward, who has been confidant as well as banker to four monarchs, has served for 23 years as Receiver-General of the Duchy of Cornwall.

Elizabeth as Queen enjoys very few windfalls from her remaining hereditary rights. By ancient tradition, she is entitled to all whales and sturgeon caught in British territorial waters—and whales, when they turn up, are now worth about £1,000 and sturgeon about £55. The crown still owns all land left bare by the slipping away of the sea, any island which suddenly springs up in territorial waters, and the foreshore—the land between high and low tide—around Britain's perimeter; wreck in its various forms belongs to the crown; so does the property of any person who dies without leaving kin or claims upon their estate; so also does all "treasure trove," gold or silver coins, bullion or ancient relics hidden in the earth or in a secret place with the intention of being recovered later. The crown also owns, by tradition, all gold and silver mines in Britain (there are none to speak of), and the exclusive right to search for oil in the United Kingdom. In theory, these possessions and rights can still be claimed by Elizabeth II but in practice the monarch turns over all proceeds to the Treasury or, in the case of "treasure trove" and ancient relics, to museums. The sovereign still owns some 600 of the Thames River's 800 swans and all white swans swimming in open or common rivers, provided they are wild and unmarked, presumably because, like whales and sturgeon, they are not depositable in the Treasury.

If Elizabeth II could sell her family heirlooms she would certainly rank among the world's multi-millionaires, if not as the richest individual in the world. Apart from the crown jewels, which are the property of the state, the reigning sovereign inherits almost priceless treasures.

The royal picture collection, housed at Buckingham Palace and at Windsor Castle, is the finest private collection in the world. Handed down and added to without interruption by every monarch since Henry VIII (except when Cromwell sold some of the masterpieces), it includes prized canvases by most of the old masters—Titian, Rembrandt, Velasquez, Canaletto, Rubens, Holbein, Breughel, Tintoretto, Van Dyck and Vermeer among them—and many by British painters—Reynolds, Gainsborough, Ramsay—as well as new paintings by contemporary artists added to the collection by Victoria, Queen Mary and the present Queen Mother. In 1946 the estimated value of 506 of the paintings in the collection was put at £2,000,000.

Before the Second World War the Buckingham Palace collection of gold plate alone was worth more than £2,000,000. Placed together, it would weigh five tons. It is impossible to price-tag the royal library at Windsor, which contains upwards of 100,000 volumes. George VI's stamp collection of 330 volumes, inherited from his father and now passed on to Elizabeth II, is valued by the Keeper of the Philatelic Collection at around £1,000,000.

Despite her seemingly flush financial position Elizabeth II, like her father, contends that she has to struggle to make her expenditure match her income. In order to cut down his tremendous overheads George VI instituted strict economies in his household and personal expenditure, and the select committee which examined the royal books in the summer of 1952 expressed its satisfaction with the economical administration of the royal household and its belief that no further large-scale economies could be made in the new Queen's homes. At George VI's request Palace officials after the war worked out the cost of living for his family, his household and his domestic staff to a fraction of a penny a day, and in 1949 the managing director of London's Savoy Hotel was called in to suggest economies for the royal kitchens. The Keeper of the Privy Purse and the assistant Treasurer run the Palace finances on a strictly counting-house basis. A detailed invoice has to accompany all goods ordered and all accounts are filed so that current expenditure can be checked against similar items bought in previous years.

Privately George VI used to declare that he could not afford to lose money, even on his pleasures. He insisted that the royal racing stable pay its own way, and managed to net a nice profit from his shooting at Balmoral and Sandringham by the sale of part of the yearly bag of grouse, partridge, pheasant and duck and the use of the remainder in the royal kitchens.

These economies, continued by Queen Elizabeth II, while they may help preserve her private fortune, have also served to bring the royal establishment more in tune with the post-war mood of the majority of Britons, who, in their uphill battle to regain an adequate standard of life, are dead against over-spending and too-obvious royal luxury.

XXIII

ROYAL HOMES

THOSE who don't live in royal palaces are apt to think of
them as beautiful, spacious buildings in which life is lived at
the highest level of elegance. Those who do live in them know
that they can be as uncomfortable and unhomelike as museums.[1]
Every occupant of Buckingham Palace since Queen Victoria has
complained that it has a dank, musty, institutional smell, which
led Edward VII to refer to it always as "The Sepulchre."

It is a peculiarity of the British monarchic system, at least
since it was transformed from an absolute to a constitutional
monarchy, that most of the royal residences are so far behind the
times in modern improvements that thousands of the subjects
live in greater comfort than the sovereigns. At a time when bathrooms had become commonplace installations in London's working-class flats, for instance, there was not one bathroom in
Windsor Castle, and there is still no central heating inside the
cold, thick-walled fortress. Clarence House was not provided
with central heating or a modern bathtub until it was renovated
in 1949 for Princess Elizabeth and the Duke of Edinburgh, and
to this day there is no running water in Queen Mary's suite at
Marlborough House.

According to the custom established by Victoria and given
the authority of tradition by yearly repetition during the reigns
of Edward VII, George V and George VI the royal year runs on
a fixed and regular pattern, and the migrations of the royal
family to its various residences around Britain are as unvarying
and as certain as the seasons.

In the course of a normal year Elizabeth II and her family
occupy for varying lengths of time a total of five royal residences.[2]
Only two of these—Buckingham Palace and Windsor Castle—
are state palaces, however.

The bulk of their time—most of the first six months of each year and a shorter period at the end—is spent at Buckingham Palace, which is the head office of the monarchy as well as the Queen's principal home. Whenever the court is in London Elizabeth and her husband and their children, usually accompanied by the Queen Mother and Princess Margaret, escape each week-end to the seclusion of Royal Lodge, tucked away in the privacy of Windsor Great Park, which they regard as their real family home.

Usually twice each year—generally at Easter and invariably during the week of racing at nearby Ascot in June—the Queen moves her court to her ancestral home, storied Windsor Castle, which has been used by an unbroken procession of England's kings and queens since William the Conqueror cut trees from the surrounding forest and built himself a fortress on the site. For the late summer and early autumn months the royal family moves north in a body for their holiday at Scotland's Balmoral Castle, built by Victoria and Albert as their summer retreat. The royal Christmas generally means Sandringham, the comfortable country home built by Edward VII in his princely days, where the whole family traditionally gathers for the season's celebrations.

Foreign diplomats are accredited to the Court of St. James's because the official London residence of Elizabeth II's court is still the Palace of St. James's, a sombrely-attractive, toy-soldier castle in aged red brick, but it is at Buckingham Palace that they present their letters of credence to the Queen. Ever since young Victoria, then a girl of 18, imperiously decided to move into it three weeks after her accession to the throne in 1837 Buckingham Palace has been the symbolic seat of British sovereignty and the London home of the reigning monarch. It has been the home of eight successive generations of the royal family, the birthplace of two monarchs, William IV and Edward VII, and one king-to-be, Prince Charles, the present Duke of Cornwall.

Buckingham Palace is the most famed royal residence in the world. From the time Victoria took up her residence there it became the very heart of an expanding Empire, as later it has served as a symbol of unity to the British Commonwealth. In modern times, particularly in the last 40 years, it has become the focus of public celebration, the gathering point at which the nation assembles to express its emotions on occasions of great national sorrow or rejoicing. Its familiar setting—the stern, greyish-white, rectangular façade, topped by the royal standard at the masthead; the wide, sweeping courtyard, held in by the ornamental iron gates and the gilt-tipped railings; the little wooden sentry boxes and the scarlet-coated sentries; the baroque fountain of the Queen Victoria memorial dominating the wide roadway that fronts the Palace, with the larger-than-life statue of the old queen sitting cosily in her robes, surrounded by improbable mermaids and tritons, as she gazes down the long, broad, tree-lined avenue of the Mall—invariably conjures up a satisfying picture of Britain in her rich and illustrious heyday, the long near-century of the Victorian and Edwardian reigns.

This 602 roomed building,[3] a combination of state showpiece, business offices and family mansion, is easily the most valuable piece of real estate in the monarchy's portfolio—its 45-acre site, in a superb position in central London, was valued at £3,000,000 before the Second World War and has perhaps doubled in value over the intervening years—and successive monarchs who have been stuck with the burden of living in it have toyed with the idea of disposing of it. George V used to tell friends that his life-long ambition was to pull down "Buck House" and use the money obtained from the sale of its grounds to reconstruct the smaller, more intimate Kensington Palace as the town residence of the sovereign.

By British standards of antiquity, Buckingham Palace is a fairly recent acquisition of the monarchy. In the seventeenth century the land on which it now stands was planted with mulberry trees, an experiment encouraged by James I, who thought that the cultivation of silk worms would be a profitable investment. The industry failed—some say because the wrong kind of trees were planted—and a decade or two later the "Mulberry Garden" became a public entertainment ground, which was the scene of raffish escapades during the days of the diarists Pepys and Evelyn. In 1703 the property was sold to John Sheffield, the Duke of Buckingham, who built on it Buckingham House, a commodious mansion of red brick designed for him by a Dutch architect, where he lived until his death in 1720. The first two Georges had their eyes on it as a possible royal residence, but the aged Duchess of Buckingham, who survived her husband by 23 years, asked a high price for the property and the deal fell through. Finally, in 1761, George III persuaded the Duke's descendants to sell him the original Buckingham House and grounds for the sum of £21,000. George III's intention was to settle the mansion on his wife, Queen Charlotte, as a dower house in the event of her widowhood, but they liked it so much that they made their home there and twelve of their thirteen children were born in it. Queen Charlotte died before her husband, however, and on his death it passed to George IV.

"The First Gentleman of Europe," whose tastes were nothing if not expensive, had the ambitious idea of building a metropolitan palace in the heart of London, a palatial residence in the capital as the appropriate background for the monarchical office, but after his extravagance in erecting the Royal Pavilion at Brighton, Parliament balked at his proposal to provide funds for a new palace. In 1819, while he was still acting as Prince Regent on his father's behalf and a year before he came to the throne in his own right, Parliament agreed to let him remodel and re-furnish Buckingham House as the King's residence. The royal architect John Nash, the designer of London's Regent Street, was instructed to prepare plans for enlarging and modernizing the mansion at a proposed cost of £200,000.

George IV and Nash thereupon entered into a friendly con-spiracy. By adding a wing here and a courtyard there and building on a few new extensions the sovereign and his architect agreed that it was possible to create a building that looked like a palace. Despite repeated protests from Parliament the transformation was undertaken, but progress was painfully slow because of frequent changes in Nash's plans. At one period, when as many as 1,000 workmen laboured on the building, working until late in the evening by the light of candles, the project was costing £10,000 a week and by 1828, to Parliament's astonishment, George IV had spent more than £600,000, three times the original estimate, on a palace that was not yet completed. When Nash announced his intention of tearing down some of the new structure because he was not satisfied with it, Parliament in-dignantly set up a commission to inquire into the royal expendi-ture. At this point George IV died, without having lived in his new palace, and Nash was promptly dismissed.

George IV's brother and successor, William IV, embarrassed by his legacy, disliked the building so much that he refused to live in it. He tried to foist it on the Army as a barracks and then on the Government as a House of Parliament, but there were no takers and he was finally persuaded to complete it. The final architectural touches were provided by Edward Blore, who designed Abbotsford, the home of Sir Walter Scott. During the seven years of William IV's reign the palace stood empty, an expensive white elephant, while the workmen gave it the finishing touches.

Much to the country's astonishment young Victoria, who followed William IV, announced that it was from the new Buckingham Palace and not from St. James's or Kensington Palace that she and her successors would rule and on the twenty-third day of her reign she drove over from Kensington with her mother and took possession of her new home. At that time the Palace consisted of buildings ranged around only three sides of a central courtyard, with the open side of the quadrangle facing down the Mall. The main entrance to the courtyard was formed by a huge marble arch, from which flew the Queen's standard. Within ten years Her Majesty was complaining that the Palace had become too small for her growing family and Parliament, pleased to hide George IV's original structure from view, granted an additional sum of £150,000 to build a fourth wing, the east front, which was grafted on to the Georgian buildings and enclosed the quadrangle. Parliament got its own back on George IV when his Royal Pavilion at Brighton was sold to defray part of the cost of the new wing, and a number of magnificent fireplaces, mirrors and fixtures were removed from the Pavilion to grace the state rooms of the Palace. The central archway, which was to be dignified by the name of the Marble Arch, gave its name to an area of London when it was removed in 1847 from the courtyard to make way for the new wing and transplanted to its present position at the north-east entrance to Hyde Park.

The new wing, designed by Blore, presented a very shoddy façade and weathered badly over half a century and in 1913 it was redesigned by Sir Aston Webb and refaced—without disturbing the glass in the windows—in Portland stone to present the porticoed, judicial-looking front of the present day.

The Palace has three main floors, known as the ground, the principal and the bedchamber floors. Roughly one half of its interior space is occupied by great state and semi-state apartments, one quarter by crown and household offices and less than a quarter by actual living accommodation for the Queen, her family and the household.

The east front, facing down the Mall, contains on its principal floor the Balcony Room, which Queen Mary remodelled about 25 years ago in Chinese style. It is from this room that the royal family emerges on to the famed balcony directly under the flag-staff on special occasions. On either side of the Balcony Room are two suites for state visitors, only one of which is kept in commission, due to the small number of royal visitors now received at the Palace. These rooms open on to the Principal Corridor, a magnificent passageway 20 feet wide and 240 feet long, divided into three sections by mirror-glass doors, which runs the entire length of the east wing. On the bedchamber floor above are guest suites, the rooms of the lady-in-waiting, and, at the Constitution Hill end, the sitting-room, bedroom and bathroom now occupied by Princess Margaret. The east front also has an additional top floor of small rooms, mainly devoted to staff and storage.

The ground floor of the east wing is broken up by archway entrances, which correspond to the gateways in the ornamental railings that surround the gravelled forecourt.[4] The large centre gate is opened only when the sovereign drives through in state: on other occasions even royalty uses one of the side gates. The small archway on the left as you face the Palace from the Mall is known as the Visitors' Entrance. Inside this entrance is kept the visitors' book, which is signed not only by those visiting by appointment but also by all who keep up the old custom of "calling" to leave their card as a mark of respect after a royal birth, death or illness. Following George VI's death there was a constant stream of callers for days. Each visitors' book, a specially-made, 500-paged, gilt-edged volume bound in red leather and stamped with the royal cipher in gold, lasts for about two years and when full is sent to be preserved with the monarchy's archives at Windsor Castle.

On the right-hand side of the ground floor is the Privy Purse entrance, used by household officials and those with business at the Palace. Visitors are met by the footman on duty, shown into a waiting-room while their arrival is notified on the house telephone, and then conducted to their destination by footmen. No one is allowed to wander around the Palace without an escort, both for security reasons and to prevent their getting lost in the maze of corridors and staircases. Even Queen Mary, who had known the Palace all her life, got lost one day soon after she moved in when she ventured up a little-used staircase.

Apart from these precautions there is far less rigmarole involved in visiting Buckingham Palace than there is in entering the White House, or even the U.S. Embassy in London. Elizabeth II's telephone number (Whitehall 4832) is listed in the London phone directory. However, only personal friends and relatives who know the "code"—a particular way of asking for a member of the royal family—are put directly through by the Palace switchboard to the Queen or her husband or a member of the family.

The north wing of the Palace, which looks out on Constitution Hill and Green Park, contains on the ground floor the administrative offices of the secretariat, on the principal floor Elizabeth and Philip's royal suite, the Queen's study, the Queen Mother's suite of apartments, and the family's private dining-room, known as the Chinese Luncheon Room, and on the bedchamber floor the nursery suite, some private guest-rooms and servants' quarters.

The south front, overlooking Buckingham Palace Road, is given over to the household offices, bedrooms of the live-in members of the staff, and the Palace kitchens. Beyond the Entrée door are various entrances for staff and tradesmen.

The west wing, which fronts on to the rolling lawns of the Palace gardens, is architecturally the best of Nash's contribution to "Buck House." As the showpiece of the building, it houses all the state apartments, which open on to central corridors so that some face the gardens and some the quadrangle. On the ground floor the corridor is known as the Marble Hall, on to which open a number of semi-state rooms, including the magnificently-proportioned Bow Room, across which garden-party guests pass to emerge through its deep bow-windowed glass doors on to the terrace, the "1844" and the "1855" drawing-rooms flanking the Bow Room, as well as the stately dining-room where members of the household take their meals. On the principal floor of the west front the 150-foot-long corridor serves as the Picture Gallery, the black-and-gold walls of which are hung with some of the most valuable works of art from the royal collection. In Edwardian days the gallery was a museum-like passageway in which a profusion of pictures covered every inch of wall space. Under Queen Mary's direction its roof was re-modelled to admit more light, concealed electric lighting was introduced and its display of pictures reduced to a few important canvases which now hang at eye-level. Surplus pictures and paintings of historical rather than artistic interest—likenesses of former sovereigns, distant royal relatives and pictures of royal yachts and race horses—were distributed among other rooms and corridors in the Palace. After the Second World War, when the pictures were again rehung after being stored for safety, Queen Elizabeth further reduced the number in the Gallery from 120 to about 50, giving each room to be seen. Next to the Picture Gallery is the Silk Tapestry Room, the walls of which are covered with French silk Gobelins, treasured French tapestries from the seventeenth century.

Elizabeth II still holds court in the same suite of twelve state apartments used by Victoria, although they were all redecorated under Queen Mary's supervision after the First World War. The most important of these, on the principal floor of the west wing, are the Throne Room, the State Dining Room, the State Ball-room, the Music Room, the White Drawing Room, the Blue Drawing Room and the Green Drawing Room. Most of these salons are connected by a series of high Spanish mahogany doors, 12 feet high by 7 feet wide, mounted in ormolu and fitted with mirror-glass panels which reflect the ornate splendour of the interior appointments and give the effect of even greater spacious-ness to the outsize rooms. The floors are of marble and parquet.

The royal throne at the Palace is used only on occasions of great state by the Queen, but the Throne Room, an eye-filling chamber some 65 feet long, is always kept in order and readiness. Its white-painted walls are richly ornamented in gold. Around the walls, just below the ornate ceiling, runs a frieze depicting scenes from the Wars of the Roses. The huge Brussels carpet is in crimson, decorated with Tudor roses. At one end of the room, raised upon a crimson-covered dais and under an elaborate canopy of crimson and gold, stands the throne—a straight-backed, crimson-upholstered armchair with arms of plain wood. Flanking the dais are the thrones of George V and Queen Mary and two carved gilt council chairs made for George IV's throne room. In an alcove to the side sits the massive single throne, topped by its crown, which was used by Victoria.

The State Dining Room is another immense chamber. Its centrepiece, dwarfed by the overwhelming dimensions of the room, is a massive dining-table, 8 feet 3 inches wide, which can seat 24 guests comfortably when it is unexpanded and can be extended to 80 feet in length with the insertion of 19 additional leaves. Ornate flower designs, picked out in gold, decorate the plaster work around the domes in the ceiling, and around the walls stand no fewer than ten resplendent sideboards.

The State Ballroom, which used to be the scene of evening courts and is now used for occasional investitures and the more elaborate state banquets, was added to the Palace by Victoria in 1847 and stands at the junction of the west and south wings, directly over the Palace kitchens. A room of truly majestic proportions—123 feet long, almost 60 feet in width and 45 feet high—it contains another throne, which stands at one end of the long room in a recess enclosed by tall pilasters of gold. Along the sides of the room are rose-coloured, damask-covered, tiered couches, similar to those in the House of Commons.

The Music Room, where guests are presented prior to a state banquet, is perhaps the most impressive of Nash's interiors. Located in the middle of the west front, directly over the Bow Room, its five great bow windows look out over the Palace gardens. Its ceiling, from which hang two magnificent chandeliers, is domed and richly encrusted with gold, and around its walls are set 18 tall gold-topped colums of *scagliola*, which imitates *lapis lazuli*. Besides a unique four-sided clock designed by George III and a brass-inlaid walnut piano specially made for the Prince Regent, the room's furnishings include 120 Louis XIV chairs, each of which is worth a small fortune. Flanking the Music Room are the White Drawing Room, a 48-foot-long room decorated in white and gold, with its furnishings upholstered in deep ivory satin brocade, and the 68-foot-long Blue Drawing Room, intended by Nash as the ballroom, which takes its name from the pale blue of its walls and upholstery. The Green Drawing Room, a smaller salon, serves as an ante-room to the Throne Room.

Honeycombing the Palace are more than a mile and a half of

white-painted, red-carpeted corridors, most of them more than 20 feet wide and between 200 and 240 feet in length. Given names for convenience—there is also a King's Corridor and a Household Corridor in addition to the Principal Corridor, the Marble Hall and the Picture Gallery—they have been converted into ante-rooms to house the royal treasures.[5]

Tacked on to the extremes of the west front are two former conservatories. One was converted more than a century ago into the Palace chapel, and until the death of George V the custom of saying morning prayers there was maintained. The chapel was damaged by a bomb during the war, but because the royal family are seldom at the Palace for Sunday services it has been last on the schedule for repairs. The other conservatory was converted by George VI into a swimming pool soon after he took the throne. It, too, was bomb-damaged, but the pool has been restored and the building now houses in addition a squash rackets court, where the Duke of Edinburgh plays with his Palace cronies.

Except for tantalizing glimpses from the top of a bus, few Londoners ever see behind the high, spiked walls that surround the Palace's 40-acre garden. These quiet, leafy grounds, a park without a public, contain a large ornamental lake, an octagonal, glass-sided pavilion where the royal family takes tea on pleasant summer days, the shallow bunkers that remain from the now-disused nine-hole pitch-and-putt golf course which George VI built for himself before the war, and the Palace tennis courts.

During most of the long years of Victoria's widowhood Buckingham Palace stood empty, except for servants and a few royal guests, while the old Queen brooded in the greater seclusion of Windsor Castle, Balmoral and her summer residence at Osborne, in the Isle of Wight. Edward VII brought "Buck House" back to life, instituted the social highspots of evening courts and in his brief reign of nine years initiated a few overdue improvements in the building, but it was during the reign of George V and Queen Mary that the biggest changes were made. The east front was remodelled three years after they came to the throne, and new gates and railings were installed to offset the memorial to Victoria in front of the Palace. Under Queen Mary's expert eye the state apartments were refurbished in a style more consistent with the Prince Regent's grand ideas. A housewife as well as a decorator, Queen Mary also modernized the domestic offices. The antiquated kitchens were remodelled and the Palace's primitive plumbing was overhauled at her insistence.

Apart from repairs necessitated by bomb damage no important structural changes were made during George VI's reign. The state apartments—the furnishings of which are handed down from reign to reign—remain much as Queen Mary arranged them, and George VI and his wife confined their alterations to their private apartments. When Elizabeth II and the Duke of Edinburgh moved into the Palace the antiquated central heating system was in process of conversion from coke furnaces to oil burners and the Palace's electrical system was being modernized, but they have made few changes in the private quarters of the building, merely taking over as the royal suite the bedrooms, sitting-rooms and dressing-rooms used by Elizabeth's mother and father and reconverting the former nursery suite which Elizabeth and Margaret had used, to accommodate Prince Charles and Princess Anne.

As a break from their official life, which necessarily involves meeting and being agreeable to thousands of people, most of whom they have never met before, Elizabeth and her family cherish the complete privacy and protection against intrusion which is theirs at Royal Lodge, their week-end home. An angular, three-floored building, painted pink to suit the Queen Mother's taste, it stands secluded amid the trees of the Great Park that spreads south from Windsor Castle.

Royal Lodge was originally built by Nash in 1810 as a shooting "box" for George IV, who liked it so much that he lived there for some time while additions were being made to Windsor. Much of it has since been pulled down and rebuilt and of the original lodge only a large drawing-room, known as the "saloon," a unique octagonal sun room and the wine-cellars remain. When George V gave it to the then Duke and Duchess of York in 1931 Bertie and Elizabeth set about converting it into their own home and their improvements have made it perhaps the most up-to-date of the royal residences. Royal Lodge still belongs to the Queen Mother, but as Elizabeth and Philip have had no country house of their own since Sunninghill Park, the 25-roomed Ascot mansion which the late King provided for them, burned down in 1947, they still regard Royal Lodge as their week-end home.

Royal Lodge was George VI's favourite spot for rest and relaxation and it was there that he went for his convalescence after his leg operation and his first outings after his lung resection. Requiring only a small staff, it is run like a private house. All equerries and ladies-in-waiting are dismissed, no flag flies from the masthead, and the few servants on duty wear the plain black of private service instead of the liveries of Windsor Castle. Court etiquette is dropped in favour of the informal, homey atmosphere of family life.

The workers on the great Windsor estate and farm and their families who live in the grounds regard the royal family more in their week-end role as the local landowners than as royalty. Elizabeth II, like her father, knows most of her workers by name, and the Queen Mother takes time to visit their homes and interest herself in their families. Like a good squire, George VI rehoused his workers after the war in a new model village, complete with social club and recreational centre, inside the Great Park. This little community has its own royal school, the original of which was started more than 100 years ago by the Prince Consort to make sure that the royal households never ran short of properly-educated servants. The first curriculum was drawn up by Victoria herself and emphasized such useful domestic arts as needlework, spinning, gardening and carpentry. Today the royal school instructs a yearly average of some 60 pupils, all of them children of men and women in the royal service.

Four miles by road from Royal Lodge, but only a mile and a quarter as the crow flies, the massive, turreted battlements of Windsor Castle stand out against the sky. Rising majestically from its commanding position, a chalk hill on the Berkshire bank of the River Thames, between the river and the old town of Windsor, it is the largest castle still surviving in Europe and the most imposing and most ancient royal palace in existence.

The thick grey walls of Windsor enclose a storehouse of British royal history. For more than 800 years an unbroken line of kings and queens have used it as a royal residence, weaving its golden story into the rich tapestry of their nation's past.

According to legend, King Arthur and his Knights gathered around their Round Table in the vicinity of Windsor. Because of its strategic position above a bend of the Thames, the site was probably a fortified point at the time of the Roman invasion. A few years after winning the battle of Hastings William the Conqueror, first attracted to Windsor as a possible hunting preserve, prudently converted an existing Saxon hunting lodge into a moated fortress, one of the circle of strong-points he built around London to control the defeated Saxons. His successor, William Rufus, used Windsor only as a fortress and a prison, but with the reign of Henry I, who held his inaugural court there and replaced the wooden fortifications with a stone circuit wall, it became a home for the kings of England.

It was from Windsor Castle that King John, after nine days of negotiations with his rebellious barons, rode forth on a June day in 1215 to Runnymede, four miles down river from Windsor, to sign Magna Carta. Henry III carried on a great building programme during his long reign and about 1272 began the massive Round Tower which dominates the 13-acre site, but around 1344 Edward III, who added rooms of such splendour that the Castle was turned into a palace, reconstructed and enlarged the tower, which he used as a meeting-place for his newly-founded Order of the Garter. Upriver from the Castle, overlooked from its walls, are the famed playing fields of Eton and the cluster of ancient buildings of Eton College, founded by Henry VI when he was a stripling sovereign of 19. Edward IV built within the Castle walls the graceful St. George's Chapel, a spellbinding piece of architecture regarded as one of the most perfect perpendicular buildings now in existence, in honour of the patron saint of the Order of the Garter.

Over the centuries a steady procession of kings and queens lived and loved and died in Windsor and left their marks upon the Castle. It was there that tragic Anne Boleyn first caught the lustful eye of Henry VIII as she paced the cloisters with her venerable uncle, the dean of the Chapel. It was to Windsor that Queen Elizabeth I summoned Shakespeare to write for her a play showing Falstaff in love, an imperious request to which he replied by writing and producing "The Merry Wives of Windsor" within 14 days. Charles I spent his last Christmas a prisoner in the Castle and after his execution in Whitehall his body was brought back to Windsor and secretly buried in St. George's Chapel. After the death of Queen Anne in 1714 the great Castle was neglected. The first two Georges did not like living there, but George III, who planned the great restoration of the Castle, lived out his last years of madness at Windsor and died there in 1820. The aged, unhappy monarch, who knew that he was going insane, roamed the rooms of the Castle bemoaning aloud his fate and pathetically stuffed his clothes with cushions so that his Queen should not see how his illness had wasted him. When George IV came to live at Windsor in 1823 it fell to him to complete the restoration planned by his father and, true to his extravagant form, he spent many thousands of pounds before his death in 1830, transforming the Castle into an imposing palace. He improved the skyline appearance of Windsor by connecting the confused jumble of buildings into a whole and adding towers and turrets and battlements to preserve its medieval profile. He connected the rooms of the living-quarters by passages running around three sides of the quadrangle, and created a magnificent suite of state apartments, which he filled with costly furniture and treasures of the day. He bought for the Castle the world's finest examples of Sèvres porcelain, which had been specially made for Louis XVI of France in 1784. Windsor Castle remains today much as George IV made it.

In more modern times Windsor is most closely associated with Victoria. It was there that she first met Prince Albert and became engaged to him and it was to Windsor that they returned, radiantly happy, for their brief honeymoon ("I and Albert, alone at last," the young Queen confided to her journal when the Castle doors closed behind them). It was at Windsor, too, that Victoria sat with her beloved Prince through his illness that brought his death and it was within the stout protecting walls of the old stone structure that she spent most of the sorrowful years of her widowhood. None of Victoria's heirs have shown her affection for Windsor, however. Edward VII and George V dutifully moved the court there each year for a round of social festivities, but they preferred "Buck House" as the main royal residence. Edward VIII found Windsor depressing and inhibiting to his tastes—but it was from this shrine of his nation's history, appropriately, that he made his anguished abdication broadcast.

In the Second World War Windsor's 900-year story came full circle when it was again turned into a fortress. Anti-aircraft guns were emplaced in the parks, soldiers trained in its grounds. The furnishings and fittings of the state rooms, its historic treasures and its valuable paintings, valued at more than £3,000,000, were stored away for safety and the Castle was closed to sightseers. Because its stout stone construction afforded the best protection against bombs it was chosen as the refuge for Princesses Elizabeth and Margaret, who remained there most of the war years, along with the evacuated staffs of St. James's Palace, the Lord Chamberlain's office, the King's Treasurer and the Privy Purse.

George VI was proud of this inheritance—when Mrs. Roosevelt and Mr. and Mrs. Winston Churchill were his guests there for a week-end in 1948 he personally conducted them on a two-hour tour of the state apartments—but no one could live comfortably in these historic surroundings and the late King, following the custom of his grandfather and his father, understandably limited his residence at Windsor to one or two brief periods each year, a practice which his daughter apparently intends to follow.

By long tradition the court always moves to Windsor to be on hand for Ascot week, the annual June week of racing at nearby Ascot racecourse, the richest and most fashionable race meeting of the year-round British racing calendar.[6]

Like her father, grandfather and great-grandfather, Elizabeth II plays host to a five-day house party at Windsor Castle during Ascot week. Whereas Edward VII's and George V's guests were usually their intimates among the top-drawer nobility and landed aristocrats George VI, particularly after his daughters grew up, customarily invited a score or so young men and women from the Princesses' set and the accent on youth carried over into Elizabeth II's first Ascot week after her accession.

The guests are entertained in the sumptuous royal suite of three spacious drawing-rooms in which Victoria lived. These supremely elegant apartments, a heritage from George IV, were redecorated by Queen Mary in the Regency style and outshine the state rooms at Buckingham Palace in the magnificence of their appointments. Opening on to one another through carved Chippendale doors, they are known as the Crimson Room, a chamber measuring 65 feet by 35 feet, with an elaborately carved and gilded ceiling and upholstery and wall panels of crimson silk damask; the Green Room, with an ivory and gold ceiling and

wall panels and furniture of green silk damask; and the White
Room, which is furnished in white and gold silk damask.

At dinner the Queen, accompanied by the elaborately-uniformed officials of her household in attendance, sits at the head
of the great dining table in the portrait-hung banqueting hall,
the Waterloo Chamber, where the party is waited on by men-
servants in scarlet. Instead of the gay parties of Edward VII and
the long dinners of George V's reign, the evening entertainment
at Elizabeth's and Philip's Windsor house parties is more likely
to be a session of canasta, charades and parlour games or a sing-
song round the piano with Princess Margaret. High spot of the
week is the Ascot ball at the Castle, for which the Queen invites
an additional hundred or so guests in to dance until the early
hours in the Crimson Room.

When the house party ends and the royal family departs the
furniture in the private apartments is carefully covered, the
fittings are stored and the china put away and Windsor Castle
draws back into its historic past until the next royal visit.

Balmoral, standing amid the stern Scottish hills alongside the
tumbling River Dee in Aberdeenshire, where the royal family
usually spends a long summer holiday, is a sham castle, as
counterfeit and new as Windsor is historic and real. Less than
a hundred years old, it became part of the royal inheritance
because of Victoria's and Albert's enthusiasm for the Highlands,
an infatuation which the Queen and her Consort carried to an
obsession.

Victoria and Albert first fell under the spell of the ruggedly-
beautiful, lonely hills and valleys and forests of the Highlands
when they visited Scotland in 1842. In the summer of 1848, when
the Queen's doctor urged her to go there for a tonic holiday,
Prince Albert went house-hunting and bought a four-year lease
of Balmoral House, a small country mansion and estate nestled at
a bend of the Dee, six miles from Ballatar, the nearest town.
Victoria was delighted with her retreat. "All around," she wrote,
"seemed to breathe freedom and peace and to make one forget
the world and its troubles." The Highlanders, she and Albert
agreed, were "such a chivalrous, fine, active people."

The forests around Balmoral reminded Albert of his native
Germany and in time he conceived the idea of building his royal

partner a majestic home of their own in the Highlands. When their lease expired, Albert bought the Balmoral estate for £32,000 at Victoria's suggestion. The charming Balmoral House was torn down and three years later, in 1855, the new Balmoral Castle was completed according to the Prince Consort's design. Critics said that Albert had wedded his memories of German *schlosses* to architectural conceptions of his own that were more enthusiastic than beautiful, resulting in a bastard mixture of German eccentricities and a faked Scottish baronial style, complete with a keep, numerous towers and turrets and interior winding staircases. Architecturally, about the best that can be said for it is that it is discreetly hidden from public view by a thick screen of Scotch firs.

The interior decorations were in no better taste. Stags' heads and the Queen's favourite Landseer prints predominated on the walls, and the carpets, curtains and upholstery, and even the linoleum, were in tartan—some in dress and hunting Stewart, in honour of the Queen's descent, and some in a grey-and-red Balmoral tartan, a variation designed by Albert. The Lord Rosebery of that day, who became Liberal Prime Minister for a brief period in 1894–95, was moved to remark that he had always thought the Queen's drawing-room at Osborne the ugliest in the world until he had seen the drawing-room at Balmoral.

To Victoria and Albert, however, Balmoral was their "dear paradise." It was to Balmoral that the Queen retired in 1862 in the first gloom of her widowhood and in the long years after Albert's death she was happiest in the Highlands. She perpetuated the Prince Consort's memory by continuing his customs—the guard of soldiers selected from a Scottish regiment, pipers to play at dinner—and retaining his favourite servants and ghillies. She knew every cottage and its inhabitants for miles around the estate. Over the Castle the widowed Queen imposed gloomy, rigid standards which resulted in an atmosphere derisively known as Balmorality. The sexes were discreetly separated, the male staff bedrooms being on one side of the Castle, the female staff rooms on the other. Members of her household in attendance met with her for a stiff, formal dinner, then glumly retired to their bed-sitting rooms, and her few guests chafed at her orders that the drawing-room had to be closed up at 11 p.m. and the smoking-room at midnight. Victoria insisted that she must be attended at Balmoral by a Cabinet Minister and top-ranking politicians complained bitterly, though privately, when it was their fate to be chosen Minister-in-attendance. Balmoral was "like a convent," wrote Sir Henry Campbell-Bannerman. "We meet at meals, and when we are finished each is off to his cell."

None of Victoria's successors have quite shared her enthusiasm for Balmoral—Edward VII referred to it as "a Highland barn with a thousand draughts"—but by the time of her death tradition had set in and since then every monarch has taken his family north for the holidays. George V did away with much of Victoria's ritual and Albert's baronial trappings and George VI and his wife modernized the drawing-room and dining-room, but in the upstairs rooms the tartan curtains, tartan linoleum and the old-fashioned basin-and-jug washstands remain much as Victoria left them. And inside, at the foot of the stairs, there still stands the life-sized white marble statue of Prince Albert, complete with dog and gun.

To George VI Balmoral, despite its pretensions, had two great attractions. One was that its great estate, an 80,000-acre tract of heather-covered moors, forests and craggy peaks, unsuitable for farming, is the finest shooting preserve in Britain. Red deer abound in the hills and the moors are thick with grouse.

The other attraction was that, except for their Sunday worship at nearby Crathie church, where as many as 2,000 sightseers gather each week to watch royalty enter and leave the little hillside kirk, the royal family enjoys almost complete privacy within the vast expanse of the Balmoral estate. No court circular is issued from Balmoral and no pictures are permitted unless the Queen requests them. And no reporters are assigned to cover their holiday activities.[7]

Victoria's and Albert's choice of Balmoral has caused the whole royal family to gravitate to the Dee valley—Royal Deeside, as its inhabitants proudly call it—for their holidays. Elizabeth and Philip and their children used to stay at Birkhall, a small, old-fashioned, three-storey house on the Balmoral estate. Birkhall is now available for the Queen Mother, who used to stay there with her husband when she was Duchess of York. Abergeldie, another royal house nearby, is often occupied by the Gloucesters or the Duchess of Kent and her children, and various other houses and cottages on the estate are occupied in summer by senior members of the household and their families. Even the Queen's secretary, Sir Alan Lascelles, has a summer house in the neighbourhood.

"Christmas," George VI once confided to a friend, "is the one time of the year I really enjoy—I have my family all around me and I can forget for a little while that I am King."

Christmas generally means Sandringham, the comfortable, rambling royal country home in Norfolk, 100-odd miles from London, where the four generations of the royal family traditionally assemble for the end-of-year celebrations.

A 150-roomed, three-floored mansion in red brick, vaguely Tudor in style, Sandringham is the youngest of the Queen's houses. The original 8,000-acre estate was bought for £220,000 in 1861 by Edward VII, then Prince of Wales, out of his revenues from the Duchy of Cornwall and he built the house in 1870 as a home for his bride, Princess Alexandra of Denmark. Both Edward VII and George V regarded Sandringham as their real family home ("I have a house in London and a home at Sandringham," George V used to say) and lavished their personal finances on its upkeep. It is estimated that at least £1,200,000 has been spent on the estate since Edward VII bought it.

George VI, who had to worry about money in a way his grandfather and father never did, made Sandringham pay its way. The big house was closed up during the war years—when the late King and his family went to Sandringham they stayed at the smaller Appleton House nearby, which had belonged to the King's aunt, Queen Maud of Norway—and the estate, including the small private golf course, was turned over to intensive agricultural production. Situated not far from the Norfolk coast, it lies in the heart of one of Britain's best farming areas, and most of the 17,000-acre estate, except for 200 acres of parkland around the house, is now profitably worked by tenant farmers. The upper floors of York Cottage, the small house on the estate where the late King, his sister and all his brothers, except the Duke of Windsor, were born, has been converted into apartments for estate officials and the ground floor into estate offices.

In Edwardian days Sandringham was the scene of gay house parties, at which Edward VII set the pace and at which the late Victorians looked somewhat askance. George V refused to use the big house while his mother was alive, and continued to live with his family in York Cottage until Queen Alexandra died in 1925, but with his firm, proper reign Sandringham became less of a social centre and more of a private home. The regime which this stern-willed monarch imposed on the family became a tradition which is still observed, especially at Christmas.

XXIV

ROYAL HOUSEKEEPING

BUCKINGHAM PALACE is a more or less self-contained community, a walled village on its own in the midst of London. It has its own police force, post office, emergency fire service, stables, garages and maintenance shops, and its own social and welfare activities for its staff. It even has its own labour union.

Under the prevailing austerity conditions of today the royal establishment at "Buck House" is run on more economical lines than at any time in its history, but to keep the place in running order still requires a domestic staff of some 260 footmen, porters, maids, kitchen hands and charwomen, comparable with that of a large hotel, and no one is superfluous.

At Windsor Castle the domestic staff is smaller, but the upkeep of its 700 rooms and their magnificent treasures and art works calls for a maintenance staff of 50 to 60 full-time craftsmen and women—gilders, upholsterers, cabinet makers, metalsmiths, stovesmiths, seamstresses and carpet planners. Only skeleton domestic staffs are maintained at the other royal homes—Royal Lodge, Sandringham and Balmoral—except when the royal family is in residence, when they are supplemented by servants brought from London.

In the early days of Victoria's reign Buckingham Palace extravagances were notorious. Servants and tradesmen alike profited by the lax household administration of the new regime. When the economical Prince Albert was finally permitted to examine the Palace housekeeping accounts he was horrified to find such irregularities as the daily delivery of 2,000 coloured candles, an order which had stood uncancelled since a ball eight years previously. When the great state apartments were lighted by hundreds of candles these were never used a second time. The old candles, known as "Palace ends," were the traditional perquisites of the footmen and brought a high price in local shops. The last guests to leave a Palace function frequently complained that they were almost bowled over by footmen rushing to blow out the candles and wrench them from their chandeliers.

Nowadays, however, royal housekeeping is on an efficient, business-like basis. Under the supervision of household officials, duties are rigidly defined and all departments of the Palace run on a strict budget. Expenditure has to be vetted and approved by the Keeper of the Privy Purse. All foodstuffs, equipment and supplies are ordered through a central purchasing office under the Comptroller of Supply, James Kennedy. To save money, as much food as possible is bought direct from the royal farms and estates, but even these are required to submit bills to the Palace to keep the books straight. Invoices from tradesmen are carefully checked against deliveries, and then checked again in detail by the Comptroller of Supply before the quarterly bills are paid.

The administration of the entire Palace is the responsibility of the Master of the Household, Sir Piers Legh, but even he must submit all proposals for hiring of staff, entertainment and the extra expenses of state functions to the Keeper of the Privy Purse for approval.

Under the Master of the Household's direction, the day-to-day domestic management of the Palace is shared by three officials—the Palace housekeeper, Mrs. Fergusson, who chooses the maids —of whom there are nearly 50 on the permanent staff—arranges their duties, supervises the household linen and looks after the royal family's private apartments; the Palace Steward, John R. R. Ainslie, who served as butler to the late King when George VI was Duke of York and now supervises the indoor male servants; and the Palace Superintendent, Stanley Williams, formerly Superintendent at Windsor Castle for a dozen years, who functions as a sort of head janitor and maintenance boss of the vast building.

Housekeeping at Buckingham Palace is a non-stop job. Not one of the 602 rooms is shut off or kept under dust sheets: all of them are given a weekly maintenance and spring cleaned three times a year. There are hundreds of ornaments to be dusted, scores of tables and sideboards to be polished and acres of floor to be kept spotless. There are nearly one and a half miles of corridors, mostly carpeted and heavily ornamented. About half of these are dusted and their carpets swept daily. Electric vacuum cleaners are used for the carpets, but the Palace charwomen are provided with more than a score of different types of household brushes, some specially designed for "Buck House" with extra-long handles to reach the intricate mouldings and the carved ceilings of the high state rooms. There are hundreds of windows to be cleaned, a job which takes twelve men all their time throughout the year. There are upwards of 160 clocks to be wound and regulated, many of great age and requiring expert handling, a job to which a Kensington firm assigns a special clock winder.[1] Silver polishing is a full-time job, and each day a man known as a "table decker" arranges flowers from the royal gardens and greenhouses at Windsor throughout the Palace, a chore which the Queen Mother likes to do in the private apartments. The Palace washing, except for the royal family's personal garments, is regularly sent out to a London laundry.

The indoor male staff consists of footmen (who double as waiters), valets, porters and pages. Before the Second World War they wore a handsome, gold-braided livery of scarlet and blue, but during the war years, to save laundering their white shirt fronts and stiff collars, they were put into a functional coverall of navy blue, copied from the military battledress. This economy still remains in force. The austerity battledress, with "E.R." in gold braid over the left-hand breast pocket of the jacket, is worn by the male servants for everyday use and only on ceremonial or special occasions do the Palace footmen don their old ornate livery. The Queen's personal male servants wear plain black when on duty.

The general Palace servants are assigned to their duties in shifts, but the royal family have their own personal staff, trusted retainers who have been with them for years. Elizabeth II's personal maid, a Scotch girl named Margaret MacDonald, came first to the family as under-nurse to the two Princesses, and her sister, Ruby MacDonald, who was nursery-maid to young Elizabeth and Margaret, is now Princess Margaret's personal maid. The Queen Mother's present personal maid began her service with the family as a nursery-maid in the Bowes-Lyon home. The same set of three housemaids are always assigned by the Palace housekeeper to clean the family's private apartments, regarded as an honour.

Under the Palace Superintendent are the charwomen as "daily women," who come in each morning to do th interior cleaning, the stokers and squads of full-time maintenance men—upholsterers, carpet experts and electricians—who keep the furnishings in repair and replace the 2,000 light bulbs in daily use at the Palace. Structural repairs of the Palace are the responsibility of the Ministry of Works, which keeps a superintendent of works, an engineer and a small technical staff stationed there.

A few years ago when George VI and his wife were entertaining an American visitor to tea Elizabeth suggested that the curtains should be closed. The King got up and pulled them shut himself. "No use ringing for a servant around here," he grumbled to his guest.

George VI was not reduced to doing his own household chores, but he did have a domestic worry which none of his predecessors on the throne ever faced—the difficulty of obtaining servants to keep the royal establishment going. For generations service at the royal homes and palaces has been a family tradition: sons and daughters of maids and footmen were anxious to follow their parents, and if there were any vacancies in the royal service other royal relatives or the blue-blooded household officials and wealthy aristocrats who made up the court could always fill the gaps from their own large domestic staffs.

With the post-war revolt against domestic service, a direct consequence of Britain's blessing of full employment, all this came to an end. At last count there were fewer than a dozen servants at the Palace with a tradition of long family service and only three who could boast an unbroken family link with "Buck House" of 100 years. Most of Her Majesty's new servants are now hired direct from the labour exchanges, Britain's official employment offices, or from private agencies, but as the royal budget cannot compete with the wages and inducements offered by other servant-less households the Master of the Household often has to take his labour from the bottom of the barrel. Efforts are made to check on the reliability of new employees, but occasionally slip-ups occur, to the consternation of the police authorities charged with the security of the royal homes and

23

persons. A few years ago it came to light that two people known to the police had been given jobs in one of the royal homes. They were immediately dismissed. In the summer of 1951 there was an incident in Clarence House involving a female employee who turned out to have a police record.

In 1946 George VI bowed to the times—or brought the monarchy up-to-date, depending on one's point of view—by recognizing a labour union in his own home. For some months after the end of the war members of the staff had complained that they were underpaid and overworked. Compared to the high wartime wages enjoyed by the rest of Britain, their salaries were low. Before the war the indoor servants worked only every other day, but the wartime servant shortage put an end to that: at state functions in the Palace they were often obliged to work until midnight and later. When the complaints were unheeded there were angry mutterings below stairs and in the corridors Palace officials would come upon furtive little knots of servants discussing their grievances. Finally one of the porters organized a Palace branch of the Civil Servants union and in a few months all but four among the royal domestics had joined it.

The King and his family were taken aback by this break with tradition—Princess Elizabeth privately protested that it was a personal affront to her father—but mediators from the Treasury and the Ministry of Labour advised the Keeper of the Privy Purse and the Master of the Household, the King's representatives in collective bargaining, to meet the new union's demands, on the theory that His Majesty should set an example as a good employer. Wages and hours were adjusted and a minimum union wage established. For a porter this is £4 12s. 6d. per week: for housemaids, a starting salary of £87 per year, plus room and board. George VI recognized the existence of the new union by giving it an office in the Palace for its meetings. Since that time the staffs at Windsor Castle, Sandringham and Marlborough House have been organized, and George VI was forced to grant periodic pay increases to keep up with the rising cost of living. In 1948 the Palace stokers and maintenance men, who belong to a different union, staged an unofficial one-week walk-out over higher wages and a shorter working week.

Despite their grievances, Palace servants agree that they have a considerate employer. Elizabeth II, as did her father, knows many of them by name, takes an interest in their personal lives and treats them to an annual household ball, which is organized by the staff's Royal Household Social Club.[2]

Below stairs, the servants have their own hierarchy of authority and rules of precedence. There are separate dining-rooms for senior and junior members of the staff as well as a dining-room for clerical staff, and even the coffee trays sent up to the senior employees are served in strict order of precedence. In Victoria's time the servants were quartered mainly in damp, dingy basement rooms or low-ccilinged attic cubicles that led later occupants of the Palace to suspect that she must have been waited on by a race of pygmies. Footmen were crowded ten or twelve to a dormitory and drinking, gambling and other irregularities went on during their off-duty hours. In later years wooden partitions were erected to make separate cubicles for the staff and during George VI's reign most of these were replaced with walls to provide comfortable bedrooms for the cooks, duty footmen and pages. Each housemaid on duty also has her own private bedroom. These new servants' quarters have one advantage over the state bedrooms in which royal guests sleep—they at least have their own hot and cold running water.

Shortage of staff and a general desire for economy has reduced the state entertainment of the sovereign to a bare minimum compared to the lavish balls and banquets which were the social high-spots of the reigns of Edward VII and George V.[3]

Like most functions connected with the monarchy, state banquets follow a time-honoured routine that seldom changes from reign to reign. If it is a large party the scene is always the lofty white-and-gold State Ballroom, the walls of which are panelled with huge Gobelin tapestries depicting the story of Jason and the Golden Fleece. From its ceiling hang six magnificent rose-crystal chandeliers.

Backstairs preparations begin early in the morning of the banquet day when the porters set up the long tables. The Silver Pantry staff lays the white table linen or the lace mats, whichever is to be used. Then a domestic official with the archaic title of Yeoman of the Glass and China Pantry takes charge of setting out the dishes. At state dinners the Palace's famed gold dinner service is generally used. (This is actually silver-gilt plate, except for three pieces—a salver, a tray and a cup dating from George IV's time —of pure gold.) Next, a royal servant with the title of Yeoman of the Silver Pantry takes charge of setting out the cutlery, which is known as "laying up." At each place are laid a soup spoon, two steel knives and two forks, prongs down.[4] Cutlery for the other courses is brought in with the plates.

When the tables are set the "show gold" is brought in and arranged under the supervision of the Yeoman of the Gold Pantry. Some pieces are so hefty they require four strong men to carry them. On tables around the room, against a background of red baize, are displayed the massive, hammered gold plaque known as the Achilles shield, silver-gilt salvers, flagons and loving cups inherited from Georgian days and treasures like pilgrim-bottles and antique sconces. Around the walls go potted palms and huge banks of flowers. Menus, prepared well ahead and approved by the Queen, are printed in French and distributed around the tables. Then, when everything is set, the footmen dress and powder each other's hair. On the biggest state occasions they wear ornate gold-frogged scarlet tailcoats, knee breeches and buckled shoes.

The royal procession to and from the Ballroom is a stately, formalized march that is designed to show the guests the best of the Palace's grand apartments. The Queen assembles with her family and any royal guests in an ante-room known as the Royal Closet and then, escorted by the officers of the household in their resplendent uniforms and attended by the ladies- and gentlemen-in-waiting, she leads the way into the White Drawing Room. The waiting guests form up behind and then the procession moves through the series of connecting doors into the Music Room and then the Blue Drawing Room until it reaches the Ballroom, where the national anthem is played. When the guests are seated, the footmen take up their positions behind them, one to every four or five guests, and the serving begins. Food is brought up on the run by servants from the kitchens below. Sherry and wines are served during the meal, but no cocktails are offered the guests.

Throughout the meal a military string band plays in the musician's gallery. Then, when the dinner is finished, the guests are treated to the traditional ritual of the Queen's pipers. A score or more picked pipers march into the Ballroom, their pipes skirling in unison. They march around the tables, playing all the time, and then march out again. The pipe major returns, alone, walks up to his sovereign and places one foot on a rung of Her Majesty's chair while the Queen pours him out a glass of whisky. The pipe major raises his glass high, stamps to attention, gives a loyal toast in Gaelic, tosses off the drink in one swallow, turns and marches out.

When the dinner breaks up for coffee the procedure sometimes varies. If it is a large banquet crowd, the Queen leads the way back to the Music Room—this time by way of the State Dining Room and the Blue Drawing Room. On less formal occasions the Queen leads the ladies to the Ballroom supper room for coffee while the Duke of Edinburgh takes the male guests through to the Picture Gallery, and sometimes the Queen and the Duke withdraw to a private room to which they invite special guests. Whichever variant is followed the royal couple end the evening by mingling briefly with the guests in the large Music Room. Then, escorted by the household and attendants, they retire, which is a signal that the party is over.

In pre-war days Palace catering was on such a lavish scale that large quantities of delicacies left over from state banquets were given to charitable organizations. Under the enforced austerity reign of today there is hardly enough left over to feed the servants, let alone any for charity.

The serving of food at Buckingham Palace had always been something of a problem because of the layout of the unplanned, rambling structure. When the court is in residence there six dining-rooms are in daily use and hundreds of meals are served. All the food for the royal table is prepared in the Queen's kitchen and that for the rest of the Palace staff in the staff kitchen. Outside caterers are called in to supply and serve the teas or buffets at garden parties or presentations, when the numbers involved —as many as 6,000 to 7,000 guests—swamp the facilities of the Palace.

The State Dining Room is separated from the kitchens by a good quarter mile of corridors and stone-stepped passageways. In the old days trusted and experienced servants were assigned the task of rushing the food to the table before it got cold, but now electrically-heated trolleys are used to bring the food and an adjacent serving-room has been fitted with large electric hot-plates. When the royal family lunches or dines alone they use a small, simply-furnished dining-room on the principal floor of the north wing, near their own apartments on the Constitution Hill side of "Buck House." This is inconveniently separated from the royal kitchens on the Buckingham Palace Road side by almost half a mile of corridors, but the food is brought across by footmen and left on hot-plates until needed.

The few guests privileged to join the Queen and her husband at a meal in their private apartments find that there is less formality in the royal suite at meal times than there is in the staff and household dining-rooms. Service is often somewhat cafeteria style, in which everyone is expected to get up and help themselves from the modest array of food on the sideboard.

The royal family does not have individual ration books, as commonly supposed. The Palace is run on a catering licence, which entitles it to a food allowance similar to commercial restaurants or industrial canteens, but this privilege is never abused. When restaurant meals were held to a three-course, five-shilling limit during the worst years of Britain's post-war austerity, George VI saw to it that Buckingham Palace meals conformed to the same standard. Moreover, he insisted that the family's consumption of scarce, rationed foodstuffs—meat, bacon, butter, sugar, tea, fat and cheese—remained within the weekly rations permitted his subjects. This was more of an exemplary than a physical sacrifice, however, for the royal tables are liberally supplemented with non-rationed foodstuffs—eggs, fowl and game—from the royal farms and estates.[5]

Chef de cuisine at the Palace is a hefty, chubby-faced, 39-year-old Yorkshireman, Ronald Aubrey, who served his apprenticeship at the Savoy and worked in the Palace kitchens for 14 years before he became head chef in 1947. Both of his parents at one time worked on the Palace staff. Under him are four assistant chefs, three porters, two pastry maids and two scullery maids. For state functions he is permitted to hire as much extra help as he needs from outside sources. Aubrey, who specializes in traditional English and Scotch dishes, is the first Briton in generations to hold this post in the household and his selection for the job—over the claims of many famed French chefs who coveted the position—underlined the preference of George VI and his family for plain, unadorned British fare.

Aubrey commutes to his job each morning from his home in a London suburb. In his little Palace office he makes up the day's menus and between 10.30 and 11 each morning he takes them to the Queen for her approval. Very rarely does Elizabeth II make an alteration. Until recent reigns it was the custom for the head chef to attend the Queen in her *boudoir* every morning to await her instruction for the menus, but Queen Elizabeth, the Queen Mother, decided soon after moving to the Palace that the kitchens were familiar enough with the royal taste for the chef to make up the menus himself and merely submit them for approval. Wherever the royal family goes Aubrey goes along— to Windsor, Balmoral and Sandringham. It is he who plans and prepares the family's traditional Christmas dinner at Sandringham.

During the austere war years and the rugged post-war aftermath George VI insisted that all austerity restrictions affecting his subjects apply equally to his family and his household as far as their position permitted. As an example to the country's fuel conservation programme during the war years it was much publicized that His Majesty had worked out his own fuel economy measures for the royal palaces. These included only one light in each bedroom, no fires in bedrooms except by a doctor's orders, the removal of unessential lights from corridors, and squads of fuel watchers to detect and stop waste. Ministry of Fuel and Power experts were called in to measure the absolute minimum lighting necessary at "Buck House." Palace bathtubs in London and Windsor were painted with a line at the five-inch mark, the officially commended bathing depth, to conserve hot water, and out at Windsor the occupants of the residential rooms could only obtain hot water from the kitchens on certain days each week. At the height of Britain's post-war coal shortage during the critical 1946–47 winter the King ordered that no fires were to be lighted in the palaces until four in the afternoon. The late Count Sforza, the Italian Foreign Minister, who spent a few chilly hours at Buckingham Palace in 1947, later remarked, "I can testify to the austerity practised by the royal family. The King received me in a room colder than anything I have found even in Rome, where we like cold rooms."

"Make-do and mend," another British austerity slogan, has always been practised in the present royal family. The Queen Mother, a thrifty and thoroughgoing housewife, taught her daughters to be careful with their clothes so that they can be passed down the line. Princess Margaret frequently wore clothes handed down by her elder sister until her pride was touched when the newspapers called attention to one of her hats that had been worn some time before by Princess Elizabeth. Clothes that cannot be passed down within the family or are no longer needed are packed up and sent to the Queen Mother's sisters or other relatives.

When clothing was rationed George VI made comparable economies in his personal wardrobe, though his sacrifices were not apparent to his subjects. He had many of his shirts repaired with new collars and cuffs—made from material snipped off the extra-long tails of his pre-war shirts.

Like most of their subjects, George VI and his wife enjoyed a mild grouse against austerity and were particularly pleased when they got hold of special treat to brighten their fare. Passing a plate of cakes to an American guest at tea one day during the war years, the King warned, "I don't know what's in these. Sawdust, I suppose."

When Elizabeth, the Queen Mother, made a trial run aboard her luxuriously refitted namesake, the S.S. *Queen Elizabeth*, before it began its post-war voyages, she confessed to the chief steward that the one feature that had most impressed her were the napkin-white rolls in the dining-room, which Britons had not seen for years. Later on, when she went down the gangplank she clutched a bag of white buns to take home to her husband.

During the war years the royal rule against receiving gifts from strangers was relaxed. The two Princesses in particular received many parcels, including scores from the U.S., containing everything from nylons to canned goods and old clothing. They opened them all, kept what they could use and gave the rest away.

Without the ceremonial trappings of ornate coaches, highly-educated horses and gaily-caparisoned whips, coachmen and postillions the state drives of the sovereign through her capital in the automobile age would admittedly lack much of their magic and glamour.

The duty of conveying Her Majesty in state through London belongs to the staff of the Royal Mews, or stables, at Buckingham Palace.[6] The Queen's horses are technically the responsibility of the Master of the Horse, but they are in fact in charge of the Superintendent of the Royal Mews, which also house the Queen's motor cars, under the supervision of the Crown Equerry.

The Royal Mews, a straggle of buildings running along the south side of the Palace gardens, also house a prized collection of ornate state coaches and landaus.[7] Some of the landaus are used to convey foreign ambassadors to the Palace when they present their credentials to the Queen. There is also a sedate brougham in which a Queen's Messenger travels about London daily delivering Her Majesty's despatches to Government offices.

The drive for economy has hit the Royal Mews like the rest of the royal establishment. Before the war years upwards of 85 horses were stabled in the solid, old-fashioned stalls behind the Palace, but at present, because of increased costs of maintenance, there are only 35. Ten of these are the Palace's famed greys, of which six were a post-war gift to George VI from Wilhelmina of the Netherlands. The greys are popularly known as Windsor Greys.[8]

Schooling the horses and mannering them to draw the state coaches through slippery streets lined with cheering, gesticulating crowds is an exacting task, the responsibility of head coachman Rupert Land, who has been in the service of the monarchy for some 40 years. To accustom the horses to their task they are subjected to noise tests which go on for weeks before a ceremonial drive, in which red-coated dummy soldiers are dangled before their eyes, trumpets are blared alongside them and stablehands and passers-by are invited to set up an unholy din.

Constitutionally, the security of the royal homes and palaces and the persons of the royal family is the responsibility of the Home Secretary, who delegates the job to a division of Scotland Yard, which maintains a special branch headquarters at "Buck House." On ceremonial occasions plain-clothes men from the Yard provide protection along the route and mingle with the crowds, but at Buckingham Palace and other royal residences uniformed policemen are detached from London's Metropolitan Police for guard duty. A travelling staff of half a dozen or so policemen accompany the royal family to which ever residence they are using.

At Buckingham Palace there is a police guard of 20 men, who patrol in three eight-hour shifts. The night shift patrols the

Palace gardens accompanied by trained police dogs. In addition, the Palace mounts its traditional military guard consisting of one officer, four non-commissioned officers, 18 troopers and a drummer to beat the alarm if necessary, but as the soldiers are not allowed to leave their posts even to chase after intruders their function is more decorative than practical.

A few years ago both Buckingham Palace and Windsor Castle were wired for an ingenious burglar alarm system. Activated when concealed pressure pads under the carpets are stepped upon, the alarm makes a self-announcing phone call to Scotland Yard and a number of other police stations and repeats its recorded message: "Intruders have entered Buckingham Palace (or Windsor Castle)." At Windsor the normal police guard is doubled when the royal family is in residence, and watchmen and military guards patrol the Castle corridors after dark all year round. Royal Lodge is surrounded by a 12-foot fence surmounted with barbed wire and the entrance gate is opened and closed from a police post in the grounds. A plain-clothes man is always on duty when the Queen is in residence there and uniformed policemen walk the grounds and Windsor Park rangers patrol the Great Park. Sandringham has its own staff of wardens and night watchmen and one permanently-stationed policeman, who is supplemented by the travelling staff of policemen when the royal family stays there.

The other royal palaces and homes in London are also well guarded. St. James's Palace has its police patrol and military guard and Marlborough House, across the street, has its military sentries, five policemen who patrol its grounds, and, inside, a uniformed policeman as well as a plain-clothes Yard man who acts as Queen Mary's personal attendant. The police on duty have instructions to scrutinize all callers and all tradesmen who deliver supplies to royal residences, and the men who patrol the grounds inspect every door and gate at regular intervals. Palace servants who wish to admit relatives or friends are required to obtain a special pass from the Master of the Household.[9]

In addition to their residential guards, members of the royal family have personal bodyguards who accompany them on most occasions, except purely personal visits, when they leave their homes. Elizabeth II's bodyguard, a detective inspector, is always close at hand in the background when the Queen is present. He has his own berth in the royal train, and private sleeping quarters at the Palace. He sits alongside the chauffeur in the Queen's limousine and is always the first man out when the car pulls up.

George VI's personal bodyguard was Chief Inspector Hugh Ross Cameron, an impeccable, broad-shouldered Scot, one of the crack revolver shots of the Metropolitan Police, who was picked in 1930 for the job of guarding the then Duke of York. Cameron, who retired from service a week before George VI died, performed the last melancholy duty of walking in the funeral procession immediately before the coffin of the man he had served for almost 22 years.

Queen Victoria, much to her annoyance, was thrice shot at and once hit at with a stick, and even Edward VIII, in his brief reign, had one unpleasant moment when a deranged spectator, hoping to call attention to his personal grievance against the Home Office, created a scene by hurling a revolver under the sovereign's horse as Edward rode back from presenting new colours to the Guards in Hyde Park. It was at least one measure of King George VI's universal popularity that Cameron, in his 22 years as a royal shadow, never had to report a single threatening incident.

POSTSCRIPT

XXV

THE NEW ELIZABETHAN AGE

"FAMOUS have been the reigns of our Queens," said
Winston Churchill in his broadcast tribute on the death of
George VI and the accession of Queen Elizabeth II. "Now that
we have the second Queen Elizabeth also ascending the throne in
her twenty-sixth year, our thoughts are carried back nearly four-
hundred years to the magnificent figure who presided over and in
many ways embodied and inspired the grandeur and genius of
the Elizabethan age."

To many Britons, cheerlessly plodding along their uphill path
to economic recovery, the keynote sounded by their aged Prime
Minister, himself a servant of two Queens, was both a challenge
and a stimulus, bringing to mind the old belief that Britain
prospers best when there is a woman on the throne.

It may have been no more than fortunate chance but it is a
historical truth that the great ages of Britain's history have been
usually associated with the rule of a female monarch. Of the five
ruling Queens who have occupied the British throne since 1066
three have bequeathed their names to the most glorious chapters
in Britain's long story: the heroic age of the first Elizabeth,
which founded England's sea-going might, established the beach-
heads of her future Empire and inspired the golden period of
English literature, drama and music; the age of Queen Anne, the
brief epoch which added a few more imperial milestones and
numbered among its leaders such eminent Britons as John
Churchill (the Duke of Marlborough), Sir Christopher Wren,
Locke, Swift, Addison, Pope, Steele, Defoe and Isaac Newton;
and the bustling, abundant Victorian age, which ushered in the
creative, inventive, enterprising force of the Industrial Revolution upon which a pioneering Britain surged forward to become
the richest, most powerful world-empire on the face of the globe.

Looking back from their war-weary, austerity-bound present to these great matriarchal periods of their past, Britons were inclined to hope that the new Elizabethan age augured well for their country. The more ebullient Fleet Street journals, carried away by the coincidence of name, viewed the second Queen Elizabeth as if she were gifted with the heroic inspiration of the first Elizabeth—along with the magical qualities of the legendary King Arthur.

In sober fact, the presence of Queen Elizabeth II on the throne can have little bearing on whether Britain prospers or not. Stripped since Victoria's time of its last remaining direct political power, the crown at its best can provide only the symbolic, unifying, steadying influence in the nation's life. In the complex, interdependent world of the twentieth-century there can be no true counterpart of the expansionist, adventurous, freebooting age of the first Elizabeth. And in the final analysis, whether Britain can return from the edge of bankruptcy, recover from the grievous losses of two victorious world wars within a generation, and regain a standard of life adequate to sustain an over-large population on an under-sized island depends on the exertions of the British people themselves, on their willingness to accept a far-reaching revolution in their economic structure, and, even more frustratingly, on circumstances in the outside world over which Britain has little or no control.

"A new King, a new Prime Minister, a new Parliament often marks a new epoch in politics, but seldom in the life of the people . . .," wrote G. M. Trevelyan in his great "English Social History." And yet, in the long, continuing story of the British monarchy, it has happened more often than not that the character and personality of the monarch epitomizes the spirit of his reign. Thus, as Victoria and her industrious Prince Consort expressed in their private lives and public roles the essence of what we know as Victorianism, so may Elizabeth II and her husband, in the maturer years of her reign, take on and reflect back the spirit of a new age.

Though the reign of Elizabeth II has barely begun the probable pattern of its future is already discernible.

It is likely that their family will long remain the main focus of Elizabeth's and Philip's life, as it was for George VI and his wife. Elizabeth has always told friends that she hopes for a large family, and it is unlikely that being Queen will alter her wish— though it may postpone it.

In his naval career Philip managed to see a good part of the world, and Elizabeth's travels since 1947 have whetted her desire to see more of it. Royal visits abroad will be scheduled in a steady stream, for Elizabeth is determined to visit the parts of her Commonwealth and Empire which her father, due to the inter- ruptions of the Second World War, could not see.

It may be that after the visit of the Queen and her husband to Ceylon, Australia, and New Zealand, planned to begin in November, 1953, the grand-style royal tour will become a thing of the past. In the changing, proudly-growing nations of the Commonwealth a state visit from the sovereign every dozen years or so will no longer suffice. As Queen in a jet-propelled age, it is now possible for Elizabeth II to be, in practice as well as theory, equally Queen in all her realms. By jet airliner she can travel from London to the capital of her Canadian realm or from Ottawa to Canberra in little more time than it took her great- great-grandmother to chuff by train from London to Balmoral. Instead of remaining based upon the capital of her British realm and visiting once or twice during her reign the member nations of her Commonwealth family, as her father and grand- father did, it is now possible for Elizabeth II, accompanied by her husband and children, to take up residence in turn for at least part of the year every two or three years in the most important of the nations which owe her allegiance. There she would carry out the normal duties of a constitutional monarch, not as a visiting monarch but as Queen in residence.

Consideration has also been given to the suggestion, voiced by some Commonwealth citizens, that in the absence of the Queen from their land there should be a resident member of the royal family in each of the Dominions. Unorthodox though it would be, it is not out of the question to suggest that the great ambas- sadorial talents of the Queen Mother, now in the prime of her life, might be employed in a proconsular role as Governor- General, the representative of her daughter, in a major Dominion.

Out of her experience in South Africa and their joint ex- periences in Canada Elizabeth and Philip have been made aware of the drawbacks which invariably turn royal tours into one-sided affairs, in which a limited number of people see them while they themselves see comparatively little of the country they are visiting. On the tour of South Africa, undertaken in part to broaden the education of the then Princess Elizabeth, the succession of marches past, formal garden parties and carefully-organized demonstrations by native subjects prevented the late King and his heir from getting even an inkling of the combustible human problems of the great Dominion. Elizabeth's and Philip's royal tour of Canada was crowded and monotonous beyond human endurance—the same military salutes, presentations, addresses of welcome and reply over and over again—and the Royal couple were privately unhappy about the "brass curtain" of civic dignitaries and government officials—and their wives—who monopolized their tight schedule and prevented them from seeing more of the country and its people in their own informal way.

On future royal visits reforms based on the tour post-mortems which Elizabeth and her husband have conducted will certainly be made.

Despite the prolonged ordeal of public appearances which a ceremonial royal tour necessarily involves, both Elizabeth and Philip are eagerly anticipating their postponed visit to Australia. The Duke of Edinburgh paid two visits to Australia at the end of the Second World War and fell in love with the country. To his friends he has confided that if the accidents of his life had not settled him in Britain he would have liked to have made Australia his home.

If the personalities of the young Queen and her Consort are a true guide, however, the greatest change in the new reign will lie in the direction of humanizing and broadening the monarchy, further breaking down the barriers between the crown and the people—a slow, gradual process which George V began and which George VI continued.

Elizabeth II has indicated to her Ministers that she will seek greater simplicity in court ceremonial and the social activities of Buckingham Palace, a trend which should help eradicate the suspicion (given credence by the annual social display of garden parties and presentations) that access to the Palace depends on wealth, earned or inherited. The Duke of Edinburgh has let it be known that, as a step in the same direction, he would like Prince Charles, the future King, to have a more liberal education than has heretofore been permitted for the heir to the throne. Just as Prince Albert in his time reformed and brought up to date the mechanism of court life, which had fallen into disrepute during the reigns of George III and his two sons, so Elizabeth and Philip are certain to sweep away some of the time-honoured formalities of the court, which is still too bound by practices and conventions that were old-fashioned at the end of Victoria's long reign.

Both the Queen and her Consort have the outlook of their contemporaries and are alive to the shifting social values around them as Britain passes through yet another era of transition, an awareness which is shared by the new guard of royal advisers who will in time supplant the aristocratic courtiers inherited from George VI's reign.

In any institution as old as the British monarchic system such changes as are periodically necessary to bring it into step with the times must be introduced gradually, but in time, as the last of the aristocratic barriers which tend to shut off the royal family from the people are broken down and as the circle around the throne is widened with the intake of new blood until it reflects all viewpoints and currents of opinion in Britain and the Commonwealth, the monarchy as moulded by Elizabeth and Philip will move closer to the democratic monarchies of the Scandinavian nations.

Thus, though Queen Elizabeth II is no longer able to bequeath her name to a splendid imperial age like her famed female predecessors, if she completes the process of taking the crown to the people which her grandfather began and her father so ably advanced she may yet take her place in the nation's annals as "The People's Queen," which, in the last analysis of the role of kings and queens, may prove to be the greatest glory of them all.

NOTES

I

"THE KING IS DEAD: LONG LIVE THE QUEEN!"

1. Formerly the death of a sovereign meant the dissolution of Parliament and the vacation of all offices under the crown, since Parliament meets on the personal summons of the monarch and all offices are in theory held at the sovereign's will and pleasure. Since 1867, under the Representation of the People Act, the duration of Parliament has been independent of the demise of the crown and both Houses stand adjourned only until their members have taken the oath of allegiance to the new sovereign. In 1901 the Demise of the Crown Act provided that the holding of any office should not be affected by the demise of the crown and that no fresh appointment should be necessary either in Britain or in the Commonwealth.

2. The last time that the heir to the British throne was abroad when the monarch died was in 1714, on the death of Queen Anne. News of his succession had to be conveyed to the new George I in Hanover by a letter from the Privy Council, which took several days to reach him.

3. At Charing Cross, in front of the statue of Charles I, Lancaster Herald read the proclamation from his carriage. At Temple Bar the procession halted while Portcullis Pursuivant advanced on foot to the barrier of scarlet cord stretched across the road, behind which waited the Lord Mayor of London, the Sheriffs and City officers. "Who comes there?" sang out the City Marshal, maintaining the traditional independence of the City of London. "Her Majesty's Officers of Arms," replied Portcullis Pursuivant. The Marshal permitted him to advance past the barrier without military escort to where the Lord Mayor and his Corporation, in the ancient liveries of their offices, waited. There the Pursuivant proffered an Order in Council demanding "entrance into the City of London in order to proclaim her Royal Majesty Queen Elizabeth II" and the procession was permitted to enter.

At the junction of Fleet Street and Chancery Lane Norroy and Ulster King of Arms read aloud the proclamation, and then the Lord Mayor and the civic representatives joined the procession to the Royal Exchange, where Clarenceux King of Arms read the proclamation from the steps.

A smaller proclamation ceremony took place at Westminster's Middlesex Guildhall, and at the Tower of London the Governor of the Tower led his scarlet-coated Yeomen Warders to five points in the Tower where the proclamation was read.

4. The great stone walls of Westminster Hall, one of the most beautiful buildings in all Britain, have looked down on most of the long story of Britain's monarchy. It was built by William Rufus in 1097 and 300 years later Richard II installed the magnificent hammer-beamed roof. Henry VIII played tennis in the Hall (and not long ago one of his tennis balls was found wedged far up between two of the rafters). There Charles I sat during the trial that ended in his execution in 1649, and it was there that Oliver Cromwell pointed to the Speaker's mace with the contemptuous words—"Take away that bauble"—that dismissed the Long Parliament. Apart from the crypt of St. Stephen's, Westminster Hall was the only part of the Palace of Westminster which survived the disastrous fire in 1834, and it was saved again by the efforts of the fire watchers when German bombs fell on the Houses of Parliament during the Second World War.

5. Officers of the five foot regiments of the Brigade of Guards, in scarlet and bearskins, shared the vigil with the Household Cavalry.

6. More than 700,000 mourners filed past the bier of George V, which lay on the same catafalque in Westminster Hall from January 23 to January 29, 1936, but his lying-in-state period extended over a week-end, when more people were free to attend.

7. The popular notion that no animal has been trusted to draw a hearse in a royal procession since a horse became fractious at Queen Victoria's funeral is not quite correct (the caisson bearing George VI's remains was twice drawn by horses of the King's Troop, Royal Horse Artillery). At Victoria's funeral the horses drawing the gun carriage became fractious when the massed bands began to play and the swingle-tree attached to the limber was broken. The naval guard of honour then took over the task of hauling the gun carriage. In recognition of this service, ever since it has been the tradition for naval ratings to have the honour of drawing their sovereign in the final procession to his grave.

8. If royal custom is followed the remains of George VI may lie for some years in the royal tomb house beneath St. George's Chapel, a jealously-guarded vault which can be visited by few except members of the royal family, before being transferred to a final resting place, probably in the Chapel itself. The coffin of Edward VII lay in the tomb house from 1910 until 1927, when it was removed, together with that of his Queen, Alexandra, to a new tomb near the altar of the Chapel. The body of George V remained in the tomb house from January, 1936,

until February, 1939, when it was transferred to its tomb in the nave of the Chapel. A strangely beautiful subterranean resting place, the royal tomb house, designed to contain 81 bodies, was built by George III, whose remains, along with those of George IV and William IV, lie on one of the shelves at the side of the vault.

II

THE CROWN AND THE PEOPLE

1. In fact, Elizabeth II on her accession inherited a Cabinet headed by Prime Minister Winston Churchill, the members of which had received their seals of office from the hand of her father. This carry-over, which obviates even a momentary disruption of governmental affairs on the death of one sovereign and the accession of another, is made possible by the fact that the Cabinet is technically a committee of the larger and mainly formal body known as the Privy Council, the members of which retain their office from one reign to the next.

2. Despite its almost-medieval profile, the Palace of Westminster, more familiarly known as the Houses of Parliament, is not one of London's ancient buildings. Its main architectural style is pseudo-Gothic and most of it dates only from 1850. Since the reign of Edward the Confessor in the eleventh century the present site, between the Thames and Westminster Abbey, has held a royal palace and it was there that the first Parliaments were summoned to meet. When the Commons gained a separate identity they met in the chapel of St. Stephen, one of the three churches embedded in the courts and cloisters of the palace, and for two and a half historic centuries, when the character of British government was shaped, they met in this converted medieval church. In October, 1834, a fire broke out under the House of Lords when a careless official threw into a stove a pile of wooden tallies, then used as a part of the Exchequer's accountancy system. Only the historic Westminster Hall and the crypt of St. Stephen's survived. The present structure was put up during the early years of Victoria's reign. The House of Commons, destroyed by bombs early in the Second World War, was rebuilt in the post-war years in a modified Tudor style.

III

THE MONARCHY IN ACTION

1. The sovereign is not constitutionally required to attend personally at the opening of each session. Queen Victoria on a number of occasions did not open Parliament in person and in the autumn of 1951 George VI was compelled to miss the ceremony because he was still recovering

from his lung operation. In these cases the functions of the crown are placed in the hands of a commission, headed by the Lord Chancellor, who takes on the duties the monarch would normally perform and reads the sovereign's speech.

2. Although the Judicial Committee is primarily a court of appeal, questions of great legal complexity are sometimes referred to it for opinion. It is also the interpreter of constitutions for the Dominions (except for those which have discontinued all appeals) and the colonies, and in the ecclesiastical field it is recognized as the sole interpreter of orthodoxy for the Church of England.

In its modern form the Judicial Committee dates back to the seventeenth century, when a special committee of the Privy Council was appointed to hear appeals from the king's lands overseas, but in its historical sense its roots go back to the *Curia Regis* of the Norman kings, when any subject enjoyed the right to petition his king in Council for justice. The king traditionally delegated the power to hear such appeals to his Privy Council and since 1833 jurisdiction in these cases has been formally exercised by the Judicial Committee.

Today the Judicial Committee is headed by the Lord Chancellor, the chief jurist of the nation, and includes the Lord President of the Privy Council, ex-Lord Presidents, Law Lords and judges of the Court of Appeal who are Privy Councillors, but in practice only a handful of these learned legal men sit in session when the court convenes in its austere committee room at 9 Downing Street, next door to the Prime Minister's residence.

Though there is nothing dramatic about its setting, the varied jurisdiction of the Judicial Committee makes it the most romantic tribunal in the legal world. It interprets not only Dominion and colonial statutes, but takes cognizance of legal codes as different as the Roman-Dutch law from South Africa, the recondite intricacies of Hindu and Mohammedan law as well as the infinite varieties of tribal customs in Africa and Asia.

As the final instrument of the King's and Queen's justice it has put its collective mind to work on the most astonishing collection of cases, ranging from the delicate question of the right of women to sit in the Canadian Senate to the problem of what to do with convicts who succeeded in escaping to Trinidad from Devil's Island. In one famous decision it ruled that a heathen idol and its priests were really similar to a limited company and its directors and it held that the wishes of the idol must be respected. In another it upheld the appeal of—and acquitted —an African who, convicted of the murder of a child, pleaded that he had killed the infant believing honestly that it was a water spirit and dangerous to his tribe. Cases down for hearing in one single term (1949) included a disputed income tax assessment in British Honduras; the partition of a joint family property in Bengal; execution proceedings in Madras; a claim by a daughter of a slave-concubine in Zanzibar; the law of contributory negligence in Canada; the disputed title to a cocoa farm in West Africa; appeals against murder convictions in Patna and Lahore; and a conviction for a ritual murder in Basutoland.

Not a court of law in the ordinary sense, the members of the Committee sit without any judicial trappings. Technically they are engaged in giving advice to the crown and when they have made up their minds they deliver no judgment. They humbly report to Her Majesty whether in their opinion the appeal should be allowed or dismissed. Then at a subsequent meeting of the Queen and the executive members of the Privy Council a formal Order in Council is read which recites that "Her Majesty, having taken the said report into consideration, was pleased by and with the advice of Her Privy Council to approve thereof and to order as it is hereby ordered that the same be punctually observed, obeyed and carried into execution." And the judges of the courts below and all other persons whom it may concern are enjoined to "take notice and govern themselves accordingly."

3. Colloquially, the British still use the word Empire when they mean the Commonwealth of Nations or the Empire, or both together. Strictly speaking, the Empire now comprises: Aden, Bahamas, Barbados, Bermuda, British Guiana, British Honduras, Cyprus, Falkland Islands (disputed by the Argentine), Fiji, Gambia, Gibraltar, Gilbert and Ellice Islands, Gold Coast, Hongkong, Jamaica, Kenya, Leeward Islands, Malta, Mauritius, Nigeria, North Borneo, Northern Rhodesia, Nyasaland, St. Helena, Sarawak, Seychelles, Sierra Leone, Singapore, Solomon Islands, Somaliland, Trinidad, Uganda, Windward Islands and Zanzibar. The Commonwealth includes the United Kingdom and the Empire and the self-governing nations of Australia, Canada (including the once self-governing colony of Newfoundland), Ceylon, New Zealand, South Africa, India and Pakistan as well as the self-governing colony of Southern Rhodesia and the independent states, governed under the advice of the British, of Brunei, the Malay States and Tonga.

4. When New York's Governor Dewey visited England in 1949 he staggered Members of Parliament by referring to Australia, New Zealand and Canada as "colonies."

5. The description of these self-governing nations as Dominions is obsolete. They are under the dominion of no one. The expression originated at the end of 1866 when Sir John Macdonald, the first Prime Minister of the new Dominion of Canada, came to London with his colleagues to work out the constitution of the new federation of Canada. The Canadians proposed to call their nation "The Kingdom of Canada," but the British Foreign Office feared this would antagonize American public opinion by setting up a new monarchy across the U.S. border. One of the Canadian mission, Sir Leonard Tilley, who had a habit of reading a chapter in his Bible on going to bed, on the night the conference was adjourned came across the passage in the 72nd Psalm containing the words, "He shall also have dominion from sea to sea."

Next morning he proposed "The Dominion of Canada" and the suggested name was adopted.

The self-governing Dominions, with Canada in the lead, are now anxious to drop this outmoded description. For the proclamation of Elizabeth II the British studiously avoided "dominions" and proclaimed her "Queen of this Realm and of all Her other Realms and Territories." Next step will be to change her royal style and title, which requires the agreement of all Commonwealth Parliaments. Meanwhile, until someone proposes a less mouth-filling designation than "member of the British Commonwealth of Nations" Dominion will continue in popular usage.

IV

THE MONARCHY ON PARADE

1. At Christmas-time in 1950 the stone of Scone, which remains quietly on display at Westminster Abbey between coronations, was again in the news. The stone, an ordinary-looking, heavy block of dull reddish sandstone, has come down in legend as the pillow on which the patriarch Jacob dreamed of angels at Bethel, and its subsequent migrations are supposed to have carried it to Spain and then to Ireland. Its existence there in the centuries before the Christian era is uncertain, although a stone corresponding to it, which the Irish called the stone of destiny, was preserved on the hill of Tara. It is now thought that this stone may have been taken over to the west of Scotland early in the Christian era by settlers from Ireland. At any rate, a similar stone was venerated in that part of Scotland for several centuries and in the ninth century King Kenneth removed it to the Abbey of Scone. There the tradition grew that its possession was essential to the preservation of regal power and all the kings of Scotland were successively crowned upon it until 1296, when Edward I removed it to England and left it as an offering of conquest at the shrine of Edward the Confessor in Westminster Abbey, where it was inserted under the seat in a specially-designed coronation chair.

For generations the presence of the stone in England has rankled extreme Scottish nationalists, who look upon it as a symbol of their lost independence. Early on the morning of Christmas Day, 1950, a few hotheads from the extremist fringe of the Scottish nationalist movement broke into Westminster Abbey, damaged King Edward's chair and the stone itself, and spirited the chipped relic off to a Scottish hideout. Some months later, when the public reaction to their escapade ranged between outrage and amusement even in Scotland, and with Scotland Yard hot on their trail, they quietly arranged to have the stone returned to custody.

2. These spurs, fitted with straps of crimson velvet embroidered with gold, were made for Charles II's coronation. At one time they were buckled on, but immediately removed so as not to impede the sovereign, but since the coronation of Queen Anne it has become customary merely to touch the sovereign's heels with them.

3. There are actually five swords in the house of Windsor's regalia and each plays its role in the coronation. The main one, the great two-handed sword of state, is primarily used for the royal opening of Parliament and other state occasions, when it is carried before the King, point upwards, by a peer. In the coronation it is carried in the procession, but is replaced by the jewelled state sword for the King's investment. The other three swords—copies of those sent by Pope Leo X to Henry VIII when he bestowed on him the title Defender of the Faith—were made for Charles II's coronation after the originals had been destroyed. They are the sword of Justice to the Spirituality, which is carried sheathed but point upwards throughout the coronation, and its counterpart, the sword of Justice to the Temporality, and the short, blunt-ended sword of Mercy, which is carried between the other two swords by a peer at the coronation.

When not required for state occasions the regalia and crown jewels are kept under guard at the Tower of London. Most of the regalia dates only from the seventeenth century. Nearly all the regalia that had accumulated in the previous six centuries of the monarchy was lost when imperious Oliver Cromwell seized control of the nation and, in a gesture of contempt for the monarchy, ordered it to be melted down or sold for what it would fetch—a pittance, in fact, compared to its real value, apart from its great antiquity. For the coronation of Charles II in 1661, after the restoration of the monarchy, as much as possible of the regalia was recovered and new crowns, swords, orbs and sceptres were made to resemble the old.

4. Sceptres are the most ancient emblem of royalty and no fewer than five are preserved at the Tower of London. The royal sceptre with the cross, a bejewelled baton of incalculable value, almost three feet long, with the upper and lower ends richly enamelled and studded with jewels and a middle section of plain gold for the grip, was fashioned for the coronation of Charles II but important additions have since been made to it. Most striking alteration was the insertion of the mammoth, pear-shaped, $516\frac{1}{2}$-carat diamond, the Great Star of Africa, cut from the famed Cullinan diamond of 3,025 carats, which was presented to Edward VII by the Transvaal Government in 1907. This flawless stone, which eclipses even the massive amethyst and jewelled cross mounted above it in the head of the sceptre, is held in place by ingenious movable clasps which allow the diamond to be removed so that Queen Elizabeth can wear it as a pendant on great state occasions. This great sceptre is used only at coronations and at the funeral of the monarch, when it rests with the crown and the orb on the coffin.

The second sceptre, the rod with the dove, also made for Charles II, is a gold staff three feet seven inches long, beautifully enamelled and jewelled except for the plain gold grip at the lower end. At the top is a golden orb with a band and an arch studded with diamonds, and the orb in turn is topped by a cross on which rests a white enamelled dove with outstretched wings, and feet, eyes and beak of gold, which is supposed to be symbolic of the Holy Ghost.

The Queen also has two sceptres to which a similar symbolism is attached. The Queen's sceptre with the cross, made for Mary of Modena, the wife of James II, is a gold staff somewhat shorter than the King's, topped by a golden orb with a diamond band and an arch on which is set a cross, the four arms of which are decorated with large diamonds. The Queen's ivory rod, a three-foot baton, is made of three pieces of ivory joined together with gold bands, with a golden orb and a cross at the top. Sitting on the cross is a beautifully enamelled dove with closed wings, its beak, eyes and feet also made of gold. The fifth sceptre, known as the Queen's sceptre with the dove, is a smaller version of the King's sceptre with the dove, being specially made for Mary II, who was crowned co-sovereign with her husband, William III. It is not now used at coronations.

Not technically a sceptre but accorded a place in the coronation is a long gold rod, surmounted by an orb and cross, which is known as St. Edward's staff. The present staff was made on the order of Charles II, but the original, destroyed by Cromwell, was supposed to contain a fragment from the true cross. In ancient reigns it was reputed to be a staff used to guide the King's footsteps at his coronation and at one time it was ceremoniously placed in the monarch's hand as he arrived at the door of the Abbey. In recent coronations, however, it appears only in the procession, when it is carried by a nobleman.

5. St. Edward's crown, the longest-lived national symbol in the world, derives its name from the one supposedly worn by Edward the Confessor, though it dates only from 1661. A skilled craftsman, Sir Robert Vyner, was commissioned court jeweller by Charles II and charged with creating new regalia as far as possible resembling that destroyed by Cromwell. The new ornaments were mostly given the old names.

Although it has been altered from time to time and its stones reset and rearranged, St. Edward's crown remains much as Vyner fashioned it. Wrought of gold, it is festooned with diamonds, rubies, emeralds, sapphires and pearls and at the centre of its crossed arches, the edges of which are bordered with rows of silver pearls, rests a golden orb surmounted by a cross, from which hang two large pearls. Experts do not consider it particularly artistic, however: its precious stones, though ostentatious, are of poor quality and no great value. It is unusually large, being made at a time when wigs were worn, and excessively heavy, weighing nearly seven pounds. Inside the crown is a velvet cap fringed with miniver, known as the cap of maintenance. In the Middle Ages this was accorded almost as much veneration as the crown itself and was carried in procession in front of the king, but one of the Tudor monarchs decided to wear this historic headpiece to shield his head from the sharp metal points of the crown, and this custom has been retained ever since.

From the reign of Charles II all British monarchs, except Queen Victoria, have been crowned in this successor to the ancient crown of England, although it is now replaced by the less-burdensome crown of state for the long drive back to Buckingham Palace. Victoria found the weight of St. Edward's crown too much for her: she was crowned Queen wearing the state crown and a nobleman symbolically carried St. Edward's crown for her throughout the ceremony.

As the crown of the realm, St. Edward's crown is surrendered immediately after the coronation ceremony for safekeeping, and so it was necessary to have another crown for state occasions. State crowns, known as the imperial crown of state since the reigns of the Tudors, have altered in design according to the tastes of the times, but many of the old gem stones have been re-cut and re-used. The present state crown, made in 1838 for Victoria, is a magnificent headpiece ornamented with no fewer than 2,783 diamonds, 277 pearls, 18 sapphires, 11 emeralds and 5 rubies. In its front is mounted the oblong-shaped, 309-carat diamond, the Second Star of Africa, cut from the Cullinan diamond, and above it the massive stone, the size of a hen's egg, known as the Black Prince's ruby. This is not really a ruby, but a stone of great antiquity known as a spinel. It is pierced in front and the hole has been filled with a small ruby. It was presented to the Black Prince on the battlefield after the battle of Navarette in 1367 by his ally, Don Pedro the Cruel, King of Castile, who in turn had obtained it by murdering the King of Granada and taking it from him. Henry V wore the stone in his coronet around his helmet at the battle of Agincourt in 1415. Cromwell sold it—for the sum of £4—but it was recovered. In the centre of the diamond cross which surmounts the orb atop the crown is mounted a beautiful sapphire, said to come from the ring of Edward the Confessor, and hanging from the intersection of the arches are four large, pear-shaped pearls, reputedly the earrings of Queen Elizabeth I. This crown, weighing just over 39 ounces, is used for the ceremonial state opening of Parliament and other royal occasions during a reign, and it rests on the coffin at the funeral of the monarch. The cross atop the crown jarred loose and toppled to the street when it was being carried on top of the coffin of George V on its way to Windsor, but it was recovered by a hawk-eyed marching Guardsman and restored. Edward VII used to have this crown carried before him at the openings of Parliament but George V re-adopted the practice of wearing it and George VI followed suit.

Parenthetically, the crown that is symbolically represented on coins, stamps and official documents does not correspond to either of these two real crowns, but is a conventional artist's conception of the symbol of sovereignty, the form of which used to alter from reign to reign but was more or less standardized in the reign of Edward VII.

When George V went to India for the imperial durbar announcing his coronation, it was discovered that by law neither the crown of state nor St. Edward's crown could be taken out of England and so a new crown, the imperial crown of India, was quickly made. Conventional in design, with the customary orb and cross on top, it is more dazzlingly beautiful than its older counterparts, and is studded with 6,170 diamonds, with a rare-quality, 34-carat diamond and a large Indian ruby as its centrepieces. It cost £70,000 to make and is perhaps worth double that today.

Four other crowns are included in the royal regalia. One is the crown of Queen Mary of Modena, with which this consort of James II was crowned. It was also used for the coronation of Mary II. Not particularly beautiful, set with pearls and diamonds of antique cut, it is no longer worn today. More artistic is the diadem of Queen Mary of Modena, which this Queen wore on her way to her coronation: it is set with large diamonds and large and perfectly matched pearls. Queen Mary's crown, which Queen Elizabeth wore for her Coronation in 1937 and which has now passed down to her daughter, was made under Queen Mary's direction for her own coronation in 1911. Encrusted with small diamonds, its eye-stopping centrepiece is the famous, 108-carat Koh-i-noor diamond, the greatest historical stone in existence, with a legend going back some 5,000 years. Below it is the Fourth Star of Africa, a 62-carat gem cut from the Cullinan diamond, and the centre of the cross atop the crown carries the 92-carat Third Star of Africa.

Seventh crown in the regalia is the Prince of Wales's crown, moderately jewelled in plain gold, which has more historic significance than actual value. Before Cromwell's time the Prince of Wales wore only a coronet for state occasions, but Charles II decreed that he should be provided with a crown of his own.

Aside from their symbolic worth, the crown jewels of Britain are literally priceless in value. The great and rare stones mounted in the regalia have such a limited market that ordinary rules of evaluation cannot be used for them. In 1935 a venturesome British expert, E. F. Twining, C.M.G., M.B.E., estimated that £5,000,000 would not suffice to buy the whole collection of precious stones and gold (the gems cut from the great Cullinan diamond were then said to be worth £1,000,000 alone and the Koh-i-noor was valued at £140,000) but the wartime inflation in the price of jewels has boosted this estimate considerably. Some authorities now value the entire collection at not less than £20,000,000.

The crown jewels and the regalia are the property of the realm. The monarch has no right to them, although he or she is the only person who can give the order for their removal from the Tower when they are required for state occasions.

6. The Coldstream Guards, which celebrated their tercentenary in 1950, can claim a similar origin. General Monck, an outstanding soldier, first formed his regiment and entered Oliver Cromwell's

service in 1650 and after a series of brilliant victories he and his troops were sent to Scotland to subdue the royalists and pacify the country. Early in 1660, after the abdication of Cromwell's son, Richard, who succeeded his father as head of the Commonwealth, Monck marched with his men to London. Sensing the will of the people, whose opinions he sought on his march south, he decided to use his commanding military position to back the restoration of Charles Stuart to the throne and the election of a free Parliament. Cromwell's troops were quickly disbanded, but after the out-of-work soldiery rioted in London Parliament prudently decided to retain Monck's regiment in the service of the crown. On February 14, 1661, the renowned general, advanced to the peerage as the Duke of Albemarle by a grateful Charles II, led his regiment into the service of the King as the Lord General's Regiment of Foot Guards, thereafter popularly known as the Coldstreamers.

7. The Tower gunners fire 41 rounds to mark royal births, the state openings of Parliament and on the rare occasions when the monarch prorogues or dissolves Parliament in person. They also fire a 41-gun salute whenever the monarch passes through the City of London in procession.

8. In the summer of 1951 the Yeomen Warders added a new chapter to their long history. When it was decided to open the Tower to visitors on Sunday afternoons the Warders were given the choice of working the extra half day or surrendering their proud duty of escorting visitors around the Tower to civilian guides. The Warders chose to work the Sunday shifts—but they retaliated by forming a union (a branch of the Civil Service Union) and joining it almost to a man. However, in putting forward their first unionized demand for a pay increase the Warders found it hard to break with their long tradition of service. Instead of asking for a specific sum they told their Resident-Governor in gentlemanly fashion, "We leave it to you." They got their rise.

V

OFFICES OF THE MONARCHY

1. The office of Lord High Steward is filled only temporarily on such occasions as a coronation or in the very rare case of a trial of a peer by the House of Lords, and the appointments are now strictly limited to the duration of the occasion, but in earlier reigns the Lord High Steward was a figure of immense power who claimed to rank as second person in the kingdom and the supreme judge in Parliament. After the reign of Henry IV the office was abandoned as a permanent post. At the very few modern occasions on which a Lord High Steward

has been required to preside at the trial of a peer in the Lords the Lord Chancellor of the day has been appointed.

The office of Lord High Treasurer, once the head of the king's Exchequer, has not been filled since 1714. Since that time it has been continuously held in commission by a body known as the Lords of the Treasury. Parenthetically, the office of First Lord of the Treasury is virtually a sinecure office which is generally held by the Prime Minister, and until 1937 it was this office which provided the head of the Government with a salary.

The Lord High Constable in olden days was commander of all the royal forces, which made the holder a power in the realm, but since the time of Henry VIII the office has never been filled permanently and, like the post of Lord High Steward, it is now a historic survival which is temporarily filled only at the time of a coronation.

The office of Lord High Admiral, ninth of the Great Officers of State, is no longer an active position. Except for a brief period when it was held by William IV when he was Duke of Clarence, it has been held in commission and its functions carried out by a body of deputies known as the Lords of the Admiralty since early in the eighteenth century.

2. The College of Arms is also called upon to trace family trees. Recently a wealthy American businessman came to it after having spent £1,500 on an ancestral search that had carried him back only to his grandfather. The College, without much trouble, took his pedigree back as far as the seventeenth century and then warned him that as his forbears were working-class people in the days when families were large further search would be difficult. The American asked them to continue, and the College eventually satisfied him by tracing his roots back to the twelfth century.

3. Not every peer of the United Kingdom has the right to a seat in the House of Lords. Although all the Temporal peers of England (created before the union with Scotland in 1707), Great Britain (created after the union with Scotland but before union with Ireland), and the United Kingdom (created since the union with Ireland in 1800) are entitled to seats (unless barred by any of the established disqualifications, infancy, felony, bankruptcy, or being of alien nationality), the Scottish peers vote for 16 and the Irish peers for 28 of their number to represent them in Parliament. The Lords Spiritual are represented by the Archbishops of Canterbury and York, the Bishops of London, Durham and Winchester and 21 other English diocesan bishops. Many English peers also sit under other and lesser titles than those by which they are generally known: thus, a duke may sit under his second title of earl or viscount, or an earl as a baron. Very few of those entitled to sit actually attend ordinary sessions of the Lords. Although some 850 male members hold the right (peeresses in their own right are not granted membership in the Lords), an attendance of 80 constitutes a full house, the average engaged in big debates is 50 and on most days

there are rarely more than a score present The quorum is three! A hundred qualified peers have never even bothered to take the oath of allegiance and so cannot vote in the chamber. The peers have lost most of their executive powers, but they still retain a few ancient prerogatives —among them the right to be hanged with a silken cord!

VI

MONARCHIC TRADITIONS

1. The lairds of the Fowlis estate in Scotland's Ross-shire are required to pay to the Queen's representative a token rental of one snowball, payable at midsummer, which must be obtained from the mountain forest of Ben Wyvis. This is not as difficult as it sounds, for snow never completely disappears from the 3,429-foot high peak of Ben Wyvis. Whenever the monarch visits the Duke of Atholl at his beautiful Blair Atholl estate at the foot of the Scottish Highlands the Duke must pay his rent of one white rose to the sovereign. Easy enough in summer, the ancient custom presented difficulties when Victoria suddenly turned up at Blair Atholl in mid-winter, when there was not a white rose in the country. But the Duke of that day was equal to the occasion and sent post-haste to the south of France a member of his staff, who returned with a white rose before the Queen left the castle. A red rose constitutes the rent paid for the site, in London's Seething Lane, of the one-time home of Sir Robert Knollys, a war hero of the fourteenth century, and whenever the monarch passes through the Berkshire town of Hungerford he is presented with a red rose, a tribute that goes back to the fourteenth century days of John of Gaunt, who gave fishing and other rights to the townsfolk.

2. The claims of the descendants of the Stuart pretender to the British throne have never been allowed to die out. In 1937 Prince Rupprecht of Bavaria, a descendant of the Stuart kings of England, duly sent his formal notice of protest against the coronation of King George VI.

3. The British Navy and Royal Marines drink their toasts sitting down while at sea and standing only when ashore, a variation that purportedly originated when a visiting royal personage cracked his head on a low deck beam while rising to reply to a toast. Certain Army regiments also drink their toasts seated, a hangover from the times when they served as substitute Marines on warships, while others proclaim their loyalty by *not* drinking to the health of the ruler, an exception that was made during the eighteenth century's divided loyalties between the absent Stuarts and the reigning Hanoverians, when all officers were ordered to drink the King's health as open witness of their

allegiance, a decree from which certain regiments were excused because their fidelity was beyond question. In the Gloucestershire regiment only the president and vice-president of the mess give the toast, a variant that goes back to the Peninsular War when, at the end of one day's fierce battle, only two officers remained alive to honour the toast.

Apart from the gesture over the finger-bowls, the royal toast has often been used to proclaim illicit loyalties during the monarchy's stormy history. During the years of Britain's Civil War (1642–1647) and Cromwell's subsequent Protectorate a Cavalier who supported the monarchy would covertly drop a crumb of bread into his drink and then pray, "God send this *crumb well* down!" In private, the Jacobites who supported the Stuarts had a verse-toast of their own, which ran:

> " God bless the King—I mean the Faith's defender,
> God bless (no harm in blessing), the Pretender;
> But who Pretender is, and who is King,
> God bless us all—is quite another thing."

4. In the last year of George VI's reign 56 deserving men and women received his Maundy money. For her first Maundy ceremony, on April 10, 1952, Elizabeth II's gift was bestowed on only 26 male and female recipients. However, once needy recipients are on the Royal Almonry list they receive Maundy money as long as they remain good citizens or until their conditions improve and the 30 men and women who missed out on Elizabeth's gift were given a special grant of £5 for males, £4 10s. for females, roughly equal to the Maundy allowance.

VII

FOUNTAIN OF HONOURS

1. The main orders through which honours and, in most cases, knighthoods are conferred are these:

The Most Noble Order of the Garter, which is not the most ancient order in existence—the Portuguese and the Vatican possess older orders which they still bestow—but is the most distinguished and exclusive order of chivalry in the world. Of more or less legendary origin, it was founded in 1348 by Edward III. Knights of the Garter are limited to 25 British companions, in addition to the reigning sovereign, a few members of the royal family, and a small number of foreign members. The Queen Mother, Queen Mary and ex-Queen Wilhelmina of the Netherlands are Ladies of the Garter. In the eighteenth and nineteenth centuries the Garter became a weapon in the hands of the political party in power, and was frequently held out as a political bribe, but in 1946 Attlee and Churchill in consultation agreed to remove this senior distinction from party politics and George VI was asked to fill without political advice all vacancies in the order caused by the death of knights. After the 1945 general election, which swept the Conservative Party out of power, George VI offered the Order of the Garter to Winston Churchill but Churchill asked permission to refuse. According to an unsubstantiated but likely story he is alleged to have told the King that "it would be unfitting to receive the Order of the Garter from my sovereign when I have so recently received the order of the boot from your people."

The Order of the Thistle, a Scottish chivalric order founded by James II in 1687, is also exclusive, though less prized than the Garter. Besides the sovereign, it musters 16 knights.

The Order of St. Patrick, limited to the sovereign and 22 knights, was founded by George III in 1783 to celebrate the union of the kingdoms in Great Britain.

As the three senior orders of knighthood, the Garter, Thistle and St. Patrick have for some generations past been restricted almost exclusively to peers.

The Most Honourable Order of the Bath, next in antiquity to the Garter, traces its actual origin to an even earlier date than the Garter although it was not formed into an order until 1399. In those days the decoration was intimately connected with the coronation. Those who were to be created Knights of the Bath assembled at the Tower of London the night before the coronation, where they were ceremoniously bathed before being knighted, symbolizing the purity with which the solemn coronation rite should be approached: then, having placed their weapons upon the altar, they kept vigil throughout the night and in the morning donned the robes of the order and accompanied the king in procession to Westminster Abbey. When the Tower was abandoned as a royal residence the order fell into abeyance, but it was revived in 1725 by George I and the chapel of Henry VII in the Abbey was made its headquarters. There, below the beautiful fan-tracery of the vaulted chapel roof, hang the ornate armorial banners of oil-painted silk, one for each knight. George V revived the solemn installation service at Westminster Abbey, when the banners of the deceased knights are lowered and replaced by those of the more recently created, and George VI kept up his father's practice.

The Most Distinguished Order of St. Michael and St. George, originally founded to reward the services of natives under British protection in the Ionian islands of the Mediterranean, is customarily bestowed for distinguished service within the Empire and in the field of foreign affairs. It is supposed to be limited to 1,200 knights, but this restriction was overlooked after the Second World War when so many services were rewarded that membership in the order rose to nearly 4,000. The Most Excellent Order of the British Empire, a newer and lesser decoration than the St. Michael and St. George, was instituted during the First World War and is bestowed alike on both sexes for valuable services rendered to the Empire.

There are three Indian orders originated by Queen Victoria, the Order of the Star of India, a coveted decoration which was instituted in

1857 as a reward to Indian princes and others who remained loyal during the Indian mutiny; the Order of the Indian Empire, founded when Victoria was proclaimed Empress of India in 1878; and the Imperial Order of the Crown of India, created at the same time and intended for female relatives of Indian princes or those who held high office in India, which can only be bestowed upon women.

The Royal Victorian Order, like the Garter a personal honour from the sovereign, was originated in 1896 for bestowal on those who render important or personal services to the monarch and the royal family, and the knighthoods of its highest ranks are generally conferred upon the royal doctors, the secretariat and household officials. Women admitted to this order rank on equal terms with men.

The Order of Merit, which confers no rank, title or precedence, is none the less select and prized because it is given only for service of the highest merit in art, literature, science and public service. It is limited to 24 Britons and such eminent foreigners as the monarch may designate. Founded by Edward VII, it is conferred by the sovereign without consulting the Prime Minister. The Companionship of Honour, limited to a membership of 50, likewise carries no title: in fact, it was instituted during the First World War to reward those who had rendered valuable service but were averse, for personal reasons, to receiving any distinction carrying a title. Clement Attlee, on the defeat of the Labour Government in 1951, was honoured with the Order of Merit when he relinquished his post as Prime Minister, an honour also bestowed on Winston Churchill when he handed over to Attlee in 1945. Both Attlee and Churchill are also Companions of Honour. General Dwight D. Eisenhower is an honorary member of the Order of Merit.

And, finally, there is the Imperial Service Order, a less well-known honour which Edward VII instituted at his coronation to reward members of the administrative branch of the civil service.

Apart from these orders, the British have their purely military honours which are reserved for the fighting services, graded downward from the Victoria Cross (the initials of which take precedence over all other knightly grades or decorations), given sparingly and only for the highest bravery in the field in the face of the enemy, the Distinguished Service Order, instituted in 1886 and given only to commissioned officers, and its lower-rank counterpart, the Distinguished Service Medal, awarded for distinguished service in the field, and the more common Military Cross and Military Medal. These carry no titles, but the Victoria Cross brings its holder a small life pension. In the Second World War, which brought Britain's civilians into the front line, George VI appropriately created two new awards to mark the bravery and service of his citizens, the George Cross, the civilian counterpart of the V.C., and the George Medal.

Because of the limited membership of the high, title-conferring orders, the honour of knighthood is more frequently conferred today on so-called Knights Bachelor, actually the oldest of the ten classes of knighthood. These belong to none of the orders and receive no armorial insignia, though they may buy a badge of rank from the Imperial Society of Knights Bachelor. Within most of the categories of honours there are finite gradations in rank—companions, knights, knight commanders and so on—and a deserving or ambitious recipient often finds himself possessed of two or more knighthoods (though not in the same order, except for the Order of the Bath, which has equal-ranking military and civil grades) as he advances up the hierarchy. When this happened to an elderly British admiral during the Second World War his friends sent a ribald congratulatory signal to his Mediterranean flagship: "Twice a knight—and at your age, too!"

2. Because the sovereign is Defender of the Faith, the court is compelled to uphold a rigid moral code. In Edward VII's time no divorced person, even if the innocent party, could be received at court because the Church of England does not recognize divorce. In the reigns of George V and George VI this rule was relaxed, because of the breakup of wartime marriages, and the innocent parties were often received at court—but, with few exceptions, the guilty are still beyond the royal pale. Elizabeth II has strong personal feelings against divorce, particularly when there are children of the marriage.

VIII

THE LIFE AND TIMES OF GEORGE VI

1. Explaining "what this kingship business means to us" a few days after George VI's death, A. J. Cummings, the astute columnist of the London *News Chronicle*, remarked:

"In an active political sense republicanism has ceased for us to be a controversial theme. Even as an academic exercise it is confined chiefly to stubborn old gentlemen with historical memories and to a sprinkling of theorists still able to make out a good intellectual case for a radical change in an ancient constitution. I can't imagine any general election in this country fought on such an issue. It would cut no ice with any party.

"There was a time when ardent Socialists might have been tempted to place the subject prominently in a fighting manifesto in the fear that the monarchy could be used in some way to prejudice their independence. But as the Labour movement grew in strength and in familiarity with Parliamentary procedure, more particularly as Labour Ministers discovered in practice how remote it is from the possibility of interference, and yet how conveniently it enables democracy to work, any thought of challenging boldly the monarchical idea faded silently away."

2. When the pioneering couple of British Socialism, Sidney and

Beatrice Webb, drew up their "Constitution for the Socialist Commonwealth of Great Britain" they proposed no change in the monarchy, and confessed that no one had been able to suggest a practicable way in which the British Empire could do without a symbolic head or obtain one by popular election.

IX

WARTIME MONARCH

1. The wartime royal train which George VI used was a luxury originally built for Queen Victoria, though she did not live to ride in it. Its solid carriages, with their out-of-date fittings, were replaced a few years ago with modern coaches. Elizabeth II, having discovered the time-saving feature of air travel and broken down the remaining royal taboos against flying as a means of transport, will probably call for the sovereign's special train much less frequently than her father did for getting around Britain.

2. Honorary appointments to this order do not carry the accolade of knighthood: thus General Eisenhower, while not entitled to put "Sir" in front of his name, can append his signature with the letters G.C.B. A number of Americans were made honorary Knights of the British Empire during the war and General Marshall, like Eisenhower, was made a G.C.B. Altogether, 70 Americans were made honorary knights by George VI during his reign.

X

"THE PEOPLE'S KING"

1. One of George VI's good friends among the Labour Ministers was the late George Tomlinson, the homely, humorous politician from Lancashire, who served as Minister of Works and then Minister of Education in the Attlee Government. Soon after the war's end, when Tomlinson was Minister of Works, he and the King stood looking at bomb-blasted Buckingham Palace.

"I suppose you're in charge of this place now, George?" asked the King.

"That's right, sir," said the Minister.

"Well, what about my windows?" asked George VI.

"Oh," said Tomlinson, with a nice democratic touch, "it'll come your turn."

About a year later the Palace windows were replaced and when

Tomlinson next appeared at "Buck House" the King laughingly remarked to the Queen in Tomlinson's presence, "It's come our turn!"

2. One of the first Americans to sense the liberal outlook of the late King and his Queen, particularly towards social problems, was Franklin D. Roosevelt. After King George and Queen Elizabeth had visited the U.S. in 1939 the late President wrote to Nicholas Roosevelt, a relative:
"Dear Nick,
. . . I wish that you could have met the King and Queen—they are very delightful and understanding people, and, incidentally, know a great deal not only about foreign affairs in general but also about social legislation. Actually they would qualify for inclusion in that famous book, which is constantly quoted by some of *your friends—not mine*—to the effect that Eleanor and I are Communists!"
The book referred to was "The Red Network," by Elizabeth Dilling, one of the first major efforts to apply the smear technique to modern American politics.

3. Commenting on the novel situation which confronted George VI in 1945, the election of a Labour administration backed for the first time in British history by a large Parliamentary majority and intent on making far-reaching changes in the British way of life, Clement Attlee, in a speech after the King's death, carefully remarked: "He was broadminded and tolerant. It cannot, I think, have been easy for him to have had a Government returned to power with a majority pledged to make sweeping changes, but he accepted the position. I never knew him to depart from strict constitutional propriety. He had studied economic and social questions, and whether or not he agreed with the policy of the Labour Government, he understood very well the reasons for it."

4. Earl Mountbatten later revealed that he had turned down the job when Attlee first offered it to him ("No one in his right frame of mind would dream of going out to try to settle an insoluble problem," he told the Prime Minister), and later accepted the assignment when the King pressed him to take it on.

5. The true significance of the political miracle by which George VI lost an imperial title and yet, in the words of Mr. Attlee, won "the hearts of the people of India" was not properly appreciated in the United States when it took place. It was perceived belatedly in a posthumous tribute in the Washington *Post*, an editorial comment which George VI would have appreciated.
Said the *Post:* "In the flood of American comments on King George VI and his place among British sovereigns, there seems to be an undercurrent of reproach or censure that he left the Empire smaller than when he came to the Throne. This, to our minds, is an odd revival of the Kiplingesque thinking at least 50 years behind the times.
"What is national greatness, anyway? Which was the greater

achievement—to conquer India or to set it free? Which was the more splendid—to send the Lancers charging against the dervishes at Omdurman, or to set up self-governing assemblies in West Africa, in the later years of George VI? And which was the finer act of states-manship—to crown Victoria Empress of India, or to keep India within the Commonwealth on her own terms as an equal and self-respect-ing member?

"If courage is the test of greatness, then Britons of the reign of George VI had it in supreme measure. If character is the test, the late King and all his people showed it through the hardships of the war and post-war years. If statesmanship is the test, then the Britain of George VI had it, too, especially in transforming a restless Empire into a Family of Free Nations.

"By every standard Americans respect and admire, we submit that more greatness was packed into the 15 years of George VI than in all the 63 years of Queen Victoria."

6. Other titles dropped from the royal style in the past: King of England, Jerusalem, France, Naples, Scotland; Duke of Normandy; Sovereign Protector of the United States of the Ionian Islands (Greek islands off the west coast of Greece, handed over to the protection of Britain by the Treaty of Paris in 1815 and restored to Greece in the 1860's). The sovereign's one non-regal title, Defender of the Faith, was first bestowed on Henry VIII by Pope Leo X, but when Henry changed his religious convictions to suit his matrimonial intentions the honour was indignantly withdrawn. Henry promptly persuaded his Parliament to confer upon him the style of Defender of the Faith (Protestant), which successive sovereigns have borne.

7. Out went: "O Lord our God, arise
                 Scatter his enemies
                 And make them fall;
                 Confound their politics,
                 Frustrate their knavish tricks;
                 On Thee our hopes we fix;
                 God save us all."

In went: "Nor on this land alone—
                 But be God's mercies known
                 From shore to shore.
                 Lord, make the nations see
                 That men should brothers be,
                 And form one family
                 The wide world o'er."

8. Commenting on the striking similarity between George V and George VI, Sir Owen Morshead, who served both monarchs in his capacity as librarian at Windsor Castle, remarked in a broadcast memoir

after George VI's death: "Father and son were in fact alike, as those who were about the late King noted increasingly as he grew older. Their signatures were scarcely distinguishable; their reaction to the daily round of business was similar; given their choice, both would have preferred to have passed their life in the country surroundings of their Norfolk home, where both alike developed an unusual degree of skill with the gun. Both were second sons, not intended for the Throne; both disciplined themselves to face the glare of unsought publicity and the exacting toil of a job that was never done."

9. The extent of George VI's popularity was somewhat touchingly expressed after his leg operation in 1949 when London's newsvendors scrawled on their placards the affectionate if unregal assurance, "He's all right." It was shown again more dramatically when thousands of his subjects, with deep concern written on their faces, took up their pavement vigil outside Buckingham Palace in September, 1951 when the ailing King was suddenly operated on for the removal of one of his lungs. Few of them could explain articulately why they were there but still they remained, patiently enduring the gloom and the drizzle for day after day until they were assured that the anxiety over the King's life had lifted.

Of the eulogies written and spoken at the time of George's death the most moving tribute of them all came from a London workman, who wrote an artless letter to the editor of the *News Chronicle*. It said:

"We the ordinary working-class people loved our King dearly. Somehow he seemed to get deeper into our hearts than any of the others we've had, and we don't want any of the great men to keep on telling *us* what a good King *he* was. We've known that all along.

"Didn't He stop with us through all the bombing, when He could have gone to safety, as everyone hoped He would? Maybe it was that alone that *got us* more than anything else. Remember that morning in the East-end, after one of the worst raids, when He brought the Queen with Him, and walked among the ruin and rubble, talking to anyone, comforting and consoling. Then that rough chap who couldn't hold himself any longer burst out with 'You're a *good* King, Sir.' He turned (God Bless Him) and he didn't stammer then, and said, 'And you're a *good* people.'"

10. R. Ellis Roberts, onetime literary editor of the British weekly *The New Statesman and Nation*, in a review of Hector Bolitho's book, "A Century of British Monarchy," in the *Saturday Review of Literature* put an interesting historical interpretation on the relationship between crown and people.

"During this last century the throne in England gained its freedom just as truly as did millions of its newly-enfranchised subjects," Roberts wrote. "After the departure of the Stuarts the throne was really in subjection to the great families which had got rid of James II and who fought so bitterly against all attempts to reinstate the Stuarts. This dominance of the great houses over the Crown effectually prevented any contact between the sovereign and any but a minute fraction of the people.

"The monarch, when he had the character, had power; but it was held on sufferance. Of course royal power, even some royal privileges, have been curtailed since 1851; but only so, in our age of revolutionary change, could the monarch's influence be increased and strengthened. By the complete removal of the Crown from party politics, the king has been able to influence his people in a way that was not possible when he reigned by sufferance of the great houses, Whig or Tory."

11. "There has been no King, in Britain or anywhere else, who succeeded so well in identifying himself with the lives and habits of the people," said the London *Daily Herald*, the Labour Party's newspaper, in an editorial tribute the day after George VI's death. "Although much of the elaborate pomp and exclusiveness of royal circles has been wisely modified, it is still inevitable that a king should live a life of strict routine and much ceremony. But because of King George's humanity and humility, the etiquette of the Court has never been a barrier between him and the citizens of the Commonwealth. While doing an immensely exacting job with outstanding ability, he has inspired affection equally with respect."

Within a few months of his death, however, there appeared a left-wing note of criticism that the democratizing process initiated by George V and ably advanced by George VI had not been carried far enough. When the official period of court mourning for the late King came to an end the pro-Labour *Reynold's News*, the London Sunday newspaper which serves as the organ of the influential Co-operative movement, dropped a broad hint that Queen Elizabeth II should turn out the aristocrats who traditionally make up the court and replace them with more humble working-class subjects. The journal argued that this was a good occasion "to bring the monarchy up to date" by discarding much of the "hidebound routine that creates a wide gulf between the Queen and her people."

XI

THE HAPPY FAMILY

1. Cried the president of the Protestant Truth Association after Margaret's visit to the Pope: "Queen Victoria would never have dreamed of such a thing! This is an attempt of the Romans to get a foot in!" And when the then Princess Elizabeth proposed to follow her sister's gesture in 1951 the National Union of Protestants denounced the visit as "unconstitutional . . . dangerous to the safety of the British Empire."

2. An illustration of Anglican authority in matters of royal behaviour came to light in the humiliation of the present Queen Mother at the time of the wedding of her niece, Lady Anson, in the autumn of 1950. For the marriage of Lady Anson to Prince Georg of Denmark, the Earl of Strathmore, the Queen Mother's brother, loaned his private chapel at Glamis Castle and Her Majesty announced that she would attend the wedding. The clergyman chosen to officiate was the Earl's private chaplain, who belonged to the Scottish Episcopal Church, a relatively small body in Scotland. However, Lady Anson's first marriage had been dissolved, and even though she was the innocent party the Church of England, while not explicitly forbidding it, does not approve the re-marriage of a divorced person. Although the Church of England's authority over the Scottish Episcopal Church is purely nominal the Archbishop of Canterbury intervened at the last moment, ordered the Episcopal clergyman withdrawn and "advised" the Queen Mother not to attend the ceremony. Elizabeth was compelled to announce publicly that she would only join the wedding party for the luncheon afterwards and when the ceremony finally took place at Glamis she waited patiently in an adjoining drawing room.

XII

THE KING WHO WORKED LIKE A MAN

1. Apart from his ranking role at the head of his three fighting services, George VI was honorary head of no fewer than 59 military bodies and his appointments ranged from colonel-in-chief of his Brigade of Guards to Honorary Commanding General in the Nepalese Army.

Among the military appointments held by the late King were colonel-in-chief of the Life Guards, Royal Horse Guards ("The Blues"), Grenadier Guards, Coldstream Guards, Scots Guards, Irish Guards, Welsh Guards, the 1st Royal Dragoons, 11th (Prince Albert's Own) Hussars, Royal Regiment of Artillery, Corps of Royal Engineers, Somerset Light Infantry, East Yorkshire Regiment, Royal Welch Fusiliers, King's Royal Rifle Corps, the Queen's Own Cameron Highlanders, the Royal Tank Corps, and the Royal Army Ordnance Corps; Captain General of the Honourable Artillery Company (Territorial Army); colonel-in-chief of the 16th Light Cavalry, 1st Punjab Regiment, and 13th Frontier Force Rifles of the Indian Army, colonel-in-chief of the Duke of Lancaster's Own Yeomanry, Leicestershire Yeomanry and the Officers' Training Corps; colonel-in-chief of the King's African Rifles, Royal West African Frontier Force, and the Ceylon Defence Force.

2. "Few people perhaps realized how hard he worked," said Clement Attlee after George VI's death. "They knew that he had public duties

to perform. They probably understood that there were many formalities to be observed, but they did not know the close attention which he gave to every side of public affairs. Masses of telegrams, reports and other State papers came before him and he never treated them perfunctorily. I was always careful to be up to date in my reading whenever I went to see him, for I knew that he would be well informed on everything, whether foreign or domestic. He often told me how surprised visiting statesmen were at the extent of his knowledge. 'They don't seem to realize I have to work,' he would say."

3. Aside from his military appointments, George VI was a patron of innumerable public organizations. Among the most important of his honorary roles were: Protector of the University of Wales, Bencher of the Inner Temple, Master of the Merchant Navy and Fishing Fleets, Grand Master of Windsor Great Park, Elder Brother of Trinity House, and Bailiff Grand Cross of the Order of St. John of Jerusalem in the British Realm.

He received the honorary degree of doctor of laws from Cambridge, Belfast, Brisbane, Melbourne, Adelaide and Glasgow universities, and doctor of civil law from Oxford. Among the various foreign orders he received were the Order of St. Vladimir of Russia with swords, the Chrysanthemum of Japan, Persian Cross of Carol I of Rumania, the Legion of Honour and *Croix de Guerre* of France, Grand Order of Gurtz, and the Nepalese Order of Rajanya.

4. Up to the time of writing neither the King's doctors nor Buckingham Palace officials have ever admitted the malignant nature of George VI's disease. The bulletin signed by nine doctors who examined the King on September 18, 1951 announced that examination had shown "structural changes to have developed in the lung." At this time the medical profession assumed that the King was suffering from bronchial carcinoma, a diagnosis confirmed by the urgency with which His Majesty was operated on five days later, and this the royal medical men did not deny.

5. Under the Regency Act of 1937 a Council of State must be set up whenever the sovereign is absent from his realm or temporarily incapacitated. A Council of State acted for George VI on two of the five occasions when he went overseas during the war years and again when he toured South Africa. Counsellors of State are entitled to approve Orders in Council and Government appointments, to sign commissions in the armed services and to carry out a variety of state business in the sovereign's name: however, two of the most important remaining royal powers—the right to dissolve Parliament and the right to create new peers—are not given to them.

According to the Act, the Council of State shall consist of the wife or husband of the sovereign, if the sovereign is married, and the next four adults in the line of succession, or if the number of adults in the line of succession is less than four, then all such persons. Under the procedure laid down in the Act a Regent, who must be the person next in succession to the crown, if of age, is appointed only in the event of the sovereign's madness or complete incapacitation, or if the sovereign dies leaving an heir to the throne who has not reached the age of 18.

The order of succession to the throne has been strictly established since the Act of Settlement of 1701, and it is hedged about in law with genealogical safeguards. Sons of sovereigns and their descendants have precedence over the daughters, for instance, and the daughters and their descendants have precedence over lateral lines.

According to their royal pedigree, the order of succession to the throne is at present as follows: (1) Prince Charles, the heir apparent; (2) Princess Anne, Elizabeth II's second child; (3) Princess Margaret, the Queen's sister; (4) the Duke of Gloucester; (5) Prince William of Gloucester; (6) Prince Richard of Gloucester; (7) Prince Edward, the young Duke of Kent; (8) Prince Michael of Kent; (9) Princess Alexandra of Kent; (10) the Princess Royal, George VI's only sister; (11) the Earl of Harewood, first son of the Princess Royal; (12) David, infant son of the Earl and Countess of Harewood; (13) the Honourable Gerald Lascelles, second son of the Princess Royal.

The Duke of Edinburgh ranks far down in one of the royal family's lateral lines as a descendant of Queen Victoria. In 1947 Debrett's Peerage estimated that 178 descendants of Queen Victoria were then living, although even this authority was not sure of all the obscure German lines which flowed from her.

XIII

APPRENTICE SOVEREIGN

1. Although the British people and the rest of the world for long regarded Princess Elizabeth's eventual succession as apparent and inevitable, according to the legal provisos determining dynastic succession she remained heiress presumptive until her father died, however remote was the possibility that George VI and his Queen would produce a son and heir to the throne.

The eldest son of a king is described during his father's lifetime as heir apparent because nothing but death can prevent his ultimately succeeding to the throne. Any more indirect heir—such as the brother or daughter of a king who has no son—is styled heir (or heiress) presumptive because he or she can only succeed presuming no heir apparent is born. The only way in which a woman can be heiress apparent is when she is the daughter of a sovereign's eldest son who has died before his father, which has never occurred in Britain's history. Apart from George VI, there is only one other instance in British history of a sovereign dying without male heir and leaving only daughters or sisters.

This was when Edward VI died unmarried and the only other children of Henry VIII were the Princess Mary and Princess Elizabeth.

2. On her first visit to Scotland after her accession the new Queen was about to present an archery cup when she noticed that it was engraved with the words: "Presented by Her Majesty Queen Elizabeth." Her proper style is Queen Elizabeth II, and Her Majesty promptly ordered the cup returned to the jewellers to have her numerals added.

3. As a result of these early contacts Elizabeth has always been more at ease at military ceremonies and soon after her accession she announced that she had assumed the colonelcy-in-chief of the main regiments and corps with which her father had been associated, the Life Guards, the Royal Horse Guards, the Grenadier Guards, the Coldstream Guards, the Scots Guards, the Irish Guards, the Welsh Guards, the Corps of Royal Engineers. She also assumed the appointment of Captain General of the Royal Regiment of Artillery and of the Honourable Artillery Company, both appointments held by her father. According to the War Office this is the first time a reigning British Queen has held military commands. Queen Victoria did not take military titles.

4. Many British newspapers and periodicals, which should know better, and most American publications, which are not expected to be versed in royal styles and titles, still persist—inaccurately—in referring to Elizabeth's husband as Prince Philip. Although George VI, by letters patent on November 20, 1947, conferred upon his son-in-law "the title, style and attribute of Royal Highness" this princely prefix did not create the Duke of Edinburgh a Prince. Until he became a naturalized British subject his proper style was His Royal Highness Prince Philip of Greece and Denmark. From the time of his marriage, and until such time as his wife accords him the style of Prince Consort, his correct full title has been His Royal Highness Philip, Duke of Edinburgh.

XIV

ROYAL CONSORT

1. That Philip had made the grade with the British people became evident after his wife's accession when, amid growing public speculation whether Queen Elizabeth would create him Prince Consort, there were many suggestions, some from influential quarters, that he should be given the loftier style of King or at least King Consort, bracketing him equal with the Queen in name but without her constitutional powers.

If and when the Duke of Edinburgh is to be advanced to the style and title of Prince Consort is a matter entirely for Elizabeth to decide. Many Britons feel that the title of Prince Consort leaves something to be desired and would prefer the less domestic ring of the Prince Royal.

Conferment of the title of Prince Consort or its equivalent on Philip would confirm his precedence over all other members of the royal family, although it would not change his political status at all. In the meantime, by royal warrant issued by his wife on September 30, 1952, the Duke of Edinburgh ranks as first gentleman of the British realm, taking precedence immediately after Elizabeth II. Until that ruling was made the Duke was outranked by his son as Duke of Cornwall and, when not accompanying his wife, by the Dukes of Gloucester and Windsor, who ranked first and second in accordance with the dates on which their royal dukedoms were created.

When Elizabeth ascended the throne there was some confusion in the public mind whether she would be the last sovereign of the house of Windsor. According to precedent Princess Elizabeth, even after her marriage, remained a Windsor and when she took the throne she became the fourth sovereign of the house of Windsor, for it has always been the custom to regard a Queen Regnant as belonging to her father's house. However, following ordinary English custom her children bore her husband's adopted surname of Mountbatten and her accession touched off learned debates whether her son, Prince Charles, would one day succeed to her throne as the first of a new line, the house of Mountbatten.

From the reign of Queen Anne, who was a Stuart, until 1917 the royal family had no surname. George I, the first of the house of Hanover, was a German princeling, the Elector of Hanover, whose family had not used a surname—at various times Guelph, Este or Wettin—for generations. Before 1917 all members of the British royal family were princes or princesses but in that year, when George V restricted the use of princely styles to children of the sovereign and of the sovereign's sons but not of his daughters, it became necessary to adopt a surname to be used by those who ceased to enjoy a princely prefix. By proclamation George V therefore ended the embarrassing German dynastic name of Saxe-Coburg and Gotha (Prince Albert's family name) and adopted the surname of Windsor for his royal house. It was George V's intention that the dynasty should for ever remain the house of Windsor—his proclamation categorically declared that he had "determined that henceforth Our House and Family shall be styled and known as the House and Family of Windsor"—but he left room for misunderstanding by specific reference to Queen Victoria's descendants in the male line, overlooking the possibility that in two reigns the succession would pass to a female.

Almost immediately she came to the throne Elizabeth II decided to continue the name of Windsor down her family line and by a declaration in her Privy Council on April 9, 1952, she corrected her grandfather's oversight and officially announced "her will and pleasure that she and her children shall be styled and known as the House and Family of Windsor, and that her descendants, other than female descendants who marry, and their descendants, shall bear the name Windsor."

XV

ELIZABETH THE QUEEN

1. Occasionally the Palace releases some of its letters to the press in a conscious effort to underline the democratic nature of the present-day monarchy and the requests or complaints contained in them reveal some of the strange tasks the sovereign is expected to perform.

An ex-G.I. in Pennsylvania lost track of a wartime friend in the British Army. He wrote George VI about it and a few weeks later received a letter from Buckingham Palace with his pal's address and Army serial number. A South African wrote in to ask if his friend, an able seaman in the Royal Navy, could be transferred to *Vanguard* so that he could visit South Africa during the royal tour. The sailor got his transfer. A crippled ex-serviceman, a veteran of both World Wars, who had an ailing wife and six youngsters, was four times refused permission to open a new pastry shop in his home town in 1948 because of the austerity shortages of fats, flour and sugar. He sat down one evening and wrote George VI all about it. Four months later, after much bureaucratic gear-grinding, he received a letter from the Food Minister's office informing him that, by His Majesty's command, special consideration had been given in his case so that a licence could be granted for his pastry shop as an exception to the rule.

The selectmen and town clerk of the little town of Bethlehem in New Hampshire appealed to George VI in 1951 to clarify their community's early history by certifying that 177 years before—in 1774—a charter of birth had been granted the town, then known as Lloyd's Hill, by one of George III's colonial governors, John Wentworth. According to their letter, which caught the late King's historic interest, the original charter had never been received from Governor Wentworth, it having been entrusted to a man who was lost at sea. Always anxious to make up for the mistakes of his great-great-great-grandfather's reign, George VI had this query seriously investigated, but a few weeks later the Bethlehem officials received a letter from Sir Alan Lascelles, which read: "His Majesty would gladly help you, but regrets that it is constitutionally impossible for him to sign the document (certificate of charter) enclosed with your letter. The King directed me to inquire at the Public Record Office if any information could be produced bearing on the charter given by Governor Wentworth in 1774, but I am sorry to say that a search reveals nothing relevant."

2. British newspapers seldom indulge in more than implied criticism of the royal family's taste in clothes, but a particularly unbecoming dress and hat which Elizabeth, the Queen Mother, chose to wear to a society wedding in the summer of 1950 caused one London popular newspaper to explode. "Who on earth advised the Queen to wear the outfit she had for the Somerset-Thynne wedding?" demanded the *Sunday Pictorial*.

"The Queen is a delightful personality. On most of her public appearances, she is superbly dressed. . . . Yet, (in this case) . . . the hat is too large, too heavy and too drooping. . . . The skimpy cape is both broadening and shortening. The dark edging makes the dress look like a dressing gown with the sash undone." All in all, clucked the newspaper, her appearance was "a misguided effort that will not enhance our growing reputation as a fashion-conscious nation. . . ."

Such press criticism of the royal taste invariably brings a flood of protesting letters-to-the-editors. A few years ago when the *Daily Express* pointed out a few fashion mistakes in a spring ensemble which the then Princess Elizabeth chose to wear to a horse show (over-emphatic decorations, high-heeled, ankle-strap shoes) its readers protested by a majority of seven to one against the paper's "impertinence and rudeness." Wrote one huffy reader: "It is abominable that you should allow such disgusting criticism of the dress of the daughter of the King of England. I should imagine the author is either a Communist or a foreigner."

XVI

THE QUEEN MOTHER (I)

1. The widow of a sovereign is customarily given the courtesy title of the Queen Dowager or, in appropriate circumstances, the Queen Mother. She may also use her own name prefixed by the word Queen. After the accession of Queen Elizabeth II it was formally announced that her mother's formal title would be Queen Elizabeth, the Queen Mother, and her grandmother would henceforth be formally styled Queen Mary, the Queen Dowager.

Queen Mary for long disliked the title of Queen Mother and by her own wish, publicly announced, she was known by the style of Queen Mary. The widowed Queen Elizabeth does not like the title of Queen Mother either, but she had not much choice in accepting it. She could not follow her mother-in-law's example and be known merely as Queen Elizabeth because that would cause confusion with her daughter's title.

The position of Elizabeth as Queen Mother remains much the same as when she was Queen Consort. She is still entitled to the royal style of Her Majesty and is still entitled to sign herself Elizabeth Regina. From a legal point of view, it is no longer high treason to conspire her death. About the only limitation placed upon her is that she has to have the consent of the sovereign before she marries again, but she does not forfeit her royal status if she marries a commoner. Parenthetically, few Dowager Queens or Queen Mothers in British history have ever married again. Last to do so was Queen Katharine Parr, who, having successfully survived two previous husbands, lived through matrimony with Henry VIII and then a few months later married again to Lord Seymour of Sudeley, brother of one of Henry's previous wives, Jane Seymour.

2. British genealogical authorities claim to have established that the Queen Mother is distantly related to Shakespeare (the fourth Earl of Strathmore married one of Shakespeare's descendants) and American family-tree experts, not to be outdone, have demonstrated to their satisfaction that Elizabeth is a second cousin six times removed to George Washington and a fifth cousin four times removed to Robert E. Lee.

3. With such a stormy and romantic past Glamis is well-endowed with legends. One is that it is held by the Bowes-Lyon family for a purely nominal rent, the nature of which is known only to the family members. Another is that there is a secret haunted chamber, which is unlocked by the estate factor and revealed to the heir when he attains his majority, both of them being sworn to silence. And, of course, Glamis is reputed to have its ghost—although this one is supposed to be a beautiful, smiling apparition, known as the Grey Lady, which makes its appearance whenever some singular good fortune is imminent.

XVIII

DOWAGER QUEEN (I)

1. Although she herself held such powers as could influence the destiny of her nation, the great Queen Victoria was not amused at the suggestion of giving the vote to women. She wrote: "The Queen is most anxious to enlist everyone who can speak or write to join in checking this mad wicked folly of Women's Rights with all its attendant horrors, on which her poor feeble sex is bent, forgetting every sense of womanly feeling and propriety. . . . It is a subject that makes the Queen so furious that she cannot contain herself. God created men and women *different !*"

2. While remaining strictly non-political in her friendships, Queen Mary has long had a soft spot in her heart for Labour's leader, Clement Attlee. "Queen Mary admires Mr. Attlee's character so much," confessed one of her entourage, "that in her view, he can do nothing wrong."

3. The public was given a choice of two legends—that Princess May had really loved the elder brother, or that she had secretly always loved Prince George—but it was difficult to accept the union as a real love match. Years later when Prince George became George V one of his first acts was to take into court a slanderer who had repeated the nasty 20-year-old rumour that, as a young man in Malta, he had another wife, daughter of an admiral, whom he had been compelled to abandon when he became heir to the throne. George V won his case and cleared his name.

XIX

DOWAGER QUEEN (II)

1. The foundations of the royal family fortune passed on to Queen Mary were laid by Queen Victoria. In the 70 years of royal extravagance preceding her reign the private coffers of the sovereign were emptied (George IV ran up debts of £522,000 through his rollicksome enthusiasm for horses, women and Oriental architecture), but long years of careful husbandry and semi-retirement from public life during her widowhood enabled Victoria to replenish the family fortune, and eventually, as biographer Lytton Strachey commented, she found herself "a person of great wealth," with a reputed personal fortune of £2,000,000.

Although he lived high and spent freely Edward VII probably added to the family inheritance, for he numbered among his cronies some of the shrewdest financiers of Europe, men like Jewish-born Sir Ernest Cassel (grandfather of Edwina Ashley, who married Louis Mountbatten), who advised him on his investments. He was once reputed to have made £1,000,000 in one day on a stock market jump in steel shares. Edward's fortune was passed down to his son, George V, and the major share of it reverted to Queen Mary on her husband's death.

XX

ROYAL RELATIVES

1. How much of the yearly royal allowances to persons other than the sovereign is taxable is a secret kept within the bosom of Britain's Inland Revenue department. As an unmarried person with no dependants, Princess Margaret's yearly £6,000 at full rate of British tax would dwindle to about £2,600.

When Princess Elizabeth was voted a £40,000 yearly grant upon her marriage and the Duke of Edinburgh was given a £10,000 annual allowance, the Chancellor of the Exchequer then ruled that all but £4,000 of Elizabeth's grant should be considered tax-free and that the Duke should be relieved of tax on four-fifths of his income, giving the royal couple a tax-free joint income at that time of £44,000.

During the Parliamentary haggling over the new Civil List proposal to increase the Duke of Edinburgh's allowance to £40,000 a year for life as the consort to the Queen a Socialist income-tax expert in the House of Commons estimated that as much as £38,000 of this would be regarded as tax-free in order to cover the Duke's household, travel and living expenses. The Chancellor of the Exchequer refused to divulge the precise figure, although he conceded that the expert's estimation was not quite correct. Although the Inland Revenue decision varies from case to case, it is generally assumed that the members of the royal family are granted around 80 per cent. of their income free of tax to cover their expenses.

2. The heir to the throne is *born* a member of the House of Lords and does not have to wait until he is legally of age before taking his seat, although in the past it has been customary to wait until the royal legal age of 18.

3. The Marquis, a white-bearded old man who looked like a grumpy version of George Bernard Shaw, was one of London's eccentric characters in the years before the First World War. Although he owned 50,000 acres in Ireland, a 200-roomed Irish castle and enjoyed a yearly income of some £80,000, he remained an absentee landlord, a hermit and a notorious miser who preferred to live alone in filthy, dust-covered rooms in London. His one indulgence was membership in London's famous social clubs, the members of which not unnaturally shunned him because of his obnoxious habits. He would forage in the dustbins for kitchen refuse and when he dined at his clubs he usually brought scraps of food along in paper bags. He would sit for hours in the window alcove of one club overlooking the street, licking the tip of his long nose with his tongue, and whenever he took a dislike to a fellow member he would thumb his nose at him when they met.

Home on leave from the First World War, where he served with distinction in the Grenadier Guards, winning the D.S.O., Lord Lascelles saw his great-uncle sitting in a club and on a sudden impulse greeted him and told him about the war in the trenches. A few months later, when the Marquis of Clanricarde died, his will revealed that he had altered it in his nephew's favour, making him heir to the Clanricarde fortune of £2,500,000.

4. The Princess Royal's two sons have no royal titles because of the 1917 edict of George V, who limited the title of prince or princess to children of the sovereign and of the sovereign's sons, but not of his daughters. George VI exercised his right to amend this decree a few days before Princess Elizabeth's first child was born.

XXI

THE ROYAL HOUSEHOLD

1. The Lord Steward was originally a deputy of the Lord High Steward, the ranking post of the nine Great Officers of State, and in time he became a permanent officer of the household, chief judge of the Court of the Palace of Westminster (originally a court for determining actions

against members of the household, it subsequently grew into comparatively extensive jurisdiction, but was abolished in 1849) and the first dignitary at court. During the present century the Lord Steward has been superseded as first dignitary at court by the Lord Chamberlain, who is now the senior officer of the royal household.

2. Until this century the Mistress of the Robes was a political appointee and went out of office whenever the Government changed. Her badge of office used to be a golden key, which was passed from one holder to the next until the custom had to be discontinued when the notorious Sarah, Duchess of Marlborough, who served as Mistress of the Robes to her great friend Queen Anne, refused to part with the key. Since then the badge of the office has been a miniature of the queen set in brilliants.

3. Technically, the royal household also includes a variety of institutions that were once either attached to the court or dependent on royal patronage. For instance, the Royal Academy of Art is, properly speaking, part of the Queen's household. There is also the Royal School of Needlework, which has been one of Queen Mary's lifelong interests. Members of the Royal School of Needlework were given the assignment of working the decorative design on the gold cloth canopy held over George VI and Queen Elizabeth during the anointing ceremony at their coronation, and they also embroidered Queen Elizabeth's coronation robe.

4. It was estimated that if George VI had paid their top fees for private patients to the nine physicians and surgeons, including his household medical men, who carried out his leg operation in 1949 the bill would have run to £4,000 to £5,000. In fact, his bill was only a small part of this sum.

XXII

THE PRIVY PURSE

1. George III gets credit for the bargain which set the pattern for future Civil Lists because he was the first to surrender his rights to most of the crown lands and revenues. In fact, his bargain was merely a slight variation in the arrangement made for the reign of his grandfather, George II. Parliament guaranteed George II an income of £800,000 a year if the hereditary revenues together with those provided by Parliament fell short of that sum, but George II was to take the benefit of any surplus.

2. The amount determined is not always the same from reign to

reign. Edward VII received £470,000 yearly from his 1901 Civil List, only £5,000 less than the sum voted for Elizabeth II in 1952, although living costs have increased three-fold since the turn of the century. George V also received £470,000 yearly. Edward VIII, as a bachelor king, was expected to get along on less than his father had done. George VI's Civil List was fixed in 1937 at an annual £410,000, but in 1947, 1948 and 1951 he was relieved of certain expenditure by the state, which in effect gave him an additional £83,000 yearly.

3. Elizabeth II's Civil List also provides that any further children which she and her husband may have will be adequately taken care of. Younger sons, other than Prince Charles, will get £10,000 per year when they reach the age of 21 and £25,000 per year upon marriage. Princess Anne and any further daughters born to the royal couple will receive £6,000 yearly at the age of 21 and £15,000 per year upon marriage, the same provision that has been made for Princess Margaret.

4. The first son born to a reigning sovereign is born with certain titles in the peerage. Likewise, the eldest son of the heir or heiress to the throne succeeds automatically to the same titles the moment his father or mother ascends the throne. Thus four-year-old Prince Charles became, at the moment of his mother's accession as Elizabeth II, Duke of Cornwall in the peerage of England, Duke of Rothesay, Earl of Carrick and Baron of Renfrew in the peerage of Scotland, and Lord of the Isles and Prince and Great Steward, or Seneschal, of Scotland. The heir to the throne is not born Prince of Wales or Earl of Chester. Those titles are created for him at the sovereign's pleasure, and not until he is so created does he automatically become a Knight of the Garter.

5. The Civil List of 1952, looking far into the future, also made provision for the Duke of Cornwall's possible marriage. If he marries after attaining his majority at the age of 21 the Duke is expected to provide for his wife and himself out of the revenues of the Duchy of Cornwall, which will then accrue to him in full. If he should predecease his wife, however, his widow is to draw an annuity of £30,000, provided by Parliament. If the Duke of Cornwall dies before coming to the throne the entire revenues of the Duchy revert to the Exchequer, to be used in relief of the Civil List.

6. In contrast to Britain's expenditure on the monarchy, Germany's ex-Kaiser got £770,000 yearly and Italy's King Victor Emmanuel drew £782,000 per year. Little Belgium, with a population only slightly larger than New York city, allows its royal family an expenditure of £396,428 per year, plus an allowance of £42,850 yearly for its abdicated ex-King Leopold III. The Netherlands, in granting its royal family its first raise since 1938, in 1952 raised Queen Juliana's annual income from £100,000 to nearly £150,000 and that of her

consort, Prince Bernhard, from £20,000 to £30,000. In addition, Princess Beatrix, the heiress to the throne, is to have a yearly grant of £25,000 when she reaches the age of 18, and her husband, provided her marriage is approved by law, will draw another £25,000. Out of their income the Dutch royal family is expected to pay for all ceremonial costs as well as the expenses of the royal households and the wages of the staff. The maintenance of the royal palaces is covered by an additional grant of £29,166 per year.

7. Other items in George VI's £192,790 housekeeping bill for 1951 were: liveries, £5,523; laundry, £5,040; travel costs, £5,335; royal gardens, £7,237; purchase, hire and upkeep of cars, £4,210; subscriptions, cups and medals, £5,777; medical expenditure, £146; royal library, £226; royal cellars, £6,502; and sundries, including Sandringham and Balmoral expenses, garden and presentation parties, £12,602.

8. The Duchy of Lancaster is a duchy without a duke. That title became extinguished when Henry V, who, as Prince Henry, had been granted both dukedom and duchy, succeeded to the throne and it has not been re-granted since. Annexed to the crown in perpetuity, the duchy still retains a separate identity in the public mind because its principal executive officer, the Chancellor of the Duchy of Lancaster, is always a member of the Government. In fact, this is a sinecure, a ministry without portfolio.

9. As a farmer George VI followed the tradition of the British reigning monarch in developing breeds to improve the nation's stock. British breeds known the world over today owe much to royal patronage. The famous shire horse, once the heavy steed of the armoured knight, owes its development to Edward III and Henry VIII. Queen Anne, who presented prizes for distance races, did much to encourage the breeding of race horses. Queen Victoria encouraged the breeding and development of dairy cattle breeds at Windsor, and Edward VII and George V bred every kind of horse, sheep, pigs, beef and dairy cattle.

At Sandringham George VI specialized in that most English breed of sheep, the Southdown, and Red Poll cattle. The Windsor farm was the home of his shorthorn cattle and at the model farm at Stoke Climsland, on the Duchy of Cornwall estate, he specialized in the red Devon breed of beef cattle.

George VI's development work on the royal farms, now worked by his daughter, did much to make known overseas the virtues of British stock. Many of the prized specimens from the royal farms were exported and at agricultural shows in Britain his cattle, horses, sheep and pigs generally distinguished themselves and often walked off with the prizes.

XXIII

ROYAL HOMES

1. Victoria's Prince Albert once plaintively remarked, "Food always tastes so much better in small houses." This rather pathetic complaint was apparently occasioned by the fact that dishes often arrived cold at the royal table at Buckingham Palace despite the efforts of footmen to bring them at a trot up 72 steps and through the quarter-mile of warren-like corridors that separated the kitchens from the royal dining-room.

2. The Queen's Scottish Palace, used at the most for a few days each year, is the Palace of Holyroodhouse in the heart of Edinburgh. A cold, gloomy pile of history in stone, architecturally a mixture of French and native Scots, Holyroodhouse has historically romantic associations—in it lived Mary, Queen of Scots and it was there that Bonnie Prince Charlie danced the nights away—and a majestic setting in a natural amphitheatre at the foot of a volcanic crag known as Arthur's Seat.

It is a touchy point with Scots that the Palace of Holyroodhouse is so little used as a royal residence.

3. No two persons, even when taking an inventory together, have ever seemed to agree on the exact number of rooms, ante-rooms, storage rooms and cubicles in Buckingham Palace. Estimates range from 564 rooms to 615. Most commonly accepted count: 602.

4. When garden parties or presentations are held at the Palace an elaborate protocol determines who enters by what gate. Only royalty—members of the British royal family and visiting royal persons—may use the gate opening directly into the Palace gardens on the Constitution Hill side of the grounds. Those who hold the right of "Entrée"—diplomats, members of the household, leading members of the Government and ex-Ministers—are entitled to enter by the so-called Entrée door on the south front of the Palace, along Buckingham Palace Road. Ordinary guests are rewarded with a peek at the Palace's interior. They are permitted to drive their cars into the quadrangle and alight under the portico on the quadrangle side of the west wing at the entrance to the white and gold Grand Hall, which gives them a quick glance at the magnificent crimson-carpeted, white-marble Grand Staircase and some of the great state apartments as they cross through the west front to emerge into the gardens.

If Elizabeth II's gold-emblazoned standard is flying from the flag-staff atop the centre of the east wing it indicates that Her Majesty is "in residence" at the Palace, though it does not necessarily mean that she is at home at the moment. It is lowered only when she departs to spend the night elsewhere.

5. Thanks to the acquisitiveness of earlier monarchs Buckingham Palace is a veritable museum stuffed with antiques. The furniture in the

state rooms is mainly French, bought by George IV, and the other parts of the Palace contain many pieces of English furniture made by those consummate craftsmen—Robert Adam, Hepplewhite, Chippendale and Sheraton. The whole Palace collection of treasures, including the old masters in the royal gallery, the antique furniture and the vast hoard of costly china and ornate bric-a-brac, is conservatively valued at almost £5,000,000.

During the war years most of the contents of the state rooms and many of the royal treasures were removed from the Palace and stored in safety. They were carefully replaced in their former positions, a job that took several months, in time for the state functions that marked Princess Elizabeth's wedding.

6. Elizabeth II is the only monarch to own her own racecourse. Royal Ascot, to give it its correct name, belongs entirely to the sovereign—course, stables, grandstand and amenities—and although it has a total income of some £500,000 a year it is run on a no-rent, non-profit basis and all surplus earnings are ploughed back into course improvements.

The royal connection with Ascot goes back to the days of fat Queen Anne. Driving out from Windsor one fine summer day in 1711 she raced her horses across the smooth expanse of turf on Ascot Heath and impulsively decided then and there to hold a race meeting on the beautiful spot. On an August Saturday in 1711 the first horses raced for a plate valued at £100, presented by Her Majesty, and the Queen and her suite drove over from Windsor to watch them.

Under successive monarchs Royal Ascot flourished. George III was a regular attendant at the heath, George IV bowled over the course in a horse-drawn carriage and William IV, who smartly made the Jockey Club jointly responsible with his Master of the Buckhounds for running the enterprise, instituted the royal procession in which the sovereign and the royal family drive along the course in open carriages, one of the attractions of the meeting. Victoria had little patience with the sport of kings, but she made her visits to Ascot her one regular racing activity.

Because of its royal patronage, Ascot race week has become a social occasion, a fashion parade with horses, and among the glossy magazine set the competition is fierce for the coveted 2,000 to 3,000 crown-embossed cardboard badges which permit the wearer to enter the royal enclosure in front of the royal box.

Applications for admission to the enclosure are submitted through the Duke of Norfolk, senior trustee of the Ascot Authority and the Queen's Representative at Ascot, but the Queen, through her Lord Chamberlain, is the final arbiter of who shall enter or be debarred from the enclosure. Following court etiquette, those who have been the guilty parties in divorce cases are not granted admission. The Queen also determines the dress to be worn and the official invitations to the enclosure command: "Ladies will wear day dress with hats—gentlemen, morning dress or service dress."

NOTES

Bookmakers, legal in Britain, are not permitted in the royal enclosure, but backers may confide their wishes to bookies' representatives at the rails. Ladies admitted to the enclosure are not supposed to make bets (though an increasing number do), but they are permitted to entrust their escorts with their commissions. Members of the royal family never make their own bets, a chore they delegate to the equerries.

On certain days of the meeting, and sometimes on all four days of racing, the royal family and their guests drive over from Windsor. Outside the course the Queen and other members of the family take their places, strictly in order of precedence, in open landaus for the royal procession along the course to the royal box. The carriages are drawn by so-called Windsor greys and bays from the royal stables, ridden by velvet-capped, bewigged postillions decked out in their Ascot liveries of scarlet and gold.

7. This tradition of privacy, which dates from Victoria's wish for seclusion on Deeside, was breached in the summer of 1951 when Princess Margaret celebrated her twenty-first birthday at Balmoral. Certain London newspapers sent photographers and reporters to break through the iron curtain of privacy that surrounds the Castle, a journalistic enterprise that was not approved by many of their readers.

XXIV

ROYAL HOUSEKEEPING

1. There are altogether some 600 clocks in the royal homes and palaces, 250 of them at Windsor Castle. Some of these timepieces are horological rarities, part of the unique collection started by George III, which go for a year on one winding, but all of them have to be adjusted when Britain switches from Greenwich to daylight saving time and back again.

2. It was a tribute to George VI's standing as an employer that only 17 servants from all departments at "Buck House" chose not to return to the Palace service on their demobilization after the war.

A greater consideration for the servants has marked the last few reigns. Queen Victoria thought it unqueenly to take notice of the servants, except for one or two highly favoured exceptions. No maidservant was allowed to address Victoria except through a lady-in-waiting or a household official. One day when the old Queen was dozing in front of the fire in the Bow Room a live cinder from an explosive hunk of coal popped out and landed in the fold of her skirt. An alert maid, deciding to forget the no-speaking rule in the emergency, told the Queen what had happened—and was sharply rebuked for her impudence.

3. A special staff problem which the Master of the Household occasionally has to meet is the hiring of extra footmen to serve at state banquets at Buckingham Palace. These auxiliary waiters must be specially trained and at least six feet tall to fit the scarlet-and-blue state liveries from the Palace wardrobe. They must also be prepared to have their hair dressed and powdered with flour. Their fee for the night is £3, in addition to dinner and the choice of a bottle of beer or a double whisky. Before the Second World War the extra staff required for state banquets was drawn from among the retired footmen who lived in or near London, but their numbers have dwindled in recent years.

4. Even in its "laying up" the Palace has its peculiarities. Forks have been placed prongs down ever since one of the Georges, haranguing his guests at the table, brought his fist down with a painful wallop on the upturned points of his fork. Another of the Georges, trying to tackle a pippin with a gold knife, bent it out of shape and called in disgust for a steel knife. Ever since both gold and steel knives have been served with the fruit.

5. Despite the introduction of post-war economies the Treasury experts who examine the Privy Purse accounts discovered that the Palace kitchens and dining-rooms were consistently running over their budgets. In the summer of 1949 the Master of the Household called in Hugh Wontner, managing director of London's Savoy Hotel, to recommend how meals at the Palace could be run on a business-like footing. Wontner instituted several new money-saving ideas. The junior staff members were put on board wages: they were given higher salaries but required to pay for their food from their kitchen. A chit system was also introduced which requires the Palace staff to sign individual receipts for their morning coffee and afternoon tea. For his economy efforts Wontner was made a Member of the Victorian Order by George VI.

6. The Royal Mews were not always the monarch's stables. The description has been associated with horses only since Henry VIII, after a fire in 1537 burned down the royal stables in Bloomsbury, ordered the horses stabled in an area of central London (where the National Gallery now stands) known as the Royal Mews, which was where all the kings of England—from Richard II to Henry VIII—kept their falcons. The word mew has nothing to do with horses. It means to moult or shed.

7. There are three great state coaches which can be used for ceremonial drives. One is the four-ton Gold State Coach, a huge-wheeled carriage originally designed for George III's coronation. It is elaborately carved and gilded, and on its panelled sides and doors are exquisite allegorical paintings by Cypriani. It is traditionally drawn by eight grey horses, four of which are ridden by postillions and all of which

have a walking man at their head. Their eight sets of red morocco leather harness, elaborately ornamented and polished, are claimed by the royal stable staff to be the finest in the world. They were made for George III, each set being cut out of a single hide, at a cost of £14,000. When the harness was recently re-leathered the firm of famous saddlers entrusted with the work found that it had to call its pensioned old-timers out of retirement to do the fine stitching and ornamentation because the modern craftsmen were not sufficiently skilled. Unfortunately, the coach has no brakes and is so heavy that it is unsafe to drag it at more than a walking pace.

Then there is the Irish State Coach, so called because Victoria bought it after seeing it at a Dublin exhibition, which is less elaborate than the Gold State Coach. George VI preferred to use it for such state drives as the opening of Parliament because, being beautifully sprung, it can be drawn by the horses at a trot. It was in this coach that Princess Elizabeth rode with her father to her wedding at Westminster Abbey. The third of the ceremonial coaches is known as the Glass Coach, which carries other members of the royal family in processions. It was in the Glass Coach, in which royalty are more readily seen, that Elizabeth and Philip returned to the Palace from the Abbey as man and wife.

8. The name was tagged on to them by the newspapers because, until the abdication, the sovereign's grey horses were always stabled at Windsor. After the abdication they were all moved to the Buckingham Palace stables. Before the First World War the state coaches were usually drawn by cream-coloured horses, mostly imported from Hanover, but when the war with Germany cut off this supply a switch was made to greys. Nowadays, the Queen's coach is customarily drawn by greys, while the following state landaus are horsed by bays.

9. Despite these elaborate precautions a number of intruders, most of them cranks or crackpots, have succeeded in getting in to the royal homes and gardens—on nine occasions in 1950 and 1951 alone.

A few years ago two American touring students slithered over the garden wall at the Palace for a look at George VI's backyard but were apprehended before they could get their bearings. In December, 1950, another American wandered into Sandringham when the late King was in residence but he was politely escorted off the grounds when he described himself as "a nosey American hoping to have a word or two with the royal family."

A year or so ago a man entered Buckingham Palace and stole a diplomatic box and another male intruder, who confessed he did it for a bet, eluded the guards, used a builder's ladder to gain access to a Palace balcony and was finally found hiding in a room near George VI's apartments. In 1950 a man got into Marlborough House and attacked and injured Queen Mary's housekeeper and her assistant. In June, 1951, three toughs who were surprised by a policeman patrolling the grounds of the Duchess of Kent's country house beat him up and got away. A month later a young man scaled a Palace balcony, entered a maid's room at 3 o'clock in the morning and announced that he had come to call on Princess Margaret. The quick-witted maid asked him to wait while she informed the Princess and then phoned for the Palace police.

To forestall further wall-scaling break-ins at Buckingham Palace the authorities at the end of 1951 installed yet another security system, twin copper wires along the top of the Palace garden walls which activate a radar-like screen in the Palace police room whenever they are touched or approached by intruders.

"Buck House" records show, however, that intruders have always been a Palace problem. The most persistently enterprising of them was a young man named Jones, who was first discovered hiding in the Marble Hall in December, 1838, soon after the young Queen Victoria had moved into the new building. Jones claimed to have lived in the Palace for a year, living on food stolen from the kitchens, and to have ·overheard conversations between Victoria and her Ministers. This tale proved false and Jones was acquitted. Two years later he was found in the Palace again—this time hiding under a sofa in the Queen's dressing-room. He was examined by the Privy Council and sent to prison for three months as a rogue. The Palace guards were strengthened, but in March, 1841, Jones was back inside the Palace: he was caught by a policeman in the Grand Hall. Again he was taken before the Privy Council and once again he was packed off to prison. The guards were doubled—but Jones never came back.

INDEX

413

INDEX

419